# GLOBAL CORPORATE
## INTELLIGENCE

# GLOBAL CORPORATE
# INTELLIGENCE

. . . . .

## Opportunities,
## TECHNOLOGIES,
## AND THREATS
## IN THE
## 1990s

. . . . .

edited by George S. Roukis,
Hugh Conway, and Bruce H. Charnov

**Quorum Books**
New York • Westport, Connecticut • London

**Library of Congress Cataloging-in-Publication Data**

Global corporate intelligence : opportunities, technologies, and
   threats in the 1990s / edited by George S. Roukis, Hugh Conway, and
   Bruce Charnov.
      p.   cm.
    Includes bibliographical references (p.   ).
    ISBN 0–89930–220–3 (lib. bdg. : alk. paper)
    1. Business intelligence.   2. Business communication.
   3. Communication in management.   4. Management information systems.
   I. Roukis, George S.   II. Conway, Hugh.   III. Charnov,
   Bruce H.
   HD38.7.G62   1990
   658.4′7—dc20         89–27240

British Library Cataloguing in Publication Data is available.

Copyright © 1990 by George S. Roukis, Hugh Conway, and Bruce Charnov

Library of Congress Catalog Card Number: 89–27240
ISBN: 0–89930–220–3

First published in 1990

Quorum Books, 88 Post Road West, Westport, CT 06881
An imprint of Greenwood Publishing Group, Inc.

Printed in the United States of America

∞

The paper used in this book complies with the
Permanent Paper Standard issued by the National
Information Standards Organization (Z39.48–1984).

10 9 8 7 6 5 4 3 2 1

**Copyright Acknowledgment**

Grateful acknowledgment is extended by Ewan Anderson for extracted material in chapter 15,
originally published in *Strategic Minerals: The Geopolitical Problems for the United States*
(Praeger Publishers, New York, a division of Greenwood Publishing Group, 1988). Copyright ©
1988 by Ewan Anderson. Reprinted with permission of Praeger Publishers.

To my late parents, Steven and Jennie Roukis

To my wife, June

To two wonderful people, the best in-laws one could hope for,
Sylvia and Jerry Schlesinger. Thank you for all your help,
encouragement, and most of all, for your daughter,
Gail J. Charnov.

# Contents

# Tables and Figures

**TABLES**

**FIGURES**

# Acknowledgments

In the preparation of a book, the main focus of intellectual attention is centered on substantive concerns. The administrative and secretarial support functions are invariably taken for granted. Special thanks are due to those unsung heroes who provided us with diligent assistance during the preparation of this book. These include Geeta Kudva, Linda Cossen, and Jean Quaranta of Hofstra University. Appreciation is also extended to Marilyn Gallo Gould and Pauline Travis.

# Introduction

There can be little doubt that the world is changing more quickly and dramatically than at any other time in history. It may well be that scholars, decades from now, in evaluating the changes that have virtually engulfed the latter half of this century, will describe these changes as the "information revolution." This revolution has been characterized by two opposite yet strangely complementary trends. The first trend is the changes in technology that have served to link the world and, in effect, to make it smaller. One need only consider, as millions did on a daily basis, the interrelationship between the various national economies as the last stock market crisis rippled around the world from market to market, and the growing reality of those interrelationships upon the investor in even the smallest rural hamlet. Similarly, we have seen the emergence of a truly global view encompassing an enlarged perspective of the world and the complexity of its myriad interrelationships. It is these two forces, philosophical and technical, that are shaping the world, creating its challenges, and leading to new opportunities.

The evolution of computing power forecasts the coming revolution. In 1947 ENIAC, the first computer operated with vacuum tubes, generated a great deal of heat, filled two stories in a large building, weighed over 60,000 pounds, and cost almost $487,000. Yet today the multifaceted digital watch worn by children, costing only a few dollars, contains more sophisticated computing power. Historians of technology have estimated that the cost of computing power has fallen so precipitously that had a Rolls Royce automobile kept pace, its cost today would be only $5.00.

But the reductions in the cost of computing power, however dramatic, cannot begin to indicate the significance of this revolution. It is but the latest evolutionary stage in the revolution that has served to separate the modern metropolis from the medieval village. In that world the few great libraries cataloged their literary holdings in bound books, listing each new acquisition in sequence. As these catalogs continue, even after centuries, to prove invaluable to medieval scholars and librarians, it is evident that they were designed to be maximally durable. But it is less evident that they were minimally useful in evoking the value of their information. The lists lacked even the slightest flexibility—information was static, and these catalogs limited both the acquisition of information and its usefulness. It is apparent that even the simplest card catalog in the local public library possesses the flexibility for information organization, manipulation, and use that was lacking even in the great libraries of the past.

The U.S. Patent Office accepted the first patent application for a flexible card system in 1849, but it took almost fifty years before the Library of Congress adopted the practice of distributing book cards cataloging books in a uniform manner to local libraries. These movable cards, adaptable to the organization and manipulation of information, are a worthy if overlooked symbol of the division between the medieval world of static facts and the hallmark of modernity—a dynamic manipulation of increasing amounts of information.

A philosophical revolution in the way in which information is viewed has accompanied the technological advances that have increased both the amount of data available and the ability of the user to manipulate that data. The world has progressed from the vision of noted science fiction grandmaster Arthur C. Clarke in the late 1940s of satellites in permanent orbits capable of facilitating communication to every point on earth to the reality of direct dialing to even the farthest reach and to the smallest village. Such technology, suspended above the earth in geosynchronous orbit, has made the acquisition of "real-time" data a reality that will alter the way in which the world is perceived and the manner in which individuals interact with it.

But the impact of information-processing technologies, especially the personal computer, has not been limited to merely increasing the currency and amount of information, as was aptly observed in an interview by Apple Computer's irrepressible executive, technology advocate, and sometimes seer, Jean-Louis Gassee:

Do we really think we can measure productivity in the information age as Frederick Taylor did with manufacturing in the industrial age, by the mile of text produced? Information should not be evaluated by volume alone. Do we evaluate a meal by the number of calories ingested? The point of personal computers is precisely to enhance content as well as production. In that way, personal computers become true intellectual power tools. (Speech at World Affairs Council, Fall 1986)

If Gassee is correct, and many feel that he is, the utilization of these emerging technologies will lead to increased productivity by means of enhanced creativity. But the Consulting Division of Arthur Andersen and Company, utilizing this dynamic view of information, has stressed that this creative utilization of information confers a competitive edge—and these corporate visionaries have designated this principle as IFCA, information for competitive advantage. Other more contentious commentators have gone so far as to assert that information is, or will become, not a managerial tool but a corporate weapon to be wielded in the commercial struggle.

The focus of this collection is to be found precisely in the interplay of these forces that are daily shaping the emerging reality. At its core is the essential belief in the value of information and corporate intelligence to the modern business enterprise. This is not to imply a traditional narrow view of intelligence, but rather to embody the principle that intelligence encompasses any information needed by the contemporary organization. Concomitant with the belief in the acquisition and effective use of information are both the assertion that such a result will confer a critical advantage and the assertion that a global view will hallmark the emerging information. Today the corporate intelligence function must cope with the changing reality produced by the new technology. This new reality consists of international markets linked more closely than ever before as a result of the internationalization of financial and information industries. Communications and corporate technology have transformed both services, making their products ubiquitous. Technology and the globalization of money and information have transformed or affected virtually every sector of industry, and the total represents an industrial revolution. Sophisticated new machinery has provided the vehicle or means for transforming the financial, information, and other service industries. New technology has internationalized capital and allowed universal access to new information. The universality of money and information in turn has reshaped the global economy and led to a restructuring of traditional closed political systems (USSR) and economic associations (European Common Market). Social conflict theory appears to be particularly relevant and analytically useful for evaluating these changes.

The revolution is producing corporate structural change, with large companies seeking to expand their global influence and merging with other very large corporations. Simultaneously the technology has created innumerable applications opportunities and has brought into existence an industry of entrepreneurs to service "niche" markets between the components of the new technology and potential users. The technical service capability has been identified as the real source of future economic power. The flurry of corporate acquisitions involving this expertise appears to support this belief.

Before the description of how each chapter serves to advance the authors' viewpoints, there is an additional observation that deserves comment. The changing philosophy and emerging technologies previously discussed and embodied in the vision of virtually every chapter must be viewed as an ominous cloud upon the horizon of totalitarian states and an irresistible force opposing dictatorial rule. Such police states are universally distinguished by strict control of information, from state control of the media to strict penalties for unsanctioned data dissemination. But control of information is antagonistic to the emerging technologies that promote and facilitate information proliferation. It is significant not only that many totalitarian states lag behind the Western world in the use of computer technology, but also that the gap is growing. While the military authorities in such states have acquired the latest in technological wonder, such technology has failed to penetrate the larger society, and rightly so, for to allow the proliferation of computer technology would represent letting the technological genie out of the proverbial bottle, never to return. As experience in contemporary American society with the "computer hacker" has amply demonstrated, networked computers in almost every school, if not every individual classroom, have invited the most clever to "crack" remote data bases. Even the military has learned that its computers are not immune from such attempts at uninvited entry. This lesson has surely not been lost on those already fearful of what data technologies can accomplish in willing hands, yet the limiting of information technologies in the wider society can only serve to discourage if not actually retard productivity resulting from enhanced creativity. Totalitarianism and technology would seem to be on a collision course.

This book begins with two chapters on the emerging interrelated global world order, a hallmark of the information revolution. George Roukis systematically discusses the intelligence process as it embodies the global view and presents approaches that are inherent in and the result of such a view. His analysis of the impact of far-flung events upon the contemporary corporate decision-making process serves to aptly illustrate that no modern enterprise can ignore the larger world. Alluding to the growing gap in computer utilization in the Soviet Union, Roukis points to the opinion that this may even threaten its status as a superpower and diminish its prestige.in the eyes of the world. He insightfully points out that intelligence resources are regularly devoted to the acquisition of the latest technology and predicts that such efforts at gaining the newest computers will accelerate. Yet as the remaining chapters in the book amply assert, the real problem will be to allow a climate encouraging widespread use of such information technologies.

In a supportive chapter, Hugh Conway shows how modern technology has changed the corporate intelligence function. He notes that whereas previously the tools and methods of analysis were comparatively primitive and typically focused on a small number of competitors acting in a relatively stable environment, communications and computer technology have unalterably changed that environment. In effect, he maintains that information made available through new technology is the staple in the diet of the modern corporate intelligence function. Conway asserts that in a global environment there is an ever-increasing tide of information requiring identification, selection, systematic review, and analysis. For information to become intelligence, less useful information must be systematically culled from more useful information, with the latter hierarchically arranged to reflect the potentially most useful combinations, associations, causal relationships, and interconnections of facts. He provides a well-structured analytical framework for corporate intelligence practitioners to view more particular, company-specific concerns. Technology has created the modern information industry, and to succeed, modern corporate intelligence must master the techniques and assimilate the products of the transforming technology.

The importance of the global perspective having been established, the second part deals with the emerging technologies and information application. Robert Gordon's chapter points out that the word "intelligence" is used in several different contexts. It can refer to the process of gathering data; it can refer to the data itself; and it can refer to the application of knowledge to produce useful information from the data. In well-developed illustrative language he shows how the computer can be used to further all these aspects of intelligence and further provides the perspective for the executive to determine the use of these concepts for the organization and to understand the choices open to it in today's technology. Mahesh Chandra and Shivaji Rao consider the evolving application of technology and discuss the development and implications of artificial intelligence. These so-called "thinking computers," actually software applications, will greatly enhance the value of information, and the point is not lost upon industrialists and innovators alike that the ability to better utilize information may well lead to crucial advantages that determine the difference between success and failure. Artificial intelligence goes hand in hand with the advances being made in the development of expert systems whereby the rules of thumb and other decision-making parameters are being reduced to an operations set that can intake, process, and evaluate information much like an actual expert. Although these systems are in their infancy, the promise is for the inexpensive proliferation and application of knowledge to pragmatic issues and in circumstances where it was not previously possible or cost effective.

As the chapters in this book echo a leitmotif revolving around the use by business of information, it is natural to speak of the business of information as new entrepreneurial opportunities emerge daily for those prescient to envision them. Paul G. Zurkowski writes of the emerging business of information and, by implication, of those wise enough to make use of the information systems. His chapter will serve as an invaluable primer and guide for even the technically unsophisticated looking toward the acquisition and effective utilization of an information-providing service and the information thus acquired.

David Flynn's contribution makes the telling point that the development and utilization of state-of-the-art technology confer its crucial advantage precisely because the effective use of current information leads to greater certainty of managerial decision making. On the other hand, Akira Tomioka's analysis of Japanese decision making in part 5 takes the opposite track and is sure to provoke comment from most readers. He asserts that Japanese business leaders have been so successful because of the application of technology and the use of information, but that this leads to uncertainty, which in turn creates new opportunities. Cultural differences would allow for such a divergence of opinion, but a comparison of these two chapters should inevitably lead to new ways of looking at the application of technology and its impact upon the contemporary enterprise, even though many must perforce disagree with either Flynn or Tomioka.

John E. Ullmann's chapter deals with the problem of bad news. As the ancient myth of the Persian Messenger who was killed for delivering bad news to the ruler amply illustrates, bad news carries with it an often unique liability for all concerned. Professor Ullmann provides genuine insight into how organizations can deal with negative information, and therein he makes an even more significant impact than the topic of his chapter would initially indicate. He reminds the reader that the production of information, both acquisition and analysis, is only part of the story. That information must then be used by people, and all who design management information systems must consider how information will be used. The human elements of the management information system will be as important as any hardware or software.

Mamdouh Farid presents a concise view of the structure of the corporate intelligence system and a thoughtful discussion of how the organization goes about gathering its information. His point, often woefully overlooked in the actions of even sophisticated executives, is that intelligence gathering is a necessary precursor to intelligence usage. He argues forcefully that the gathering process, the product of a comprehensive system, must not be neglected in the emphasis on how to effectively use intelligence. He also describes the interrelationship between information needs and information-system design, a factor that must be considered before implementing either individually.

Henry Berszinn and his firm are in the forefront of the development and application of information-gathering methodologies and are achieving notable success in introducing such methodologies into many different kinds of economic entities. His in-depth description of the ''nuts and bolts'' of one such application forces the thoughtful reader to consider the human side of such applications—that state-of-the-art technology realizes its potential only when the human component achieves its potential. Berszinn provides the reader with easy-to-grasp concepts and practical techniques with which information can be generated from the field by leveraging other existing programs.

In the fourth part of the book, Bruce Charnov presents a systematic approach to intelligence data security. Although the intent of this chapter is toward the pragmatic, the point is made that computer and data security begins with a corporate commitment and an affirmative philosophical stance. He demonstrates how such a commitment can be actualized at virtually every organizational level to achieve an overall state of data security. The threats that confront a modern business mandate such a total approach, for to ignore even a single avenue of approach, given the fact that the firm's entire data base can be purloined by a skilled thief on a disk in a shirt pocket, is to court disaster. Charnov's chapter should be, and may become, required reading for all management information systems (MIS) and information-related executives.

Robert S. Redmond reminds us all that computer security is not merely a local concern but a major facet of the growing international intelligence-gathering efforts of foreign and, to varying degrees, hostile nations. While his focus is on defense-related threats to computer security, the implications of his insightful commentary will profit the corporate executive in general but prove of specific and immediate value to those companies who are increasingly entering the international arena in search of expanded markets or production advantage. In a similar and perhaps even more sinister vein, the international terrorist threat is portrayed by Joseph E. Goldberg of the National Defense University. Professor Goldberg's chilling topic belies his academic pursuit and will probably be read at a single sitting. It is riveting in detail and compels attention. No company expects such disaster, but his chapter will help in preparing should it come.

Robert Kühne, a noted expert in international management and marketing, details the pragmatic concerns of intelligence management in confrontation with the international terrorist threat. He argues that even though the number of incidents involving terrorists is quite small, the international corporation can adequately prepare for any eventuality. While Goldberg approaches the terrorist threat from a macro level, Kühne's contribution approaches the problem from a micro level, and the combination of the two will serve as an effective primer. Kühne's planning for executive protection should be required reading before every international assignment.

The final part of this book, dealing with strategic intelligence, presents an enigma even to an experienced reader, for its chapters are not easily classified by content or sophistication.

Akira Tomioka's chapter has already been described, as it contrasts powerfully with the one by David Flynn, but its controversy is presented in this final part of the book. This is stylistically correct because of its focus on Japan, which is in concert with the international and nontraditional focus that marks this part. Additionally, Tomioka's assertion that there is no conspiracy between the Japanese government and industry will surely be characterized as national apology by some or truthful revelation by others, but it will not be ignored. Tomioka, an American Ph.D., has returned to his native land to teach at the Tokyo University of Information Science, but American and international thinkers on data security and utilization have not heard the last from this insightful and provocative academic.

Evan W. Anderson presents a superb and stimulating discussion of the influence of geography upon corporate risk assessment, making real and immediate the esoteric and formerly arcane discipline. It will literally open new vistas for corporate security planners. Joshua N. Feinman, Peter M. Garber, and Michelle R. Garfinkel have been equally innovative in their analysis of financial warfare and the corporate response. Their depiction of the shadowy world of financial warfare, previously known only to a few and suspected by academics, will give pause to those who consider current events; and the guidelines for corporate response will cast light into dark corners.

The book concludes with Marshall Lee Miller's comprehensive overview of the Soviet foreign intelligence-gathering apparatus, even in the *glasnost* era, continues to be a potent and ongoing effort to acquire by stealth where innovation has failed, this chapter could serve as an authoritative briefing for all those seeking to write thrilling novels of international intrigue.

The four chapters in the last part aptly illustrate both the directionality and inherent uncertainty confronted by those seeking to deal with management of corporate intelligence in the 1990s. Unconventional, provocative, philosophical, pragmatic, and sometimes contradictory—this is the nature of the challenge to those who would manage the information that is both the lifeblood of the modern business and its competitive advantage in the future. To lumber along, a mighty commercial colossus relying on past success, is to imitate the dinosaur, and the lesson of that ancient beast's extinction is not lost on even the schoolchild. The corporation must adapt to the changing world described in the chapters of this book, and its authors provide a starting point for that adaptation.

# Part I

## GLOBAL OPPORTUNITY AND ANALYTICAL FRAMEWORK

# 1

# The Corporate Intelligence Process: Global Perspectives and Approaches

## *George S. Roukis*

Intelligence from a practical perspective has to take into consideration the changing contours of the international environment. For American firms, traditionally used to market dominance in the 1950s and 1960s, the dialectical reconfiguration of the world economy in the 1990s and early twenty-first century poses problems and challenges of an unprecedented nature. If both the Soviet Union and the United States are devoting a proportionally larger share of their economic resources to military preparedness, their investment base for economic development is thus marginally reduced. In the long run both are palpably handicapped, though not in the superpower (military) sphere.[1] Further, as this diminution in economic capability occurs, the economic strength of Western Europe, particularly after the integration of the European Economic Community (EEC) countries in 1992, and the continued exemplary economic performance of Japan will intensify the present disquieting competition. Armament investments might enhance short-term national security, but over time they may diminish the commercial effectiveness of the American economy.[2] This will be further compounded by the sustained industrialization of such Third World countries as South Korea, Taiwan, Singapore, Indonesia, India, and Brazil. Economic domination is perceptibly shifting to Western Europe and the Pacific Basic countries. In essence, as the rest of the world develops, the economic pie for American firms shrinks. Other problems that overhang these profound macro changes are the relative undevelopment of American human resources, the widespread illegal drug trade, terrorism, acquired immune deficiency syndrome (AIDS), and the unresolved regional conflicts in the Middle East, Southeast Asia, and Latin America.[3] The Philippines, South Africa, Mexico, and post-Khomeini Iran are inherently fraught with uncertain dangers.

Until recently the drug war has been rather one-sided. The United States was concerned about supply and provided generous assistance to Latin American governments for crop destruction. The governments of the region, on the contrary, perceived the drug problem as demand in the United States. Controversy centered on the relative weight of supply and demand. However, the geographical extent of drug trafficking in the Latin American region is massive. Mexico, Colombia, Jamaica, and Belize are the main suppliers of marijuana to the U.S. market. Peru, Bolivia, and Colombia grow nearly all of the cocaine that the Colombian drug lords ship to the United States. Forty percent of the heroin entering the United States comes from Mexico. It is estimated that the U.S. retail market for illegal drugs is $130 billion. In Bolivia alone the value of cocaine production in 1988 was approximately $1 billion, of which $250 million circulated in the country, constituting nearly one-quarter of Bolivia's foreign exchange earnings. Perhaps 300,000 jobs were directly or indirectly linked to cocaine production. Unfortunately, the judicial systems in many of these countries suffer the same maladies: a frightened judiciary, untrained police, and ineffective laws. Bank secrecy laws frequently prevent comprehensive money-laundering investigations. Adding to these woes is the corruption drug money wreaks upon the country's leadership.[4] Corrupt officials can impose unreasonable demands on foreign firms or extract exorbitant extortion payments. They can also front for foreign intelligence services and subvert American business operations and influence. The drug trade is a danger that affects the productivity of the American domestic economy as well as foreign commercial activities.

Another major problem facing American firms, especially in East Africa, is AIDS. Pandemics like AIDS have often begun with a viral mutation that permits a microorganism to attack humans as well as animals. In past centuries a new disease oftentimes killed a substantial portion of the affected population. The bubonic plague in Europe in the fourteenth century wiped out more than 60 percent of the population. In the case of AIDS, the incubation period is remarkably long, making effective detection difficult.[5] In parts of East Africa, where the AIDS epidemic is serious, economic and social dislocations have occurred. According to NBC science correspondent Robert Bazell, "Millions, if not tens of millions, will die of AIDS in Africa. The Rakai district of Uganda near the Tanzanian border seems to have been affected the hardest. Formerly a busy commercial hub, Rakai is now almost deserted."[6] A 1988 sampling of sixty-eight truck drivers passing through Entebbe, Uganda, revealed that 45.5 percent were infected. A study at the largest morgue in Abidjan, Ivory Coast, showed an infection rate of 66 percent among adults thirty to thirty-nine years old who had died in the hospital. The World Health Organization (WHO) projects that by 1992 a quarter of a million African infants will have acquired AIDS from their mothers.[7] If these examples are an indication of what this dreaded disease can do, imagine its continued spreading on the African continent and beyond. How will this affect human resource management, and at what point is a country's national security at stake? If a cure is not forthcoming in the next decade, and the disease remains unchecked, how will business firms operating in highly contagious areas maintain normal operations? What impact will the AIDS epidemic in the United States have on insurance costs? The AIDS question could be the sleeper of our times.

To be sure, the U.S. government intelligence agencies will still provide sound and accurate analyses of world developments and trends, but corporations, particularly the large multinational corporations (MNCs) will need timely data. It will not be enough for companies to have just accurate esoteric information about a specific country, person, or event. Corporate management will have to be prepared to take swift preclusive or remedial action. Firms cannot wait for a government agency's opinion or decision to take quick action. Regrettably, unlike the Japanese, we have not developed the planning capabilities and processes to implement systemic adaptations to fast-paced changes. We have also not assessed the future significance of present events. For example, in 1986 Japan replaced the United States as the world's leading creditor nation. It has surpassed the United States in industrial production, though not in total gross national product (GNP), where services are included. The Japanese-owned portion of American business is growing at four times the rate of the U.S. economy. Japan now finances 30 percent of the American government deficit. Thirty years ago not a single Japanese bank was included in the world's top fifty banks. In 1987 the ten largest banks in the world were Japanese.[8] As these changes occurred, the United States became a debtor nation and lost its ability to exercise a leadership role in the international financial marketplace. If one compares Japan's high savings, trade surplus, and low interest rates with America's low savings, structural trade deficit, and high interest rates, it is easy to conclude that Japan has the competitive cost advantages.[9] If there is a single lesson to be learned from these facts, it is that Japan's success pivots on its perception that economic growth is a matter of survival. Hence its information- or intelligence-gathering systems have distinct national security objectives. The Japanese employ the term comprehensive security as a work of art. It includes economic as well as physical security. In the latter category it is understood to encompass more than defense against invasion. It entails planning for wider range of contingencies, including natural disasters.[10]

In recent years we have witnessed the emergence of labor militancy in two pivotal countries, South Africa and South Korea. We have also seen how a well-organized, highly motivated labor movement can bring about change in a Communist country. Solidarity, the independent Polish labor organization, won a majority of the seats in the country's 1989 national parliamentary elections, and a non-Communist government is now in power.[11] Recent strikes in South Africa and South Korea have gone beyond traditional collective bargaining issues to encompass major political objectives. In South Africa the National Union of Mineworkers, a black union formed in 1982, undertook a twenty-one-day strike in August 1987 that cost hundreds of millions of dollars in physical damage and lost production. It also resulted in a loss of lives and jobs for mineworkers. However, far from producing a workable adversarial bargaining relationship, the strike hardened the parties' attitudes and negotiating positions. The Sullivan codes adopted in the early 1970s and the 1979 Wiehahn reforms, which provided for improvements in economic and social developments and new mechanisms for regulating industrial relations, were unable to prevent potent political demands. The stoppage was essentially a dress rehearsal for future strikes with an emphasis on ending the system of apartheid.[12] In South Korea the bitter strike against Motorola Korea in December 1988 was not only waged for higher compensation and better working conditions but also sought to overcome a legacy of authoritarianism in labor relations and politics. Companies like Motorola that paid higher wages in the United States obtained cost advantages from locating production operations in South Korea. As the South Korean labor movement developed, particularly with the encouragement of newly enacted labor laws, disputes over bread-and-butter issues spilled over into strident anti-American sentiments. Workers viewed Motorola's bargaining objectives as a form of neo-imperialism.[13]

It is too early to predict how indigenous employees in host countries will react over time to multinational corporations, but the growing power of these firms creates and produces political responses. As democratization proceeds in totalitarian or authoritarian countries, the initial reaction of suppressed or government-managed labor organizations is to seek greater political participation. This quest for political influence was visible in South Africa, South Korea, Poland, and, in part, mainland China among some workers who supported the student demonstrations for democracy in May and June 1989.[14] The recent economic and political changes in Eastern Europe will, at some point, produce labor conflict.

For American firms operating in postauthoritarian business environments, it is not unreasonable to predict that labor militancy will increase as it has in South Korea. Workers will seek wages and benefits that no longer reflect a low-wage country where wages in the first instance were conceived or acquiesced in by the authoritarian host government. Wage competition will intensify. This same form of competition will also increase in the industrialized high-tech countries of the world economy as Western European, Japanese, and American firms implement cost-containment measures to maintain competitive advantages. Globalization, modernization, and democracy will bring significant benefits to many workers, but not equitably across the board. This will precipitate labor dissonance in countries or regional areas where low-wage policies are the central focus of corporate strategic planning. Consequently, a need is now emerging for timely intelligence on labor in both developing and developed countries, with an emphasis on several key questions:

1. How have the labor policies of host governments encouraged or precipitated labor disturbances?

2. Have the labor policies of multinational firms been perceived as supportive of worker aspirations or as developmental impediments?

3. What role does labor play in the politics of the host country, and conversely, what role does government play in the labor management relations process?

4. What indicators or event series portend labor problems?

5. What techniques—education, political participation, mediation, fact-finding, arbitration, labor courts, effective labor standards, and so on—best resolve labor disputes?

6. Where applicable, how does the Soviet Union view labor developments in selected developing and developed countries where American multinational firms are located, and what has been the impact of the Soviet-dominated World Federation of Trade Unions on the political and economic climate in these identified countries?[15]

These questions are not exhaustive; they do indicate the nature and direction of thoughtful inquiry.

As a primary corporate support function, the intelligence process basically observes the same organizational format as a government intelligence agency. The collection of raw data must relate to specific predetermined targets, and sources and methods of collection must be assiduously identified. In the business world sources normally include customers, suppliers, competitors, trade shows, government, technical meetings, publications, experts, former employees of competitor companies, and union officials. Other vital sources of information are service organizations. These can be financial institutions, advertising agencies, and consulting firms. Service organizations usually have to monitor regulations, judicial decisions, and legislative enactments in foreign countries and, as a rule, accumulate large amounts of information concerning foreign investment climates and competitor capabilities.[16] Also, the intelligence function interfaces with external data bases and outside research firms. In addition, it insures that all relevant segments of the company are sensitive and responsive to the intelligence-gathering imperative, and it collects operational assessments data from these intraorganizational sources. It is therefore essential that managers at all levels of the planning process are involved in determining what critical information is needed. A succinct but powerful study by Herbert E. Meyer, who was vice president of the National Intelligence Council, underscores the relevancy of timely intelligence in the international business world. His comment captures the essence of the process: "The global nature of economic activity has also linked us together, irrevocably, to a degree that has never before existed. A strike, coup, currency shift, or technological breakthrough in one country has an impact beyond that country's border."[17]

By itself, raw information is without practical effect until it is converted into intelligence. The finished product now supports the policy-making process. The product (intelligence) could relate to a market research survey, socio-economic analysis, new product development, or assessment of a political risk. It could also provide support for an acquisition strategy. The Japanese Trading Companies, the Japanese External Trade Organization (JETRO), the major oil companies, and the privately owned grain companies provide examples of well-managed and effective business intelligence operations. Each grain-trading company, for example, has branch offices throughout the world, and each branch is responsible for collecting and transmitting information to corporate headquarters. Cargill, Inc., receives about 14,000 daily messages from its 250 branches. It has the ability to provide high-quality timely warnings on impending changes and to sort high volumes of information.[18] JETRO has an information-gathering network of approximately 270 employees assigned to 81 cities in 59 countries. Twelve hundred analysts then review the collected data.[19] In these cases the intelligence function is integrally related to the long-term strategic planning process.

There are several interesting developments that warrant further comment. Marxism has become discredited as an economic growth model, and Soviet intervention in regional conflicts has abated, as witnessed by Soviet withdrawal from Afghanistan. Democracies have replaced authoritarian regimes in several key countries (Philippines, Turkey, Paraguay, and South Korea), and left-wing totalitarianism has lost its intellectual appeal. The market economy with particular modifications has been adopted in several prominent Communist countries, and free-market policies have been implemented in heretofore state-managed Third World economies. Despite these encouraging developments, there are two broad trends in this evolving competitive international economy that restrict free trade. The first trend is toward managed trade, whereby particular nations agree to buy and sell from each other specified amounts of goods and services. The second is toward the globalization of production, whereby goods are manufactured throughout the world on carefully calculated cost considerations. The post–World War II rules of free trade are not being observed as intended, since managed trade leads to dumping, tariffs, and special industry subsidization. Under these circumstances, those governments that offer the best trade inducements will profit; those governments that have minimal political risk will attract investment.[20] Moreover, an intense competitive environment will inevitably produce conflict as perceived business gains or losses are emotionally intertwined with historical political concerns such as national liberation movements, irredentism, and ethnic rivalries. Terrorist attacks against a rival's business interests will most likely increase. By the end of the twentieth century, the United States will face Third World states with comparable armaments, including nuclear, chemical, and bacteriological weapons. The Iraqi Exocet missile that hit the USS *Stark* in the Persian Gulf in 1988 is a dramatic example of this new reality.[21] If corporations can develop business intelligence units that can track, monitor, and accurately assess these developments, they will have a better chance to survive and prosper in this volatile environment. If they do not, they will miss the intricacies of the value systems that lie beneath the comfortable veneer of the modern buildings and new boulevards in many Third World countries. Piercing these mysterious veils will be the litmus test of success.

Before proceeding to a discussion of political risk, it is important to distinguish political uncertainty from political risk. Policy decisions flow from this semantic analysis. Political uncertainty describes an unmeasured subjective doubt about an environment, while political risk describes a relatively objective measurement. A change in government, for example, will perhaps generate a feeling of uncertainty as to the prospective intentions and policies of the new leadership. This is a subjective assessment. Until a thoughtful analysis is made of the potential risks, uncertainty will prevail as to the government's future policies. Once an analysis has been conducted, risks can be identified and weighed. If the new government issues regulations that require a significant increase in the use of indigenous managers or requires local indigenous firms to supply more of the parts and raw materials for the finished fabricated product, a measurable political risk is present. This allows the affected firm the opportunity to assess the impact of the potential risk. However, without some type of objective assessment technique, comparisons of country risk levels become exceedingly difficult.

A well-designed corporate intelligence system permits management to develop an extensive list of specific types of risks. These risks can be conceptualized as events or a series of events in the national or international environments that can affect the physical assets, personnel, and operations of the firm.[22] In some cases, where an intelligence analysis indicates that a particular nation is interested in encouraging a specific type of direct investment, joint venture, or licensing arrangement, the leadership of the firm might be in a good position to negotiate a favorable agreement. In other cases, where the intelligence data indicates that numerous indigenous special-interest groups are competing at cross-purposes, the firm might decide not to locate in that country because some important divisive group disagrees with the firm's operational and employment policies. Sometimes a national government is apprehensive that the firm is gaining too much influence in the host country's domestic affairs, which could lead to the imposition of controls and onerous regulations, such as expropriation, price controls, adverse tax changes, production restrictions, profit-repatriation limitations, currency devaluation, export restrictions, local content usage, and restrictive labor standards.

At other times the political climate of the host country portends a turbulent future. If there is a continued discrepancy between the expected and realized living standards of the indigenous population, the perceived or forced suppression of upward socio-economic mobility, the restriction of certain groups from participating in the political process, or high levels of unemployment and inflation, dissatisfaction can easily precipitate mass civil disorders, including riots, sabotage, insurrection, terrorism, and guerrilla warfare. The range of potential risks is virtually unlimited. If corporate managements can establish the caliber of intelligence systems that identify correctly those elements of political risks associated with overseas investment and also incorporate these ongoing intelligence findings into their strategic planning systems, they can devise competent adjusting tactics and strategies. Examples of effective coping responses would be investment guarantees, timing and entry strategies, sourcing and moving of funds, and establishing an international production network strategy. Sometimes, where funds are involved, a company would be wise to enact policies on fund movements. For example, policies on transfer pricing, royalty payments, interest charges, and the allocation of companywide overhead expenses minimize financial exposure. At other times direct lobbying can be effective in preventing burdensome changes. If the firm and the host country are on relatively good terms, it becomes easier to persuade government officials to reconsider questionable policies. Small dependent countries are less likely to seek major changes, but over time there is a shift in the parties' bargaining leverage.[23]

On the other hand, corporate intelligence officials will still have to be mindful of current research trends and new product developments. This will necessitate careful monitoring of the scientific literature and competitor product policies. The information revolution is changing our global economy and transforming national political and business institutions. Scientific knowledge is currently doubling every thirteen to fifteen years. Today, information regarding all nations' diplomatic, fiscal, and monetary policies is instantly transmitted to more than two hundred thousand screens in hundreds of trading rooms in dozens of countries. There is virtually no place on earth that is not electronically linked.[24] In fact, it is estimated that the number of digital computers—from microprocessors to mainframes—in use today exceeds the total population on earth.[25] Yet important as these developments are for strategic business planning, it may become more difficult to discern meaningful patterns if the tendency is to store an abundance of information indiscriminately. Planting false information or willfully subverting a competitor's data-base systems is possible under these circumstances. Information acquisition will also require tighter security measures to insure that employees or individuals with access to trade and technological secrets are not compromised or suborned by competitor firms or foreign intelligence agencies. The recent cases involving William Peter Kampiles, Joseph G. Helmick, Christopher Boyce-Lee, Andrew Daulton, Michael Lance Walker, Jerry Alfred Whitworth, and Ronald W. Pelton attest to this frightening reality. Greed was the primary motivator of these betrayals.

Marketplace espionage has many variations—bankers taking on the KGB as a silent partner, Silicon Valley executives smuggling chips to the Soviet Union, and sailors on warships stealing parts for Iran. As Real Admiral William O. Studeman, director of Naval Intelligence, stated, the espionage of the Walker spy ring "was of the highest value to the intelligence services of the Soviet Union with the potential, had conflict erupted between the superpowers, to have powerful war-winning implications for the Soviet side."[26] Soviet intelligence did not steal the secrets, American traitors did in the pursuit of fast money. Once the Soviets recruited spies on the basis of ideological affinity; now they depend on walk-ins with information to sell. As part of the corporate intelligence function, the information-collection and analysis process should also be strongly supported by thoughtful counterintelligence policies. Hopefully this will prevent or minimize trade-secret theft.

The Soviet Union, facing a growing technological gap, has deployed its best intelligence assets to obtain the latest high-technology research and advanced high-tech products. In the future, especially as the Soviets try to reorganize and revitalize their economy, the technological espionage threat will intensify. *Glasnost* and *perestroika*, at least for the short run, are not meant to transform the Soviet economy into a capitalistic state but are intended to reform what exists, that is, to make the system more effective and productive. General Secretary Mikhail Gorbachev's highest priority is to revitalize the Soviet economy. The changes he calls for are as follows:

• Transferring decision-making authority from government ministries to enterprise directors
• Offering material inducements to enhance labor productivity
• Encouraging industrywide efficiencies by competing in the international marketplace
• Shifting resources from the military to the consumer goods sector[27]

A transformed Soviet system resting on greater openness and political participation does not presuppose that the ideological goals of Soviet foreign policy have been discarded, but it does improve the prospects for a less confrontational environment. In the final analysis we are dealing with a state and a political system, not an individual, no matter how charismatic and impressive General Secretary Gorbachev appears. A major problem facing the Soviets is the ever-growing friction between computer technology and the rigid conservative structure of the Communist government. In relation to other leading Western countries, the Soviet Union has not been able to fully utilize the capabilities of the computer. In fact, a recent study observed that given the pace of computer technology advancements, the Soviet Union's inability to incorporate this technology could threaten its position as a superpower:

As the pace of computer applications accelerates in the industrialized countries of the West—as it does each year—the USSR will fall further and further behind in its goal of reviving a sluggish national economy and maintaining its prestige in the eyes of the world.[28]

The Soviets are aware of this dilemma and thus devote considerable intelligence resources to obtain the latest advances in computer technology. Other targets include microelectronics and materials technology. It would be a formidable task to develop this technology in the Soviet Union; thus the pronounced emphasis on high-tech espionage. In the following years industrial espionage will increase as the Soviet Union and other nations struggle for political and economic supremacy.

Another aspect of the changing international environment is the growing conflict between the multinational corporation (MNC) and hostile governments. Despite the mammoth size of many MNCs, the world-state system is still characterized by distinct nation-states exercising coercive power. As part of the corporate intelligence and political risk assessment function, corporations will still have to deal with foreign government and business leaders. In the international marketplace there will be common interests and issues of conflict demanding astute negotiating skills. When an intelligence system determines that a particular risk or problem is present in a country, the company's management might decide to negotiate a disposition that satisfies both parties. The key, of course, is the negotiator's ability to turn around a seemingly intractable problem. Assessment is also a communications process that emphasizes societal conflict analysis. By understanding a country's key risk factors, management is capable of exercising bargaining leverage. Negotiations are necessary for any arrangement that establishes complicated forms of collaboration, including attempts by corporations to reverse or modify decisions antithetical to their interests.[29]

If a government, for example, decides to restrict profit repatriation or requires that 50 percent of the top managers be native, the corporation has the option to accept this arrangement or leave the country. Either choice may be disadvantageous. Instead, if the corporate intelligence system generated sufficient background data about the government's key officials and the overall needs and problems of the country, the company's leadership might be in a position to negotiate a compromise settlement. In the years ahead, given the intense global business competition, firms should carefully train managers to conduct quasi-diplomatic relations. With the surge of overseas investments, American firms are shedding the banner of nationalism and assuming the posture of global enterprises. In this milieu these firms are not so dependent upon the American economy. As a practical consequence, they will have to develop the panoply of information resources that will permit expansion and survival.

Nearly 17 percent of current total corporate assets were overseas in 1989, as compared to 14.4 percent in 1984, and the trend will continue.[30] The globalization of business requires new organizational structures and effective information systems to govern operations. In the past, American firms operating overseas did not have to be as productive and modern, since using low-wage labor compensated for the lack of sophisticated machinery and equipment. Today higher wage rates in South Korea, Taiwan, Indonesia, and other Third World countries have eliminated this advantage. The emphasis is now on high-technology production, and this requires prompt adjustments to changing circumstances. Suppose that a manufacturing firm located in an Asian Third World country decides that expanding operations and utilizing state-of-the-art equipment is promising. Suppose further that it learns that the government and indigenous business community are lukewarm or opposed to this expansion. If its intelligence operatives also learn that a particular indigenous firm would like to acquire (surreptitiously) this technology so as to use it itself, how could the firm achieve its objective? First, it is self-evident that the firm will do everything possible to protect its trade secrets (security and counterintelligence). Second, it will try to identify those government and business leaders amenable to the expansion. It will then undertake efforts (persuasion) to induce these leaders to take an active supportive role. It will then inform the wavering or opposition elements that losing the opportunity will cause unemployment and loss of needed revenue, and it will also utilize the media, if friendly, to support the project. If the firm has had a constructive or at least nonantagonistic relationship with its workers, it can utilize them to support the project. In any event, this basic illustration indicates that firms operating as independent entities are compelled to employ the same range of resources as governments. In this case the corporate intelligence system provides the data needed by policymakers to carry out the diplomatic and activist responses. For the firm, intelligence is clearly more than just collecting a broad range of data.

By and large, American corporations have established intelligence systems that gather needed decision support data, but they have not been as effective in preempting threatening actions. An active negotiating policy that elicits the support of the host country's key players or at least neutralizes the suspicions of the opposition is a necessary imperative in this environment. Co-optation in this context is an important policy tool. Negotiations must also be utilized to change negative perceptions. Suppose the intelligence unit learns that a significant portion of the host country's population views the company's policies as adversely affecting cultural values. A low-keyed approach, avoiding strong patronizing statements, though emphasizing the company's enhancement of the host country's well-being, could produce better results. It must be stressed that negotiations must be consonant with the host country's methods of bargaining and respectful of that country's heritage. For maximum success, it is up to the corporate management to ascertain the subtleties and nuances of the host country's negotiating climate. Effective negotiations relate to effective intelligence. A good corporate negotiator should never take a situation for granted. He or she must recognize that his or her opponent's evaluations and positions are subject to change. Issues are not created by natural forces but by the parties themselves. This simple understanding is too often forgotten by negotiators in critical situations. A balanced mixture of expediential calculations and moral convictions, premised upon an understanding that the rules promulgated by others can condition and define the bargaining agenda, should guide the negotiating process. Agreements occur when the parties decide to settle for available terms rather than incur the risks and costs of doing better. In the international business world where risks are always present, negotiations become the primary means to attain normalization of relations, enhanced terms of trade, resolution of complex problems, new commitments, and clarification of points of disagreement. Corporate negotiators must have a clear understanding of the operational environment and an ability to compromise within the limits of nonessentiality.

Generally speaking, it is not unusual for business leaders to make decisions with the expectations that they will work. A feeling of confidence pervades their actions, predicated, in part, upon past successes. In a large strategic setting, sudden and unexpected moves by competitors or adversaries sometimes catch them by surprise, notwithstanding a contrary intelligence report. Suddenly there is a realization that management has been operating on the basis of a faulty threat perception and a myopic understanding of a competitor's intentions. What has gone awry? An intelligence unit was established that methodically observed the tenets of intelligence collection and analysis, but a failure of significant proportions occurred. As Ariel Levite ably points out in his seminal book on strategic surprise, "The capacity of any intelligence service to provide high-quality, timely warnings of impending strategic threats depends on more than its ability to develop and sustain sophisticated collection assets. It also hinges on its capacity to sort high volumes of information and provide constant training and intellectual invigoration to the intelligence analysis."[31] The cause of the disaster might have stemmed from the leaders' oversimplified belief about the strategic environment, or the consensus of the intelligence unit might have been based upon ambiguous assumptions. If the corporation has not considered alternative responses, its viability and survival may be at stake. An effective corporation must have leaders who are capable of adapting to environmental changes. This entails an ability to avoid miscalculation, rash decision, and faulty policy implementation. As a basic step, it is not only important for policymakers to formulate the main problems, it is also incumbent upon them to determine the main dangers to be averted, the minimum gains to be expected, and the maximum costs that the firm can tolerate. If the intelligence data is analyzed within this basic framework, free from any ideological predispositions or supposed commonsense perspective, the chances of reaching a sound policy decision increase. Raising skeptical questions about the intelligence findings enhances the data's usefulness. Advising all pertinent members of the organization to be on the alert for new information enriches the quality of the final intelligence report. Calling on the best expert advice for immediate consultation when an unforeseen problem arises insures accurate decision making.

The findings of the intelligence unit should also be challenged, but within the parameters of the strategic policy process. The lead policymaker must know how to ask the right questions and how to encourage the other members of the policy group to do the same. This rigorous analysis will insure that the latest intelligence findings are subjected to an in-depth comprehensive policy review. Even when there is minimal time to decide what to do in a rapidly escalating crisis, particularly where an intelligence report is suspect, resources can be quickly mobilized to assess competently the dimensions of the crisis. Knowledgeable experts can supply timely substantive briefings, while advocates of different policy options can assess the benefits and drawbacks of their positions. A few hours' time is usually sufficient to conduct a thorough problem-solving analysis of the crisis. The emphasis should be on identifying the diagnostic and information-processing errors that affected the preliminary intelligence report and discerning the faulty assumptions and other conceptual mistakes of the report. Failure to collect and assess in-depth information on a crisis can produce an inadequate understanding of the problem and a poorly conceived remedial response. Intelligence and sound decision making are integrally related. Complementing this linkage should also be a process for assessing current and programmed collection against critical strategic objectives. This would allow for adjustments in collection, processing, and production where new developments or unforeseen incidents or crises arise. A periodic internal accountability review will discern the vulnerabilities of the system, if any, and reveal organizational weaknesses, such as faulty collection methods or dubious sources of collection.[32]

Moreover, to further insure that sensitive information is protected, the intelligence unit should establish a classification system that defines different levels of information access. Adopting in some modified format the classifications used by governments (confidential, secret, and top secret) would enhance security. Confidential information is defined as information "the unauthorized disclosure of which reasonably could be expected to cause damage to the national security." Secret information presupposes that the expected damage from unauthorized disclosure would be "serious." The effects of disclosure of top secret information would be exceptionally "grave."[33] For employees with access to sensitive information, background checks (full field investigations) would be desirable. Signing nondisclosure agreements would also heighten security. It should be pointed out that such security measures define different levels of data sensitivity and restrict access to those who have been cleared on a need-to-know basis. Hence guidelines regarding classification, data protection, and access levels are extremely important. Installing shredding devices for disposal of confidential data and conducting periodic checks for wiretapping and bugging can also minimize trade-secret thefts.

A corporate spy's primary mission is to acquire a rival's secret proprietary information (software, inventions, prototypes, concepts, designs, blueprints, and drawings), and innovative methods will be used to obtain this data.[34] Depending on the circumstances, these methods might include planting an agent on the competitor's property, false job interviews with a competitor's employee(s), hiring away a strategically placed competitor's employee, or outright theft of documents, samples, and drawings.[35] Irrespective of the method used, it would be unwise for corporate managements to assume that industrial espionage is a low-risk contingency. Trade-secret thefts cost American firms billions of dollars annually, and the costs will escalate as the computer becomes easier to penetrate. Industrial espionage will assume greater importance than military or political espionage in future years, and this threat must be forthrightly addressed by concerned corporate managements. Since business is not as encumbered as government in policy making and administration, it can more readily adapt to changing circumstances and situations. An effective all-embracing corporate intelligence system is crucial for survival.

## NOTES

1. For an excellent account of this thesis, see Paul Kennedy, *The Rise and Fall of the Great Powers* (New York: Random House, 1987). According to Kennedy, "Simply

because it is the global superpower, with far more extensive military commitments than a regional power like Japan or West Germany, it requires much larger defense forces—in just the same way as imperial Spain felt it needed a far larger army than its counterparts and Victorian Britain insisted upon a much bigger navy than any other country. Furthermore, since the USSR is seen to be the major military threat to American interests across the globe and is clearly devoting a far greater proportion of its GNP to defense, American decision-makers are inevitably worried about losing the arms race with Russia. Yet the more sensible among these decision-makers can also perceive that the burden of armaments is debilitating the Soviet economy and that if the two superpowers continue to allocate ever-larger shares of their national wealth into the unproductive field of armaments, the critical question might soon be: 'Whose economy will decline fastest relative to such expanding states as Japan, China, etc?' " (p. 532). For an interesting analysis of the declining Communist system, see Zbigniew Brzezinski, *The Grand Failure: The Birth and Death of Communism in the Twentieth Century* (New York: Charles Scribner's Sons, 1989).

2. Kennedy, *Rise and Fall*, p. 533. On this point, Kennedy states: "Here, too, the historical precedents are not encouraging. For it has been a common dilemma facing previous number one countries that even as their relative economic strength is ebbing, the growing foreign challenges to their position have compelled them to allocate more and more of their resources into the military sector, which in turn squeezes out productive investments and, over time, leads to the downward spiral of slower growth, heavier taxes, domestic splits over spending priorities and a weakening capacity to bear the burdens of defense" (p. 533).

3. For a succinct but compelling assessment of the declining American work force, see Bruce Nussbaum's article, "Needed: Human Capital," *Business Week*, September 19, 1988, pp. 100–103. Nussbaum writes: "In the final analysis, wage gains and losses mirror what is happening to worker productivity. The high decline in the wages of the unskilled labor force shows that it is no longer competitive in the international economy. The productivity of the unskilled is plummeting, while worker productivity abroad is soaring. This could signal major losses in the battle for world markets. The U.S. may now be entering an era where neglect of the bottom half of society begins to threaten the welfare of the entire nation" (p. 103).

4. Margaret Daley Hayes, "The U.S. and Latin America: A Lost Decade," in (Special edition), "America and the World" *Foreign Affairs*, 1988/89, pp. 187–89. This very perceptive article covers the full range of Latin America's basic problems. Concerning a more cooperative regional approach, she writes: "The OAS [Organization of American States] in the drug issue is encouraging, but it will have to be much more active to have a measurable impact on the problem. One area in which the OAS might take the initiative is in developing region-wide protocols for handling accused criminals and extradition requests" (p. 189).

5. Edward Teller, "Science, Technology, and Policy in the 1980's," in "American Foreign Policy: Toward the 1990's" (Tenth anniversary issue), *Harvard International Review*, 1989, p. 114.

6. Robert Bazell (science correspondent for NBC), "The Plague," *New Republic*, June 1, 1987, p. 15.

7. Marilyn Chase, "WHO's AIDS Chief Faces Major Task," *Wall Street Journal*, June 20, 1989, Sec. B p. 9. As to the further dimensions of this problem, Chase notes: "Yet Africa bears its misery with the scantiest of resources. In the U.S. government

spends $500 a year on each citizen's health care; many African governments can afford only $1 per capita. In the U.S. some AIDS patients are sustained by AZT, a drug costing $8,000 a year; in Africa, most cannot afford condoms to prevent transmission of AIDS or common antibiotics to ease AIDS symptoms'' (p. 89).

8. Daniel Burstein, *Yen: Japan's New Financial Empire and Its Threat to America* (New York: Simon and Schuster, 1988), pp. 36–41. Burstein's analysis is indeed stimulating. As an illustration of Japan's new financial strength, he writes: "Money has always 'made the world go round,' but never more so than today. Japan has become the leading creditor nation not just at any random time in history, but at a time when a single world financial supermarket and a single world economy are being forged'' (p. 42).

9. Ibid., p. 44.

10. David M. Abshire, "Toward a Grand Strategy," in "American Foreign Policy: Toward the 1990's" (Tenth anniversary issue), *Harvard International Review*, 1989, p. 81. Abshire recommends a comprehensive U.S.-Japanese strategy that builds upon the Japanese concept of security.

11. See John Tagliabue, "Pressures Rising for Polish Party," *New York Times*, June 18, 1989, p. 6. Tagliabue further notes, "The Communist Party's predicament is further complicated by Solidarity's rising expectations. Having swept 92 of 100 seats in the upper house or Senate in the first round of voting June 4, and all but one of the 161 seats accorded it in the lower house or Assembly, Solidarity officials intend to move into the last remaining citadel of the party—its network of patronage within the bureaucracy and the economy'' (p. 9).

12. For a well-balanced analysis of the rising tensions between the mine companies and black workers, see John F. Burns, "South Africa's Economy Faces an Unsteady Future," *New York Times*, March 13, 1988, p. 10. See also Diane B. Bendahamane and Anthony G. Freeman, eds. *Black Labor Unions in South Africa* (Washington, D.C.: Foreign Service Institute, United States Department of State, 1987), and Ned Tomke, "Politics Overrides Economics as Key Issue in South Africa," *Christian Science Monitor*, August 28, 1987, pp. 16–17.

13. Susan Chira, "Motorola's Labor Woes," *New York Times*, February 19, 1989, sec. 3, pp. 1, 10. A significant point made in this article is the ineffectiveness of existing labor laws to resolve labor management conflict: "Fewer strikes are breaking out these days than in 1987, when there was a total of about 3,700 labor disputes. But one of the reasons that such disputes can spiral out of control here is that labor and management have not agreed on standard procedures for resolving strikes."

14. It is difficult to predict what changes the 1989 student demonstration will have on the government. The protestors were defeated and retaliatory measures were swiftly imposed. For a contemporary on-the-spot view of how the government treated arrested dissidents, see Nicholas D. Kristoff, "Unleashing the Darker Methods of the Cultural Revolution," *New York Times*, June 18, 1989, sec. 4, pp. 1, 3. An interesting comment underscores the historical continuity of repression: "The scene could have come straight from the Cultural Revolution: 26 workers who had participated in the democracy movement were forced onto a stage before a packed meeting hall, so the masses could jeer at them. The workers' heads had been shaven, and some of them wore placards around their necks, giving their names and 'crimes.' Their public humiliation was a prelude to the next punishment: reform through hard labor in a work camp'' (p. 1). Others arrested and charged with acts of sabotage were executed.

15. See Roy Godson, *The Kremlin and Labor: A Study in National Security Policy*

(New York: Crane, Russak and Company, 1977). Though this study is somewhat dated, it does provide an informative overview of the Soviet Union's world labor strategy. His chapter entitled "Labor as an Instrument of Soviet National Security Policy" is particularly interesting. He notes the distinction in training methods between the programs offered by the World Federation of Trade Unions (WFTU) and those of the AFL-CIO: "Usually the training—whether conducted in a Soviet-bloc school or at a regional seminar—is almost completely ideological and political. Unlike the foreign labor education projects of the AFL-CIO, for example, little or no attention is devoted to the rudiments of organizing, negotiation, collective bargaining, and grievance procedures—the bread and butter concerns of unionists. Rather, they are designed to improve the propaganda skills and orientation as opposed to the technical skills of the student" (p. 40).

16.  Three studies that deal quite comprehensively with the corporate intelligence function, especially the organization of the process and source targeting, are Richard Eells and Peter Nehemkis, *Corporate Intelligence and Espionage: A Blueprint for Executive Decision Making* (New York: Macmillan, 1984); Benjamin Gilad and Tamar Gilard, *The Business Intelligence System: A New Tool for Competitive Advantage* (New York: American Management Association, 1988); and Leonard M. Fuld, *Competitor Intelligence: How to Get It—How to Use It* (New York: John Wiley and Sons, 1985).

17.  Herbert E. Meyer, *Real-World Intelligence* (New York: Weidenfeld and Nicolson, 1987).

18.  Dan Morgan, *Merchants of Grain* (New York: Penguin, 1980), p. 283. The other major grain companies are Continental, Louis Dreyfus, Bunge, and André. Morgan is uneasy with the grain companies' secrecy, he writes in his introduction: "But most large American companies today take the view that they have some responsibility to account to the public, to disclose and explain their actions. This is not the prevailing view among the five major grain companies. The code of secrecy that applied in 1844 has been not only perpetuated but fortified as the control of the major companies became centralized in the hands of a few people. The result is often suspicion, reticence—and arrogance" (p. 17).

19.  Jeffrey T. Richelson, *Foreign Intelligence Organizations* (Cambridge, Mass.: Ballinger, 1988), p. 263. Richelson provides a detailed analytical breakdown of the British, Canadian, Italian, West German, French, Israeli, and Japanese intelligence organizations. While these are governmental intelligence systems, their organizational structures and guiding philosophies provide a useful format for corporate intelligence executives.

20.  Robert B. Reich, "Whither Protectionism?" in "American Foreign Policy: Toward the 1990's" (Tenth anniversary issue), *Harvard International Review*, 1989, pp. 100–102. Reich's comment is interesting: "The playing field of international trade no longer even appears level. The exceptions are now the rule, and the old post-war rules now the exception. One consequence of this trend is that governments are beginning to judge the openness of their trading partners' markets on the basis of results—how much the other nation imports from them—rather than by reference to neutral rules. Thus a failure to import enough is taken as a sure sign of unfair protection" (p. 100).

21.  U.S. Congressman Lee H. Hamilton, "America's Role in the World: A Congressional Perspective," in "American Foreign Policy: Toward the 1990's," (Tenth anniversary issue) of the *Harvard International Review*, 1989, p. 37.

22.  David A. Jodice, *Political Risk Assessment: An Annotated Bibliography* (Westport, Conn.: Greenwood Press, 1985), p. 5. This is perhaps the best bibliography on the political risk literature. The book's value is well expressed in its introduction: "This volume

reviews analytic works and methodologies appropriate for the assessment and forecasting of political risk. It will serve as a guide to the field for corporate decision makers and managers of country/political risk assessment teams. Students of the environmental assessment practices of U.S.-based firms will find this a convenient introduction to the field. Analysts and managers in the international affairs agencies of the U.S. government will turn to these references and their authors as they struggle to incorporate techniques from private industry into governmental assessments of foreign political developments" (p. xi).

23. Ibid., p. 28.

24. Walter B. Wriston, "Technology and Sovereignty," *Foreign Affairs*, Winter 1988/89, pp. 65, 71. As Wriston points out, "Today we are witnessing a galloping new system of international finance. Our new international financial regime differs radically from its precursors in that it was not built by politicians, economists, central bankers or financial ministers, nor did high-level, international conferences produce a master plan. It was built by technology. It is doubtful if the men and women who interconnected the planet with telecommunications and computers realized that they were assembling a global financial marketplace that would replace the Bretton Woods agreements, and over time, alter political structures" (p. 71).

25. Leon Martel, *Mastering Change: The Key to Business Success* (New York: Simon and Schuster, 1986), p. 55. Martel notes: "Today, little more than a third of a century later, the number of digital computers in use—from microprocessors to main-frame—exceeds the number of people on earth. But even such a staggering total soon will be surpassed several times over. The post-industrial era—with information its transforming resource—has only just begun, and the electronic information business, already high, is still in its infancy" (p. 55).

26. Thomas B. Allen and Norman Polmar, *Merchants of Treason: America's Secrets for Sale* (New York: Delacorte Press, 1988), p. 4. The authors further assert, "The modern world of espionage never was a James Bond world of professional, stereotype spies and high-level defections. Spying has become profitable part-time work for faceless, unglamorous people who, in their routine jobs, have access to their nation's secrets."

27. Claiborne Pell, "A New Era in US-Soviet Relations," in "American Foreign Policy: Toward the 1990's" (Tenth anniversary issue), *Harvard International Review*, 1989, p. 87. The Soviet Union's need for respite is well stated by U.S. Senator Pell: "From the Soviet point of view, the restructuring of their economy requires a period of reduced superpower tension—a breathing space. In an environment of East-West conflict, Moscow would find it difficult to move resources from the military to the civilian sector. They would be less likely to achieve the expansion of trade, technology and credits that they used to strengthen their economy" (p. 87). See also, Eliot Cohen, "Analysis," in Roy Godson, ed., *Intelligence Requirements for 1990s: Collection, Analysis, Counterintelligence and Covert Action* (Lexington, Mass.: D.C. Heath, 1989), p. 89.

28. David A. Wellman, *A Chip in the Curtain: Computer Technology in the Soviet Union* (Washington, D.C.: National Defense University Press, 1989), p. 17. Wellman interestingly notes, "It is an ironic state of affairs for the Soviets that their own ideology, which places science and progress on the altar of public worship, has been unable to absorb and exploit the computer—the basic tool of today's technology age" (p. 17).

29. There are many excellent books on the negotiating process, but two books provide a good understanding of the conceptual nature of negotiations: Fred Charles Iklé, *How*

*Nations Negotiate* (New York: Frederick A. Praeger, 1964), and Henry A. Kissinger, *American Foreign Policy* (New York: W. W. Norton and Company, 1974).

30. Louis Uchitelle, "U.S. Businesses Loosen Ties to Mother Country," *New York Times*, May 21, 1989, pp. 1, 30.

31. Ariel Levite, *Intelligence and Strategic Surprises* (New York: Columbia University Press, 1987), p. 185.

32. Irving L. Janis, *Crucial Decisions: Leadership in Policymaking and Crisis Management* (New York: Free Press, 1989). This is a well-written detailed book and must reading for analysts and executives. Using evidence and concrete examples from real-life crises, Janis capably demonstrates how failure can be substantially reduced if sound procedures of information acquisition, analysis, and planning are used. His new theoretical framework, "The Constraints Model of Policymaking Processes," has practical application to crisis situations. Another book recommended is Richard E. Neustadt and Ernest R. May, *Thinking in Time: The Use of History for Decision Makers* (New York: Free Press, 1986).

33. Jeffrey T. Richelson, *The U.S. Intelligence Community*, 2d ed. (Cambridge, Mass.: Ballinger, 1989), p. 414.

34. Eells and Nehemkis, *Corporate Intelligence and Espionage*, p. 110. According to the authors the restatement of Torts says categorically that an exact definition of trade secrets is not possible. However, it suggests that courts consider the following factors when adjudicating trade-secret cases: "(1) The extent to which the information is known outside his business; (2) the extent to which it is known by employees and others involved in his business; (3) the extent of measures taken by him to guard the secrecy of the information; (4) the value of the information to him and his competitors; (5) the amount of effort or money expended by him in developing the information; (6) the ease or difficulty with which the information could be properly acquired or duplicated by others" (p. 111).

35. Ibid., p. 139.

# 2

# Analytical Framework for Corporate Intelligence

## *Hugh Conway*

Corporate intelligence, like most other corporate functions, has been radically changed by modern technology. Formerly the function had to cope with change executed at a relatively slow pace. The tools and methods of analysis were often secretive, were comparatively uncomplicated, and typically were focused on a small number of competitors acting in a relatively stable environment. Communications and computer technology has unalterably changed that environment and, consequently, corporate intelligence activity bounded by it.

Today the corporate intelligence function must cope with the changing reality produced by the new technology. This new reality consists of international markets linked more closely than ever before as a result of the internationalization of financial and information industries. Communication/computer technology has transformed both services, making their products ubiquitous. Technology and the globalization of money and information have affected virtually every sector of industry, and the total represents an industrial revolution.

Within an increasingly complex and competitive global environment the daunting job for corporate intelligence is to identify opportunities and threats. Information, made available through new technology, is the staple in the diet of the modern corporate intelligence function. The sheer volume of this staple, however, would make it undigestible without the help of computer technology. To manage large amounts of information requires the automated capability to receive, sort, save, and retrieve data. Transforming information into intelligence provides the intelligence function with its ultimate challenge and increasingly will become the value-added yardstick against which its utility and expectations will be measured.

The process of turning information into intelligence involves identifying useful information and processing that information in a way that helps to solve a corporate problem. It sounds simple and it is not.

Consider the steps in the process:

- In a global environment there is an ever-increasing tide of information requiring identification, selection, systematic review, and analysis.

- For information to become intelligence, less useful information must be systematically culled from more useful information, with the latter hierarchically arranged to reflect the potentially most useful combinations, associations, causal relationships, and interconnections of facts that will improve corporate insight and understanding of events and help problem solving.

To provide this service, the best corporate intelligence practitioners will rely on experience, wisdom, and hard work. They will be the most adept at looking beyond the surface of facts and best able to identify meaning and relevance.

The remainder of this chapter presents an analysis of technological change and social reactions to change. It is intended to serve as an analytical framework within which current corporate intelligence practitioners can view more particular, company-specific concerns. The analytical framework itself does not provide a company-specific prescription for conducting corporate intelligence. Its intended value is in demonstrating an analytical approach to examining, evaluating, and understanding change. The level of analysis may be inappropriate for much corporate analysis, and its findings and associations may not be relevant for specific operations and intelligence concerns. Rather, the analysis is meant to stimulate thinking about new approaches and to encourage the development of conceptual frameworks within which the importance of certain facts becomes more apparent.

In the past such an exercise would have been criticized as being too theoretical; there was not enough available data, and the relatively slow pace of change made modeling theoretical constructs impractical. The current industrial revolution created by communications and computer technology makes the exercise a necessity in today's corporate environment; a necessity in order to cope with the plethora of data internationally available; a necessity to the design of increasingly more sophisticated computer programs; and a necessity to improve our appreciation of the process of obsolescence, regeneration, and change.

Technology has created the modern information industry and placed it in a competitive setting characterized by nearly universal access to its products. To succeed, modern corporate intelligence must master the techniques and assimilate the products of the transforming technology. More prescience and creativity will be demanded.

A brief historical overview of technological change is presented in the sections that follow. Major revolutions in technological change are noted along with some discussion as to why technological change takes place at all; arguments that seek to explain the pace of change are considered along with factors or conditions that seem to explain the levels of inventiveness that exist at any point in time. While theories are helpful in explaining the parts and timing of certain changes, no single theory or set of explanatory variables has succeeded in anticipating the arrival of revolutionary technology, technology that has transformed economic enterprise and led to sociopolitical adjustments and reforms. Technology remains an exogenous variable in theories that attempt to predict or explain major industrial change. However, once the process of major industrial change has begun, there is considerable opportunity for theoretical analysis and speculation.

In the current communication/computer technology revolution, sophisticated new machinery has provided the vehicle for transforming the financial, information, and other service industries. New technology has internationalized capital and allowed universal access to new information. The universality of these products, in turn, has shaped the global economy and led to a restructuring of traditional closed political systems (USSR) and the development of new economic coalitions (European Common Market). Social conflict theory appears to be particularly relevant and analytically useful for evaluating these changes.

The revolution is producing corporate structural change, with large companies seeking to expand their global influence and merging with other very large corporations. Simultaneously the technology has created innumerable applications opportunities and has brought into existence an entire industry of entrepreneurs to service "niche" markets between the components of the new technology and potential users.

Technical expertise in the new technology and a service capability have been identified as the real source of future economic power. The flurry of corporate acquisitions involving this expertise appears to support this belief. Social and political adjustments to the technical and economic revolution are well under way. Correctly identifying the vital signs of the adjustment process and responding to them provide a challenge on which future corporate profitability and success will rest.

## TECHNOLOGICAL CHANGE

The development of an analytical frame for corporate intelligence should take into account historical facts and considerations. To help in predicting new technology changes and their implications, the occurrence of major breakthroughs in the past and their rate of diffusion are considered.

Daniel Bell of Harvard University has identified three major technological revolutions that have created and are changing modern industrial society. The first revolution occurred about two hundred years ago with the application of steam power to transportation, manufacturing, and mining.[1] By the middle of the nineteenth century the importance of this technological revolution was appreciated by the great social thinkers of that time, including Karl Marx, who noted that societies had been forced to rearrange themselves and their economic and social relations in order to accommodate the new technology. The objective technology and the new arrangement of people were collectively referred to as the "mode of production."[2] Moreover, technological change was seen to be virtually self-sustaining in the new capitalist economies in order to offset declining profit margins over time. Increased competition and declining profits provided the motivation to develop new labor-saving technologies.

Bell identifies a second technological revolution occurring about one hundred years ago with developments involving electricity and chemistry. Electrically transmitted messages, turbines, plastic, and synthetic fibers resulted from the new technologies.[3] Entrepreneurs who comprehended the market potential of the new technologies pioneered their diffusion. Nevertheless, anomalies in the speed with which certain technologies were adopted, while others languished, proved perplexing.

In a recent essay Brian Winston commented upon the relatively slow pace and the late introduction of television in the U.S. consumer market. Although very few sets were available in this country by the mid–1930s, "20,000 sets were operating in Britain and 180,000 people saw television images of the Berlin Olympics in 1936."[4] According to Winston, the constraints on the introduction of television were related to corporate strategy and interests; attention at the time was focused on the mass marketing of radios. He concludes that the constraints on early television diffusion were the result of the "law of suppression of radical potential." "This 'law' implies that technologies are introduced into society only when they do not disturb preexisting arrangements of all kinds."[5] While potentially useful in explaining why some technologies are not adopted more quickly and diffused more generally, the law does not explain the arrival of technologies that do disturb preexisting arrangements.

Commenting on the rate of new discovery and technological change, Ralph Landau relates such change (but not breakthrough innovations) to government fiscal policies that nurture and encourage experimentation, invention, and implementation. The level of capital gains taxation is identified as an important variable explaining future levels of investment in research and, consequently, technological change.[6]

Landau sees "correct government policies" as a prerequisite for technological change and identifies large budget deficits and "excessively high apparent real interest rates" as products of bad policy that threaten research and development in the future.[7] In the context of globalization, however, it is no longer clear that U.S. fiscal policy can single-handedly influence events as it did in the past.

"By 2013 the third technological revolution the joining of computers and telecommunications (image television, voice telephone, data information computers, text facsimile) into a single yet differentiated system, that of the 'wired nation' and even the 'world society'—will have matured." This future will be characterized by "robotics, electronic mail and messages, information retrieved on call, services organized through interactive terminals.''[8] Bell predicts that the joining of computers and telecommunications technology will have fundamental social consequences. "Communications networks, interactive in real time, with bursts of data speeding thousands of miles, mean the breakup of old geographical habits and locations. Thus, we see a change of extraordinary historical and sociological importance—the change in the nature of markets from 'place' to 'networks.' ''[9]

Illustrating the point has been the emergence of the global office. New technology has allowed service industries to follow the example set a decade earlier by manufacturing industries; office jobs have been moved abroad in order to take advantage of cheaper operating costs including lower pay scales. The New York Life Insurance Company processes insurance claims in rural Ireland along with Hartford-based Travelers Corporation. McGraw-Hill processes subscription-renewal and marketing information for several of its publications in Galway. A subsidiary of American Airlines employs over one thousand workers in Barbados and the Dominican Republic, processing ticket information. "The additional technological advances of satellite communications and trans-ocean fiber optic cables now make it reasonable for corporations to view each of their many service functions separately and ask: Where in the world can a certain task be done most efficiently and at the lowest cost?''[10]

Over the last five years changes in communications technology have led to a 50 percent increase in the number of long-distance transmissions in the United States, both domestic and international. The introduction of fiber-optic and other digital technology has resulted in greatly increased telecommunications capacity at lower rates. "A single optical fiber can carry more than 8,000 calls, compared with 48 for a copper wire.''[11] Rate reductions worth hundreds of millions of dollars have been passed on to consumers, thereby offsetting the cost of increased usage.

The emergence of communication/computer technology has taken place within the context of increasing global wealth. Joseph Nye attributes this wealth to U.S. foreign policy. "To the extent that the U.S. has had a grand strategy for foreign policy over the past 40 years, it has been to promote economic prosperity and political stability in Western Europe and Japan and a close alliance with them.''[12] The spread of prosperity, however, has led to "increased complexity of international interdependence which has reduced the potential for any country to exercise decisive influence over the whole system. Complexity derives from more actors, more issues, greater interactions, and less hierarchy in international politics.''[13]

Nevertheless, a major new influence has emerged within the system; money has moved overtly to center stage. The "internationalization of capital''[14] relates to the vast amount of Eurodollars held by banks and countries outside the United States and not covered by U.S. financial regulations. This internationalization of capital is the single most important development with which corporate intelligence in the 1990s must contend.

The existence of this vast hoard [means] that banking and corporate groups [can] direct their capital in search of higher returns, even when such action [goes] against the domestic interest of individual countries. This means that few countries, if any, are able to control their own currency. There is a loss of one of the main levers of power and influence.[15]

## Internationalization of Capital

Joan Spero has analyzed the extent and effect of the globalization of money. "World financial flows now dwarf goods flows by a factor of 50 to 1. Integrated global markets such as the Eurobond and Euroequity markets have developed; national markets now welcome foreign international participation; and increasingly national markets are joined electronically."[16]

Three key developments have created the conditions for global financial markets and money movement:

• Deregulation during the past ten years in many countries has ended controls on financial investment and services and has encouraged the flow of capital.

• Communication technology and computers have enabled financial markets to link and conduct daily business.

• Risk-reduction strategies employed by the financial managers of large pension funds and money market and equity funds include diversifying risk across several financial markets by means of innovative hedging techniques.[17]

Increasingly U.S. companies raise capital outside the United States. By the end of 1986, 516 foreign corporations listed securities on the London Stock Exchange; 59 foreign companies were listed on the New York Stock Exchange; and 52 foreign companies were listed on the Tokyo Stock Exchange.[18] Within the financial maelstrom, Japan has emerged as the world's largest creditor. International assets of Japanese banks have reached two trillion dollars, over two and one-half times those of U.S. banks.

Increasingly securities such as bonds and equities are the preferred means of raising and investing capital rather than direct bank borrowing. "Securitized financings accounted for only 44 percent of funds raised on the international financial markets in 1982. By the end of 1986 this figure was 87 percent."[19] In the United States, West Germany's Deutsche Bank earned $464 million in net income on assets of over $110 billion in 1988. Future plans call for continued U.S. expansion in the investment banking and securities markets.[20]

In the United States, the sheer magnitude and volume of daily money transactions made possible by communication/computer technology are difficult to comprehend. According to Spero, U.S. banks settle payments with each other through Fedwire, operated by the twelve Federal Reserve Banks and the Clearing House Interbank Payments System (CHIPS) operated by the New York Clearing House Association. Together "Fedwire and CHIPS handle an average daily volume of almost $700 billion in interbank settlements. The overwhelming majority of CHIPS activities is related to international markets. Eurodollars and foreign exchange transactions now account for 82.4 percent of CHIPS dollar volume."[21]

The large volume of these daily transactions, coupled with the speed with which information can be transmitted, has raised concerns over the stability of the global financial market. The speed with which information is transmitted can produce and exacerbate market shocks and vulnerability.

## Information

Complementing money, information has been given new value as a result of the communication/computer technological revolution. Computers have allowed the development and processing of much more data than was possible in the past, and communications technology has permitted its quick transmittal and universal access. In the United States alone there are between 4,000 and 5,000 data bases available on some 500 to 600 different computer systems. Data bases are continually being developed and designed to provide more specific, tailored information. The U.S. Information Industry Association (IIA) believes that this increase is in response to the growing demand for customized, quality information service.

To satisfy this demand, "infopreneurial" skills are being built on the knowledge of where data are and the ability to develop intelligence from information and to protect the resulting product. Computerized information systems are commonplace within large corporations. The technology has been applied in manufacturing in order to improve information flow, development, and analysis. For example, General Motors (GM) has spent over $40 billion in recent years on computer-integrated manufacturing (CIM). The GM information network now ties GM supplies to the manufacturers, with productivity improvements related to reduced bottlenecks and cost savings through better inventory control and improved equipment-replacement schedules.[22] During the 1980s the Ford Motor Company set up its Corporate Technical Information System (CTIS) to manage its information technology system. The automaker had literally hundreds of information sources, from highly technical engineering reports to the business sections of daily newspapers across the United States; the daily information flow included reports from overseas operations in the Pacific and Western Europe. Yet information was difficult to retrieve and seldom shared.[23] By 1989 CTIS had rationalized the system, creating thirty action files shared among four thousand corporate users.

The challenge facing all major corporations today is to maximize the usefulness of their own internal marketing information and data. The realization has dawned that stored data can be converted into valuable market-oriented intelligence. This discovery has elevated the importance of records management and has created a new service niche within the fast-growing information service industry.

Once internal information systems have been developed, the logic of competition has drawn the focus for new technology applications outward. Corporate intelligence analysts rely on outside data-base services for current information on industry trends and competitors' financial performance. To satisfy this interest, data bases have been built on information contained in trade and business publications, corporate annual reports, and Securities and Exchange Commission (SEC) filings.[24] A typical electronic report in the 1990s will cover current operating and cost data on competitors, their acquisition history, and background information on company executives.

The fledgling information service industry now must address a serious threat created by global information access. Spurred on by the Information Industry Association, the United States (effective March 1989) became the eightieth country to ratify the 1886 Berne Convention, thereby strengthening copyright relations with twenty-four countries. The World Intellectual Property Organization (WIPO), the United Nations agency that administers the Berne Convention, has also formulated a model national copyright law to protect electronic data bases and software.

It is estimated that the United States currently loses about $50 billion a year in sales through pirating of intellectual property.[25] Without international agreement and enforcement of standards regulating conduct in this area, the figure for lost sales will rise in the future. The issue has been discussed during the Uruguay round of talks under the General Agreement on Tariffs and Trade (GATT). U.S. companies are pressing for international standards and codes for trade in intellectual property, including the right to sue in the pirater's home country when theft is discovered.

## Technical Expertise and Corporate Structure

New technology has made possible the international markets for money and information; these in turn are forcing institutional changes and creating new corporate centers of influence and power based on technical expertise. The need to solve developmental problems involving technology, money, and information has greatly enhanced the status of professionals with knowledge in these areas. Such expertise could serve as the basis for economic power in the future.

Throughout the centuries statesmen and other observers have made mistakes in perceiving the metric of economic power. For example, in the 17th century, mercantilist theorists who focused on Spain's resources of gold bullion would not have understood the rise of France with its strategic administrative and commercial structure, or later, Britain with its conditions favorable to political stability and the industrial revolution. At the turn of the century, when the historian Brooks Adams used the control of metals and minerals as the predictive index of future military and economic power, he was led to expect the ascendency of Russia and China. But as the Harvard University social scientist Daniel Bell has pointed out, the core of postindustrial societies lies in the professional and technical services, and in that realm the United States and Japan are the two leading countries.[26]

These services have become the object of acquisition and merger interest. During 1988 four Arthur Andersen and Company partners quit in order to form a consulting subsidiary to a major British advertising firm. The expertise of the defecting partners was in the field of information technology and system integration, involving the design and operation of complex computer systems. In 1990 the management information consulting business is projected to gross $200 billion worldwide.[27]

A wave of acquisitions and mergers has transformed the advertising, marketing, and accounting industries, with very large companies joining together and pooling resources. The logic behind the mergers, according to one corporate executive, is to "benefit from the continuing rapid globalization of world economies, the accelerating pace of technological change and the broad based need for new services and investments."[28] Large size in a service corporation is seen as the natural complement to the advertising/accounting/marketing requirements of multinational consumer products companies operating in a global communication network environment. "One-stop" client service is the goal of the emerging service-sector conglomerates.

Increased concentration at the top should be accompanied by a similar rationalization among small and medium-sized service businesses. Throughout the 1990s the service opportunities and requirements of global markets should perpetuate the merger/acquisition trend.

## SOCIAL AND POLITICAL CHANGE

Societies have responded differently to the third industrial revolution now under way. Relatively open societies appear to be adjusting rapidly to change. More structured societies are in the process of removing barriers that inhibit change. Communist countries have a particularly difficult problem in adjusting to the communication/computer revolution. The enhanced value of money and information that the new technology has created appears antithetical to ideas and values traditionally associated with these societies. In the past, information has been strictly controlled and selectively distributed. Production and distribution systems for most goods and services appear to operate outside the boundaries of conventional microeconomic theory.

For ideologues with an appreciation of the logic of "historical materialism," these are unsettling times. If the new technology represents a new evolutionary plateau of the "material forces of production," and if theory is correct in predicting that superior productive force supplants lesser versions and forces change within the existing "relations of production," the implication for radical change within Communist societies appears inescapable. The distortion of money and information value in Communist states is not reconcilable with the new technology and its attendant products and values. From the perspective of U.S. corporations, technology forcing change in foreign countries is creating new opportunities and problems.

### The European Common Market

The Single European Act (July 1987) created a target date of December 31, 1992, for the implementation of an internal market, defined as an area without internal frontiers in which the free movement of goods, persons, services, and capital is insured. If all goes according to plan, in 1992 the European Economic Community will become a unified market of 320 million people, about the size of the combined U.S. and Japanese markets, with an annual gross domestic product (GDP) of $2.7 trillion, exports of $680 billion, and imports of $708 billion.[29] The political, social, and economic changes represented in this move toward unity are in response to the current technological revolution.

European corporate executives have long appreciated the disadvantages of the balkanized, fractious European markets compared to the relative homogeneity of the North American market. The inconvenience of trade barriers became intolerable with the new demands and opportunities inherent in the new communication/computer technology. Huge money pools require very large multifaceted markets to efficiently manage and place the sums being invested. Integrated communication and computer systems across country borders are essential in order to eliminate delays and inconvenience for banks and managers of money funds.

Proposed Common Market reforms are contained in about three hundred policy directives in the white paper ''Completing the Internal Market.'' These reforms are designed to reduce and eliminate nontariff trade barriers between the European partners. The directives call for the standardization of European laws covering intellectual property, corporate mergers, and public procurement policies. Several 1992 initiations form component parts of an integrated information technology strategy. These include the following:

- Development of machine translation systems to minimize language barriers
- Programs to promote a single information market and electronic data exchange
- The creation of pan-European data bases

Impediments that inhibit the diffusion of communication/computer technology are targeted for elimination in order to achieve the mass market consistent with technology's capabilities and its derivative capital-information components.

Increasingly U.S. companies are establishing a presence in Brussels, Belgium (EEC headquarters), either directly or through law/lobbying firms, in order to keep appraised of 1992 initiatives. The prospect of serving a market of 320 million people has obvious attractions for most large companies. Demographically, the population cohort aged sixty-five and over is growing rapidly, creating a potentially lucrative financial services market for savings, investments, and insurance. Lump-sum retirement payments in one country (Italy) are often spent on large purchases.

It is not clear, however, just how accessible this new super market will be to

U.S. companies. The purpose behind unification is to keep money, jobs, and technology in Europe. Early signals indicate that reciprocity will be a requirement for market access. For interested U.S. firms, selling in Europe may require producing goods and services in Europe. "A new business paradigm is developing defined by joint ventures and cooperative R & D efforts by ostensible rivals, vertical alliances between producers and customers and international sharing of products and technologies."[30]

But there is no guarantee that the European initiative will succeed. Modern social theory would caution that the objective of reaching consensus on three hundred policy directives places a considerable strain on the nascent alliance.

The greater the structural or cultural diversity of those who unite in a coalition, the more their interests other than in the immediate purpose are likely to be divergent if not antagonistic. Such a coalition, if it is not to fall apart, must attempt to keep close to the purposes for which it was formed.[31]

A corollary to this is that the larger the coalition, the simpler and fewer its obligatory rules must be.

Also, the act of forming an association "is itself creative of new association." The act of unification "calls forth some kind of unification of those other groups and individuals who feel themselves threatened by the coalition."[32] In this context, corporate intelligence analysts should anticipate change and opportunity among non-EEC European nations who comprise the European Free Trade Association (EFTA members include Austria, Finland, Iceland, Norway, Sweden, and Switzerland).

## Soviet Russia

The USSR is in the midst of a Herculean effort to reconcile, through political, social, and economic reform, the new technology with the vestiges of a Communist nation-state. The job is particularly difficult because of the fundamental ideological challenge that the changes represent. Ironically, the logic of Marxist theory makes the changes unavoidable. "Historical materialism" predicts that superior productive forces (computers and telecommunications) supplant lesser versions and forces change within existing social, political, and economic relations and institutions. The effort by the Soviet leadership to guide the change and adjustment to the realities of the new industrial revolution represents an experiment in social engineering, based upon social conflict theory, probably the most significant experiment of its kind ever attempted.

The deteriorating performance of the Soviet economy during the 1980s has been identified as the catalyst behind recent economic and social reforms.

The economic slowdown was compounded by technological backwardness, creating a second "gap" of profound political and psychological importance: the gap that increasingly separated the Soviet economy from those of other advanced industrial societies, as well as from the dynamic newly industrialized countries of Asia, from South Korea to Singapore. As a new industrial revolution transformed the international economy, placing a high premium on rapid technological innovation, speedy communication, and high-quality products, the Soviet system increasingly appeared to be relegated to marginality, a comparative backwater whose economic performance was increasingly incommensurate with its political ambitions, and threatened to jeopardize its military prowess.[33]

To counter stagnation, a new economic strategy has been adopted that centers around joint ventures with international partners. The joint venture as a corporate entity in the USSR was legalized in 1987; early in 1989 rules requiring that the Soviets own at least 51 percent of any enterprise were dropped. Joint ventures are to be entered into for the express purpose of attracting Western capital, technology, entrepreneurship, and managerial skills. It is intended that they produce for an international market and meet international standards of quality. In short, the purpose of this economic reform is to introduce Soviet industry to the economic rigor and discipline of the marketplace.

Joint-venture agreements between U.S. companies and USSR enterprises are proceeding at a tentative pace. The Soviet Institute for Automated Systems has negotiated joint-venture agreements with U.S. firms to supply personal computers and computer communications services. As of midyear 1989 about forty joint-venture agreements with American companies had been initiated.[34] (A practical problem that has to be overcome in effecting these arrangements concerns repatriation of profits.)

Increased communication is perhaps the centerpiece of the Soviet reform movement. The effort appears to acknowledge the irreconcilable difference between traditional Soviet information suppression and the information access capability inherent in new technology. There is no way to import the hardware without simultaneously importing its information-processing function.

Soviet leaders appear to have made a virtue of necessity. Gail Lapidus notes that endorsement of *glasnost* and its connotation of candor was a preemptive strike intended to reduce reliance on foreign and unofficial sources of information.

The Chernobyl experience gave enormous impetus to this effort. The fact that the Soviet people first learned of a major domestic catastrophe with far-reaching implications for their own welfare from foreign broadcasts, and that the news was initially denied by their own government, was a major political embarrassment.[35]

The fact that such broadcasts were being received signalled the presence of modern technology. The options were to attempt to eliminate the presence or endorse it and attempt to harness its power. Soviet leaders chose the second option.

Embrace of the new communication/computer technology has taken several forms. A new satellite computer communications link now exists between the United States and the USSR. During 1988 representatives of the U.S. information industry met with their Soviet counterparts to decide upon the ground rules for future exchanges and cooperative efforts. Jointly agreed-upon recommendations of the delegation included the following:

- The United States and the USSR should work to establish and enforce standards for telecommunication systems.
- The United States and the USSR should access information on electronic data bases and establish an electronic network to serve as an information link between scientists and engineers.[36]

The recommendations were mutually endorsed by the U.S. American Center for International Leadership (ACIL) and the Soviet Union's Committee of Youth Organizations (CYO).

Within the U.S. government the Bureau of the Census has a written agreement to exchange information with the Soviet State Committee on Statistics (Gloskomstat). In the Soviet Union the Institute for Automated Systems and the USSR National Center for Automated Data Exchange are promoting commercial network and data-base enterprises. The effort includes linking the scientific community within the Soviet-bloc countries.

With more information available, the Soviet leadership has adopted a more sophisticated approach to information management. General Secretary Mikhail Gorbachev has placed loyal supporters to administer the ideological and cultural department within the Central Committee; loyalists have also been placed as editors of the country's most important journals, *Kommunist* and *Pravda*.[37] In place of embargo, news will now be monitored, selectively sanitized, and shaped.

Accompanying economic and communications reform has been a more subtle campaign designed to project a new political-cultural awareness. The campaign recognizes ethnic and cultural divisions within the Soviet Union, a recognition that heretofore was not encouraged. More candid discussion of problems now appears to be officially accepted, along with greater tolerance of ethnic aspirations.

On the surface, the democratization taking place seems radical and ultimately inimical to Communist Party interests. Social conflict theory offers another perspective by pointing out that group conflict and values can serve a positive function within society.

Multiple group affiliations of individuals make for a multiplicity of conflicts criss-crossing society. Such segmental participation, then, can result in a kind of balancing mechanism, preventing deep cleavages along one axis.[38]

Rigid totalitarian societies lack mechanisms for adjusting to change and consequently permit the accumulation of hostilities that may eventually threaten basic consensual agreement. Seen in this light, the promotion of democratic reform by recognizing ethnic and cultural differences has the intended consequence of generating antagonism and conflict situations. Given the disaggregated level of antagonism, the threat to higher-level political-social consensus is reduced.

Democratization, ethnic relations, and unrest will be ongoing topics of debate in the Soviet Union. The discussion itself is an affirmation of multiplicity and opportunity; sporadic conflict and even violence among ethnic and cultural divisions provides an opportunity for the Party to assert and affirm its moderating influence.

The Soviet leadership recognizes that the new industrial revolution requires a fundamental restructuring of the Soviet economy; the logic of its own ideology forces that conclusion. Democratic reforms have been selectively put in place. These reforms present business opportunities in the form of joint-venture arrangements for U.S. companies. If the analysis presented here is correct, corporate intelligence staff would advise cautious optimism about the prospects of success for such joint ventures and stress the bottom line—make sure the profit-repatriation clause is airtight.

## NOTES

1. Daniel Bell, "The World and the United States in 2013," *Daedalus: Journal of the American Academy of Arts and Sciences* 116, no. 3 (Summer 1987): 11.

2. Karl Marx, "A Contribution to the Critique of Political Economy," cited in Robert Freedman, *Marx on Economics* (New York: Harcourt, Brace and World, 1961), 6–7.

3. Bell, "The World and the United States in 2013," 11.

4. Brian Winston, "A Mirror for Brunelleschi," *Daedalus: Journal of the American Academy of Arts and Sciences* 116, no. 3 (Summer 1987): 192.

5. Ibid.

6. Ralph Landau, "Technology, Economics, and Public Policy," in *Technology and Economic Policy*, ed. Ralph Landau and Dale W. Jorgenson (Cambridge, Mass.: Ballinger, 1986), 30.

7. Ibid., 32.

8. Bell, "The World and the United States in 2013," 11.

9. Ibid., 12.

10. *New York Times*, October 18, 1988, D25.

11. Ibid., May 22, 1989, D4.

12. Joseph S. Nye, Jr., "Understanding U.S. Strength," *Foreign Policy*, no. 72 (Fall 1988): 107.

13. Ibid., 108.

14. Bell, "The World and the United States in 2013," 2.

15. Ibid., 9.

16. Joan E. Spero, "Guiding Global Finance," *Foreign Policy*, no. 73 (Winter 1988–89): 114.

17. Ibid., 114–19.

18. Ibid., 117.

19. Ibid., 119.

20. *New York Times*, May 22, 1989, p. D5.

21. Spero, "Guiding Global Finance," 125.

22. August 23, 1986, "Survey" section, *Economist*, 15.

23. *Information Times* (Information Industry Association), Supplement, April 1989, S1.

24. James M. McGrane, "Going On-Line for Planning and Competitive Intelligence," *Management Review*, October 1987, 55.

25. David Peyton, "Converging Intellectual Property Protective Instruments," *Information Times*, January 1989, S3.

26. Nye, "Understanding U.S. Strength," 121–22.

27. "Washington Business" section, *Washington Post*, June 12, 1989, 1.

28. *New York Times*, July 7, 1989, D4, quoting a joint statement issued by Joseph E. Connor, chairman of Price Waterhouse, and Lawrence A. Weinback, chief executive of Arthur Andersen and Company.

29. The European Economic Community is made up of twelve countries: Belgium, Denmark, France, Great Britain, Greece, Italy, Ireland, Luxembourg, Netherlands, Portugal, Spain, and West Germany.

30. W. John Moore, "Sprouting in Brussels," *National Journal*, May 13, 1989, 1187.

31. Lewis Coser, *The Functions of Social Conflict* (New York and London: Free Press, 1956), 144.

32. Ibid., 148.

33. Gail W. Lapidus, "Gorbachev and the Reform of the Soviet System," *Daedalus: Journal of the American Academy of Arts and Sciences* 116, no. 2 (Spring 1987): 5–6.

34. "Perestroika's Yankee Partner," *New York Times Magazine*, June 11, 1989, 20.

35. Ibid., 16–17.

36. *Information Times* January 1989, 23.

37. Lapidus, "Gorbachev and the Reform of the Soviet System," 24.

38. Coser, *Functions of Social Conflict*, 78–79.

# Part II

## New Technology and Information

# 3

# Management Information Sources and Corporate Intelligence Systems

## *Robert F. Gordon*

In this book the word ''intelligence'' is used in several different contexts. Intelligence can refer to the process of gathering data; it can refer to the data itself; and it can refer to the application of knowledge to produce useful information from the data. We will see in this chapter how the computer can be used in business to further all three aspects of intelligence: capturing the data, storing the data in an accessible form, and adding value to the data by transforming it into useful information for decision making. This chapter is organized according to these three areas of computer support for business intelligence:

1. Transaction processing and intelligence capture
2. Data-base management and intelligence storage and retrieval
3. Decision support systems and intelligence processing

We provide an overview of the concepts in transaction processing, data-base management, and decision support systems. References are listed in each of these areas for further details. Our purpose is to provide the perspective for the executive to determine the use of these concepts for his or her company and to understand the choices open to him or her in today's technology.

In discussing the application of computer systems to the intelligence function, it is important to distinguish between ''data'' and ''information.'' The term ''data'' is used to refer to raw facts, such as individual sales transactions, bank transactions, or employee time cards. On the other hand, the term ''information'' is used to denote the result of processing these facts in a meaningful way to lead to a decision. With respect to the given examples of data, the corresponding information could be the percent change in sales this year compared to last, the volume of bank transactions from each automated teller machine, or the number of employees late by day of the week. This information might help management decide, respectively, on marketing strategies for a product, the distribution of automated teller machines, and personnel policy.

Data and information are relative terms in that the material changes from one type to the other based on the current need of the individual in the company. What is information for someone at the level of operations control (such as hourly call demand to a reservations center) may be just data that needs further processing to be useful to higher levels of management. In this case the further processing might be to convert the hourly call demand into a schedule of operators for the supervisor by incorporating service-time information and union requirements. Middle management might require further processing to convert the hourly call demand to historical monthly demand and then to monthly forecasts that would then be converted to manpower projections for the next year. Here data external to the company, related to the industry and the economy, would be used to produce the forecast.

The conversion of data to information thus goes through several levels of information. It can involve accumulating or sorting the data, but more often the conversion requires incorporating other data as well as logic and mathematical algorithms.

Value is added when data is transformed into information, added again through each level of information, and added again when the information is transformed into decisions. The company gains value from transforming the transaction data of individual calls into hourly call demand to schedule the reservation agents, then into monthly demand (accumulation) and into monthly forecasts (external data capture and mathematical algorithms) to determine future requirements in staffing and equipment at the reservations center.

These value-added transformations are accomplished sometimes by the computer, sometimes by humans, and often by a combination of both. In the human/computer process, humans initially supply the objectives, criteria, and the process logic to the computer. Such specifications determine the software to be run by the computer. Once the software is programmed and tested, the computer provides the fast, accurate calculations, the execution of the specified algorithms, the storage and access of data, and the display of the resulting information. The human often interacts with the executing software, providing inputs (data and commands), viewing the results or partial results, and then evaluating them. This may lead him or her to change the input (what-if questions) or perhaps the algorithm, or perhaps to override the results. The human serves as the control when he or she makes these changes, and at times he or she may be able to program this control into the computer so it can be self-adapting. Iteratively and interactively the human/computer process leads to information and to decisions.

We call this process computer-based information systems and describe it in the next three sections.

## TRANSACTION PROCESSING AND INTELLIGENCE CAPTURE

First, we discuss the input component of computer-based information systems. Transaction processing involves the capture, error checking, and updating of data.

A transaction is a grouping of data items (also referred to as fields). The data items define the various attributes of some entity. For example, an employee transaction is a grouping of the data items associated with a particular employee, such as employee number, last name, first name, address, department, and salary. An employee transaction would consist of these six data items. In determining the data items, we look at the requirements for the data and then set up each data item so that it is at the lowest level, that is, it does not have to be subdivided. Therefore, if we anticipate a need to access employees by city, address should not be a single data item, as in the example, but should be composed of several data items, perhaps street, city, state, and zip code.

The purpose of a transaction is to make a change to the data stored in the computer. This change can be an addition, a modification, or a deletion of data. Thus an employee transaction might add a new employee, change the pay rate of an existing employee, or remove a transferred employee from the employee data base. For now we will call data stored in a computer a ''data base'' and will define this term in the next section. Other examples of transactions are reservations, deposits, withdrawals, customer orders, and purchase orders.

Companies can enter transactions into a computer in several ways. We identify variations in terms of hardware as well as processing methods. In terms of hardware, companies often utilize other computers, terminals, or sensors at remote sites to capture data. Communications networks are used to transmit data between terminal and computer, as well as for computer-to-computer links. A company may retrieve the data from another site to store and process in its own computer, or it may use the processing power of another computer to both extract and manipulate the information needed.

In terms of processing methods, companies may use interactive processing, batch processing, or a combination of both. Interactive processing allows the user to enter and edit individual transactions, getting immediate feedback during the process. Batch processing allows for bulk updates with feedback after all transactions are processed.

In interactive processing, transactions are entered at a terminal. Typically a program displays prompts and information on a terminal, and the operator at the terminal enters replies and commands. The operator interacts with the program in an iterative loop of entering data and getting feedback (information). The program allows the operator to edit the responses and transmits the operator's input to the computer, where it can be checked and perhaps, after several iterations of input and response, used to update the data base. Based on the operator's replies and/or the result of the update, the program displays the appropriate prompts and information back to the terminal.

As an example, a customer may telephone a hotel reservations center and provide the reservations agent with the date items for a reservation transaction. The agent utilizing a software program is prompted first for the type of reservations transaction: make a reservation, modify a reservation, delete a reservation. If the agent selects "make a reservation," the program displays a template, prompting for the customer's name, hotel, expected arrival date and time, expected departure date and time, room type, number of people in the party, credit card type and number, and rate code. When completed by the operator, this transaction is transmitted to the computer, where availability at that hotel for those dates and room type can be checked. If a room is available, the transaction can update the reservations data base, and a confirmation message can be sent back to the agent at the terminal. Thus the reservation can be made and confirmed while the customer is on the line.

In addition to fast feedback, another benefit of interactive processing is that previously stored data can be used to guide the input. Thus, if a customer calls to modify a reservation, the reservations agent enters the customer's identification, such as a reservation number. When the agent enters this identification, the data corresponding to that reservation are displayed, serving as verification and prompt information for talking with the customer and as a basis for modifying the reservation. The agent avoids having to ask the customer and reenter previously stored data.

A similar interaction occurs when a terminal is used to enter customer orders or to record shipments or payments. As the data is received, it is entered, edited, and used to update the data base. There is relatively small delay between data entry and use in these types of systems; thus availability of rooms, inventory, and orders are kept up to date with the activity. Furthermore, interactive processing allows the corrections to the input to be made at the time of data entry, before the update of the data base.

Some business environments lend themselves to direct input of data by the customer, rather than having the customer go through an intermediary. Thus a bank customer might enter a withdrawal or deposit transaction directly into the terminal (automated teller machine) instead of giving it to the bank teller to enter. A traveler might reserve an airline seat by interacting with a touch-screen terminal that displays a diagram of the airplane's seating. A visitor might find a list of restaurants by selecting items from menus on a terminal screen or find travel directions by selecting one of a set of sites on a map displayed on the terminal screen. In the hotel reservations example, instead of the customer giving the reservations agent the data, he might use a touch-tone phone to input the information directly to the computer.

To further reduce the delay between an event and its entry into the computer, the data capture might be automated. Sensors can capture the data instantaneously and send it to the computer, avoiding the time to communicate it to the terminal operator and to have it typed into the terminal. Applications of sensors are radar to transmit air traffic control programs, onboard instruments to capture positional data for missile guidance control, road sensors to control traffic lights, measurement probes sending data to control a chemical process, and optical scanners to read product bar codes on a shipping/receiving dock. The term "real-time" might be best applied to these systems; the computer data is updated as the event (transaction) takes place.

In other cases the data might already be in a form readable by computer but might be at another site or in another company's computer. A company with branch computers might store local data in each branch computer and connect the local computers through a communications network. This distributed processing allows local processing of data as well as the transmission of data to the other computers for processing and/or display.

News services, stock trading, government statistics, financial data, and economic projections often are put in computer-readable form. Companies can access this data for a fee through a telecommunications link to the service's computer. The service's computer provides the data and the access program. A company can extract selected data from a service's computer data base to be used in its own computer data base.

In contrast to the given examples of data entry, companies may want to use batch processing for some updating of their data bases. In batch processing all the transactions for a given period are converted to machine-readable form, such as on tape or disk. Usually an operator using a key-to-tape or key-to-disk machine enters and verifies the transaction data. The resulting tape or disk is read by a program that updates the whole data base with the transactions. This approach is best suited for a large number of transactions when most of the data base must be updated and there is no need for immediate response or prompting for input. Neither the computer nor the communications line is tied up for data entry as in interactive processing. Batch processing is typically used to update data bases to produce periodic reports. Most accounting applications, such as general ledger, accounts receivable, accounts payable, and payroll, are effectively handled in this way.

Getting the data into computer-readable form is often the most time-consuming and error-prone part of using a computer system. In addition to key-to-disk and key-to-tape entry, optical scanning and optical reading can be used to capture the data. Optical scanning programs identify the presence or absence of markings (whether penciled multiple-choice answers or bar codes). Optical reading, on the other hand, requires that the computer identify specific characters or numbers. Optical reading is thus more processor intensive than optical scanning.

Voice input is beginning to be used in some applications. Discrete speech recognition (recognizing speech with distinct pauses between words) is an alternative means of data entry. Programs exist that can recognize a large number of words. Most often these recognition programs are voice-dependent. They may be useful, for example, on an assembly line where the operator's hands are not free to input data. Continuous speech recognition is much more difficult to accomplish by computer, requiring very large processing capability.

For some applications, it is not necessary that the computer recognize the content of the data, whether it be text, voice, graphics, or images, but only that the computer be able to store and retrieve it. Thus pages of text, voice, graphics, and images can be scanned and digitized to be stored (and/or transmitted) in a computer. Programs retrieve the items and present them to the user; it is left to the user to process them.

## DATA-BASE MANAGEMENT AND INTELLIGENCE STORAGE AND RETRIEVAL

Once the data is captured for computer use, it is necessary to store it in a form that makes it easily accessible. Different storage methods and means of structuring the data are used to organize the data for fast retrieval. The particular storage method and data structure depend on the retrieval needs. We will describe several storage methods and data structures and discuss the conditions under which to use each. In doing so, we will concentrate on the important data-base concepts.

First, some terminology is necessary. We spoke about data items comprising a transaction in the previous section. It is common to refer to the data items as fields and transactions as a type of record and to think in terms of the following hierarchy: a file is made up of records that are made up of fields. Thus an employee file is composed of employee records (one for each employee), each of which is composed of fields (each field containing the value of a data item for that employee). Typically the format of each record in the file is the same. In this case each employee record has the same number, type, and size of fields. The first field of every employee record may be employee number, the second field may be employee last name, and so on. The format of the fields forms a template, more precisely called a record type, to be followed by each record. When the actual values for fields are supplied, such as employee number: 83067, employee last name: Jones, and so on, a record is created. Each record is an example or, more precisely, an instance of the record type. A file usually has one record type and contains many instances (one for each employee in the example) of that type. Usually one field of the record type is denoted as the key field; it is a field that can be used to order the records in the file. Typically a field that has a unique value for each record is chosen to be the key field. In the example, employee number would be a good candidate for the key field.

Just as an executive might have memos organized in a file folder, the computer has records organized in a file. The executive might have organized memos in one file folder in chronological order, in another file folder by subject, and in another by sender. Similarly, if we consider each memo to be a record and its date, subject, and sender to be three different key fields, then the computer can be instructed to store the data in one of these key sequences. Given any of these keys, this could provide any of these organizations of the memos.

It is important to realize that it is not necessary to physically store the same data in three different ways (three files) in order to access it efficiently in each way. Furthermore, we may not want to store the data in any of these sequential orders, and yet we may want to be able to utilize the three orderings.

As an example, if the executive only stored the memos chronologically in one file folder but prepared a list (index) by subject showing the dates associated with each subject, he could use the index to point him to the appropriate memo in the chronological file, thereby accessing the memos in subject order. Of course this would be slower than having the file in subject order for this purpose, but this procedure eliminates the need to duplicate the memos. Similarly, indices and pointer fields allow the computer to access data in many different ways even though the data is stored only once.

The access method refers to how to find the record physically on the storage medium. The storage medium is usually tape or disk. The data structure of the records refers to the organization of the data: the order of fields within a record, the connection between records in the file, and the use of indices and pointers to reach a record.

Regardless of the organization of the data, there are two data access methods: sequential access and direct access. In sequential access, each record is retrieved in sequence as it is stored. A typical sequential access method device is a tape drive. The data structure for sequential access is usually also sequential; that is, the records are usually in some meaningful order (alphabetical, chronological, or the like). In direct access, any record can be retrieved without having to retrieve the prior records in the file. This method allows the computer to go directly to the address (location) of the desired record. The records need not be in any specific order required by the application; that is, the physical location of the records need not be determined by the logical relation of the records. A typical direct access method device is a disk drive.

Sequential access can be compared to a cassette player. To play the fifth song on the cassette or to edit it, you must play or fast-forward through the first four songs. In contrast, direct access is similar to a record player; you can play the fifth song directly by moving the record arm to that song. The listing of the songs on the album cover provides the index to each song on the record, and you can play them in any order.

To get an appreciation of the benefits and limitations of each method, consider the playing of one particular song in the album. Sequential access (cassette player) would require playing all prior songs; on the average, half the songs would be played before reaching the desired song. Direct access allows us to move the record arm to the selection without playing through the previous songs. In this case (specific selection), direct access is superior. On the other hand, suppose we wanted to play every song on the cassette. We would start the cassette and sit back and listen to each song in sequence until the cassette ended.

If we were to follow the direct access scheme, manually we would check the album index and pick up and place the record arm before each song. In this case (all selections), sequential access is better. Of course, with the phonograph record we could let the record arm start at the beginning of the record and play through all of the songs automatically. This points out that a direct access device, such as the record player, often can be used for both direct access and sequential access.

There are many ways (data structures) to organize and store company data. Which structure to use depends on the retrieval requirements for that data. In a sequential device there is basically only one type of data organization, and that is called a sequential file. In this data organization each record is sequenced by a key field. The records could be in alphabetical order if, for example, last name were the key field. The records could be in chronological order if date were the key field. Accounting applications often use sequential files because the application is run periodically, and for each period, most of the records in the file need to be accessed. For example, a payroll system will have to read the record for each employee to produce the paychecks each period. As we saw earlier, when most of the records need to be accessed, a sequential file structure is best.

Sometimes there are several different and possibly conflicting retrieval requirements for a given set of data. A limitation in the payroll sequential file structure is that if we wanted the payroll to be produced in employee number order and a payroll report to be ordered by employee last name, then we would have to store the same data twice, once for each order required. With a direct access method device, we can handle this and only store the data once. In the example of the record album, if we wanted to play all the songs but in a different order, we could use the index on the album cover to point us to move the record arm to each song in the desired order. This is true for computer direct access devices as well.

For a direct access method device, there are many choices of data organizations. This flexibility allows the design of the data structures to fit the multiple needs of the company. As we saw earlier, a sequential data structure can be handled on a direct access method device. For other data structures, the computer must be supplied with the location of the record desired. This can be provided by giving the computer access program the desired record's key and having the program transform the key algebraically to arrive at a number that will be assigned as its location. Such a technique is called basic direct access method (BDAM), and typically the key is divided by a prime and the remainder is the recorded location.

Another technique utilizes an index. The indexed random structure has an index stored with the records on the file. The index contains two columns (like the index of a book or album cover); the first column contains the key values in sequence, and the second column contains the corresponding location of that record. To retrieve a record, the computer program finds the desired key value in the index and retrieves the record from the corresponding location.

A third method utilizes a field in each record to point to the location of the next record to process. Once the computer retrieves a record, one of its fields contains all the information necessary to retrieve the next record. Pointers in records avoid the need to use keys. With several pointer fields in a record, the computer can process the data in many different ways, although the data is stored only once. All that is necessary is to be given the field to use for the pointer and the initial record's location. Even parts of a record (segments) could be stored separately, as long as there is a pointer from one segment to another. This is the basis of a data base.

A data base is the data together with a description of how the data is organized. The description of the data organization is called the schema. A program, called a data-base management system, reads the schema and uses it, as one would use a road map, to find the data in the data base. The schema tells the data-base management system the location, or how to find the location through other records (using pointers), of the desired record or record segment. The files that we described previously (such as a payroll file) have one record type. These files also are organized in one way (for example, sequentially, one record after the other) and are called flat files. With pointers, the file can have a more complicated and more versatile organization. Its structures could have some records at a different level of importance than others or a different grouping of records.

The data-base management system provides the ability to specify the schema, load the data base (instances), update the data base, and retrieve information from the data base on the schema. It is this last function that is the purpose of setting up the data base and the one in which we are most interested. The purpose of a retrieval might be to produce a report from the data base by finding (and perhaps accumulating) all records that satisfy a particular criterion (request). Alternatively, we may want to interactively query the data base with an English-like language to display specific fields from all records that meet a criterion.

The two most popular kinds of data bases in industry are hierarchical data bases and relational data bases. A hierarchical data base is used when the data organization required for retrieval follows a natural hierarchy, similar to a company's organization chart. The schema for a hierarchical data base starts at the top of the organization (root segment) and provides pointers to each succeeding level. Thus, to use the personnel organization chart as an example, the root might be the president record (it might contain fields referring to name, office location, duties, and so on), the next level might be the vice president record (it might contain different types of fields, such as functional department name), the next level might be the director level, and so on. This schema provides an outline of the data in the data base. When the actual fields are completed, the resulting instances of the data make up the data base. There may be one instance of president, ten instances of vice president, and so on, just as there were many instances of the employee record type in the payroll flat file. This hierarchical data base is useful for retrieving all employees working for the marketing vice president, for example, because they are all in the levels pointed to by that vice president's record.

Applications that lend themselves to hierarchical retrieval are reporting systems: division, region, and territory for sales reporting or for financial statements. Thus, to retrieve a salesperson's activity, the data-base management system will select from the data base the appropriate division, which will point it to the appropriate region, which will point it to the appropriate territory, which will contain the salesperson's activity in one of its fields. This structure allows fast retrieval of all salespersons in a particular region. The reverse retrieval, to find a particular salesperson without knowing his or her division and/or region, would be difficult (time-consuming), because the hierarchical structure does not help the search.

Relational data-base organization is preferable when we want the capability to change the order of retrieval based on the request. For example, sometimes we may want to retrieve information about all the customers who bought a specific product; at other times we may want to get information about all the products bought by a particular customer. Customer and product form a different hierarchy in these two cases. In the first case it would be better for retrieval efficiency to have customer at a higher level. Then getting all the product records under a specific customer would be easy; however, with that organization it would be very time-consuming to determine all the customers for a given product.

A relational data base is designed to handle situations like this, where the hierarchy needs to be changed for different retrievals. A relation is simply a flat file or a table of records. A relational data base has one or more relations. The schema for a relational data base defines each relation or table by identifying the fields that each record in that table will contain and which field will be the key. The relational data-base management system provides functions to manipulate the tables, such as selecting the instances of a table that meet certain criteria for their fields (all employees with salary field above $50,000), or joining instances from two tables that have a field value in common to form a third table.

In the example there could be three relations: product, customer, and purchases. The product relation might be a table of all product records, each with fields such as product code (key), price, and inventory amount. Similarly, the customer relation might be a table of all customer records, each with fields such as customer name (key), address, and balance. In order for the data-base management system to retrieve product information about all products purchased by a given customer or customer information for all customers who purchased a given product, we need to provide it with information from both relations. A purchase relation might contain all purchase records with fields such as customer name, product code, and amount.

To answer the request for all product information for products purchased by customer A, the program would first search the purchase relation for all instances of customer A and from the resulting product code in each one of these instances would retrieve from the product relation the information for that product. To get the customer information for all customers that purchased product 001, the program would first search the purchase relation for all instances of product 001 and from the resulting customer name in each one of these instances would retrieve from the customer relation the information for that customer.

Thus a relational data-base management system finds the necessary links between the relations as it processes the request. It is therefore more flexible than a hierarchical data base. The hierarchical data-base management system has the links already defined between the levels of the hierarchy. It is thus able to find the desired records faster than a relational data base, provided that the request is based on those predetermined links.

The data-base management system (whether hierarchical or relational or other) then allows management to query the data base and provides the results of a wide range of searches through the large number of instances in the data base. Management can get information in the form of reports or interactive answers to queries. The information is based on selection criteria and can consist of details of individuals as well as group summaries, subtotals, and comparisons. Basic arithmetical and logical combinations of the fields in the selected records can be produced for management decision making.

For example, personnel management might ask to select from their employee data the employees who have experience in certain areas, high ratings, and certain aptitudes as a basis for filing a job application. Marketing management, for advertising decisions, might query the reservations data base to calculate the mean lead time between reservation booking date and arrival date for a particular time of the year and region of the country. A customer service agent might ask for the billing information to be displayed for a particular customer to answer a complaint.

Typically the data stored in data bases are internal to the company, historical, and very detailed (at the individual transaction level). The data-base management system searches and combines the data to answer the query or to fill the report. This is useful to help solve the types of problems and information needs at the lower levels of the company, where the internal, historical, detailed information can be used as a basis for decisions. Specific employees, customers, or products can be selected that meet criteria. Summary and statistical information can be provided based on the detailed field values, such as lead-time information. Management has complete access to, and the ability to select and combine all of, the data captured in its data base.

Sometimes the extracted information completely answers the problem (list of employee candidates); sometimes further transformations are necessary to arrive at a decision (the lead time is just one input to determine the media plan). We will describe in the next section decision support systems to apply to the extracted information that evaluate alternatives and help management determine actions.

It is important to realize that top-management decisions usually involve long-term estimates that cross a wide number of functional areas in the company. These decisions require less detailed information than those at lower levels of the company; they can often be based on approximate and summary data. However, they usually require additional external data (economy, competition, government), as well as future-oriented data.

For example, to predict the next several years of company sales might require thirty-six numbers (the last thirty-six monthly sales figures) and economic and competitive action projections for the next several years. The individual detailed transactions that make up these thirty-six numbers are of little value in this case except in aggregate, so the thirty-six numbers might more practically be kept on a piece of paper (or duplicated in some other file) than calculated each time from the data base. Add to this that the external projection data are typically not even in the data base, and we see that in this case the data-base retrieval is not the important contribution of the computer; it is the decision methodology that is important. Given that these are the kinds of problems (long-term, future-oriented, requiring external data) that top management faces, top management benefits less from transaction processing and data-base management than the lower levels of the company.

Top management can, however, benefit as much as the other levels from the use of decision support systems. We will describe some of the most often used decision support systems in the next section and indicate the type of real-world problems that they should be used to solve.

## DECISION SUPPORT SYSTEMS
## AND INTELLIGENCE PROCESSING

Decision support systems is a term used to describe a wide range of computerized solution techniques that can be applied to solve business problems. The solution techniques may describe alternative scenarios (answer what-if questions) or produce optimal solutions. Some may merely be data-base query routines, while others may incorporate complex mathematical algorithms. Some techniques may be developed for a company's specific problems; others may be general techniques that can be applied to similar kinds of problems in many companies.

We will describe at a high level three different and widely used techniques to give an idea of the type and range of methods available. For each technique we give a brief background of the concept and assumptions followed by an example of its use in business. In order to show a manual solution we simplify the real-world problem here, reducing its complexity in terms of the number of variables, number of outcomes and options, and number of time periods; the computer is required for most realistic business applications of these solution techniques, but the computer solution techniques follow the principles shown here.

Given a problem, the decision maker needs to determine what solution technique to use and then to abstract from the real world the important aspects of the problem required by that solution technique. The result of this abstraction is called a model.

The model is a representation of the real system, that is, a simplification of the real system, including only those aspects that are considered important to the problem at hand. The model might be a graphical representation of the problem to be solved (such as an architectural drawing of the building or an engineering drawing of a machine part), or it might be a mathematical representation (such as a profit function with production constraints or a queuing equation). The resulting model can be analyzed and revised to examine alternatives. The desired objective is that the best alternative be identified by using the model and then translated to the real system and implemented.

We can categorize business problems into decision making under certainty, decision making under risk, and decision making under uncertainty, based on how much information is known. Each of the first two categories has a set of solution techniques that have been found most useful in solving that category's problems. In the third category, decision making under uncertainty, there is insufficient data to make a decision without imposing some outside conditions or spending some money to get the additional data.

For decision making under certainty, it is assumed that the decision maker knows all the possible actions that can be taken, that for each action there is only one outcome, and that the payoff for that outcome is known. The problem is to determine the action, perhaps from an infinite number of possible actions, with the best payoff. Many problems in decision making under certainty in industry have been solved by applications of differential calculus or by mathematical programming. These techniques have been used to solve problems ranging from inventory management and distribution to production planning and scheduling.

For decision making under risk, it is assumed that the decision maker knows all the possible actions that can be taken and that for each action he knows all the possible outcomes with the payoff and probability of each. Two solution techniques for solving very different kinds of decision-making-under-risk problems are decision trees and simulation. Decision trees have been used to solve problems involving media selection, pricing, new-product introduction, and investment decisions. Simulation has been used to analyze performance-improvement decisions in areas ranging from transportation systems and communications networks to manufacturing lines.

For decision making under uncertainty, it is again assumed that the decision maker knows all the possible actions that can be taken and that for each action he knows all the possible outcomes, but he does not know the probability associated with each outcome. In decision making under uncertainty, the technique of payoff matrices is often used as a starting point.

In each category, when we say that the decision maker knows all the actions or outcomes or that he knows the payoffs or the probability, we mean realistically that he knows the important action choices and outcomes and that he can reasonably estimate the payoffs and probabilities in a range that is accurate enough to make the decision. We describe a popular solution method used on the com-

puter for solving problems in decision making under certainty and two methods
for solving problems in decision making under risk.

## Decision Making Under Certainty

In decision making under certainty, there are a number of optimization methods
available for solving business problems by computer. We discuss here a special
case of mathematical programming, called linear programming, that has been
successfully used in optimizing the refinement of oil, the production of feed mix,
and the manufacture of pharmaceuticals.

### Linear Programming: Brief Background

Mathematical programming is a solution technique applied to decision problems where entities are competing for limited resources, whether those resources
are labor, machines, storage, or demand. In mathematical programming the real
system is modeled by an objective function that is to be optimized (either maximized or minimized) subject to a set of constraints. The general formulation of
a mathematical program is to optimize

$$f(x_1, \ldots, x_n)$$

subject to

$$g_1(x_1, \ldots, x_n) \leq b_1$$
$$g_m(x_1, \ldots, x_n) \leq b_m,$$

where $x_1, \ldots, x_n \geq 0$. In this formulation, any constraint $g_i$ can be less than or
equal (as shown), equal, or greater than or equal to $b_i$. We want to find non-
negative values of $x_1, \ldots, x_n$ that will optimize the function $f$ while satisfying
all the constraints $g_1, \ldots, g_m$.

A linear function is one that is a sum of terms each of which is a constant
times a variable raised to the first power. A linear function of two variables set
equal to a constant is a straight line; a linear function of three variables set equal
to a constant is a plane; a linear function of more than three variables set equal
to a constant is a hyperplane. In particular, if both the objective function $f$ and
the constraint functions $g_1, \ldots, g_m$ are linear functions, then the model formulation is a linear program. A linear program with even a large number of
variables and a large number of constraints can be quickly solved by computer
(using the Simplex Method or some variation of it) to provide the optimal
solution. The basic assumption to use this method is linearity of the objective
function and the constraints; that is, a change of one unit in the value of a variable
produces a constant change regardless of the value of the variable. Thus there
can be no diminishing returns and no economies of scale.

**Figure 3.1**
**Feasible Region**

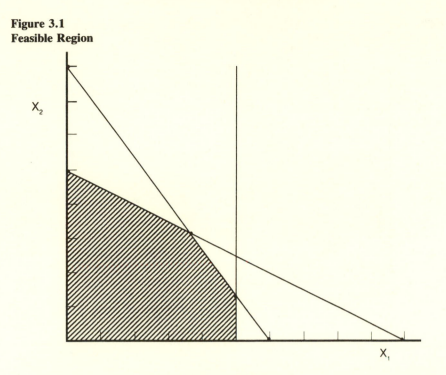

To get an idea of how the Simplex Method produces an optimal solution, consider the case of two variables and the following linear program: maximize

$$f(x_1,x_2) = 10x_1 + 15x_2$$

subject to

$$g_1(x_1,x_2) = 4x_1 + 8x_2 \leq 40$$
$$g_2(x_1,x_2) = 6x_1 + 4x_2 \leq 36$$
$$g_3(x_1,x_2) = 1x_1 + 0x_2 \leq 5,$$

where $x_1, \ldots, x_n \geq 0$.

Figure 3.1 shows the region of $x_1$ and $x_2$ values that satisfy the three constraints (feasible region). We then want to determine which of this infinite number of points optimizes the objective function. Figure 3.2 shows some possible curves for the objective function obtained by setting $f(x_1,x_2)$ to some test values. All the possible objective function curves are parallel to each other, and their values increase as we move toward the top right of the figure. Overlaying the possible objective function curves of figure 3.2 on the feasible region of figure 3.1, we see that the optimal solution is at the point where the objective function last cuts

**Figure 3.2**
**Objective Function Values**

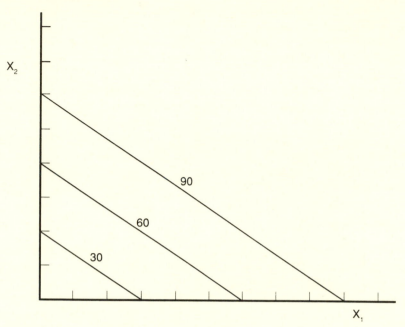

the feasible region as we move toward the top right. This occurs at the corner $x_1 = 4$, $x_2 = 3$ of the feasible region.

In the two-dimensional case, because the constraints are all linear, the feasible region is bounded by straight lines, and because the objective function is linear, the objective function is a straight line. If we move the objective function line until it last intersects the feasible region, then the optimal solution will always occur at a corner (or, in the case where the objective function is parallel to the boundary line, at the whole boundary line as well as its corners) of the feasible region. This is true whether we are maximizing the objective function or minimizing it and generalizes to any number of variables and any number of constraints. Since the number of corners in a feasible region (regardless of the number of variables and the number of constraints) is finite (whereas the number of points that make up the feasible region is infinite), an algorithm can solve the problem by testing the corners. The Simplex Method starts at one corner, tests the direction that will most improve the objective function, and moves to that corner. It continues this process until it reaches a corner where going in any direction can no longer improve the objective function.

### Linear Programming: Example

Let us say that we have two products A and B that we can produce, and let $x_1$ represent the amount of product A to produce and $x_2$ represent the amount of product B. Suppose that we will get a profit of $10 per barrel of product A and $15 per barrel of product B that we produce. Obviously there are constraints on how much we can produce. Suppose that the production of each product requires time on the same two machines and that machine 1 is available for 40 minutes per hour and machine 2 is available for 36 minutes per hour. Suppose that to produce a barrel of product A requires 4 minutes on machine 1 and 6 minutes on machine 2. To produce a barrel of product B requires 8 minutes on machine 1 and 4 minutes on machine 2. Suppose also that the number of barrels of product A must be less than 5 per hour because of demand limits. The resulting linear program representation of this problem is the one shown in the "Brief Background" section. The optimal solution is the corner point $x_1 = 4$ barrels of product A, $x_2 = 3$ barrels of product B, and the profit at that production level is $85 per hour (see figures 3.1 and 3.2). There is no other combination level that will give a better profit.

## Decision Making Under Risk

We describe the main aspects of decision trees and simulation as examples of two very different and widely used solution techniques for decision making under risk. Decision trees are usually used to make marketing decisions on price, advertising, and product introductions and financial decisions on investment alternatives. Simulation is often used to make production and staffing decisions.

### Decision Trees: Brief Background

In decision making under risk, it is assumed that the decision maker knows all the possible actions, the possible outcomes for each action, and the associated probability and payoff of each action. The decision tree is a technique of diagramming these alternatives and applying a rule (expected value) to eliminate those actions that are not part of the optimal strategy.

The decision tree displays the possible actions for each time period (shown as branches emanating from an action point) and, for each action, the possible outcomes with their probabilities. Each path, consisting of alternating action and outcome branches for each period, results in a specific cumulative payoff. To solve the decision tree, we start at the last period and calculate the expected value of each action in that period. The expected value is the weighted sum of the probabilities and the cumulative payoffs:

$$\text{Expected Value} = p_1 P_1 + \ldots + p_n P_n$$

where $p_i$ is the probability of outcome $i$, and $P$ is the payoff for that branch of the tree.

The expected values of each possible action at an action point are compared and the best one selected; all other action branches are eliminated at that action point. This selected expected value is then used as the payoff in the calculation of expected value for the prior period, and the process is repeated for the next-to-last period. The result (paths remaining) after completing all the time periods is the optimal strategy.

Inherent in this process is the assumption that the action with the best expected value is the best action. First of all, since the expected value is a weighted average of the payoffs, it is most likely the case that the actual payoff will not be equal to the expected value. The expected value of an action with two equally likely outcomes, one with payoff $2,000 and the other with payoff $1,000, is $500. That payoff will never be obtained. If the action can be repeated over and over again under the same conditions (a rare situation in business), the long-run average payoff will be $500. However, given that the action is to be made once, is that action better than one with a guaranteed payoff of $400? In reality, the answer depends on your situation: whether you can or want to risk losing $1,000; whether you have a requirement to choose only those actions that have a chance of returning at least $2,000; and so on. Often utility is substituted for dollars in measuring payoffs to account for some of the limitations in using expected value.

### Decision Trees: Example

As an example, suppose that a company wants to determine an advertising strategy. Let us assume that it needs to decide between three advertising plans, A, B, and C, for the first month and D and E for the second month. Its estimates of the possible outcomes and the probabilities and the resulting two-month payoffs are shown in figure 3.3 for every realistic combination of action and outcome. We work backwards from period 2. At each point either action D or E is selected based on the higher expected value. The remaining action's expected value is used as the payoff for period 1. As a result, action A in period 1 gives the highest expected value, $1,320. For action A, the expected value of D is better than E if outcome 1 results in period 1 and the reverse if outcome 2 results. The optimal strategy, therefore, is to choose A in period 1 and then if outcome 1 results, choose D in period 2; otherwise choose E. We point out again that given the assumptions, there is no better strategy. Note, however, that the results of this strategy could never produce the highest possible payoff ($4,000) as with action B, nor guarantee a positive payoff as in the case of action C.

### Simulation: Brief Background

Simulation is a solution technique that mimics the real system by describing the activity flow in a model. A discrete event simulation program generates an artificial flow of customers in the model, tracks them as it advances time in the model, and determines the resulting performance of the system in terms of measures such as delay time and waiting-line lengths. The model can then be changed by revising conditions, such as adding more servers, changing the arrival pattern, or changing the service rules. The resulting performance measures can then be compared to see which combination provides the desired performance at a reasonable cost.

**Figure 3.3**
**Decision Tree**

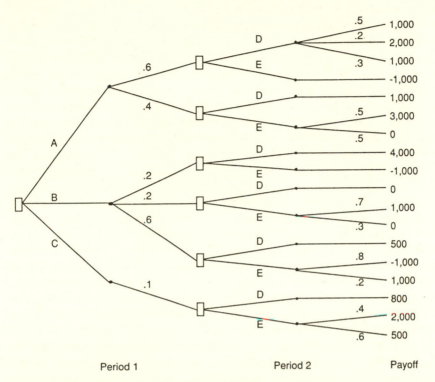

Period 1                          Period 2                    Payoff

*Source:* John A. Campbell, James R. Hemsley, David Burris Windsor, *Articial Intelligence and Management*, The Institute of Management Sciences, August 1986, p. 65.

Simulation can be applied to investigate any system where there are limited resources that provide service, thereby resulting in delays. Examples of such systems are assembly and manufacturing lines, traffic flow (vehicles, voice and data messages, computer instructions), and customer service.

The important objects to abstract from the real system are the jobs (customers that flow through the system) and the service centers (where the jobs are processed). The primary data that needs to be extracted from the real system about the jobs is their arrival-time pattern. For each service center, we must input to the model the number of servers, the rule for selecting jobs for service, and the service-time distribution. Jobs may go through several centers before leaving the system. The conditions to send a job to a particular service center must be input. Given these specifications from the real system or from a proposed variation of the real system, the computer will then follow the jobs through the service centers, measuring such statistics as waiting time, queue length, and throughput.

The simulation program produces the flow of jobs through the network by using a random number generator to sample from distributions, a clock to advance time, and a bookkeeping code to track the individual movement of jobs and accumulate the resulting performance measures. It is important to realize that since we are using random numbers to sample from our abstraction of the real system's distribution, the output results also contain randomness. That is, the results of the simulation cannot be taken as exact, but must be considered estimates of the actual value. Typically the estimates can be made more accurate by statistical methods of designing the simulation experiment. This may involve repeating the simulation run many times using different random numbers to get several estimates, or comparing results from different portions of one run, or using longer runs.

### Simulation: Example

As an example, let us assume that we want to determine the appropriate number of check-out workers in a supermarket. We look at the real system and determine that the important characteristics for the model are the arrival pattern of customers, the time they shop, the service rules and time distribution at the check-out counters, and the number of check-out counters. Further suppose that we find that the shopping time depends according to some equation on the number of items that the customer purchases, and similarly the service time depends on the number of items purchased. We then (perhaps by observing the system with a stopwatch) identify the arrival pattern by measuring the time between arrivals, estimate the shopping-time equation by measuring the shopping time and comparing it to the number of items purchased, and similarly determine the service-time equation.

Of course, not every customer arrives within a fixed number of minutes of the previous customer, nor does every customer purchase the same number of items. We would like the computer simulation, though, to use the data collected to artificially create a flow of customers that follow the actual arrival pattern and then purchase items according to the actual distribution. We therefore use the information collected to set up the pattern (or use some known distribution that closely fits the empirical data) and then sample at random from that pattern for each customer.

Suppose we capture the data and summarize it as shown in table 3.1. Furthermore, suppose that we estimate the shopping-time equation and the service-time equation to be shopping time $= 5 + 2$ x number of items and service time $= 1 + .5$ x number of items. This does not include waiting time on line, which will be determined for us by the simulation program.

Our assumption that all the important outcomes are known means that the sum of the probabilities is 1. If we have the computer program generate random integers between 0 and 9, the probability of a particular one of those ten integers being generated at any point is .1. Therefore, if we assign the integers 0, 1, 2, and 3 to the first item under Arrival Pattern in table 3.1 (that is, when 0, 1, 2,

**Table 3.1**
**Arrival and Purchase Patterns**

ARRIVAL PATTERN

| Interarrival Time (minutes) | Prob. | Random Number |
|---|---|---|
| 1 | .4 | 0,1,2,3 |
| 2 | .3 | 4,5,6 |
| 3 | .1 | 7 |
| 4 | .1 | 8 |
| 5 | .1 | 9 |
|   | 1.0 |   |

PURCHASE PATTERN

| Number of Items | Prob. | Random Number |
|---|---|---|
| 5 | .2 | 0,1 |
| 7 | .1 | 2 |
| 10 | .1 | 3 |
| 14 | .5 | 4,5,6,7,8 |
| 20 | .1 | 9 |
|   | 1.0 |   |

or 3 is generated, we select the result of 1 minute), the probability that the first item will be selected will be .4, as in the real system. This process is called sampling from the distribution and, over a large number of random number generations, will approximate the real system.

To see how the simulation program uses this information, let us suppose that the following two streams of random numbers are generated (stream RN1 for sampling from the arrival pattern and stream RN2 for sampling from the pattern of items purchased):

RN1: 4 7 0 3 2 8

RN2: 9 1 7 8 6 3

The simulation clock is set to 9 A.M. when the supermarket opens, and we decide to simulate the activity with two check-out counters open, one express (10 items or less) and one regular. Using the first random numbers from stream RN1 and the Arrival Pattern in table 3.1, we assign customer 1 to arrive at 9:02 (random number 4 is assigned to the second item, 2 minutes). Customer 1 shops for 20 items (random number 9 is assigned to 20 items in the Purchase Pattern in table 3.1), requiring 45 minutes (shopping-time equation) and check-out service time of 11 minutes. Customer 1 is ready to go to the regular check-out at 9:47. Waiting time is not yet known, for other customers may get in line ahead of customer 1, and therefore the time this customer leaves the supermarket is not yet known but will be determined when other customers are processed. Similarly, following this procedure, customer 2 arrives at 9:05, shops for 5 items, and requires 15 minutes shopping time and 3.5 minutes service time at the express counter. Customer 2 is ready to go to the express check-out counter at 9:30. Customer 3 is ready to go to the regular check-out counter at 9:30, ahead of customer 1.

The simulation program thus generates the random numbers, samples from the input distributions to generate the events in the model, advances time to the next event, and then tracks the movement of the customers and accounts for the delays. The simulation experiment must be run for long clock times and/or repeated several times with different random numbers to accurately estimate the results to reduce the error in using random sampling. Getting summaries of throughput and waiting times for the two counters and then comparing these to either more counters or different service selection rules (and accounting for sampling error) will provide management with the information necessary to schedule the counter workers.

We have described some very often used computer solution methods to indicate the range of techniques, the inherent assumptions when using these techniques, and the types of applications that can be handled by decision support systems. Linear programming and decision trees provide optimal solutions for relatively static problems, whereas simulation is a descriptive technique for dynamic problems. Linear programming handles deterministic problems, whereas decision trees and simulation handle probabilistic problems. These are some of the programmable solution techniques. Decision support systems make available many operations research techniques, including different types of forecasting systems, dynamic programming, cluster analysis, and discriminant analysis, for management decision making.

The computer can support management in its need for fast, accurate, and cogent information to efficiently operate, manage, and plan the business. The combined human/computer intelligence system captures the data, stores the data for quick access, and converts the data into useful information for correct decisions. The computer provides the means to gather data, especially internal data, but also, and not necessarily for top-management decisions, to access external economic, government, and business-sector data and forecasts. Once the data is in a computer-readable form, data-base management systems provide fast access to answer queries and produce reports. Decision support systems combine mathematical solution techniques with computer computation speed and data access to assist in decision making. The technology exists to effectively use the computer to monitor day-to-day operations and support tactical and strategic planning. On the other hand, if used incorrectly, it can cause an increasing drain on capital, manpower, and time.

# REFERENCES

## Transaction Processing

Kroeber, D., and Watson, H. (1987). *Computer-Based Information Systems*. 2nd ed. New York: Macmillan.

McLeod, R., Jr. (1986). *Management Information Systems*. 3rd ed. Chicago: Science Research Associates.

Senn, J. A. (1982). *Information Systems in Management*. 2nd ed. Belmont, Calif.: Wadsworth Publishing Company.

Sherman, K. (1983). *Data Communications: A Users Guide*. Reston, Va.: Reston Publishing Company.

## Data Base Management

Aho, A. V., Hopcroft, J. E., and Ullman, J. D. (1983). *Data Structures and Algorithms*. Reading, Mass.: Addison-Wesley.

Kapp, D., and Leben, J. F. (1978). *IMS Programming Techniques*. New York: Van Nostrand Reinhold Co.

Kroenke, D. M. (1983). *Database Processing*. 2nd ed. Chicago: Science Research Associates.

## Decision Support Systems

Gordon, G. (1978). *Systems Simulation*. 2nd ed. Englewood Cliffs, N.J.: Prentice-Hall.

Hamburg, M. (1977). *Statistical Analysis for Decision Making*. 2nd ed. New York: Harcourt Brace Jovanovich.

Kwak, N. K. (1973). *Mathematical Programming with Business Applications*. New York: McGraw-Hill.

Law, A. M., and Kelton, W. D. (1982). *Simulation Modeling and Analysis*. New York: McGraw-Hill.

Loomba, N. P., and Turban, E. (1974). *Applied Programming for Management*. Holt, Rinehart and Winston.

McMillan, C., Jr. (1975). *Mathematical Programming*. 2nd ed. New York: John Wiley and Sons.

# 4

# Artificial Intelligence: The Emerging Corporate Knowledge Frontier

*Mahesh Chandra and Shivaji Rao*

> As everybody knows, knowledge is power. Machines that can amplify human knowledge will amplify every dimension of power.
> —Feigenbaum and McCorduck 1983, p. 8

> The Japanese are planning the miracle product. It will not come from their mines, their wells, their fields, or even their seas. It comes from their brains, the miracle product is knowledge and the Japanese are planning to package and sell it the way other nations package and sell energy, food or manufactured goods. They are going to give the world the next generation— Fifth Generation of Computers, and these machines are going to be intelligent.
> —Feigenbaum, McCorduck, and Nii 1988, p. 12

Two recent areas of advances in computing technology, supercomputing, and artificial intelligence (AI) in general and expert systems in particular, are helping companies to increase their productivity at enormous rates. Feigenbaum, McCorduck, and Nii (1988) mention that many of the companies surveyed with regard to the use of expert systems are realizing great economic gains for themselves and their customers by factors of ten or more in the productivity of human knowledge workers.

Expert systems have found use in areas such as electronics, engineering, geology, and business. However, not all problems can be handled well by expert systems. Problems that can be handled well by expert systems have the following characteristics (Ellis 1983): (*a*) the solution of the problem requires scarce human expertise; (*b*) the problem is too complicated for the manager to handle in a short period of time; (*c*) the problem's current computer solution is inscrutable to the users (difficult to interact with, and difficult to comprehend); and (*d*) a wrong solution to the problem is expensive to the user, for example, air traffic control or a false missile alert.

A survey of the application of the expert-system technology in the insurance industry conducted by Coopers and Lybrand in 1987 revealed that almost two-thirds of the country's largest insurance companies are using, developing, or actively exploring expert-system applications; the move toward expert-system development among large insurance companies is primarily driven by a desire for a strategic and a competitive advantage (almost three-fourths believe that expert systems are crucial for their companies; and improved quality and consistency and increased productivity are the two most important criteria for expert-system applications). A recent book, *The Rise of the Expert Company*, by Feigenbaum, McCorduck, and Nii (1988) has many examples of successful expert systems being used in companies in the United States, England, and Japan. We briefly mention some of these applications.

The Logistics Management System (LMS) and IBM, based in Burlington, Vermont, helps managers and operators control processes. It advises operators and managers on the prioritization of work in the queues and on the rerouting of work if a problem develops at one of the work stations, and it automatically sends messages to work stations upstream and downstream of the problem advising them of a specific change in schedule.

Another expert system named Diagnostic Expert for Final Test (DEFT) is being used by IBM at its San Jose plant for detecting errors in the assembly of storage devices such as the 3380 disk drive. This system is able to perform diagnostic tests of 98 percent of the problems that occur, and within the 98 percent it is always correct (100 percent). The 98 percent accuracy compares well with the best techniques, and the average consultation of DEFT by a technician takes one minute or less.

The FMC corporation uses Pocatello Burden Advisor (PBA) for acquiring and monitoring data to control the process of manufacturing phosphorus and reduce the cost of production by optimizing the mix of raw materials. It functions as an advisory system, notifying operators of abnormal conditions and recommending corrective actions. FMC's potential returns on proposed AI projects are evaluated just like those of any other corporate project. FMC believes that by using expert systems it can protect the knowledge the firm already has to maintain its competitive advantage in the world market.

Credit Authorizer's Assistant (AA), developed by American Express, helps American Express credit authorizers make quick decisions about authorizing purchases for card holders who are at or beyond their normal limit. The AA automatically handles between 25 and 35 percent of the current traffic and contributes to a 20 percent reduction in the handling time for transactions that go to authorizers. The losses avoided through this improved handling are in excess of five times the size of productivity savings; further, it is believed that American Express is saving $27 million annually through the use of this expert system.

Automated Cable Expertise (ACE) is a signal-processing system that analyzes phone company repair data and identifies areas for preventive maintenance and further repair. The system operates without human intervention, analyzing maintenance reports generated on a daily basis by Cable Repair Administrative System (CRAS), a cable-repair-administration computer program. ACE delivers five different reports: (*a*) found trouble analysis, where the program searches the CRAS data base for equipment associated with a large number of customer trouble reports; (*b*) trouble report improvement methodology, where the program analyzes fixed, not-fixed, and not-found troubles; (*c*) troubles in tracked complements, where the program selects user-selected complements for trouble reports; (*d*) plus 3, where the program analyzes each customer who has reported three or more troubles in the past thirty days; and (*e*) pair transportation analysis, where the program looks for two or more specific types of repair procedures that have been performed in the last sixty days. ACE was developed by AT & T Bell Labs, and currently there are thirty-five systems installed in five Bell operating companies.

COMPASS analyzes telephone switching systems maintenance messages for GTE's No. 2 EAX Switch and suggests maintenance actions to perform. The system examines maintenance messages describing error situations that occurred during the telephone call–processing operation of the switch. The system embodies the expertise of a top switch expert and integrates knowledge about individual switch structure, switch faults, maintenance messages, and possible maintenance actions. COMPASS was developed by the GTE telephone companies.

DELTA has been developed by the General Electric Research and Development Center in Schenectady, New York. The system is designed to assist diesel locomotive personnel to diagnose maintenance needs and prescribe appropriate maintenance actions. The basic expert system is interfaced with a device that allows the system to print out diagrams and a video disc player that allows the system to display diagrams to show where particular components are located on the locomotive. Thus the expert system helps the maintenance person figure out what the problem is and, if necessary, switches over to the video system to show how to make the checks or measurements to generate information DELTA needs to make a diagnosis.

COOKER ADVISOR was developed by Campbell Soup Company, which maintains numerous plants around the world that prepare and package canned soup. An important step in the canning process is to sterilize the soup after it has been sealed in the can. The machines that perform the sterilizing function are called cookers. Campbell had one employee (Aldo Cimino) with extensive knowledge of all the cookers currently in operation. Maintenance engineers in the various plants turned to this person when they encountered an unusual operating problem with their cookers, and when Aldo Cimino was approaching retirement, Campbell decided to drain his brain—that is, to ''can'' Cimino's accumulated knowledge into a personal computer expert system. For about seven months, beginning in November 1984, Cimino was a tutor to ''knowledge engineer'' Michael Smith of Texas Instruments. The first prototype used 32 rules. Based on a wealth of knowledge gathered during a three-day review of the prototype with Campbell management, TI enlarged the system to 66 rules. Currently there are 151 rules, and the expert system has been distributed to various Campbell factory locations. Campbell, encouraged by the success of the COOKER ADVISOR, has continued its experimentation with building other expert systems.

XCON is an expert system that routinely configures Digital Equipment Corporation's (DEC) VAX 11/780 computer systems. XCON's input is a customer's order, and its output is a set of diagrams displaying the spatial relationships among the components on an order. XCON configures the systems at a very detailed level; for each order it determines necessary modifications, produces diagrams showing the spatial and logical relationships between the hundreds of components that comprise a complete system, and handles other jobs usually relegated to skilled technicians. XCON performs at the level of an experienced technical editor, but it operates much faster. XCON can typically configure in less than 1.5 minutes.

PROSPECTOR estimates the likelihood of finding particular types of mineral deposits, given field data of a geological region. The expert system can identify particular types of mineral ores, such as massive sulfide, sandstone uranium, and porphyry molybdenum deposits. The expertise is based on geological rules that form models of ore deposits and on a taxonomy of rocks and minerals. PROSPECTOR was developed by Stanford Research Institute (SRI) International.

However, the mere mimicking of intelligence is not the sole purpose of artificial intelligence. Instead, computer scientists believe that by making computers intelligent, they will be able to better understand the human intelligence function.

The *New York Times* (March 6, 1989) reported that the National Aeronautics and Space Administration (NASA) is developing expert systems to utilize the knowledge and experience of its agencies and its top- and middle-level managers and scientists, most of whom will be eligible for retirement within the next five years. Without the development of such systems, the agency feels that the retirement of experienced personnel will cripple its operations.

Forecasts of AI technologies indicate a continuing surge of interest in expert-system development, followed closely in the 1990s by natural language processing (see figure 4.1). Expert systems have a unique ability to merge the

**Figure 4.1**
**Projected Artificial Intelligence Market Development by Technical Area**

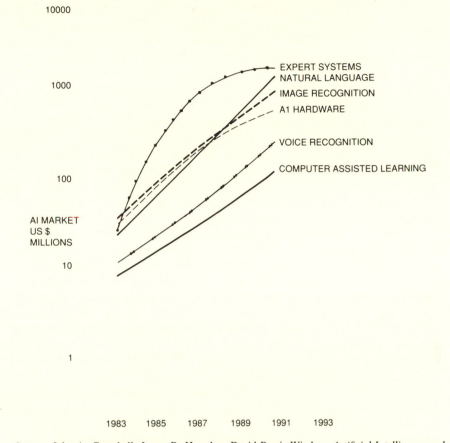

*Source:* John A. Campbell, James R. Hemsley, David Burris Windsor, *Artificial Intelligence and Management*, The Institute of Management Sciences, August 1986, p. 65.

computing technology available at hand with the problem-solving processes of a human expert. Given the nature of problems faced by organizations, which are usually ill structured, nonprogrammable, and ill defined and require the intuitive talents of an expert, expert-system applications in business (both large and small) are growing at a very rapid pace. Natural language interfaces are providing front-end query systems for data bases. The first such tool for the IBM Mainframe was Intellect from AI Corporation. We briefly discuss several expert systems in business in the Appendix. For details of these and other expert systems the reader is referred to Feigenbaum, McCorduck, and Nii (1988).

**Figure 4.2**
**The Players in the Expert-System Game**

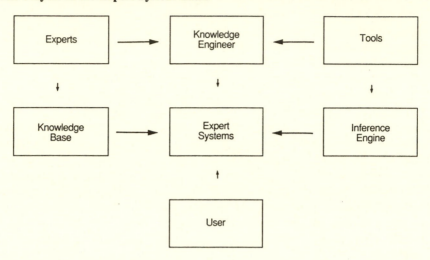

## EXPERT SYSTEMS: WHAT ARE THEY?

Artificial intelligence (AI) is a subfield of computer science that attempts to study ideas that enable computers to be intelligent. Barr and Feigenbaum (1981) define AI as "that part of computer science concerned with designing intelligent computer systems, that is, systems that exhibit the characteristics we associate with intelligence in human behavior—understanding language, learning, reasoning, solving problems and so on."

AI, since its inception in the 1950s, has been scrambling for ideas, and expert systems was a conceptual breakthrough that reinvigorated this fledgling field of computer science. Jackson (1986) defines an expert system as "a computing system capable of representing and reasoning about some knowledge-rich domain, such as internal medicine or geology, with a view to solving problems and giving advice" (p. 1).

Even though expertise for most expert systems is acquired from human experts, the expertise can also be obtained from textbooks, policy guidelines, and manuals describing standards and other sources. The main players in the expert-system game are the expert system, the domain expert, the knowledge engineer, the expert-system building tool, and the user (see figure 4.2).

The knowledge engineer is a human who extracts and organizes the knowledge from the domain expert and may even help programmers write the code. The expert-system building tool is the programming language used to build the expert system, and the user may be a scientist using the system to help discover new mineral deposits, a lawyer using it to help settle a case, or a student using it to learn more about organic chemistry (Waterman 1986).

The task of building an expert consulting system is often called a knowledge-engineering process. It requires a special kind of interaction between the domain expert and the expert-system builder—the knowledge engineer. The knowledge engineer extracts from the domain expert the intuitive solution procedures to solve problems and builds this knowledge into the expert system.

An expert is defined as "a person who, because of training and experience, is able to do things the rest of us cannot; experts are not only proficient but also smooth and efficient in the actions they take. . . . they are good at plowing through irrelevant information in order to get at basic issues, and they are good at recognizing problems they face as instances of types with which they are familiar" (Waterman 1986, p. 5).

The expert-system building process is also called the knowledge-engineering process, and knowledge engineering consists of three principal subcomponents; knowledge acquisition, knowledge representation, and knowledge application (Jackson 1986). The three subcomponents are briefly discussed in the following paragraphs.

Two of the most widely used methods of knowledge acquisition are observation and inquiry. In the first approach, knowledge engineers monitor and record the actions taken by the expert while analyzing a problem. But passively observing the expert's actions does little to identify decisions that are the result of a complex reasoning process or are a function of compressed knowledge. The inquiry approach, however, relies on introspection by the expert and inquisition by the knowledge engineer on the decision-making processes used in arriving at a solution. Unlike the other method, this method requires the expert to take a more active role, directly aiding the knowledge engineer in creating the model of his or her cognitive processes. Here again, the difficulty lies in the fact that the expert may be unaware of any automatic preprocessing of knowledge or of the presence of "compressed data" within his or her problem-solving framework. The knowledge is so well compiled that the expert accesses and manipulates it without thinking.

It is an easy task to store names and numbers in a computer. But knowledge is not data, and therefore representation is significant; otherwise it would be an impossible task to build an intelligent information system. Over the years, AI scientists have resorted to a number of techniques to represent knowledge, such as logic programming, production systems, semantic nets, and frames.

Logic programming in its purest form (standard symbolic logic) is standard predicate calculus (Nilsson 1980), where knowledge or statements are precise and well defined. Moreover, logical deductions are easy to automate. Powerful algorithms (Unification and Resolution) exist (Nilsson 1980), and the conclusions are guaranteed correct (Waldrop 1984). PROLOG, a logic-programming language, is widely used in Europe and Japan. In the United States personal-

**Figure 4.3**
**A Simple Semantic Net for the Concept of a Ship**

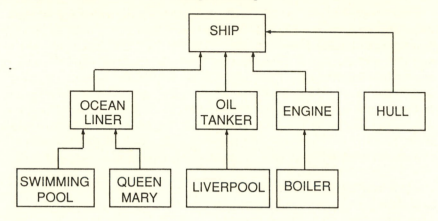

computer–based PROLOG compilers are widely available as well (Robinson 1987).

The most popular alternative to logic is the production-system approach. In a production system we have only certain kinds of rules or statements, of the form "IF this is true, THEN do that," and only certain types of logical deductions. A production system is much easier to handle and is less subject to the combinatorial explosion all too common while undertaking heuristic search. Moreover, it can handle statements about the reliability of the rules as well.

An alternative mode of representation is using semantic nets, where the knowledge is represented using a network structure. Semantic nets were originally developed for use as psychological models of human memory but are now a standard representation method for AI and expert systems. A typical example is given in figure 4.3, where the simple semantic net for the concept of a ship is defined.

Finally, a frame in the field of AI refers to a special way of representing common concepts and situations. Marvin Minsky (1975) describes it as "a data-structure for representing a stereotyped situation, like being in a certain kind of living room, or going to a child's birthday party. Attached to each frame are several kinds of information. Some of this information is about how to use the frame. Some is about what one can expect to happen next. Some is about what to do if these expectations are not confirmed" (p. 212). A frame looks just like a semantic net, except that at each node a concept is defined by a collection of attributes called slots. Each slot has procedures attached to it that are executed when information in the slot is changed.

Knowledge application pertains to the issues of planning and control in the area of problem solving. In the design of expert systems particular attention must be given to how the knowledge is accessed and applied during the search for a solution.

## EXPERT-SYSTEM DEVELOPMENT TOOLS

Even though it is possible to build expert systems using traditional programming languages, such as COBOL, FORTRAN, C, and so on, most large-scale development of expert systems utilizes AI languages (LISP, PROLOG, and so on), and most small-scale prototypes are built using personal computer–based expert shells for their greater flexibility. Moreover, the use of expert shells fits quite well with the growing trend: the increase in the number of computer systems on the desktop. E. I. du Pont de Nemours and Company, for example, has built hundreds of small-scale expert systems, and most of these have been built using shells.

A list of PC-based expert-system tools/languages and their developers follows.

1st-Class: 1st-Class, 286 Boston Post Road, Wayland, MA 01778. (617) 358–7722.

ADS-MVS and ADS-PC: Aion Corporation, 101 University Avenue, Palo Alto, CA 94301. (415) 328–9595.

ART: Inference Corporation, 5300 West Century Blvd., 5th Floor, Los Angeles, CA 90045. (213) 417–7997.

ES Environment VM and MVS: IBM, P.O. Box 5577, 2321 Whitney Avenue, Hamden, CT 06518. (203) 287–7127.

Exsys: Exsys Inc., P.O. Box 112477, Albuquerque, NM 87192. (505) 256–8356.

GoldWorks and Golden Common Lisp: Gold Hill Computers, 26 Landsdowne St., Cambridge, MA 02139. (800) 242–LISP.

GURU: Micro Data Base Systems, Inc., P.O. Box 248, Lafayette, IN 47902. (317) 447–1122.

HP-RL: Hewlett-Packard, 4 Choke Cherry Road, Rockville, MD 20850. (301) 258–2000.

KEE: Intellicorp, 1975 El Camino Real West, Mountain View, CA 94040–2216. (415) 965–5683.

Loops and Interlisp-D: Xerox Corporation, 250 N. Halstead Street, P. O. Box 7018, Pasadena, CA 91109. (818) 351–2351.

M.1 and S.1: Teknowledge Inc., 1850 Embarcadaro Road, P.O. Box 10119, Palo Alto, CA 94303. (415) 327–6600.

Personal Consultant Easy and Personal Consultant Plus: Texas Instruments, 12501 Research Blvd., MS 2244, P.O. Box 2909, Austin TX 78769. (800) 527–3500.

STROBE (developed by Schlumberger): Sun Microsystems Inc., 2550 Garcia Avenue, Mountain View, CA 94043. (800) 821–4643.

TIMM: General Research, 7655 Old Springhouse Rd., McLean, VA 22101. (703) 893–5915.

We are now entering the second era of knowledge processing, in which, according to Feigenbaum, McCorduck, and Nii (1988), "the intelligent system will be conceived as the colleagues' relationship between a computer agent and an intelligent person. The computer and the person will each perform tasks that it/he does best, and the intelligence of the system will emerge from the collaboration. If the interaction is seamless and natural, then it will hardly matter whether the relevant knowledge or the reasoning skills needed are in the head of the person or in the knowledge structures of the computer'' (p. 251).

Artificial intelligence is helping companies to produce better-quality products and thus increase their productivity and profits. It is important that corporations understand the use of artificial intelligence as a weapon to stay ahead of their competition. The companies that are using expert systems have realized remarkable results in terms of return on investment, productivity increase, consistency of decision making, and enhancement of the quality of products and services. We conclude the chapter with Tom Peters' remarks about artificial intelligence from his foreword to the book *The Rise of the Expert Company* by Feigenbaum, McCorduck, and Nii (1988): ''Any senior manager in any business of almost any size who is not at least learning about artificial intelligence, and sticking a tentative toe or two in AI's waters, is simply out of step, dangerously so'' (p. xiii).

# APPENDIX
# Expert Systems in Business

*TIARA* (*The Internal Audit Risk Assessor*). TIARA was developed for internal use by the Equitable. The application area is auditing. TIARA identifies units within the company to be audited in the next audit cycle. TIARA was written with ART (an expert shell developed and sold by Inference Corporation).

*California Sales Tax Advisor*. The application area is taxation. The system advises on the status of financial transactions involving advertising agencies, commercial artists, and designers in California. The development environment is 1st-Class, and the system runs on IBM/XT or compatible.

*ExperTAX*. This system is used internally by Coopers and Lybrand. The application area is taxation. The expert system was developed to assist audit and tax staff evaluate the application of U.S. tax laws to clients of the firm. The knowledge base incorporates the knowledge of forty top partners of the firm. It replaces a written questionnaire that could run up to two hundred pages and had to be analyzed by one of the firm's senior tax experts. The development environment was Q Shell, written by Golden Common Lisp, and the system is a proprietary product of the company.

*TAXADVISOR* (Waterman 1986). TAXADVISOR assists an attorney with tax and estate planning for clients with large estates (greater than $175,000). The system collects client data and infers actions the clients need to take to settle their financial profile, including insurance purchases, retirement actions, transfer of wealth, and modifications to gift and will provisions. TAXADVISOR uses knowledge about estate planning based on attorneys' experiences and strategies as well as generally accepted knowledge from textbooks.

*Can Am Treaty*. This system was developed and marketed by Buyers Casgrain. The application area is law. Can Am Treaty gives advice on the legal aspects of trade transactions between the United States and Canada. The program was developed with the aid of GURU (an expert shell developed and sold by Micro Data Base Systems Inc.)

*BEST MIX Portfolio Management System*. This system was developed for use by Sanwa Bank and Tokyo Information Systems. It advises on conservative management for private accounts with large deposits. It selects investments from tax-free products, a variety of time deposits, government bonds, and so on. The development environment is Brain.

*Underwriter*. This system is sold by General Data Systems. The application area is insurance. The expert system performs the task of senior underwriters and is used for both commercial and personal lines of insurance. The development environment is GDX (a proprietary shell of General Data Corporation).

*Capital Expert System*. This system is used internally by Texas Instruments Defense System and Electronics Group. It enables a novice to prepare a standardized, comprehensive capital package for the company's decision maker. The development environment is TI-Consultant Plus (an expert shell developed by Texas Instruments, commonly used on IBM PC/XT or compatible machines).

*Financial Advisor*. This system is currently sold by Palladian Software. Financial

(Source: Feigenbaum, McCorduck, and Nii 1988)

Advisor assists top management in evaluating complex business proposals, where the manager can consider alternative approaches to new product-development proposals, evaluate major strategic investments, and consider the consequences of cost-reduction plans and buying and leasing equipment. The development environment is LISP, and the system runs on Symbolics or Explorer Lisp machines.

*Financial Statement Analyzer (FSA)*. This system was developed with the aid of the Securities and Exchange Commission (SEC) and piloted in a hundred companies. The expert system captures the information embedded in the financial statements that companies file with the SEC. It is able to extract this information from a variety of formats used by the different companies and perform automated numerical analyses of standard financial ratios such as the quick ratio. The development environment is KEE, and the system runs on a Symbolics Lisp Machine.

*Manager's Broker Monitoring System*. This expert system was developed for Bear Sterns and Company, to expedite the monitoring of a broker's discretionary accounts. Discretionary accounts allow brokers to invest clients' funds without prior investor approval. The expert system maintains a profile of broker activity for compliance managers to evaluate. The development environment is GoldWorks, fielded in Lisp and C with Gold Hill 386 Humming Board.

*Mortgage Loan Analyzer*. This expert system was developed by Arthur Andersen and Company for sale by other companies. The Mortgage Loan Analyzer helps underwriters assess residential mortgage loan applications. The development environment is Aion's PC version ADS and requires a fully IBM-compatible PC.

*Client Profiling*. This system is for sale by Applied Expert Systems (APEX) and is designed to assist field sales representatives of insurance companies, banks, and other financial institutions to tailor packages of financial products for middle-income clients. The system was able to cut twenty hours worth of work time to only fifteen minutes. The development environment is LISP, and the system runs on the VAX.

*PlanPower*. This system is for sale by Applied Expert Systems (APEX). The PlanPower expert system assists specialists in financial organizations and independent financial consultants in the preparation of financial plans for high-income clients. The expert system's knowledge base is made up of 6,000 rules and can provide advice on 125 different investment products. The development environment is LISP, and the system runs on a XEROX 1186 Lisp Machine.

*Foreign Exchange Options Advisory System*. This expert system is for sale by the Athena Group. It helps in the development of strategies in trading foreign currency options. It provides recommendations based on market outlook, expected price movements, price volatility, and the investor's risk profile. The system was developed in ART, an expert shell developed by Inference Corporation.

*Portfolio Management Advisor*. This expert system is for sale by the Athena Group. It searches for the optimal investment solutions and evaluates a broad range of alternative strategies within the constraints relevant to each individual client's institutional policy, legal limitations, cost and tax concerns, investment goals, and so on. These recommendations are based on extensive macroeconomic and microeconomic models of the economy and the stock market, which constitute the knowledge base of the expert system. The system was developed in ART, an expert shell marketed by Inference Corporation.

*Lending Advisor*. This expert system is for sale by Syntelligence Inc. It was developed to evaluate the risk of mid-size commercial borrowers and to assist lending officers to evaluate loans on a consistent basis and insure that all relevant variables are considered in the decision-making process. It was developed using Syntel ES shell and runs on IBM Mainframe environment with PC terminals.

*Underwriting Advisor*. This system is for sale by Syntelligence Inc. The primary purpose of this expert system is to assist underwriters in underwriting commercial insurance lines of property, general liability, workers' compensation, inland marine, and commercial auto. The system was developed using Syntel ES shell and runs on IBM Mainframe environment with PC terminals.

*CASES (Capital Asset Expert System)*. This system was developed for internal use by IBM Endicott. It assists in the transfer or disposition of pieces of equipment or machinery and determines what forms are needed, what must be filled in, whose approvals are required, and where the completed form should be sent. CASES was developed in ES environment.

*Employment Law: Clarifying Dismissal*. This system is sold by Expertech Ltd. It helps determine whether an employee is covered under the rules of the Wages Act of 1986 and the Sex Discrimination Act of 1986. The system was developed with XI Plus to run on IBM PC or compatible.

*Prohibited Transaction Exemption (PTE) Analyst*. This system is for sale by Computer Law Systems. It assists attorneys in analyzing employee benefits accruing from the Employment Retirement Income Security Act of 1974. The system was developed using PC Consultant Plus and runs on a PC.

*Inner Budget*. This system was developed for internal use at Georgia Institute of Technology. It analyzes budgets generated by the Lotus 1–2–3 spreadsheet program. The knowledge base incorporates the expertise of senior accounting and financial staff. The system was developed using Interlisp and runs on the Xerox Lisp machine.

*More*. This system is sold by Persoft Inc. It determines the most profitable prospects on a large-scale mailing list. More was written in COBOL and runs on an IBM Mainframe 4300.

## REFERENCES

Barr, A., and Feigenbaum, E. A. 1981. *The Handbook of Artificial Intelligence*. Vols. 1–3. Los Altos, Calif.: William Kaufman.

Ellis, P. January 1983. "Expert Systems—A Key Innovation in Professional and Managerial Problem Solving." *Information Age*, pp. 2–6.

Feigenbaum, E., and McCorduck, P. 1983. *The Fifth Generation: Artificial Intelligence and Japan's Computer Challenge to the World*. Reading, Mass.: Addison-Wesley.

Feigenbaum, E., McCorduck, P., and Nii, H. Penny. 1988. *The Rise of the Expert Company*. New York: Times Books.

Jackson, P. 1986. *Introduction to Expert Systems*. Reading, Mass.: Addison-Wesley.

Minsky, M. 1975. "A Framework for Representing Knowledge." In P. Winston (ed.), *The Psychology of Computer Vision*, pp. 211–77. New York: McGraw-Hill.

Nilsson, N. J. 1980. *Principles of Artificial Intelligence*. Los Altos, Calif.: Morgan Kaufmann.

Robinson, P. R. 1987. *Using Turbo Prolog*. Berkeley, Calif.: Osborne/McGraw-Hill.

Waldrop, M. March 23, 1984. "The Necessity of Knowledge." *Science*, pp. 6–9.

Waterman, D. A. 1986. *A Guide to Expert Systems*. Reading, Mass.: Addison-Wesley.

## BIBLIOGRAPHY

Blanning, R. W. "Conversing with Management Information Systems in Natural Language." *Communications of the ACM* 27, no. 3 (March 1984): 201–7.

DELTA/CATS–1. *Artificial Intelligence Report*, Vol. 1, No. 1, January 1984.

Duda, R. O., and Reboh, R. "AI and Decision Making: The PROSPECTOR Experience." In W. Reitman (ed.), *Artificial Intelligence Applications in Business*. Norwood, N.J.: Ablex, 1984.

Engelberger, J. F. "The Ultimate Worker." In M. Minsky, (ed.), *Robotics*, 213. Garden City, N.Y.: Omni Press, 1985.

Fersko-Weiss, H. "Expert Systems: Decision-Making Power." *Personal Computing*, November 1985, 97–105.

Goyal, S. K., Prerau, D. S., Lemmon, A. V., Gunderson, A. S., and Geinke, R. E. "COMPASS: An Expert System for Telephone Cable Maintenance." *Report Computer Science Laboratory*, Waltham, Mass.: GTE Laboratories, 1985.

Harmon, P., Maus, R., and Morrissey, W. *Expert Systems: Tools and Applications*. New York: John Wiley & Sons, 1988.

Leonard-Barton, D., and Sviokla, J. J. "Putting Expert Systems to Work." *Harvard Business Review*, March–April 1988, 91–98.

Marr, D., and Nishihara, H. "Visual Information Processing: Artificial Intelligence Applications in Business." *Technology Review*, October 1978, 28–49.

Minsky, M. (ed.). *Semantic Information Processing*. Cambridge, Mass.: MIT Press, 1968.

Newell, A., and Simon, H. "GPS, a Program That Simulates Human Thought." In E. Feigenbaum and J. Feldman (eds.), *Computer and Thought*, 279–96. New York: McGraw-Hill, 1963.

Obermeier, K. K. "Natural-Language Processing." *Byte*, December 1987, 225–32.

Quillian, M. R. "Semantic Memory." In M. Minsky (ed.), *Semantic Information Processing*. Cambridge, Mass.: MIT Press, 1968.

Reitman, W., (ed.). *Artificial Intelligence Applications for Business*. Norwood, N.J.: Ablex, 1984.

Samuel, A. L. "Some Studies in Machine Learning Using the Game of Checkers. II—Recent Progress." *IBM Journal of Research and Development*, November 1967, 601–17.

———. "Some Studies in Machine Learning Using the Game of Checkers." *IBM Journal of Research and Development*, July 1959, 211–30.

Tennant, H. *Natural Language Processing*. New York: Petrocelli, 1981.

Turban, E. *Decision Support and Expert Systems: A Managerial Perspective*. New York: Macmillan, 1988.

Vesonder, G., Stolfo, T., Salvatore, J., Zielinski, J. E., Miller, F. D., and Copp, D. H. "ACE: An Expert System for Telephone Cable Maintenance." *Proceedings of the International Joint Conference on Artificial Intelligence, 1983*, 116–21.

Wright, J. R., Miller, F. D., Otto, G., Siegfried, E. M., Vesonder, G. T., and Zielinski, J. E. "ACE: Going from Prototype to Product with an Expert System." *ACM Conference Proceedings*, October 1984.

# 5

# The Business of Information: The New Competitive Challenge

## Paul G. Zurkowski

The exciting thing about information is that it creates change. When people learn something, they live differently. Information services help people learn and must change as their users change in order to continue to offer value in the marketplace. To be involved in this business is both challenging and stimulating.

Information services are driven by the marketplace. There are no guarantees in the marketplace; information services have the right to fail as well as the right to succeed. In theory, information should be of interest to people generally. In practice, information has value in direct proportion to what is at stake in a decision. The value of information is in its application; standing alone it has little value.

Information directed at decisions becomes a part of that decision process and contributes critical value. It is an element of production and, like labor, materials, and capital, it generates wealth. This wealth-generating function is the new competitive force challenging management, worldwide, today.

### HOW INFORMATION IMPACTS A PRODUCT OR SERVICE

Fundamental to understanding the wealth-generating function of information is an understanding of the effect information has on a product or service. Paul Hawken, in his book *The Next Economy*,[1] points out that there is more information in a reflex camera than there is in a pound of lead. The reflex camera embodies both scientific and technical information inherent in its operation as well as physiological and psychological information affecting the man/machine relationship created by the camera's physical and operational features. Information content in the camera is reflected in design and operational features essential to effective use of its capabilities. Clean design and smooth operation distinguish an information-endowed product.

Competitive products of all kinds, from automobiles to computers, depend not only on access to information but also on a recognition of what information is essential to a clean design and smooth operation. Successful competitors have separated out this critical new element of production. They have developed a high degree of information competence. They recognize and act upon the fact that the careful application of information is essential to winning, competitive products.

## ACHIEVING INFORMATION COMPETENCE

Every industry today has information service companies which have targeted that industry by offering participants in that industry access to an on-going process developing and delivering information.

Fundamentally, information services address a basic human condition, the human cognitive screen. Each of us is a product of our past, of our individual life experiences. Our minds are conditioned to screen out information deemed to be irrelevant to our current concerns, thereby focusing only on "relevant" information.

We have all experienced picking up an "old" journal or newspaper only to find in it something of vital interest that we had completely missed during our earlier reading. This is an example of the working of our cognitive screen. Since reading the publication, we learned something that opened our minds to different information. With a new insight we accepted and processed information different from what we were prepared to accept earlier.

The information services business, begun in the late 1960s, emerged in the 1970s as a new business. This business creates and markets information equivalents or counterparts of events, people, and artifacts. These information companies identify groups of people with common cognitive screens, most often through a simple and direct marketing approach. Such groups constitute niche markets for information services.

Information services businesses identify the information needed by decision makers in their respective niche markets and they create, gather, organize, and package relevant information so as to penetrate the cognitive screens of people for whom the information has value. Each niche market is in a different state of preparedness to use information. Some want it delivered electronically; others can use it only if it is provided in printed form. These differences, user-by-user and niche-by-niche, force the information provider to provide information in several media. To be successful, the information provider must start from a totally media-independent perspective. It cannot insist that its users take the information in only one medium. Such a policy would open the door to competitors to offer information in other media and to claim a market share in that niche market.

The result is information companies which smother a niche market with services in appropriate media to ensure they do not have to share their market with competitors. Another result is that these companies do not advertise. They already know their market; many created their markets in the first place by educating every user in the niche market personally. To promote their products or services to their niche market requires no advertising in the way consumer goods, vying for shelf space and market share, must be advertised. As a result, there are no advertising-supported media educating the world to the nature or even the existence of the information services business. That, plus the fact that those who have discovered its power want to keep it a secret, accounts for the fact that you hear so little about it.

Turning to the users for a moment, we find that most have a trained incapacity to use modern information service capabilities because they were not exposed to or trained in the use of such services while in school. Even people who gained computer literacy in school know little about information services themselves or how and when to use them. In fact, such computer-literate people often have the greatest difficulty grasping the challenge that information itself provides.

Information competency involves more than computer literacy. It involves not only how to access information, wherever it is stored and how; it requires an awareness of what information is available, how it is organized, how it is intended to be used, and how it can contribute to wealth-generating efforts in specific situations. This is a cerebral activity that requires education and training.

Mead Data Central, in the mid-1970s, built its marketing strategy for its new service, LEXIS—a full-text, online legal data base covering the nation's case law—on providing subsidized access to LEXIS to law students while they were in law school. They built into the ensuing generations of the nation's lawyers great information competencies. After becoming trained in and dependent upon doing legal research electronically, graduate lawyers demanded of their law-firm employers access to LEXIS. Today, Mead and West Publishing are providing legal services to law firms large and small built on the Mead marketing strategy of getting professionals trained while in school.

Few other fields of professional activity have been so well-served by the information providers. A feature of the information field is that no one user needs to know about all the data bases that are available. The field has grown to the point today that there are over 4,000 data bases available for searching on over 600 different computer systems, according to Carlos Cuadra's *Directory of Online Databases*. Decision makers need only concern themselves with the information services of direct importance to their businesses. Just as there is reason to subscribe only to those journals and trade publications of specific

**Table 5.1**
**Eleven Years of Data Base Growth**

| Directory Issue | Number of Databases* | Number of Database Producers | Number of Online Services | Number of Gateways |
|---|---|---|---|---|
| 1979/80 | 400 | 221 | 59 | |
| 1980/81 | 600 | 340 | 93 | |
| 1981/82 | 965 | 512 | 170 | |
| 1982/83 | 1350 | 718 | 213 | |
| 1983/84 | 1878 | 927 | 272 | |
| 1984/85 | 2453 | 1189 | 362 | |
| 1986 | 2901 | 1379 | 454 | 35 |
| 1987 | 3369 | 1568 | 528 | 44 |
| 1988 | 3699 | 1685 | 555 | 59 |
| 1989 (current) | 4245 | 1870 | 622 | 83 |

* Includes distinctly named files within database families.

*Source:* Carlos Cuadra, *Directory of Online Databases*. New York: Cuadra/Elsevier, 1989, Vol. 10, No. 3, p. v.

interest to you, so there is reason to become knowledgeable first in the use of specifically relevant information services. Outside search services can be called upon to do other searches when needed.

It is also vital to understand the intended purposes of specific data bases, as well. Sam Wolpert, founder of Predicasts, always maintained that less is worth more; that the precise information needed for a decision, not the universe of relevant information, was the most valuable. Predicasts' objective, Wolpert said, was to come as close as possible to providing the information needed for a "yes or no" answer. This, he figured, is the most valuable information. Every data base was developed for a particular objective, like Wolpert's. Making effective use of a specific data base often is facilitated by knowing not only its subject area, but the objectives for the data base as set out by its founder as well. This enables a user to "go with the flow" and to get the most out of a data base.

It helps to know about several other characteristics that distinguish information businesses:

• They create their own products rather than rely on outside authors. This provides greater control of the works as the assets of the company.

• The key to maintaining good working relationships with users in the niche market served by the company is staying close to the customer and responding promptly to new needs and opportunities. As a result, the customer often controls many aspects of the product development and service functions of the information company unlike other businesses where customers are not all so directly involved. In information, the customer's needs, changing as they are, drive the company and its products. This fact gives users great leverage in getting what they want.

• By definition, products offered in a niche market are customized to meet the specific needs and user patterns of the customer. Expect this from your suppliers and learn to participate with them in customizing the services offered to meet your specific needs.

• Information companies are often respositories of what is "known or knowable" in a given field. This is a function of maintaining their basic product-line in a machine-readable form. As time passes and their files grow, their knowledge base grows. Often they can be called on for specialized services to meet your needs based on their experience and contacts in your field of interest.

• The most important characteristic is that they perceive their product to be information. If the perception exists, the pattern of behavior distinctive to an information company is sure to follow. If you understand these characteristics you can make them work more effectively for you.

Understanding these characteristics is important to managers since a principal marketing device of the industry is to function like a chameleon, taking on the protective coloration of the market being served. It may be necessary for you to closely examine the sources of services being offered to be able to recognize the source as an information company. With that recognition comes an ability to interact more effectively with the information source.

It wasn't until the mid-1960s that one of America's oldest and largest information companies came to realize that it was not in the credit business but was indeed in the information business. Over one hundred years after Dun and Bradstreet was founded it came to recognize that the files it held on businesses in America constituted incredibly valuable data bases from which more than credit information could be extracted. When it gained this perception, it quickly moved to identify itself as an information company and to offer a wide range of services to the business world. Recognizing such developments early can give you a competitive edge by enabling you to tap into resources others haven't yet even thought about.

## THE INFORMATION INDUSTRY INFRASTRUCTURE

While the 1970s saw the emergence of information services as a separately identifiable business, the 1980s saw the development of an information infrastructure increasingly being tailored to support information handling and delivery. This infrastructure can be seen in the two-dimensional map provided in Figure 5.1.

It should be clear from this map, that the information industry is not just the computer industry. Often people respond to the concept of the information business as if it were the computer business. The significant influence of the computer in the information revolution makes this an understandable response. Professor Anthony Oettinger's Program on Information Resources Policy, Harvard University, developed the first map of this kind based on the relationship of various economic activities to computers. He placed the computer at the center of the

**Figure 5.1**
**The Information Industry Map**

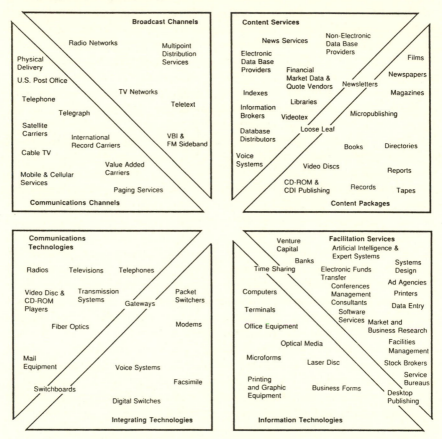

*Source:* This map was designed by Larry Day, Vice President, Information Handling Sources, Denver, Colorado, with modifications by Paul G. Zurkowski, President, Information Industry Association. The concept was based on the work of John F. McLaughlin with Ann Louise Antonoff, *Maping the Information Business* (Cambridge, Mass.: Program on Information Resources Policy, Harvard University, 1986).

map and arranged the other elements of the business around it, moving from the left side of the map, which he designated conduit, to the right side, which he called content, and from the top, which he called products, to the bottom, which he called services. The logic of this map enabled planners to "map" the growth and direction of specific companies as they acquired companies or launched new products.

The information industry map was developed by Larry Day when he was a corporate planner at the Information Technology Group (he now is President and CEO of Dealer's Digest, a financial information service company). The

Information Industry Association adopted Day's map and over the years has modified it to reflect the latest developments in the business.[2]

The eight segments of the map each involve different skills, investments, and operations, not all of which are directly involved in information handling as discussed here. However, every activity listed in each of the segments, in one way or another, offers services or capabilities essential to the businesses we are discussing here.

A brief tour of the map (proceeding clockwise and starting with Content Services) provides a useful survey of the information infrastructure in the United States.

• Content Services: The businesses listed in this sector comprise the core of the information provider community.

• Content Packages: Stand-alone packages tied to and identified with specific publishing media in many cases are the cornerstone of new information businesses offering content services in a media-independent information business.

• Facilitation Services: A vast array of close-to-the-content-services which include four kinds of activities carrying products to market, supporting information products and businesses: (a) The processing of other people's information; (b) Transaction processing; (c) Turnkey services; and (d) Support services.

The next three sections of the map represent a variety of information technology businesses, essential to the creation, packaging and distribution of information.

• Information technologies: These are the technologies giving us the capability to record, store, and process large quantities of information.

• Integrating technologies: These technologies connect information technologies to communications technologies to facilitate the flow of information from source to user.

• Communications Technologies: These are the reception equipment and the point-to-point communications tools.

Two final sections provide delivery channels.

• Communications Channels: Channels for either physical or digital delivery of information products and services.

• Broadcast Channels: Channels for either broadcasting or narrowcasting to specific audiences.

The most visible new interest in the information services business among infrastructure companies in the 1980s has come from the telecommunications companies. The Bell Holding Companies, separated from AT & T by a federal court's decision in an antitrust case, were forbidden to own the information that their systems transport. The court views the prospect of extending the monopoly that the local telephone loop enjoys to the business of information as sure to bring with it many new antitrust complaints, law suits, and service turmoil.

Particularly nettlesome to these companies is the frustration they experience in not being free to develop electronic versions of their yellow-page directories. While AT & T was subject to a seven-year prohibition against offering information services, the Bell Holding Companies have no fixed date to look forward to as a time when they could begin offering information services like electronic yellow pages. This controversy continues to focus attention, however, on information services and how best to deliver them. It reflects the continuing development of the information age.

This controversy, involving the courts, Congress, and executive agencies involved in one way or another in the information infrastructure, masks the fact that a critical mass of information services and information handling and transport facilities has been created. We see the turmoil and not the accomplishment: the 1980s have produced a critical mass of information services and capabilities.

## WHAT THE 1990s HAVE IN STORE

The 1970s produced the information business. The 1980s have built on that continually growing business by evolving a complex information infrastructure. The resulting critical mass of services and capabilities will be incorporated into the government, academia, business, and industry in the 1990s.

Chief information officers are beginning the process of educating corporate decision makers in the use of comprehensive, but largely internal, data files for planning, marketing, and managing. This is a vital effort that will pay off with highly competitive businesses. For some, integration of external sources of information at the senior business levels apparently will come only after the internal data applications have been developed, refined, and put into day-to-day use. Companies which defer that long will face increased pressure from their information competent competitors.

Workers with training in professional disciplines are becoming information integrators within organizations. Just as information services were created in various subject areas by professionals knowledgeable of the professional discipline covered by the service, so there are professionals with subject disciplines who are reaching out to external information sources for support in running their operations.

Present college marketing graduates, with software and computer expertise, are developing subject expertise and functioning as translators or integrators within organizations. They are positioning themselves to translate to the data-processing professionals what information and software support is needed by the marketing departments and, in turn, to the marketing department what capabilities data processing offers. If data processing isn't currently equipped to provide the necessary support to the marketing people, these integrators often are turning to their own PCs to develop the customized service needed by marketing. They are information-knowledge workers increasing both their subject expertise and their computerization skills. They are building their careers on the contribution they make to integrating the process of information with those corporate functions, like marketing, requiring information support. A solid middle class of information workers, based on this approach, will be needed and is beginning to emerge.

When measured against the full potential, today only small steps are being taken, here and there, to achieve the productivity-gains information services offer. This is only the beginning of the effort in the 1990s to take full advantage of the critical mass of capabilities built up over the last two decades.

## A HUNDRED-YEAR COMPARISON

If the 1990s are to realize the full integration of the growing critical mass of information capabilities, a catalyst must be found to precipitate these developments.

One hundred years ago, conditions were far different, in information and communications terms, from what they are today. For example:

• One hundred years ago, there were no child labor laws. Until well into the second decade of the twentieth century, children just approaching their teens worked in the mills twelve hours a day, six days a week. Not much time was left for the three Rs. My own father and mother, born shortly after the turn of the century, had an eighth-grade and third-grade education, respectively. Living in the lumbering areas of northern Wisconsin, their families needed their support. My mother and one of her sisters, who left school after the second grade, worked as cooks in a lumber camp where my grandfather worked as a lumberjack.

• Women had not been emancipated. They were considered to be chattels and were precluded from an active economic life outside the family.

• Large numbers of immigrants gathered in various ghettos and they continued to speak their native tongues. Only gradually did they enter the economic, social, and political life of the country.

• Universities were more like divinity schools than the sophisticated scientific and technical activities they are today. The Morrill Act, establishing the land-grant-college system, only recently celebrated its centennial.

• America had little scientific publishing apparatus. It relied heavily on German scientific publishing until after World War I.

• Public schools and communities had few, if any, library facilities.

• Western Union spanned the nation as a precursor of communications capabilities yet undreamed of. There were no radio, television, and telephone facilities.

• Transportation was limited to horse and carriage, steam engines, and canal and river travel. People lived out their lives within three to five miles of the place of their birth.

In short there was a knowledge vacuum. Under these conditions few ideas were widely shared and progress was slow. How did we deal with that vacuum? One catalyst was the Carnegie Public Library initiative. It brought to the attention of people throughout society an ever-increasing awareness of the power of information in printed form and how to use it. By the time of World War I, libraries had become known as the "arsenals of democracy."

Today, however, we face a different challenge, certainly not that of a knowledge vacuum. We are awash in knowledge and information. Today we face what can only be called a "creativity vacuum." The information tools and resources are available, but only a small part, perhaps 5 to 6 percent of the population, is sufficiently experienced and skilled in their use, having the necessary information competencies to apply these resources as elements of production. The great majority of workers do not. This lack of an information-competent population limits our ability to create our future and could be a tragedy for our society and our economy.

The in-house information-handling information integrators described earlier illustrate in a microscopic way the kind of effort and imagination needed to realize the benefits of information and to achieve an informed, creative society. In a sense, information is becoming everyone's business, with an emphasis on the word business. Not too long ago the Xerox Corporation heralded the fact that everyone could now be his or her own publisher. Today, everyone can be a part of the information business. Information-service companies are different from industrial-age companies who buy raw materials with which to build their widgets. Most industrial companies do not have the potential of selling anything back to their materials suppliers. In the information age the application of information to a company decision-making process may distill out a file of enhanced information having more value than the original data for which even the original supplier may be a market. This creates the opportunity to develop new information services. In fact, some large information businesses are the by-products of industrial operations.

In addition, the chief information officer or the information integrator who develops information for internal use faces the same business problems as outside vendors. How do you overcome the trained incapacities of the work force to use the information service? How do you demonstrate and dramatize the value of information when it is immediately subsumed into the business decision at hand? How do you "price" your service so as to continue to be a player in the decision-making process?

Everyone is seeking answers to questions like these and is coming up with entrepreneurial answers. This, in turn, leads to consideration of information as a business. The operation of these information enterprises, whether run internally or externally, is neither self-evident nor well documented. In fact, because of the unique characteristics of information (its use often enhances rather than exhausts its value; it can be used without diminishing the supply, etc.), an information operation does not fit the business patterns inherent in industrial-age enterprises.

## MEASURING THE SUCCESS POTENTIAL OF AN INFORMATION ENTERPRISE

A two-part mathematical formula can be used for measuring the success potential of an information product or service whether for in-house use or for commercial sale. Part 1 is based on an assessment of the effectiveness and capabilities of the information-service company. Three elements are assessed and assigned a value of from 1 to 10, and these values are totaled. Part 2 is based on an assessment of the multiplier factors in the marketplace that stimulate and enhance or block and undermine the service. Five such elements are assessed and assigned values of 1 to 10 and totaled.

The total points in Part 1, rating the relative effectiveness of the product and the enterprise, are then multiplied by the total number of points credited to the multiplier factors of the marketplace in part 2. The two values when multiplied together could produce a perfect score of 1,500 points. Candid evaluations based on this formula have resulted in profitable products receiving a score of as few as 300 points. This indicates that there is great room for growth both in the professional skills needed to run such businesses and in the development of the leverage factors in the information-age marketplace.

Part 1 consists of three measurements of an effective product and company.

1. THE PRODUCT ITSELF. Is the information content of the service inherently valuable? Does it relate to and affect economically valuable decisions? Will customers or in-house clients pay for or support the value-added features of the service?
2. MANAGEMENT'S MARKETING SKILLS. What entrepreneurial skills does management bring to promoting the product? Does it know the customer base? Is the product geared to user need? Is the product market driven or technology driven? If it is technology driven, beware of future problems. Look out, too, if management says that this is how people *should* or *ought* to use information. Few people do what they "should" or "ought," much less figure out how to use a new and unprecedented information product.
3. BUSINESS ACUMEN. What level of experience and acumen is available inside management? In this business, management must deal effectively with the awesome challenges of talent, technology, communications, and government.

If your evaluation says that (1) the service is new, but directed at a major high-value decision process, you may have given it 5 points (taking into consideration it has not been tested and may or may not respond to the needs of the decision process); (2) the service is more market driven than technology driven and you feel it deserves credit for that at about 5 points; and (3) the management team is a moxie group of three people, a technologically competent leader, a financial wizard, and a marketing pro, but all new to the information business and you gave it another 5 points. You gave the product and company a total of 15 points out of a possible 30 points based on what is being brought to the market. Fifteen is a high score for a new product. While that appeared easy on paper, in practice it calls for a real experienced eye to identify and quantify the merits of particular product ideas and their producers.

Moving on to the more complex matter of assessing multiplier factors in the marketplace, it should be clear from the earlier discussion of the information industry map that there are many factors and insights involved.

Part 2 consists of multiplier factors in the marketplace.

1. COMMUNICATIONS. How fulsome are the communications capabilities as they apply to the service in question? Does the service rely for its full potential on communications capabilities still on the drawing board? In market test? Or is there experience out there that can be called on to utilize the current state of the art communications capabilities to achieve maximum success?

2. INFORMATION TECHNOLOGY. The same questions pertain. Is the service based on simple tree-structure gateway services or can it use the existing Boolean-logic searching of remote data bases based on packet switching? Does it rely on the intelligence built into the personal computer of the user? Is this capability well-established in the targeted user market? Is the technology needed available? Or does the product have to "make do" with less-than-optimum technology support?

3. INFORMATION COMPETENCE. How ready is the market to receive, understand, and make immediate use of the service? How much reeducation about how to use this service will be needed? Are the schools training students to use this service as the law schools do now on LEXIS? Are there textbooks that explain to students similar kinds of services, or does this product face a market of people with trained incapacities to use it?

4. THE PLAYING FIELD. Will the competition this product faces play on a level playing field or is it tilted to the advantage of other players? For these services to succeed, a competitive marketplace is needed, not a monopoly-controlled or government-dominated marketplace. Are conditions such that a monopolist is in position to "steal" the product once it is launched? Is the government inclined to "fight" private businesses by offering services priced below cost and by tagging along the privately funded marketing of an innovation so as to undermine the long-term market for the product?

5. COMMUNITY ATTITUDE. Does the community surrounding the market targeted by this product place a high value on information? Is it in the financial markets arena where information is everyday currency? Does the community recognize information as a wealth-generating activity creating new jobs and paying taxes? Does the community value access to information? Is it important?

Each of these five multiplier factors can be decisive in the success or failure of a basically sound product. In some cases, the score assigned one or more of these factors may be a negative number because certain conditions are not just unsupportive, but are actively antagonistic to the product or service. If one assigned as high as a 6 (better than average) to three of the factors and a 2 and a 3 to the other two factors, the total multiplier factors number is 23. By multiplying these 23 points by the 15 points assigned as a measure of the quality of the product, a total point value of 345 will result. While this is slightly better than a 20-percent rating against a possible total of 1,500 points, industry experience suggests this could be a profitable product over time.

Whatever your approach to evaluating these developments, it should be evident that more and more effort is going into the process of making sense out of the information business. This, in turn, is leading to an expansion of the total number of information businesses. Even twenty years into the life of this amazing business, many are just getting started now in information ventures. This development is reflected in the fact that the Information Industry Association has grown in membership today from less than 300 in 1984 to over 800 companies (1989).

## LOOKING TO THE YEAR 2000

One of the information services the Bell Holding Companies have been permitted to engage in is provision of voice and data gateway services. Gateway services enable the telephone companies to provide message transport, billing, and some directorylike services in support of vendors of information services. The goal of this combination of services, like the initial goal of Viewdata, or Videotex as it was later called, is the creation of a mass market for information. Learning from the niche market experience of the information business, however, has led some telephone executives to talk about "masses of markets" rather than the industrial age concept of a single "mass market."

While many efforts are being made today, it is likely that a "personal use" market, whether involving "masses of markets" or a "mass market," won't emerge fully until after the turn of the century. Not only do consumer-related information services need to be created (not many proven services exist today and separate services for each local market may be needed), but alternative ways of funding their use also need to be developed to achieve an appealing and compelling array of services for individual decision making.

## THE WORLD-WIDE CHALLENGE

Information is increasingly a global business. The global integration of stock-market operations is a good example. Information development around the globe corresponds to developments in the United States. First, entrepreneurs discover information as a business. In China, even today, the government has sponsored venture-capital funds to stimulate the creation of information services for development. Second, infrastructure companies recognize the information business and develop the techniques and technologies for supporting information transport and handling. Postal, telephone, and telegraph authorities around the world are concentrating on how to service (and, in some countries, how to regulate) this business, particularly in regard to the type and quality of communications services required. Third, as a critical mass of services becomes available, they begin to be applied across the board to decision-making processes in industry, business, and government. This, in time, further feeds the growth and development of an information-handling-services sector in the economy, a vital sector to all progressive and growing countries. Fourth, consumer-related information services are developing as new funding mechanisms are provided. In France, decisions to provide a simple terminal for telephone directory information access has generated a funding technique by providing the basic communications channel for personal-use information services as an extension of the telephone itself. In response, hundreds of data bases have been created and added to the network along with the original telephone directory services.

While no one in this business, no one engaged in providing information services, is suggesting that information will displace industrial activities as the major economic activity in the global economy, it is clear that information services do contribute to and enhance all aspects of industrial life, and in so doing they generate wealth.

Information leverages materials, labor, and capital. By so doing, it offers a competitive challenge to every business. It is not surprising that a bandwagon is forming that will, in the 1990s, extend the reach and power of information into the far reaches of our economy and the economies of the rest of the world.

## NOTES

1. Paul Hawken, *The Next Economy* (New York: Holt, Rinehart and Winston, 1983).

2. For a more detailed description of the components of the Information Industry Map see Paul G. Zurkowski, "Integrating America's Infostructure," *The Journal of the American Society for Information Science*, vol. 35, no. 3 (1984).

# Part III

## ADJUSTING TO CHANGE

# 6

# Intelligence for Strategic Decision Making in Multinational Corporations

## David M. Flynn

The nature of strategic decision making requires organizations to make decisions under uncertainty. To help reduce uncertainty, various types of intelligence, that is, information-processing methods, are employed. Intelligence is the problem of gathering, processing, interpreting, and communicating the economic, social, technical, and political information needed in the decision-making process. Formal methods of intelligence include management information systems (MIS) (Huber 1984) and the decision support systems (DSS) (Keen and Scott-Morton 1978; Minch and Sanders 1986). Informal methods include external boundary-spanning activity by professionals (Keegan 1974), communication among intra-company personnel (Keegan 1974; Kobrin et al. 1980), and the internalization of uncertainty (that is, uncertainty absorption) by strategic planners (Boulton et al. 1982; March and Simon 1958).

In considering the application of formal information-processing methods to strategic decision making, this chapter focuses on several important issues. First, it provides the rationale for the extension of formal information-processing methods (FIM) to the complex environments facing multinational firms. It then identifies individual (cognitive) and organizational factors that impede the use of formal information-processing methods. Next, based on a review of the literature, it posits that these impediments combine to create a "threshold of uncertainty" for both individuals and organizations. The threshold represents a specific level of uncertainty where formal and informal information-processing methods are used equally. Below the threshold, at low levels of uncertainty, formal methods are more heavily relied on by decision makers. Above the threshold, at higher levels of uncertainty, informal methods (IM) provide the primary source of information for decision making. This concept provides an effective framework for understanding the relationship between uncertainty and formal and informal information-processing methods. Finally, currently available computer-based information-processing technologies are identified, including decision support systems, knowledge-based systems, and graphics for moving the threshold to a position where strategic decision makers use formal information-processing methods more often. Throughout the chapter information processing and intelligence will be used interchangeably. However, it must be noted that the literature on information processing is more extensive and rigorous.

## STRATEGIC PLANNING UNDER UNCERTAINTY

Strategic planning's main purpose is the determination of an organization's relationship to its environment in pursuit of its goals (Bourgeois 1980). Environments can be described on various dimensions or continua such as simple/complex, stable/unstable, concentrated/dispersed, and lean/rich (Aldrich 1979; Duncan 1972; Lawrence and Lorsch 1967; Thompson 1967). The more complex, unstable, dispersed, and lean the environment, the higher the level of uncertainty faced by strategic decision makers. Therefore, within this definition, the environment of the multinational corporation (MNC) is more uncertain. The MNC is distinguished from a domestic corporation by its complexity and dispersion (Kolde 1982). The task environment (customers, competitors, and suppliers) and general environment (economic, legal, political, social, and technological factors) are combined as part of the firm's enacted environment (Dill 1958). Uncertainty for multinational firms includes input and output uncertainty. Input uncertainty includes availability and sourcing of raw materials, skill and availability of local labor, and infrastructure (roads, airports, machinery, and so on) necessary for construction of facilities. Output uncertainty includes the expected demand, production flexibility necessary to fill demand, the level of integration of the distribution channels for the local and export market, and the stability of the local currency. In addition, political risk is a fundamental factor of uncertainty that affects operating and strategic decisions. It is within these more uncertain environments that decision makers often adjust their information-processing strategies to less formal procedures, for example, informal discussions with coworkers, consultations with dominant power coalitions, and reliance on past experience (Aguilar 1967; Fredrickson 1984; Fredrickson and Mitchell 1984; Kobrin et al. 1980; Miller and Friesen 1984).

The inverse relationship between uncertainty and the utilization of formal information-processing procedures in strategic planning may exist for several reasons. These reasons can be grouped into either individual or organizational factors that influence the strategic decision-making process. In terms of individual factors, the psychological limitations of individuals in dealing with complex and nonroutine issues have long been recognized as impediments (March and Simon 1958). When causal linkages among the numerous decision variables are unknown, simple responses to complex problems may result. In addition, individuals within organizations may feel that the sources that provide formal reports can be biased by the process that generates them (March and Shapira 1982). For example, the social construction of reality makes it difficult to validate facts that are obtained through formal methods and that are based on a limited sample of events (Davis 1982). With regard to organizational factors, the absence of a suitable organizational framework for planning and control is one important consideration. This may exist because of the existence of different types of organizations, such as entrepreneurial versus conglomerate, or differing techniques used for diagnosis of strategic issues (Dutton and Duncan 1987a, 1987b). Another factor is difficulty of using formal information-processing methods that are not suitably designed to support the analysis of unique and unstructured problems (Nutt 1984).

Although formal and informal information-processing methods may coexist within organizations, one must recognize the need for increased dependence on more formal information-processing methods (FIM) as organizations become more decentralized and their environments become increasingly complex (Huber 1984). Specifically, information requirements increase as task and general environmental uncertainty increase (Culnan 1983; Galbraith 1973; O'Reilly 1982). Furthermore, organizational effectiveness is a function of the uncertainty caused by the complexity and interdependence of tasks (Tushman and Nadler 1978; Daft and McIntosh 1981; Perrow 1967) and the ability of the organizational structure to provide participants with information. Information gathered from external sources with rigorous analysis has been shown to improve strategic decision making in dynamic environments (Bourgeois 1985). Also, quantitative and qualitative methods of analysis (that is, FIM) are necessary for the systematic and rigorous assessment of the firm's environment (Downey and Ireland 1979; Huber 1984; Kobrin 1979). This includes country and industry factors that affect a multinational firm's operations. Political risk assessment is one specific factor that has been subject to extensive analysis (Fitzpatrick 1983).

In summary, there exists a curvilinear relationship between uncertainty and information-processing strategies. As uncertainty increases, individuals increase the type and amount of information-processing strategies. However, at higher levels of uncertainty, especially in the multinational strategic decision environment, the information-processing strategies become decreasingly sophisticated. There are individual and organizational factors that impede the use of more sophisticated and formal information-processing methods. Rigorous and diverse information-processing methods are critical to decision making, particularly in complex environments. For individuals and organizations to formulate effective strategic plans, they must begin to employ formal intelligence methods that facilitate the rigorous analysis of strategic issues.

## INDIVIDUAL IMPEDIMENTS TO COMPUTER USAGE FOR STRATEGIC ANALYSIS

Individuals categorize and consider the significance of task and environmental factors in an enactment process. Because the enactment process involves filtering through individuals, preferences and cognitive frameworks elicit different perceptions of the problem environment and the usefulness of different information (Kiesler and Sproull 1982; Ungson, Braunstein, and Hall 1981).

Individual differences and limits to rational decision processes have been discussed often (for example, Cyert and March 1963; March and Shapira 1982; Simon 1982, 1977). These authors suggest that there are limits to the diversity and amount of information individuals can handle. Also, individuals often are not capable of perfect recollection of past actions (that is, individuals do not recall information in its original form) but only recognize familiar patterns (Rosenfield 1986). This perspective on human memory suggests that for individuals, information does not exist as a fixed record but changes as new information, experience, and learning occur. In addition, even nonconscious mental structures and processes affect an individual's conscious thought and action (Kihlstrom 1987). These different factors contribute to a high level of diversity among decision makers.

Furthermore, different human biasing behaviors reduce the breadth and rigor of data/information use and analysis (Davis 1982). Individuals may be anchored to a perspective and evaluate currently available information from that anchor point. Individuals may ignore events of the past and assign causality between events based on little, if any, statistical validation. Recognition of these sources of bias through the discussion of an individual's assumptions about the completion of complex tasks may permit the design of information systems that build upon differences among individual information-processing strategies. As a possible solution, decision makers could be grouped according to common perceptions of information items (Van de Ven 1986). Reports could then be tailored to homogeneous groups of decision makers. Although such a strategy seems possible, the difficulty of measurement and the cost of implementation reduce its plausibility. Alternatively, even brief training in logical thought may enhance individuals' use of reasoning about organizational events (Howard 1988). Inferences can be made about past organization/environment outcomes and taught to individual decision makers. Previous theorists have been mistaken about trainability, in part because they misidentified the kind of rules that people use naturally (Nisbett et al. 1987).

The cognitive limitations of human beings in their ability to handle complexity and pay attention to nonroutine strategic issues are a central problem affecting information-processing routines. A primary issue is how to trigger individuals to appreciate and pay attention to nonroutine issues (Van de Ven 1986). Institutionalizing the process through training and reward systems for incumbent and new managers would enhance their information-processing abilities. Also, participation in the design of complex computer programs improves the systems' acceptance and effectiveness (Campbell and Gingrich 1986).

Various factors, a few of which were identified earlier, affect the use of FIM by individuals. However, recent software technologies, discussed in the section on computer-based technologies, introduce improved methods of formal information processing. These technologies are flexible enough to address unique differences among decision makers and provide features for overcoming cognitive limits of individuals. The next section identifies organizational factors affecting the type of information-processing strategies used for coping with uncertainty.

## ORGANIZATIONAL IMPEDIMENTS TO EFFECTIVE INFORMATION PROCESSING

As an open system subject to influences from the environment, an organization develops intelligence-gathering and information-processing mechanisms, for example, strategic management information systems (SMIS), as a means of dealing with internal and external sources of uncertainty (Tushman and Nadler 1978, 614; Zaltman, Duncan, and Holbek 1973). Information processing entails the gathering, interpreting, and synthesis of information for decision making (March and Simon 1958; Tushman and Nadler 1978). It has been shown that an organization challenged by higher levels of uncertainty in the environment will increase its information-processing activities (Galbraith 1973; Tushman and Nadler 1978). Included among these activities is the usage of externally generated reports from industry specialists such as forecasts and future scenarios of industry-specific environmental factors. These data are usually integrated into centralized data bases for analysis.

Large integrated systems to collect and store data have been especially useful in environments with low uncertainty (Fredrickson 1984; Henderson and Nutt 1980). Environments with low uncertainty are defined as predictable and analyzable. Therefore, data that is externally generated is considered reliable, or at least its validity can be easily established. One may conclude that these systems, associated with tightly structured and formal information-processing systems cannot cope with highly uncertain strategic problems. However, alternative explanations may also be plausible. For example, more complete planning processes, including the use of computer systems, were not used due to their poor implementation (Nutt 1984). Furthermore, the lack of training, support, feedback, and rewards is viewed as inhibiting the successful implementation of a strategic computer-based information system (Gunawardare 1985). Organizations do not recognize the need to manage equivocality as well as uncertainty in the attempt to be effective information processors (Daft and Lengel 1986). Equivocality exists because of the existence of multiple and conflicting interpretations among individuals about the organization's situation. Also, these data bases are often highly subjective because the information is filtered through the organization's belief system.

In another context, user involvement affects the perception of usefulness of formal information methods (Franz and Robey 1986). These findings were moderated by the negative relationship between perceived usefulness and both age of the MIS department and managerial level in the organization. Specifically, the older the department, the lower the perception of usefulness of the information system. The negative relationship between level in the organization and perceived usefulness suggests that upper-level managers are reluctant to use formal information-processing methods. One could speculate that higher-level managers rely more on their intuition to solve complex problems than on unproven formal methods of information processing such as DSS.

While the impediments to the use of sophisticated intelligence systems are formidable, computer-based tools can be used to augment an experienced manager's abilities so that the overall quality of decisions can be improved. For instance, formal methods of information processing provide a means to examine many more alternatives than a manager can analyze alone. Formal management information systems have greater capacity to provide useful data quickly to managers, especially about the external environment and competition. It is critical, however, that MIS departments provide education and training programs that facilitate implementation and increase end-user awareness of computer technologies.

## INFORMATION THRESHOLD

Individual and organizational factors that impede the use of formal information-processing methods (FIM) create a "threshold of uncertainty." The threshold of uncertainty describes the relationship between uncertainty and the relative dependence on formal and informal methods. This concept suggests that both formal and informal methods are used in varying degrees as determined by the extent of perceived uncertainty faced by decision makers.

Formal methods have predominated at low levels of uncertainty caused by individual and organizational impediments. As the level of uncertainty increases, as illustrated in figure 6.1, panel A, the extent to which a decision maker uses formal information decreases. In contrast, informal information-processing methods predominate at high levels of uncertainty. As illustrated by the formal usage function in figure 6.1, panel B, the decision maker's dependence on informal methods increases directly with the levels of uncertainty.

The intersection of these information-usage functions defines the "threshold of uncertainty," point AB in figure 6.1, panel C. At the threshold of uncertainty, equal amounts of formal and informal information-processing methods are used by decision makers. Beyond this point, informal intelligence gathering prevails. Strategic decisions are based more on information gathered through informal means, such as interpersonal interaction, than on the analysis of printed data. The threshold of uncertainty will be different for individual decision makers as a function of their perceived levels of uncertainty according to their underlying perceptions and other cognitive abilities.

Increasing the threshold of uncertainty would benefit decision makers since de-

**Figure 6.1**
**Threshold of Uncertainty**

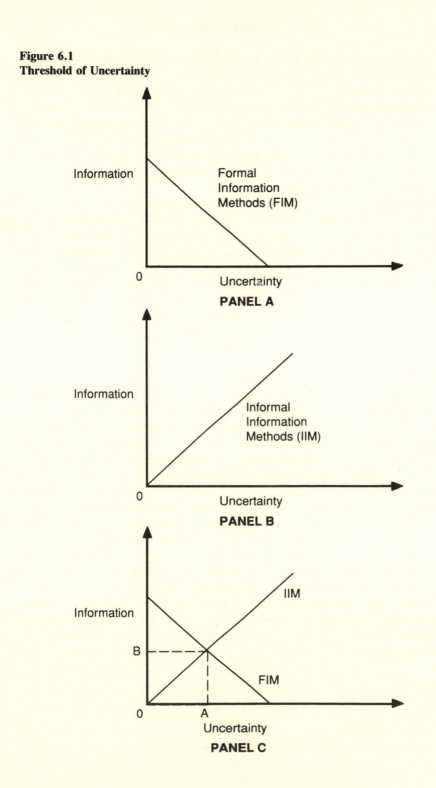

cisions would be based on objective information sources gathered outside the firm and through rigorous analysis, imparting more validity to the strategic plans developed (Bourgeois 1985). By providing more information, better methods of information management, and more powerful decision support capabilities, computer-based technologies (see the next section, "Computer-based Technologies to Support Strategic Decision Making") are capable of shifting the threshold of uncertainty to the right so that more sophisticated computer-based intelligence systems are used at higher levels of uncertainty. These technologies change the structure of information usage in two ways. First, they increase the amount of formal information available to a decision maker across all levels of uncertainty. This is represented by a parallel upward shift in the formal information-usage function. By shifting the line in this direction, the threshold of uncertainty moves from point AB to point A'B' in figure 6.2, panel A. Second, they improve a decision maker's ability to use formal information sources and effectively integrate them into the decision-making process. This is represented by the change in slope of the formal and informal information lines that results in a higher threshold of uncertainty (see figure 6.2, panel B, point A'B'). If the slope of the formal information-usage function is decreased, the rate at which formal information usage decreases is lower (less steep) at all levels of uncertainty. One could also posit that as the amount of FIM increases, there is a corresponding decrease in the amount of informal information processing, suggesting a cognitive limit to the amount of information that an individual can effectively analyze (Simon 1977). Thus the absolute change in slope is equivalent for both lines. This is represented by no change in point 0B in panel C.

In summary, the "threshold of uncertainty" concept provides a model for understanding the relationship between the uncertainty inherent in a strategic problem and a decision maker's reliance on formal and informal information-processing methods. Established planning systems tend to rely more on informal methods for numerous reasons previously cited on the individual and organizational levels, including cognitive differences, familiarity with existing methods, and the lack of organizational training and support. However, decision makers, especially planners, need to institute improved methods to cope with increasingly complex environments facing most organizations. The methods for increasing information-processing thresholds involve computer technologies that support decision makers with models, analysis, and easy access to relevant information. An increase in the threshold of uncertainty is a more desirable position for individual decision makers since decisions are based on objective information sources gathered outside the firm and on rigorous internal analysis imparting more validity to the strategic plans developed.

## COMPUTER-BASED TECHNOLOGIES TO SUPPORT STRATEGIC DECISION MAKING

There has also been an increased diffusion of computer technologies for improving personal productivity and decision making available in the marketplace.

**Figure 6.2**
**The Effects of Increased Usage of Computer-based Technologies on the Threshold of Uncertainty**

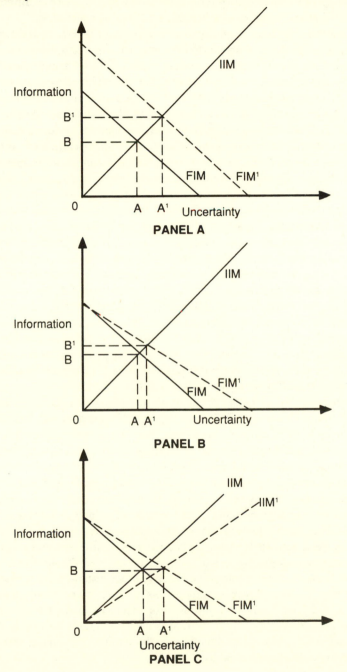

This phenomenon should provide the rationale for using formal information-processing systems in the strategic planning process. As noted earlier, there remain impediments to this proliferation, including individual differences in cognitive abilities resulting in different thresholds of uncertainty.

Moving the threshold of uncertainty to a position where strategic decisions are supported by more sophisticated computer-based intelligence requires the implementation of new computer-based technologies that combine data collected internally and externally with modeling capabilities that allow decision makers to analyze problems in a faster and more rigorous way. Huber (1984) presented several design features such as advanced communication and computing technologies and decision-process management for supporting decision making in dynamic and complex environments, for example, the operating environment of multinational corporations. However, many of the technologies he describes are normative and exploratory. Several technologies currently available can facilitate moving an individual's threshold of uncertainty to a position where computer-based information-processing (intelligence) technologies are used.

Recent developments in artificial intelligence, with increased user friendliness, may also contribute to increased proliferation of computer technology for decision making under uncertainty. For example, natural language programming and expert systems are making DSS technically feasible for unstructured decision making on the strategic level (Huber 1984; Rosenfield 1986; Rucks and Ginter 1982; Vazsonyi 1982; Watkins 1982). DSS are designed to assist or enhance a manager's decision-making ability in ill-structured and complex decision tasks (Keen and Scott-Morton 1978). They are intended to (1) give managers access to a variety of data, (2) facilitate the use of analytical operations and models for analyzing the data, and (3) do so in a fast and flexible manner to permit repeated use of the system (Sprague and Carlson 1982).

Knowledge-based systems can facilitate the intellectual processes needed to examine strategic issues in a DSS environment (Waterman 1982; Rauch-Hinden 1986; Hayes-Roth, Waterman, and Lenat 1983). The development of knowledge-based systems that simulate expert consulting and problem solving is an active area of research and development. Methods have been developed to acquire and represent knowledge and to employ it with reasoning strategies to solve complex problems and provide advice. These systems can incorporate rules and heuristics borrowed from experts working in the domain of strategic planning. The state of the art permits the development of knowledge-based systems for supporting the use of DSS. Knowledge-based systems can help structure DSS problems and provide advice on formulating analyses and on using available data.

Through a knowledge-explanation facility, these systems are also available to explain their results. This feature maintains a "line of reasoning" that can be called upon by the users at any time. For instance, managers can obtain an explanation of why a specific procedure is used and query the system for alternative techniques. Moreover, directions on how to use the models and interpret their results could be provided by this component.

Knowledge-based systems combined with DSS improve a decision maker's ability to work with models and data. They impact the structure of information usage by providing decision makers with more information and with better facilities for analyzing data. These features shift the formal information-usage function upwards and decrease the slope of the formal information-usage function. Thus these technologies move the threshold of uncertainty to a position where decision makers are more apt to use objective information and analysis at higher levels of uncertainty.

Also of importance is the presentation of the information for analysis. Recent developments in software and hardware technologies are making graphics a standard tool for decision support applications. Computer graphics present large amounts of data in an effective format that is easily understood by decision makers, who can then quickly identify trends in performance and initiate appropriate action. By providing decision makers with a means to absorb more information, these developments move the threshold of uncertainty to the right through an upward shift in the formal information-usage function. Cleveland and McGill (1985) have provided basic principles of graphical perception for the effective presentation of quantitative and qualitative data.

These automated decision aids can contain up-to-date data that are both internal and external to the organization. For instance, external information could be supplied to these systems by boundary spanners, who would serve as information processors, gathering and disseminating information from the external environment into the organization (Katz and Tushman 1983; Tushman and Scanlan 1981; Tushman and Nadler 1978). Boundary spanners keep abreast of new technical developments and organizational demands through informal contacts and personal associations.

Electronic mail facilities provide the capability to communicate with others in an efficient manner. By standardizing intracompany communication through a common processing system, these systems create a structure for formal and informal information flows. Users can quickly gather information sent by a variety of sources and make requests for other data in an electronic setting. These features facilitate the strategic planning process through increased accessibility, efficiency of communication, and timeliness of data. A related technology, electronic bulletin boards, provides the means to gain access or provide input to a subject of interest to a group of people. These systems promote sharing of information among people interested in a common subject area or involved in a common decision task.

Emerging computer-based technologies can provide a structured environment for more continuous, more complex, and higher-quality strategic decision making through formal information sources and powerful decision aids. They provide a means of moving the threshold of uncertainty to the right, where formal information-processing methods support strategic decision making. By doing so, they have direct implications for the design of strategic planning systems. For instance, communication technologies such as electronic mail and bulletin boards should increase the number of persons outside of the primary decision unit contributing to a strategic decision. The marriage of DSS and knowledge-based systems should provide automated expertise for supporting more rigorous analysis of strategic issues and problems. Moreover, through knowledge-explanation facilities, knowledge-based systems provide greater insight into the decision process, including assumptions, logic, and alternate viewpoints. Automated expertise should reduce the heterogeneity and size of "formal" decision units in terms of people but increase the resources utilized (Howard 1988). Moreover, the processes through which experts influence decisions will be less direct as a result of this technology.

## IMPLEMENTATION OF AN INTELLIGENCE SYSTEM

Effective strategic planning can be a delicate process due to the requisite involvement of many organizational members. As suggested earlier, the planning process requires a continuous flow of relevant information between subunits and a centralized planning unit. Recent research indicates that more centralization of this intelligence process contributes to more effective strategic planning and performance. Specifically, since the overthrow of the shah of Iran in 1978, more organizations have formally established a centralized environmental scanning unit to monitor environmental and competitive trends (Kennedy 1984). This scanning function may occur through individual intelligence efforts, externally generated reports, and internal analysis of socioeconomic, political, technological, and competitive trend data. It is critical that the raw data be standardized and disseminated to the relevant subunits for interpretation prior to the implementation of any strategy. Increasingly organizations are using full-time risk coordinators who integrate the specific country and industry data into an operational intelligence system.

Effective intelligence systems must also recognize the need for parsimonious data bases. If the number of variables included increases beyond a "manageable limit," the data base will become useless. Also, the data base must include narrowly defined variables for easy monitoring. This monitoring process considers the predicted versus actual outcomes among the relevant variables. Additionally, variables that are shown to have insignificant effects on organizational performance must be replaced. Effectively managed data bases minimize the threats of low usage among decision makers.

An example of an effective computer-based intelligence system for political risk analysis is the Conflict and Peace Data Bank (COPDAB) (Azar 1975). COPDAB employs the following three steps in compiling data for usage in the strategic planning function: (1) daily event statements are collected from public sources; (2) the event statements are coded to produce descriptive events that are computer stored; and (3) the descriptive events are scaled, weighted, and aggregated to produce the dimensions of interaction. This information is easily stored in a computer-based information system (CBIS) for access and analysis within particular problem domains.

Another example of an accessible source of information for multinational firms involved with Asian business is Nikkei Telecom's Japan News and Retrieval System. This online data service provides access to the Nikkei Economic Electronic Database System, which is Asia's largest depository of current and historical information on the socioeconomic and political operating environment in Japan and other Asian countries. In addition, information is provided for particular companies operating in this area. These data can be monitored on a regular basis for analysis and dissemination to the relevant strategic business units.

Some of the more relevant issues for monitoring would be changes in the ruling political party, currency fluctuations, monetary and fiscal policy, trade policy, balance of payments, competitive collaborations (joint ventures), and so on. Some of these issues may need only quarterly reviews, while others, such as currency values, need daily attention. These factors would then need to be analyzed for their potential impact on tactical and strategic decisions. As suggested earlier, these monitoring tasks are handled more often in the strategic planning department.

The future survival of multinational organizations is a function of their ability to formulate effective strategic plans and to take advantage of new opportunities. As environments become increasingly complex, a firm's ability to incorporate external sources of information with rigorous analysis in the strategic planning process becomes more important. However, there exist certain organizational and individual impediments to the use of formal methods for strategic planning. These impediments are responsible for the greater reliance on informal methods as uncertainty associated with the problem increases. The net effect of these impediments is to create a threshold of uncertainty, which was described as the relationship between uncertainty and a decision maker's utilization of formal and informal information-processing methods. Although formal and informal methods will both be used by decision makers, the threshold can be moved through sophisticated intelligence systems, such as DSS, knowledge-based systems, and electronic communication technologies.

One may also expect that as multinational organizations increase in size and complexity, computer-based intelligence systems will be required to integrate the multidivisional, multinational organization into a strategic form. Information processing through computer-based systems facilitates control of subunits and provides necessary links for integrating complex strategic decision-making processes. Loosely coupled organizations not integrated through formal information methods are maladaptive, creating a facade of system effectiveness (Kmetz 1984). The facade results from simpleminded intelligence methods that ignore the complexity of problems facing multinational firms.

## REFERENCES

Aguilar, J. (1967). *Scanning the Business Environment*. New York: Macmillan.
Aldrich, H. E. (1979). *Organizations and Environments*. Englewood Cliffs, N.J.: Prentice-Hall.

Azar, E. E. (1975). "The Conflict and Peace Data Bank (COPDAB) Project." *Journal of Conflict Resolution*, 24, 143–152.

Boulton, N. R., Lindsay, W. M., Franklin, S. G., and Rue, L. W. (1982). "Strategic Planning: Determining the Impact of Environmental Characteristics and Uncertainty." *Academy of Management Journal*, 25(3), 500–509.

Bourgeois, L. J. (1980). "Strategy and Environment: A Conceptual Integration." *Academy of Management Review*, 5(1), 25–39.

———. (1985). "Strategic Goals, Perceived Uncertainty, and Economic Performance in Volatile Environments." *Academy of Management Journal*, 28(3), 548–573.

Campbell, D. J., and Gingrich, K. F. (1986). "The Interactive Effects of Task Complexity and Participation on Task Performance: A Field Experiment." *Organizational Performance and Human Decision Processes*, 38(1), 162–180.

Cleveland, W. S., and McGill, R. (1985). "Graphical Perception and Graphical Methods for Analyzing Scientific Data." *Science*, 229(4716), 828–833.

Culnan, M. J. (1983). "Environmental Scanning: The Effects of Task Complexity and Source Accessibility on Information Gathering Behavior." *Decision Sciences*, 14, 194–206.

Cyert, R. M., and March, J. G. (1963). *A Behavioral Theory of the Firm*. Englewood Cliffs, N.J.: Prentice-Hall.

Daft, R. L., and Lengel, R. H. (1986). "Organizational Information Requirements." *Management Science*, 32(5), 554–571.

Daft, R. L., and McIntosh, N. B. (1981). "A Tentative Exploration into the Amount and Equivocality of Information Processing in Organizational Work Units." *Administrative Science Quarterly*, 26, 207–224.

Davis, G. B. (1982). "Strategies for Information Requirements Detection." *IBM Systems Journal*, 21(1), 4–30.

Dill, W. R. (1958). "Environment as an Influence on Managerial Autonomy." *Administrative Science Quarterly*, 2, 409–443.

Downey, H. K., and Ireland, R. D. (1979). "Quantitative versus Qualitative Environmental Assessment in Organizational Studies." *Administrative Science Quarterly*, 24, 630–637.

Duncan, R. B. (1972). "Characteristics of Organizational Environments and Perceived Environmental Uncertainty." *Administrative Science Quarterly*, 17, 313–337.

Dutton, J. E., and Duncan, R. B. (1987a). "The Creation of Momentum for Change through the Process of Strategic Issue Diagnosis." *Strategic Management Journal*, 8, 279–295.

———. (1987b). "The Influence of the Strategic Planning Process on Strategic Change." *Strategic Management Journal*, 8, 103–116.

Fitzpatrick, M. (1983). "The Definition and Assessment of Political Risk in International Business: A Review of the Literature." *Academy of Management Review*, 8(2), 249–254.

Franz, C. R., and Robey, D. (1986). "Organizational Context, User Involvement, and the Usefulness of Information Systems." *Decision Sciences*, 17(3), 329–356.

Fredrickson, J. W. (1984). "The Completeness of Strategic Decision Processes: Extensions, Observations, Future Directions." *Academy of Management Journal*, 27(3), 445–466.

Fredrickson, J. W., and Mitchell, J. (1984). "Strategic Decision Processes: Comprehensiveness and Performance in an Industry with an Unstable Environment.'' *Academy of Management Journal*, 27(2), 399–423.

Galbraith, J. (1973). *Designing Complex Organizations*. Reading, Mass.: Addison-Wesley.

Gunawardare, G. (1985). ''Implementing a Management Information System in an Extremely Dynamic (and Somewhat Hostile) Environment—A Case Study.'' *Interfaces*, 15, 95–99.

Hayes-Roth, F., Waterman, D. A., and Lenat, D. B. (1983). *Building Expert Systems*. Reading, Mass.: Addison-Wesley.

Henderson, J. W., and Nutt, P. C. (1980). ''The Influence of Decision Style on Decision Making Behavior.'' *Management Science*, 26, 371–386.

Howard, R. A. (1988). ''Decision Analysis: Practice and Promise.'' *Management Science*, 34(6), 679–695.

Huber, G. P. (1983). ''Cognitive Style as a Basis for MIS and DSS Designs: Much Ado about Nothing.'' *Management Science*, 19, 567–579.

———. (1984). ''The Nature and Design of Post-Industrial Organizations.'' *Management Science*, 30(8), 928–951.

Katz, R., and Tushman, M. L. (1983). ''A Longitudinal Study of the Effects of Boundary Spanning Supervision on Turnover and Promotion in Research and Development.'' *Academy of Management Journal*, 26(3), 437–456.

Keegan, W. J. (1974). ''Multinational Scanning: A Study of Information Sources Utilized by Headquarter Executives in Multinational Companies.'' *Administrative Science Quarterly*, 19, 411–421.

Keen, P.G.W., and Scott-Morton, M. S. (1978). *Decision Support Systems: An Organizational Perspective*. Reading, Mass.: Addison-Wesley.

Kennedy, C. R. (1984). ''The External Environment–Strategic Planning Interface: U.S. Multinational Corporate Practices in the 1980s.'' *Journal of International Business Studies*, 15(2), 99–108.

Kiesler, S., and Sproull, L. (1982). ''Managerial Responses to Changing Environments: Perspectives on Problem Sensing from Social Cognition.'' *Administrative Science Quarterly*, 27, 548–570.

Kihlstrom, J. F. (1987). ''The Cognitive Unconscious.'' *Science*, 237(4821), 1445–1452.

Kmetz, J. L. (1984). ''An Information-processing Study of Complex Workflow in Aircraft Electronics Repair.'' *Administrative Science Quarterly*, 29(2), 255–280.

Kobrin, S. J. (1979). ''Political Risk: A Review and Reconsideration.'' *Journal of International Business Studies*, 10, 67–80.

Kobrin, S. J., Basek, J., Blank, S., and La Palombara, J. (1980). ''The Assessment and Evaluation of Non-economic Environments by American Firms: A Preliminary Report.'' *Journal of International Business Studies*, 11, 32–47.

Kolde, E. J. (1982). *Environment of International Business*. Boston: Kent Publishing.

Lawrence, P., and Lorsch, J. (1967). *Organization and Environment*. Boston: Harvard Business School, Division of Research.

March, J. G., and Shapira, Z. (1982). ''Behavioral Decision Theory and Organizational Decision Theory.'' In Ungson, G. R., and Braunstein, D. N. (eds.), *Decision Making*. Boston: Kent Publishing.

March, J. G., and Simon, H. A. (1958). *Organizations*. New York: J. Wiley.

Miller, D., and Friesen, P. H. (1984). *Organizations: A Quantum View*. Englewood Cliffs, N.J.: Prentice-Hall.

Minch, R. P., and Sanders, G. L. (1986). "Computerized Information Systems Supporting Multicriteria Decision Making." *Decision Sciences* 17(3), 395–413.

Nikkei Telecom, Japan News and Retrieval (an online data base covering Asia). Tokyo: Nihon Keizai Shimbum; New York: Mitsui and Company.

Nisbett, R. E., Fong, G. T., Lehman, D. R., and Cheng, P. W. (1987). "Teaching Reasoning." *Science*, 238(4827), 625–631.

Nutt, P. C. (1984). "Planning Process Archetypes and Their Effectiveness." *Decision Sciences*, 15(2), 221–238.

O'Reilly, G. A. (1982). "Variations in Decision Makers' Use of Information: The Impact of Quality and Accessibility of Information." *Academy of Management Journal*, 25(4), 756–771.

Perrow, C. (1967). "A Framework for Comparative Analysis of Organizations." *American Sociological Review*, 32, 194–208.

Rauch-Hinden, W. B. (1986). *Artificial Intelligence in Business, Science, and Industry.* Vol. 1. Englewood Cliffs, N.J.: Prentice-Hall.

Rosenfield, I. (1986). "Neural Darwinism: A New Approach to Memory and Perception." *New York Review of Books*, 33(15), 21–27.

Rucks, A. C., and Ginter, P. M. (1982). "Strategic MIS: Promises Unfulfilled." *Journal of Systems Management*, March, 16–19.

Simon, H. A. (1977). *The New Science of Management Decision.* Englewood Cliffs, N.J.: Prentice-Hall.

―――. (1982). *The Science of the Artificial.* Cambridge, Mass.: MIT Press.

Sprague, R. H., and Carlson, H. J. (1982). *Building Effective Decision Support Systems.* Englewood Cliffs, N.J.: Prentice-Hall.

Thompson, J. (1967). *Organizations in Action.* New York: McGraw-Hill.

Tushman, M. L., and Nadler, D. (1978). "Information Processing as an Integrating Concept in Organizational Design." *Academy of Management Review*, 3(4), 613–624.

Tushman, M. L., and Scanlan, T. J. (1981). "Boundary Spanning Individuals: Their Role in Information Transfer and Their Antecedents." *Academy of Management Journal*, 24(2), 289–305.

Ungson, G. R., Braunstein, D. N., and Hall, P. D. (1981). "Managerial Information Processing: A Research Review." *Administrative Science Quarterly*, 26, 116–134.

Van de Ven, A. H. (1986). "Central Problems in the Management of Innovation." *Management Science*, 32(5), 590–607.

Vazsonyi, A. (1982). "Information Systems in Management Science." *Interfaces*, 12(1), 74–78.

Waterman, D. A. (1982). *Building Expert Systems.* Reading, Mass.: Addison-Wesley.

Watkins, P. R. (1982). "Perceived Information Structure: Implications for Decision Support System Design." *Decision Sciences*, 13, 38–59.

Zaltman, G., Duncan, R., and Holbek, J. (1973). *Innovations and Organizations.* New York: J. Wiley.

# 7

# Coping with Bad News

## *John E. Ullmann*

My Lord, wise men ne'er sit and wail their woes,
But presently prevent the ways to wail.
                                        —Shakespeare, *Richard II*

## PERCEPTIONS OF BAD NEWS

The troubles that can befall business enterprises are so varied and extensive that they have spawned a veritable literary genre; disaster books and articles have become virtual staples of business publications. What is common to almost all of them, however, is that the calamities did not happen suddenly but in stages, that there were warning signs all along, and that a failure to recognize them in time was a major factor in making the disaster complete.

Moreover, these days such calamities often befall large and once-reputable entities. It is often hard to fathom how it all happened. In a review of a 1988 disaster book on Wall Street doings, John Kenneth Galbraith suggests that

we have an aberrant but inescapable tendency to associate the presence or handling of money—of large financial transactions—with acute intelligence. . . . In the highest of high finance, as we have recently seen once more, the paths of presumed financial intelligence lead regularly, if not to the grave, at least to the minimum security slammers.[1]

Similar judgments may fairly be made with respect to products, as in the regularly encountered carnage of the marketplace,[2] or in production systems, of which the most portentous and expensive current example is the environmental and functional travail of the nuclear weapons industry, or services, as in the ever more questionable performance of the airlines. Again, fair warnings abounded but were ignored. It is therefore useful to determine the characteristics and components of bad news and, in particular, to identify the many factors that encourage misinterpretations and failures to act in time to avert more serious troubles.

There is, of course, a limit to what one can fairly expect of managements. A good information system and a willingness to act appropriately can help diminish the chances of trouble or reduce its gravity, but it is inescapable that not every misfortune can be prevented. It is therefore essential to consider how to respond when reports bring what management considers bad news or what clearly qualifies as bad news by its objectively examined nature. The distinction is an important one, because how bad news is perceived is an important determinant of the ultimate response.

Information may qualify as bad news in three ways:

1. It may bring word of something that adversely affects your operations right away.
2. It may refer to a threat or calamity that befalls a similar operation to yours but has not so far had a direct impact on yours.
3. It may simply mean that something has happened that you consider a more distant threat, or that events have proved long-cherished opinions or prognoses wrong, and that all this makes for a more uncertain and threatening future.

These three different perceptions are given here in descending order of gravity. Troubles experienced directly need the most urgent attention, whereas, at least in the short run, there is the point made by the French philosopher La Rochefoucauld that ''we always have enough strength to bear the troubles of others.'' But that is not much of a response in a longer run. The second and third categories may be considered part of general worries about the future, and it may be argued that some managers, at least, are in part paid to worry. Still, these categories often concern matters that may require preventive steps internally and perhaps such external responses as trying to generate public attention or organize some sort of collective action.

There is a further crucial difference between bad news for your own organization and similar troubles that might very well have affected it but did not. Your own troubles are usually only too painfully clear, but somebody else's require an immediate and, above all, honest analysis of why your organization has been spared.

Such an assessment may be quite difficult, for two reasons. The first is the pervasive danger of assuming that being spared trouble is the result only of one's own genius. The second arises when differential luck is used as an explanation.

This amounts to a belief that what has happened was the outcome of a random process. A case can sometimes be made for sheer bad luck, for having been in the wrong place at the wrong time. Certainly, nobody could fairly require clairvoyant infallibility.

Still, the management process has a large deterministic component or certainly should have. Managements are expected to organize work and direct it in a purposeful effort to attain goals. For them to plead that reverses are the sufferings imposed by an inexorable and capricious fate in a real sense negates their basic purpose; managements hardly merit their often-generous rewards if all they can do is roll with the punches. At least, such a view contradicts the universal managerial penchant for taking credit for success; this is arguably the main purpose of at least the textual parts of annual reports.

As already noted, some managers are paid to worry. In practice, this means that they are required to deal with problems as part of their professional routine, much like doctors, maintenance workers, and industrial engineers; manufacturers and others employ the latter to look for problems and fix them in a search for greater efficiency of operations. All this is one aspect of a general approach called management by exception, sometimes popularly described as the squeaky wheel getting the grease first. It may also, unfortunately, bring forth what the comedian Fred Allen called "molehill men," that is, executives who find a molehill on their desks in the morning and have till evening to make a mountain out of it.

How important a given piece of news really is and what its effects might be are therefore important aspects of initial managerial judgment. Causation in economics and business is often tricky to establish, but the performance of managements cannot be judged unless some lines of cause and effect in their actions and policies and in their decisions and implementations exist and can be defined.

When bad news of significance goes beyond routine problems, it usually relates to some events or trends that run counter to forecasts and expectations by management. Somebody in authority has failed to identify the nature or extent of technical, marketing, economic, political, or other trouble early enough to prevent damage to the interests of the enterprise or has failed early enough to change policy in the affected activities and operations. Since in all but relatively trivial matters, professional skills or reputations will have been invested in such errors, management's response is often affected by reluctance or downright refusal to recognize mistakes or take precautions.

## CATEGORIES OF BAD NEWS

The following categories of bad news are not only varied in nature, but also call forth different perceptions of the kind noted earlier. One must also distinguish between sudden and protracted happenings.

## A Decline in Markets

### Rapid

The mortality rate of products is high; various estimates have been made, but they seem to indicate that about eight out of ten product introductions end in failure; new enterprises established in order to market new products or services have an even higher rate, estimated at some 95 percent. Failure should not therefore be regarded as particularly unusual. There is the well-known S-curve of markets over time; it consists of a phase of slow introduction, then takeoff and rapid market expansion, followed by a leveling off that signals market saturation. Such statistical representations of it as the Gompertz curve may be used to chronicle such change. The results of the analysis can signal a downturn that, if it continues, spells saturation.

The Gompertz and similar S-curves like the Pearl-Reed ultimately arrive at an asymptote, that is, at an upper limit that looks like a leveling out of demand at a cozily high level. The mathematics is not to blame, but rather this potentially dangerous interpretation of the result. There are first of all the general perils in time series of all sorts of projecting past results too far into the future, that is, of expecting that past trends will continue for excessively long times. When saturation is projected or actually experienced, it is dangerous and unrealistic for managements to believe that it will go on indefinitely or for anything but a relatively brief time. Rather, a turn toward saturation should serve as a strong signal that the end is nigh unless a real substitute product with growth potential is found.

A real new product in this sense means one that has meaningful new characteristics and is not merely a retread of the existing one, whatever its advertising message. This underlines the importance of ongoing new-product research and development. It is when things go well that managements must ask what to do for an encore rather than congratulating themselves and expecting to coast on indefinite asymptotic bliss as if it were bestowed as an act of nature or an entitlement of sorts. New developments take time, and once things go badly, neither the money nor the managerial resources may be available.

This applies to all industries, whether market declines are rapid or protracted, but there are many in which it is quickly evident that products or product lines have failed. Fashion and media industries are obvious examples, but cars, appliances, and even industrial products often simply fail to catch on. The bad news then consists of sales reports of a failure to take off. Product reviews in journals like consumer, car, hobby, or homemaker magazines or in newspaper sections often bring bad market news, although it is also true that, like political polls, they do not always predict the ultimate market correctly and may give false negatives as well as false positives.

### Protracted

The characteristics of protracted declines, that is, of what might be called slow leaks rather than blowouts, or lingering sicknesses rather than medical catastrophes, are similar to those of the rapid ones, with two exceptions that respectively work for and against an effective response. On the one hand and almost by definition, there is a significant warning period. That is an advantage, although it must be judged against the response time required for coming up with new products, strategies, or other remedies. On the other hand, protracted decline can be easily ignored or disguised. There is much to be said for patience—indeed, it is essential in many aspects of management—but it is a central element in the exercise of good judgment not to put excessive faith in the long run, in which, as John Maynard Keynes observed, we are all dead.

The general industrial decline of the United States is a case in point. It has been clearly observable since the mid-1960s, but for many years, raising the issue brought forth an awesomely varied set of excuses and rationalizations. They ranged from historical inevitabilities of various sorts like grand economic cycles and national climacterics to wrongheaded new directions like the postindustrial delusion (that manufacturing could safely be neglected by an advanced society in favor of "services") and to anecdotes of the successes of a few survivors. As to the latter, they not only called for the rather obvious "one swallow" response but implicitly fell into another error: believing that catastrophes necessarily had to be universal in order to qualify as such. Here and there the decline is still denied, though with gratifyingly reduced conviction; from an infusion of realism to effective remedies is, however, still quite a distance.

## Product Failure

### At Research and Development Stage

Product failure at the research and development stage covers the many cases in which a particular approach to new-product development fails because it does not perform as intended or turns out to be too expensive to yield a commercially viable product. Many potential products fail this way even before they have hit the market.

The bad news here always means internal turmoil within the research department and elsewhere in the company and, depending on how much is known on the outside, has external effects as well. Research managers have an obvious interest in keeping things going as long as possible and not infrequently use their progress reports to mask a conspicuous lack of progress. Top management must therefore be knowledgeable enough to read between the lines, if necessary, and to bring some independent judgment to bear.

Unfortunately, as in many cases discussed in this chapter, it is only too easy to fall into an opposite extreme. Demands for instant and constant progress are made by higher executives who may almost totally lack scientific training, or, what may be worse at times, top managers get fixed ideas as to how research should come out and ride their hobbyhorses to what is often a disastrous fall. The central problem is clearly how long to go on with something; there is a situation here much as in oil drilling or mining. If only the bore hole or shaft were made just a little deeper, there would be a gusher or pay dirt; the history of mining exploration has many such examples. There is no general way of resolving this issue; it is, as indicated, an acid test of managerial judgment and competence.

Bad news in such a case becomes worse when the company has been calling its shots in the press, in its advertising, and in its presentations to stock analysts and the like. The worst case is the one in which products are scheduled to be introduced at a certain time and price and then turn out to be not only delayed but very much more expensive. This happens so often in such areas as high technology and medical products that it may no longer be considered much of a surprise, but it certainly makes it more difficult for managements to scrap large projects quietly without damage to the company's stock price or general reputation. Sometimes the effect is less because several firms have been working on a given technology that does not work out right; the ill effects are thus shared. Still, the best strategy is probably not to call more than an absolute minimum of shots in advance.

### In the Field at an Early Stage

Product failure can occur quickly in the field. Bad news may mean that the product does not work or is not safe; it may mean excessive service for a piece of machinery, ill effects of drugs, or the first reports of people getting hurt. Such bad news may be very bad; it may not readily be possible to change the product, certainly not quickly. Still, one recalls such able responses as that of Johnson and Johnson when some Tylenol capsules were found to have been poisoned; fortunately, the company had a fallback technology in the form of caplets and package seals that could be quickly brought on line.

### In the Field after a Long Time

Product failure after a long time is a form of disaster that has hit several industries with considerable force; it sometimes concerns problems that only surface after decades, but as in protracted market failures of products, there was usually ample warning that something was amiss. Examples include asbestos and cigarettes, and, in a shorter time frame, the Dalkon Shield and Thalidomide; the long and thorough tests required for drugs largely spared the United States in the latter case, but in all of them, warning signs had appeared long before their producers had serious troubles. Such developments can readily bankrupt firms, or, as in the case of asbestos, whole industries, not only by way of market loss but by huge damage awards in cases. Such cases often turn on the kind of attention that was paid to early warnings. Evidence of their suppression, or of telling the public one thing while the interoffice memos told another story, are the kind of findings that delights negligence lawyers.

## Changes in Domestic Laws and Regulations

### On Products

Bad news in laws and regulations on products relates mainly to new legal or regulatory provisions that require major changes, raise technical and marketing problems, and increase costs that cannot readily be passed along as price increases. The changes relate to health and safety and, at times, to honesty in the marketplace, that is, the design of products and their later advertising and promotion. They often happen together with other forms of early or late product failure. Indeed, product laws and regulations often are a public reaction to a perceived failure by companies to remedy problems first brought to their attention by research, market, and field reports.

These problems involve not only manufactured products but services as well, such as banking, brokerage, insurance, and professional activities. Sometimes entire "industries" are outlawed or sharply restricted, like the consultants in "debt consolidation" some years ago and certain kinds of career counseling unrelated to finding people actual jobs. In extreme cases, "bad news" comes in the form of a visit by a postal inspector or local fraud squad.

### On Operations

Changes in laws and regulations on operations generally relate to aspects of labor relations as well as to health and safety. In the latter cases, the problems are therefore similar to product problems, but since they concern operations, they call for different managerial decisions, such as major redesigns of plant facilities.

## Local Changes

### Taxes and Zoning

Local taxation has an important bearing on the viability of industrial areas, though less so than often claimed by the real estate industry and in the fierce competition between communities for new or expanding industrial tenants. Bad news concerning local tax increases thus does not generally deserve the hysteria with which it is often received.

Zoning raises another set of issues. During the protracted decline of American manufacturing, factory buildings have been converted to other uses, such as retail centers and condominiums. There have also been actions by communities against such conversions, as in the Protected Manufacturing District established in Chicago in 1987. Bad news here consists of failures to obtain zoning variances or of successful litigation against a proposed industrial facility. Such events can be highly frustrating, and it is probably true that challenges to new projects have become more frequent and protracted over the years. Still, the objections on environmental grounds, for example, are often sound enough and should not be regarded as mere versions of NIMBY ("not in my back yard").

### Law Enforcement

This is a delicate issue and does not relate merely to how many police patrols there are in some business location. Many businesses, especially in environmentally sensitive areas and in defense contracts and local government work, operate in an atmosphere of institutionalized corruption in order to keep going. When those bribed get greedy, or when there is a new regime, or when the heat is on in response to a major accident or public outcry, this qualifies as bad news, whether it is richly deserved or not.

## International Changes

### General

The growth of substantial competition in a foreign market often qualifies as bad news to an American or other multinational firm, especially when the newcomer is favored in some way by the host government. Some of this should be regarded as part of the normal tasks of facing competition. What qualifies as "bad news" under this heading is more in the nature of a sudden discontinuity so that operations in a given country have to be sharply restricted or abandoned or can be carried on only under extreme difficulties. Examples are too numerous to list, but many of them arose because managements had tenaciously stuck with certain political patrons until it was too late to salvage the company's interests when there was a change. At times, there are the downside risks of corruption; people may not stay bought. Further, corruption itself is supposed to be illegal for American firms, a point often considered naive or hypocritical by foreign competitors.

It might not always be possible to take effective evasive action, but certain managerial mind sets are a major hindrance. The first and most important of these is a habit of judging foreign conditions by U.S. domestic standards and in the light of what managers perceive as U.S. foreign policy. The often-encountered insularity of American managers is one factor, but in many cases American "country experts" and aficionados of foreign regimes contribute their share in making matters worse.

With the sole apparent exception of one Nguema Masie, the sometime dictator of Equatorial Guinea, who had managed to murder about a quarter of his country's population before being deposed and shot in 1979, there have been no regimes or groups seeking overthrow of a regime, whether left or right, no matter how foul, that did not pick up an American cheering section somewhere along the way. One recalls the friends, high and low, of the South African regime, Chiang Kai-shek, the Shah, the Marcoses, and the Somozas, and elsewhere on the political spectrum, of Muammar Qaddafi and Idi Amin, or of the Ayatollah Khomeini, whose legal interests in the United States have been represented by a former U.S. attorney general.

For one reason or another, wrong horses were backed and losses were incurred as a result. Many of the misjudgments were the result of Cold War rigidities; anything had to be accepted as long as the local panjandrum and his gang made suitable anti-Communist noises. Such rigidities delayed for many years the American ability to adjust to and profit from the split between the Soviet Union and mainland China. They now pose the danger of similar misjudgments in the time of Mikhail Gorbachev and his reforms.

This is not in any way a plea for a value-free stance nor for business executives who would sell anything to anybody; indifference to the barbarities of the world is as unseemly for managers as for any other caring or well-informed human being. However, managers who wish to deceive themselves clearly have no shortage of experts who will tell them what they want to hear.

What makes matters worse is that insofar as they have foreign contacts at all, higher executives especially tend to be in a sort of bubble environment, the world of first-class airline seats (subject to the same kinds of delays as those occupied by lesser breeds), of the Concorde and private jets, of being met at airports by limousines or helicopters, and of luxury hotels increasingly owned or managed by international chains and therefore indistinguishable from one another. Above all, foreign contacts are almost exclusively with the private or governmental elites with which business is conducted—almost invariably in English. The latter raises the point that there are countries where the elites have taken to speaking English, French, or some other language among themselves rather than that of the local people, which some may barely understand. There are few more reliable recipes for alienation between governors and governed and thus for eventual sociopolitical instability of the kind that managers must bring themselves to recognize.

### Industry Specific

There are also many cases where bad news from abroad comes in the form of a challenge to a specific industry and product. One well-known example was the international call to boycott the Nestle Company over its sales of baby formula to countries where the local water supply was too poor to serve as a safe mixer with it. Before changing its policy, Nestle had considerable losses. The boycott lasted from 1981 to 1984, and at the end of 1988 there were signs that it might be reactivated.

Another case at the end of 1988 concerned the Western European ban of American meat imports, which promptly ignited a round of trade retaliations. The ban was imposed because American farmers use hormone supplements in cattle feed. From the American side, it was asserted that the residues were negligible, but since doses on the order of billionths of grams can have a significant clinical effect on humans, even a small residue cannot be neglected.

Whatever the scientific truth, the matter also has political overtones. Clearly there is a desire on the part of the Europeans to protect industries by cutting imports, and there may be some of what George Orwell once called "letting political cats out of scientific bags." Still, there is also the record of selective nonfeasance, cutbacks in inspection, and refusal to take further needed steps on product safety that has characterized U.S. regulation of products in the 1980s.

The effects of all these variants of bad news depend on the managerial responses. Unfortunately, as indicated in detail in the next section, effective action faces handicaps of its own.

## RESPONSES TO BAD NEWS

Responding to any of the graver calamities specified earlier is not easy but is made much more difficult not only by the self-protective defense mechanisms that managers typically put in place but by the hierarchical and authoritarian structure of management itself. Moreover, the "self" in self-protection is increasingly personal rather than institutional as traditional job security for managers, let alone their subordinates, fades amid the mergers and downsizings of our time. Reactions then quickly deteriorate to personal jockeying and covering one's exposure to blame.

Whether managements and managers attempt to follow in their behavior theories X, Y, and Z, broadly definable as hawks, doves, or something in between, managers must still give orders in the strong expectation that somebody will at least attempt to carry them out. Management styles may differ in the ways that consent is encouraged, engineered, or compelled and dissent encouraged, tolerated, or suppressed, but eventually some decisions must be made and implemented.

Unfortunately, there are many wrong ways to respond, and managements use them so often that one must assume that personal characteristics or dispositions have a great deal to do with why they are chosen. They include the following:

### "We Shoulda' "

This response can be viewed as an exercise in sentence completion, for example, "we shoulda' " bought when we sold, or sold when we bought, or invaded North Vietnam, poisoned Fidel Castro's cigars, used design A rather than B, and so on. It deserves to be relegated to an expression of frustration, but not a few managers live by such overuse of the past conditional tense and, as a result, have lives of tensions, ill temper, and fear, none of which are good business or personal advisers.

### Ignore the Problem

It is true that many problems are self-limiting and eventually go away, but before ignoring bad news it is well to recall that, echoing the old Jewish proverb that no choice is also a choice, no decision is also a decision. Ignoring a problem caters to one of the oldest of human inclinations, the desire not to have one's accustomed routine disturbed. Still, one could almost assert that knowing correctly when to take action in a problem area, and when not to, goes far toward defining managerial competence.

### Slough It Off on Subordinates

It is deplorable but true that many varieties of bad news cannot be responded to merely by someone in charge ordering somebody else to respond appropriately. Quite apart from the fact that leaders are supposed to lead, it is a basic axiom in management theory, familiar from all the textbooks in the field, that managers can delegate authority but not responsibility. It is a logical as well as equitable arrangement, but it is so often violated that it has become a major source of organizational injustice. There is nothing sadder than executives who have become stuck in the development of a company product for which they themselves, in moments of honesty, foresee a dim future. They are often quite unable to get a hearing for their misgivings; they would risk the capital crime of negative thinking instead of maintaining the enthusiasm expected by their superiors. So they have to ride the project down to ultimate disaster and may lose their jobs as a result, with even their secretaries, in extreme cases, expected to fling themselves on the funeral pyre.

Top managers are not, of course, immune from ultimate trouble; for instance, the chairman of a very large chemical company was forced out some years ago when a huge plant complex had to be shut down because the state finally agreed with the local citizenry that the air pollution could no longer be tolerated. Such actions are relatively rare, however, and more likely in the case of financial jockeyings or mishaps; what is otherwise perplexing is how some top managers get to have charmed careers, as if licensed to ruin one enterprise after another.

### Use Public Relations to Gloss Over What Has Happened

Public-relations departments have their obvious place in business, but when they are used to mask bad news, especially in cases of product failures or other major problems, they pose the clear danger that managements will come to believe their own propaganda. That, as fallen leaders, from business executives to dictators, can attest, is another prescription for disaster. Leaving aside the paranoid aspects of this process, it is a proven method for delaying remedial action until too late. It is associated with and may be a precursor of the remaining bad responses discussed in this section.

Being used to command and obedience, business leaders are often both puzzled and resentful that their explanations or public-relations initiatives go unheeded by the public. This is an old phenomenon to which William H. Whyte, Jr., first drew attention in its modern American context in *Is Anybody Listening?*[3] and his classic *The Organization Man*.[4] Such complaints are still frequent, as in the long institutional advertising campaign devised for Mobil Corporation by its former vice president, Herbert Schmertz, and the writings of neoconservatives like Herbert London, Irving Kristol, Aaron Wildavsky, and Jeane Kirkpatrick. Yet their output and viewpoints and those of conservative think tanks like the Heritage Foundation, the Hoover Institution, and the Georgetown Center are more widely disseminated than ever. One must therefore at least consider the alternative explanation that many if not most people are indifferent to the messages and that to others, including experts in the field, they simply make no sense. Unfortunately, that last factor is a frequent cue for demands that such contrary views be suppressed. Such demands also come naturally to those used to command and who expect their orders to be received with enthusiasm; at the later stages of self-deception, they tend to lose their ability to detect how much of that is synthetic and a suspension of disbelief. Such attitudes are poor guides to action or even to definitions of reality.

### Refuse to Reexamine Ideological Preconceptions

We have already noted how refusal to examine ideological preconceptions may affect the adverse perception of international changes, but this ideological fixation may affect the response to all kinds of bad news. Some things simply change, and believing that this has not happened and that business may continue to be done at the old stand is again a wrong response.

Perhaps the most potentially serious such current issue is the economic and political disarray of the socialist countries, which has led to widespread departures from Marxist orthodoxy. This is certainly welcome if it leads to a better life for the peoples involved and a more tranquil world. However, there is a dangerous and complacent tendency in some quarters to regard these changes as a legitimation of the more ruthless aspects of capitalism, especially of its American variety, such as its insecurity of employment and poor social services. It would be more constructive to remember that socialism grew out of exactly such abuses and that what appears to be at work here is a universal desire for a "human face" in government and public life, whatever the political details. If this is disregarded, trouble inevitably follows.

### Throw or Join a Political or Legal Tantrum

A tantrum in this context may be defined as a combination of ever more frenzied public relations efforts, combined with litigation designed to wear out opponents and with lobbying for legal changes. The latter often is in the venerable tradition of "when losing the game, change the rules." In part, such activities are encouraged by the litigious nature of American society. The broader issues here have been extensively discussed elsewhere.[5]

With respect to the kinds of bad news discussed in this chapter, the main question is how long such answers really last; if they attempt to redefine reality, the results are likely to be short-lived and the eventual reckoning more painful. But "eventual" here may mean that by then the executives presently responsible will have safely floated out on their golden parachutes; as Mme. Pompadour said to Louis XV: "After us, the deluge."

### Cut Legal Corners

This is the last stage in the mismanagement of bad news. Given the headlines of the past few years, examples seem superfluous. The ancient advice of Confucius in his *Histories* is most appropriate here: "Do not be afraid of your mistakes and so make them crimes".

## FACING FACTS

The problems in fashioning appropriate responses make clear that executive isolation is a major contributing factor, if not the principal one. It is not only economic, even though the gap between rich and poor has widened, but also social and political.

In *Money and Class in America*, Lewis H. Lapham describes one such executive who daily went to his office by limousine and private elevator from an upscale and therefore almost ipso facto isolated suburb: "Most days he talked to people almost identical to himself—other bankers dressed in the same suits, sharing the same barbers and opinions, belonging to the same clubs and forming their impressions of the world from the same set of statistics."[6] The executive had wanted Lapham to provide him with a monthly summary of what was happening in the outside world, because, as he said, "About the economy, I know as much as anybody else which isn't much, but at least it's something. But about the kind of political ideas that might be out there snuffling around the perimeter, I don't know anything at all. I can't guess where the next blow is likely to come from."[7]

This almost perfect description of executive isolation is part of the much broader phenomenon of ruling-class alienation and, in its virtual definition of change as threat, of the kind of fear that seems to be endemic in ruling elites. It is a fear of those on lower rungs, notably of one's own workers; the kinds of traumatic change that have beset U.S. business in the course of its protracted industrial decline and corporate turmoil have been accompanied by deterioration not only in labor relations, but in national cohesion and social solidarity. Thus the kinds of bad news defined in this chapter are viewed with fear rather than as the challenges that are an inevitable part of running an enterprise in an uncertain and often capricious world.

All this underlines precisely the difficulty in getting managements to pay proper attention to intelligence reports in general and bad news in particular. To managements stuck in their own socioeconomic bell jars, adverse reports of what has happened or is about to happen are not merely in conflict with what managements had hoped and expected would happen, but, especially in their upper authoritarian reaches, with what would be permitted to happen.

It is not easy and is often a source of pained surprise when those accustomed to command at the top of a corporate or governmental hierarchy have to recognize that on this occasion at least, things are not going to go their way and that their attempts to order markets, individuals, politicians, or even small countries around are likely to fail. Such reactions recall the reply of the feebleminded Emperor Ferdinand of Austria when he was informed at the beginning of the revolution of 1848 that the people of Vienna were tearing up cobblestones and fashioning them into barricades: "Are they allowed to do that?"

As a result, those who furnish information to managements in the media, as consultants or as staffers, constantly face obstacles to presenting unvarnished truths. Some newspapers and magazines tend toward soothing syrup; others, as well as most newsletters, thrive on alarmism and on redefining intelligence as information that the reader is really not supposed to have. Such claims are not always accurate, let alone world shaking, but they cast their purveyors as combatants in the old American battle between the document shredders and the Xerox machines. The conflict between professional integrity and safeguarding one's own "market" is thus often profound, even though it is a manifest waste of time and money to buy information and then filter out everything one does not want to hear.

There is no general magic way of fixing troubles; much of good management consists of avoiding pitfalls. As this chapter shows, these abound when trouble looms, and there are many readily definable ways to make them worse. Avoiding them and approaching troubles with a clear head and perhaps a touch of humility is still the best strategy.

## NOTES

1. J. K. Galbraith, "From Stupidity to Cupidity," *New York Review of Books*, November 24, 1988, 12.

2. For a classic collection of case studies, see, among others, T. L. Berg, *Mismarketing: Case Histories of Marketing Misfires* (New York: Anchor, 1970).

3. W. H. Whyte, Jr., *Is Anybody Listening?* (New York: Simon and Schuster, 1952).

4. W. H. Whyte, Jr., *The Organization Man* (New York: Simon and Schuster, 1954).

5. See, for example, A. A. Marcus, *The Adversary Economy* (Westport, Conn.: Quorum, 1954).

6. L. H. Lapham, *Money and Class in America* (New York: Weidenfeld and Nicolson, 1988), 160.

7. Ibid., 160–161.

# 8

# The Structure of the Corporate Intelligence System

*Mamdouh Farid*

Intelligence denotes knowledge and the process involved in the search and the reach for knowledge. Corporate intelligence or knowledge results from a process that usually includes the collection, analysis, interpretation, processing, and dissemination of information.[1] For a business firm, it is the ability to scan and interpret the external environment, monitor itself, and communicate effectively with its diverse functional parts.[2]

There are many developments that increase the importance of corporate intelligence. For example, there is broad agreement that the organizational environment is becoming increasingly more complex and uncertain regarding the future course of events.[3] With increases in environmental uncertainty, the establishment of a corporate intelligence system becomes vital. Sources of uncertainty that are subject to intelligence activities include globalization, technology, product substitutes, shifts in customer demographics, value changes, political stability, and shifts in public policy. While many of these sources of uncertainty are not novel, their pace of change and intensity are greater than ever.[4] These qualitative characteristics make prediction of the environment and its impact upon the future of the organization a difficult task. In an unpredictable environment, and this is the norm for many firms, an organization may abandon its standard operating policies and scan the environment for causes and solutions.[5]

In addition, corporate intelligence takes on a greater significance in response to the contemporary knowledge explosion. This refers to the exponential increase in data collection and technologies dealing with information and communication.[6]

By definition, a corporation should take advantage of such an information explosion; otherwise it will find itself in an inferior position with respect to competitors or changes in the external environment. The airline companies have learned this lesson, especially after the failure of the no-longer-existing People Express in its struggle against United and American Airlines. Despite its continuous expansion and aggressive pricing policy, the People Express failed mainly because of its lack of information technology. Salience of intelligence activities is obvious in the establishment of a position of chief information officer in the organizational structure. For example, Motorola Corporation has a full-service intelligence unit headed by a senior manager who reports directly to the chief executive officer. Salience of intelligence activities can also be noticed in increases in information technology, such as online and real-time data bases furnished by computerized information services like Dun and Bradstreet, TRW, McGraw-Hill, and Mead corporations.[7]

Facing an uncertain environment and aware of the importance of the data-search and knowledge explosion, the organization must also increase its analytical and dissemination capabilities. This minimizes information overload and maximizes the information yield from the data collected. In a volatile business environment the ability to assess a situation accurately and to implement decisions quickly becomes crucial,[8] since uncertainty increases information-processing requirements.[9]

This requires a complementary reinforcement of all the corporate intelligence functions. In this context, corporate intelligence becomes an imperative organizational design variable. A corporation should adopt a structure that simultaneously serves data collection, processing, and dissemination.

Therefore, the definition of a corporate intelligence system should incorporate elements of structure. The corporate intelligence system refers to information activities and how they relate to corporate communication and the decision-making structure (who needs what and how much information and when to make which decision). This view represents a point of departure in examining the structure of the intelligence system.

## THE INTELLIGENCE SYSTEM

As already defined, a corporate intelligence system refers to information activities and how they relate to the total corporate command structure. The effectiveness of the system is in its success or failure to provide decision makers with high-quality information in terms of adequacy, clarity, timeliness, range, reliability, and accuracy.[10]

### Structural Sources of Intelligence Success and Failure

Because information flows across organizational boundaries and from one organizational level to another, the organizational hierarchy and other structural features shape intelligence quality (see the Appendix for a summary of different perspectives of organizational structure). Accordingly, intelligence quality is expected to decline with inadequate information gathering and processing, with increases in information distortion, and with a blockage or delay of information dissemination as a result of structural features. One feature is the criterion used for departmentalization or grouping activities. For example, grouping activities on functional specialization (for example, production, marketing, or research and development) enhances efficiency and internal-operations intelligence. Functional specialization also results in different preconceptions and different interpretations of information from different parts of the organization. This may alert top management to diverse perspectives. However, it may also maximize the pathology of specialization in terms of intraorganizational rivalries and block vital intelligence from reaching different segments of the organization.

Another downside structural feature is the existence of a complex authority and communications system in the hierarchy, which produces a rigid communications and control system. This may decrease the accuracy and timeliness of the intelligence data. Similarly, the quality of intelligence seems to be shaped by correlates of organizational growth. Specifically, the quality of intelligence could be higher in the earlier stages of the organization's life cycle. This is explained by the fact that as organizations grow larger, they usually adopt pyramidal, multileveled centralized structures. These structures impede the information analysis and dissemination process. By comparison, young expansionist organizations in the early stages of the growth cycle are less concerned with negotiating stable arrangements with their constituents (suppliers, creditors, employees, government, and so on) than with responding effectively to a fluid environment. Their organizational design typifies flexibility and a focused awareness of the external environment. A complex bureaucratic form of organization, by contrast, is less critical and lacks the ability to respond promptly to sudden unpredictable changes. The staid nature of bureaucratic organizations increases information distortion and pathologies and reduces the accuracy, relevancy, and timeliness of intelligence data.[11]

Consequently, opening all channels of informal communication does not seem to solve all the problems that face the intelligence system in a complex structure. The egalitarian (participative and informal) structure is found to increase information overload and information redundancy (these problems will be addressed in the next section) since the structure opens all channels of communication.[12]

## Information Bigness

Since many of the strategic problems facing an organization are ill structured,[13] many of the intelligence needs are not expected to be well defined. Poor problem formulation—the range and the quality of questions that start the process of data collection and analysis—may result in irrelevant information, less efficiency, and finally information overload and confusion. With the knowledge explosion and the availability of information services and electronically delivered information, the problems of information bigness and information confusion seem to be inevitable.

To cope with information bigness, effective companies attempt to keep things simple by adopting policies that reduce the number of middle managers, staff, paperwork, and objectives. Some examples of companies that keep lean staffs are Emerson Electric, which has fewer than 100 staff members and employs 54,000 people; Intel, which has $1 billion in sales and gives staff assignments to line managers; and Dana, which has 35,000 employees and reduced staffs from 500 in 1970 to 100 in 1982. Job rotation and the movement of people among divisions on a regular basis are also helpful in achieving a lean personnel structure.[14] One may hypothesize that the flow of people around various tasks and divisions also increases the infusion of ideas and dissemination of information. This enhances intelligence quality.

Some other structural adjustments seem to be in place. The organization may respond to the problem of information overload and confusion by adopting a decentralized organic (flexible) structure. Decentralization and participation decrease individual cognitive workload and allow managers and specialists to comprehend the issues. These improve the quality of upward communication and provide responsive maneuverability to unpredictable changes.[15]

Sometimes decentralization is not feasible. This occurs when highly independent competitive units preclude cohesive and goal-focused efforts. In an analogous sense, the numerous nationalities in the Soviet Union underscore this point. Successful decentralization requires a uniform culture and a strong sense of loyalty and commitment to the headquarters' management.

A flat structure is also effective in coping with information bigness. A flat structure can be maintained by expanding the structure horizontally through continued formation of small new divisions, thus avoiding addition to the hierarchy. For example, at the 3M company, division managers must know each staff member's first name. When a division gets too big, perhaps reaching $250 to $300 million in sales, it is split up.[16] Since divisions are usually self-sustaining units, this eliminates resource and information interdependency and thus increases flexibility in dealing with market demand.[17]

## THE STRUCTURE OF THE INTELLIGENCE SYSTEM

The structure of the corporate intelligence system may be proposed in the following interrelated key issues and questions that designers of an organization should carefully consider.

### What Are Our Intelligence Needs? How Can They Be Satisfied?

The business organization's intelligence needs include desirable and undesirable changes in the areas of internal operations, products, clients, competitors, suppliers, and the general environment (political, legal, economic, and so on). Internal operations intelligence focuses on achieving high internal control and good awareness of the technical external developments. It allows for functional expertise and highly efficient operations. Budget cutbacks and shrinking resources also increase the importance of this type of intelligence.

In addition, successful business firms usually focus on customer and product intelligence. This means that they are very rich in customer contacts, have high product knowledge, and respond rapidly to changes in product-market areas.

Competitor intelligence should also be important if the market is very competitive or if it is hard to establish a pattern of competitors' initiatives, choices, or responses. A growing number of large American firms now have formal units that focus on competitor intelligence. Companies like Pfizer, IBM, and International Paper now have special small units to collect, process, and disseminate intelligence about competitor's plans, products, and financial prospects.[18]

Some of the intelligence needs may be known to the organization. Invariably, many are not. Known intelligence needs are premises that underlie strategic planning and strategic decisions. These premises include assumptions resulting from earlier environmental scanning and internal operational performance about opportunities and vulnerabilities confronting the organization. As part of the implementation and feedback-control system, relevant premises should be specified, prioritized, monitored, and updated.

The other type of intelligence needs concerns new or unknown threats that the organization may encounter. These types of unknown threats may be safeguarded by strategic surveillance. Strategic surveillance is designed to monitor a broad spectrum of events inside and outside the organization that are likely to threaten the course of strategic action. This task is ambiguous, and if strategic surveillance is to succeed, the monitoring process should be kept open. Prestructuring it by setting up in advance a list of critical control issues should therefore be avoided. Only then is there a good chance of picking up unforeseeable or previously undetected critical events.[19]

Besides differentiating between known and unknown needs, intelligence needs may also be categorized in terms of local and global. In this differentiation, organizational information processing and logical reasoning seem to take place at two levels; one is focused on analysis of a local, situation-specific nature, and the other is more global and configural. It is also argued that global needs seem to be increasing in importance, especially in the current complex environment, but unfortunately this is a neglected area in the literature.[20] While local intelligence is the task of every manager, strategic surveillance and global intelligence should be kept as the responsibility of top management. Usually this mission is assigned to a committee at the strategic apex.

Organizations identify and try to satisfy their intelligence needs by adopting information technology. Information technology (computers, communication-network technologies, and other information applications) may be broadly defined as methods or techniques of monitoring, processing, and disseminating intelligence. Management information systems (MISs) and decision support systems (DSSs) are examples of two information technology applications that assist managers by both providing information and identifying what information needs should be acquired. While MISs are used in well-structured situations, DSSs are used in situations that are ill structured.[21]

Identifying and satisfying intelligence needs should also be simultaneously pursued by means of organizational design (this will be addressed in the next section) and other quick structural arrangements. An example of a structural arrangement that attempts to identify and gather intelligence is the Ford Motor Company's senior decision-making committee. This committee is responsible for examining trends, opportunities, and threats posed by the European Economic Community (EEC) market. In addition, in 1983 the company set up a corporate strategy and analyzing management committee consisting of three units: external environment (which monitors government regulations and other outside forces); business strategy (which reviews each division's ten-year strategic plans); and product strategy (which coordinates new product ideas among operational units). Each staff member reports directly to the president.[22]

Another example is the innovative approach provided by the Motorola Corporation. The company set up full-service intelligence units headed by an information chief executive. Business officers in these units hold portfolios that correspond to the company's key objectives. One officer keeps track of European business developments in areas of particular interest to the company. Another officer does the same for Asia. Other officers may focus exclusively on developments in specific fields of technology that the company has singled out for special corporate investments, or on monitoring the trade policies of specific countries.[23]

### What Are the Optimal Criteria for Grouping Activities Along Organizational Hierarchy? What Are the Subsequent Linking Devices?

Organizational structure usually includes more than one criterion for grouping activities along the hierarchical levels (see the Appendix), and choices should be made about the criterion used at each level. Choices available to the organization include grouping activities based on functions, products, customers, or geographic locations. Each of these criteria emphasizes a particular intelligence. For example, "function" brings internal operations information, "product" is for high product intelligence, while "customer" and "geographic" are for high market intelligence. Table 8.1 shows various combinations for grouping activities at the top two levels and how they serve different intelligence needs or focuses.

The outcome of this intelligence emphasis should serve the corporation's strategic objectives and its competitive advantages. Accordingly, choices for the top two or three levels in the structure are the most important.[24] Selection is

# Table 8.1
## The Impact of Organizational Structure on Corporate Intelligence

**First/Second Level Grouping**

**Expected Effect on Intelligence**

### Function/Function

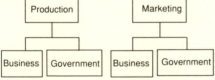

—Good market intelligence but response to market is slow.
—Good competitor intelligence but the structure does allow rapid response.
—Specialization increases internal operation intelligence, expertise, and control.
—Client knowledge lessened.
—Pathology of specialization is maximized. Structure may lead to overcentralized judgment and illusion of reliable information.

### Function/Product

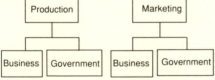

—Good existing product intelligence but slow response to competitors' product innovation.
—Strong integrated products and market intelligence.
—Specialization increase internal operation intelligence, expertise and control.
—Client knowledge lessened which may lead to neglect new product-market areas.

### Function/Customer

—High competitor intelligence but slow response to product and technology innovations.
—Good market intelligence.
—Specialization increases internal operation intelligence, expertise and control.
—Product knowledge lessened.

### Product/Product

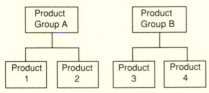

—High product intelligence.
—Rapid response to competitors' initiatives.
—Client knowledge lessened
—Lack of total market perspective but top management are alert to diverse perspective.

### Product/Function

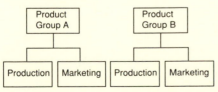

—High product intelligence.
—High function intelligence and expertise.
—Low competitive intelligence.
—Low total market intelligence.

**Table 8.1** (continued)

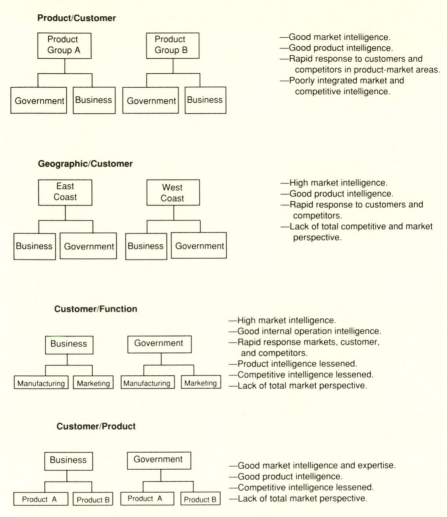

**Product/Customer**

—Good market intelligence.
—Good product intelligence.
—Rapid response to customers and competitors in product-market areas.
—Poorly integrated market and competitive intelligence.

**Geographic/Customer**

—High market intelligence.
—Good product intelligence.
—Rapid response to customers and competitors.
—Lack of total competitive and market perspective.

**Customer/Function**

—High market intelligence.
—Good internal operation intelligence.
—Rapid response markets, customer, and competitors.
—Product intelligence lessened.
—Competitive intelligence lessened.
—Lack of total market perspective.

**Customer/Product**

—Good market intelligence and expertise.
—Good product intelligence.
—Competitive intelligence lessened.
—Lack of total market perspective.

*Source:* Adapted with modification from Gregory K. Dow, ''Configurational and Coactivational Views of Organizational Structure,'' *Academy of Management Review* 13(1): 53–64.

affected by our intelligence needs (for example, internal activities, market activities, product development, and so on) and priorities of these needs (for example, whether we emphasize efficiency and economy of scale or flexibility in terms of responding quickly to changes in each market segment).[25] For example, "customer grouping" and "product grouping" may be more strongly emphasized if consumer preferences are constantly changing, and if the future progress of an organization is linked to its skills in keeping channels of consumer communication clear. Companies like 3M and General Electric represent notable examples of superior ability to stay close to the consumer. At 3M, researchers, marketers, and managers visit customers and routinely invite them to help brainstorm product ideas. At GE, products are developed jointly with customers. In conjunction with BMW, GE's plastics unit created the first panels made with thermoplastics for the BMW's Z1 two-seater.

Adopting any combination of groupings will produce a mix of outcomes (see table 8.1). Designers of organizational structure should address any substantial vulnerabilities by relying on some temporary arrangements and linking and liaison roles. For example, for "functional grouping," "customer grouping," or "geographic grouping," using a liaison device, such as product managers, will provide a linking between research activities, product development, market needs, and manufacturing needs. Solving the conflict between marketing demand for sensitivity to target market and manufacturing needs for efficiency could be achieved by such an arrangement. The creation of lateral-relation and liaison devices also increases the capacity to process and comprehend information and issues arising from intelligence gathering.[26]

## What Is the Right Information Technology, and What Costs Are Incurred In Implementing and Operating This Technology and Training Our People? How Does Information Technology Affect Organizational Design?

These are some of the critical decisions confronting the organization when it is adopting information technology. Knowing intelligence needs should guide the organization in choosing the right technology. In general, advancement in information technology should increase intelligence capability and intelligence quality. Information technology devices permit major data manipulation, such as data storage, sorting, retrieval, and processing (analysis). Much of the data manipulation, however, requires the user to quantify most of the input data. Also, data about goals and performance achievement should be declared and quantified. In addition, intelligence needs influence the operations of information technology through problem formulation. Sound problem formulation facilitates the acquisition of high-quality intelligence.

Communication and structural problems confronting the organization should also guide the selection of information technology. Technology can reduce structural barriers to the flow of information. It can solve communication and coordination problems by functioning in linking or liaison between different parts

**Figure 8.1**
**The Components of the Corporate Intelligence System**

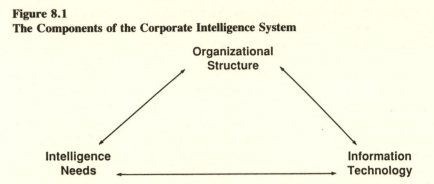

of the organization. An example is Xerox's "ethernet," which is a communication network designed for short physical distances (intrabuilding). Many pieces of office equipment are connected by coaxial cable together into one information system.

Other applications of information technology alleviate intelligence problems that result from market dispersion of the organization's activities. Information technology seems to provide a great maneuverability to the designers of the organization. It allows high coordination and control and thus permits differentiation by adopting a mixed structure in which various parts are uniquely structured. An example of such new information technology is MCI's Information Network Management Services (INMS). Adopters of this system will gain unprecedented control of network operations and management of trouble reports, performance, planning, configuration, billing, cost, and order entry and tracking. According to the system, the full spectrum of a company's voice and data traffic anywhere in the world will be handled by a single user interface—one person working at one computer terminal.

In examining the structure of the corporate intelligence system, three major aspects were identified. These are intelligence needs, organizational structure, and information technology. These are depicted in figure 8.1. The discussion shows that these elements are interrelated and affect each other. It is safe to propose that these three aspects represent the components of the intelligence system.

# APPENDIX
# Theories of Organizational Structure

Theories of organizational structure share a common concern for understanding the behavior of the organization and its members and how structure helps or hinders reaching objectives. Two distinct perspectives of organizational structure are identified: configurational and coactivational theories.[27] The features of organizational structure as viewed by each perspective are outlined in table 8.2.

The configurational view is related to the early civilizations in Egypt and China; its focus is on establishing a control system by means of a pyramidal structure. This perspective is reflected in the classical contribution.[28] According to this view, structure is designed to serve explicit goals and to reduce uncertainty by establishing control, clear accountability, and a reliable organization. A product of such effort is a blueprint or organizational chart with a static feature of fixed lines of communication and authority.

**Table 8.2**
**Perspectives of Organizational Structure**

**Configurational View of Structure**

Structure results from the following:

1. The decomposition of the organization's overall objective into subtasks.

2. The grouping of subtasks together at each level in the hierarchy on the basis of inputs (that is, functional specialization such as marketing and production), outputs (products), or market (based on customers or geographic segments).

3. The configuration of the organizational hierarchy (for example, tall, flat) as it is shaped by the number of levels in the hierarchy, the ratio of administrators to production personnel, and span of control (number of subordinates reporting to each superior).

4. Coordination and control mechanisms, such as the principles of chain of command (lines of authority and communication) and span of control, degree of centralization, and staff specialists.

**Coactivational View of Structure**

Structure involves the following features:

1. The coding systems and observed behaviors of organizational members. (These are inferred by observing the relationship between incoming information or resources and member's behavioral responses.)

2. Technological and institutional constraints on the acquisition of resources and information by members. (These constraints define the available channels of interaction and the range of possible structures.)

3. The response of the external environment to actions by organizational members. (Intraorganizational behaviors and decisions cannot be understood without studying positive and environmental reactions as well as information exchanges and power relations that link organizational members with the external environment.)

The other approach to the organizational structure is the coactivational view. This view shifts the focus from explicit goals and a fixed chart to a more dynamic view of the structure by attempting to outline the structure through observing how organizational members acquire and process information and resources when they are engaged in achieving tasks or decreasing uncertainty. Organizational structure is regarded as a fluid system that can only be understood subjectively by observing the pattern of behaviors and studying decisions of individuals and subunits within the organizational boundary (defined as a low density of exchange of information and resources).

Early contributions to this approach[29] enabled researchers to abstract organizational structure into subjective models. By extension, this has led the way to development of computer simulation of organizations,[30] their networks,[31] and their learning and unlearning.[32]

## NOTES

1. Harold L. Wilensky, *Organizational Intelligence: Knowledge and Policy in Government and Industry* (New York: Basic Books, 1967), p. viii.

2. Michael A. McGinnis, "The Key to Strategic Planning: Integrating Analysis and Intuition," *Sloan Management Review*, Fall, 1984, p. 45.

3. See, for example, H. Aldrich, B. Mckelvey and D. Ulrich, "Design Strategy from the Population Perspective," *Journal of Management*, Winter, 1984.

4. David Ulrich and Margarethe F. Wiersema, "Gaining Strategic and Organizational Capability in a Turbulent Business Environment," *Academy of Management Executive*, 3(2) (1989).

5. James March and Herbert Simon, *Organizations* (New York: Wiley, 1958).

6. It is noticeable that the availability of information goods and services is much higher than ever. See, for example, William Harris, "Collection in the Intelligence Process," in *Intelligence Requirements for the 1980's: Clandestine Collection*, ed. Roy Godson (Washington, D.C.: National Strategy Information Center, 1982). Harris shows (pp. 173–74) how information activities accounted for a significant share of gross domestic product in developed countries.

7. See, for example, Claudia H. Deutsch, "Dun & Bradstreet's Bid to Stay Ahead." *New York Times*, February 12, 1989, sec. 3, pp. 1, 6.

8. Ulrich and Wiersema, "Gaining Strategic and Organizational Capability."

9. See, for example, Paul R. Lawrence and Jay W. Lorsch, *Organization and Environment* (Boston: Harvard Business School, Division of Research, 1967).

10. Wilensky, *Organizational Intelligence*, p. viii.

11. Ibid., p. 83.

12. Thomas Peters and Robert Waterman, *In Search of Excellence: Lessons from America's Best-run Companies* (New York: Warner Books, 1984).

13. Ulrich and Wiersema, "Gaining Strategic and Organizational Capability."

14. Peters and Waterman, *In Search of Excellence*.

15. Bo Hedberg, "How Organizations Learn and Unlearn," in *Handbook of Organizational Design*, edited by Paul Nystrom and William Starbuck, (Volume 1) (New

Oxford University Press, 1981), 3–27; Henry Mintzberg, *The Structuring of Organizations* (Englewood Cliffs, N.J.: Prentice-Hall, 1979).

16. 3M Company, 1988 reports.

17. Mintzberg, *Structuring of Organizations*.

18. Herbert E. Meyer, *Real World Intelligence: Organized Information for Executives* (New York: Weidenfeld and Nicolson, 1987).

19. George Schreyogg and Horst Steinmann, "Strategic Control: A New Perspective," *Academy of Management Review* 12(1) (1987).

20. Gerald R. Salancik and Joseph F. Porac, "Distilled Ideologies: Values Derived from Causal Reasoning in Complex Environments." In *The Thinking Organization: Dynamics of Organizational Social Cognition* ed. Henry P. Sims, Jr., Dennis A. Gioia, and Associates (San Francisco: Jossey-Bass Publishers, 1986), 75–102.

21. James A. Senn, "Evolving Structures for Information Systems Management," *Journal of Management Systems* 1(1) (1989): p. 17.

22. Ford Motor Company reports, 1985, 1987.

23. Meyer, *Real World Intelligence: Organized Information for Executives*, 61.

24. Mintzberg, *Structuring of Organizations*.

25. Ian C. MacMillan and Patricia E. Jones, "Designing Organizations to Compete," *Journal of Business Strategy* 4 (Spring 1984).

26. Jay R. Galbraith, *Organizational Design* (Reading, Mass.: Addison-Wesley, 1977); Mintzberg, *Structuring of Organizations*.

27. Gregory K. Dow, "Configurational and Coactivational Views of Organizational Structure," *Academy of Management Review* 13(1) (1988).

28. Max Weber, *The Theory of Social and Economic Organization* (New York: Oxford University Press, 1947); Henry H. Fayol, *Industrial and General Administration* (London: Pitman, 1930); Luther Gulick, "Notes on the Theory of Organization," in *Papers on the Science of Administration*, ed. Luther Gulick and Lyndall Urwick (New York: Institute of Public Administration, 1937), 3–45; Lyndall L. Urwick, *The Elements of Administration* (New York: Harper and Brothers, 1943).

29. March and Simon, *Organizations*; Richard R. Cyert and James J. March, *A Behavioral Theory of the Firm* (Englewood Cliffs, N.J.: Prentice-Hall, 1963).

30. M. D. Cohn, J. G. March, and J. D. Olsen, "A Garbage Can Model of Organizational Choice," *Administrative Science Quarterly* 17 (1972): 1–25.

31. Noel M. Tichy, "Networks in Organizations," In *Handbook of Organizational Design*, ed. Paul Nystrom and William Starbuck (V. 2) (New York: Oxford University Press, 1981), pp. 225–49.

32. Hedberg, "How Organizations Learn and Unlearn."

# 9

# Field Marketing Intelligence: A Motivational Methodology

## *Henry S. Berszinn*

### WHAT IS SO IMPORTANT ABOUT FIELD MARKETING INTELLIGENCE?

You are the vice president responsible for sales and marketing. Your overall objective is to sell more products. To accomplish that, you work out a marketing plan. You review data bases, read the trade press, analyze your sales statistics, huddle with superiors and subordinates, and write and review endless drafts before putting the strategic plan into action. You implement the plan to the letter—and you find that revenues have not increased. Why not? Perhaps the answer may be that—for all the research and analysis that you have performed—you have not been working with accurate, up-to-date, relevant information. Your plan has not accurately taken into account what goes on at the point of sale of your products. You need field marketing intelligence.

What is the point of sale? It is where and when the decision is made to buy your product. It is the communication that takes place between the salesperson and the buyer that results in the buyer making a positive decision, or, even more important, the communication that takes place that results in the buyer making a decision not to buy. Information—intelligence—about the events that occur at the point of sale is a critical input into your marketing plan.

In a dynamic marketing environment, accurate information must be timely information. In order for sales-related information to be timely, intelligence about field events must be quickly gathered and transmitted from the field to the manufacturer. He or she can be trained to capture market facts and feed them back to the analytical unit at headquarters. Incentives motivate a heightened awareness of what to observe. Recognition and rewards emphasize what is important to the company and keep everyone on track.

This chapter focuses on techniques of increasing awareness of what is going on at the point of sale, that place where the prospective buyer of a product decides whether or not to make a purchase. This decision, whether or not to buy, is the vote that counts in determining the value of your marketing intelligence.

The premise of this chapter is that the more you know about what is going on at the point of sale, the better the opportunity to influence the buyer's decision in your favor through direct influence by the salesperson and indirect influence in terms of product development and marketing programs. This information about the events (and influences on events) at the point of sale is what is referred to here as field-generated marketing intelligence or field marketing intelligence.

## SUCCESS CRITERIA FOR A FIELD INTELLIGENCE SYSTEM

### Collecting Intelligence from the Field Practically

The key word in collecting field intelligence is "practically." No intelligence-generation system should cost more than it is worth. It is easy to justify a need for field intelligence. It is another story to justify the expense of development and maintenance of a system in dollars and time. The author maintains that most field intelligence can be collected as a by-product of other activities.

### Building Awareness of Information as Intelligence

Your sales people, or, more accurately, the people selling your products, need to be trained to recognize and record the important facts about sales transactions, and they need to be motivated to feed these back to you. Much of this information may be contained in a customer's objections. Information on product introductions by competitors, discounting policies, product enhancements, and so on may help explain a customer's reluctance to buy. The salesperson must be trained first to identify these objections, second to deal with them, and finally to record them for transmittal back to you.

### Motivating Participation in an Intelligence-gathering Program

That old chestnut, "Your motivation is that you get to keep your job," has little value in the often-nebulous business of field intelligence. Motivating, not compelling, is the key here. The *Wall Street Journal* points out that personal recognition topped salary four to one as the most wanted requirement for a new job according to a recent survey of fired managers.[1] Tangible rewards and recognition have a role in an intelligence program. Both must be awarded promptly and regularly to everyone involved in and contributing to the process in order to keep the information flow continuing and current.

### Collecting Information of Immediate Benefit

Immediate returns are as important as long-range strategic information to help justify the cost of a field intelligence-collection program. When companies and careers are made and broken by the quarterly income statement, both managers and the people in the field need quick, positive reinforcement that the program is working. What better way to display effectiveness than to show that information generated by the program has directly resulted in new business?

### Working within the Capabilities of the People in the Field

Great expectations and low returns will kill any program. One must carefully judge what can be realistically expected from salespeople in light of the objectives of the program. Points to be taken into consideration are whether the sales force is captive or noncaptive, agreements with distributors, and skill levels of the sales people. Not only must objectives be carefully defined at the beginning of a program, but they must also be redefined as the program progresses to bring them into line with results.

### Using an Indirect Approach to Build Support

Asking someone who depends on daily sales for his or her living to identify and collect information of global, long-term strategic value is unrealistic. It may be more practical to profile information requirements in two ways: (1) information of immediate use to the salesperson, and (2) information of value to the marketing decision maker, and then to look for areas of overlap, that is, information useful to both parties. As the process continues, the salesperson will come to the realization that intelligence gathering is in his or her own self-interest.

### Modifying Behavior with Incentives

Behavior-based systems are at the heart of our thesis. A salesperson gets rewarded for the ''outcome'' of his efforts: making the sale. To motivate salespeople to feed back information on the process of the sale, a behavior-based reward system must be established. Professional recognition, organizational identification, and plain old-fashioned greed will stimulate the grass-roots collection and communication of field intelligence.

### Appealing to the "Professionalism" in Customers and Prospects

Motivating prospects and customers to reveal their "true" buying preferences is the other side of the equation. "Just tell them that you eat liver twice a week, Mable, and they'll give you 35 dollars," headlines the ads of one marketing research firm in highlighting the biggest weakness of most marketing research. That weakness is that research subjects will try to anticipate the "correct" response, telling the researcher what they think he or she wants to hear rather than relating what they really feel or believe. This tendency can be counteracted by appealing to the respondent's sense of professionalism to get an honest answer and providing an incentive independent of the response.

### Maintaining Currency and Accuracy in a Flexible Data Base

Setting attainable objectives, exploring the relationships between the kinds of information collected, and assuring the integrity of responses are important aspects of creating a field intelligence data base. But as important is the ability to properly identify and track respondents. The data base is only as good as its sources. If the sources come to believe (by observing communications addressed to individuals no longer on staff, names and addresses misspelled, and new people ignored) that their input is taken for granted or no longer valued, they will drop out, or worse, submit garbage.

### Transmitting Intelligence to Decision Makers

The intelligence specialist (marketing manager) needs to sift through both raw field information and information from publicly available sources to assure that the intelligence he or she creates maintains vitality and relevance. The data base should have the ability to filter raw field data or text for recurring themes and vital tidbits. A communications mechanism must be established to transmit the field information to decision makers in a format that encourages utilization. This may be in the form of a regular newsletter or a compilation of highlights in hard copy or an information bank made accessible through text-searching software.

### Feeding Back Intelligence to the Field

If professional self-interest is the motivation for the information flow upward, then some flow of intelligence back down the ladder is critical to keep the pump primed and working. Program participants need to recognize that value is added to the information that they send up the ladder. Clearly there must be a benefit to them when it comes back down. A regular newsletter can provide a menu of what is available. A data base with access via modem or support service providing searching and transmission of printed material via fax can give the sales force that competitive edge in the field.

### KISSing (Keep It Simple, Stupid) for Effective Communication

The old 80-20 rule applies here as it does to any other aspect of the business. Translated for the intelligence arena, it states that 20 percent of the effort that salespeople or prospects give to a response program will yield 80 percent of the useful information. With that in mind, carefully review your collection instruments to avoid needless duplication and collection of marginal information (for instance, is it really necessary for the salesperson to document the hair color of the buyer?). Do not turn off your sources by making their intelligence-collection activities more of a chore than they need to be.

## JUSTIFICATION OF A FIELD INTELLIGENCE NETWORK

Setting up and maintaining a field intelligence network is a major commitment whether ten people or ten thousand are expected to collect and transmit information. If a wealth of information can be extracted from data bases or from a day at the library, why make the investment in field intelligence systems?

As Leonard Fuld explains, basic sources are not always adequate:

Usually any question you have about a competitor [or about what is happening at the point of sale] has two overriding requirements:

1. Currency. The information you collect must be up to date; otherwise it is useless to you.

2. Narrow focus. Your questions are specific. You are looking for a highly detailed answer to a single part of a competitor's activities [or a prospect's buying motivations].

These two requirements will often disqualify any basic source. Why? . . . Magazine articles may be three to six months old before they hit the newsstands.

Also, publishers have to meet the needs of their readership. They cannot afford to concentrate on articles of limited interest. You, for example, may be the only reader who would be interested in a story on your competitor's warehousing operation [or in the one feature of your product that prospects consider the most superfluous].[2]

## LEVERAGING FIELD INTELLIGENCE FROM OTHER PROGRAMS

If you are worried about cost, a field intelligence network need not be a stand-alone, single-objective program. In fact, identification as a field intelligence network may be counterproductive. If many of the people from whom you hope to be gathering intelligence are selling your competitors' products as well as your own, why tip off your competitors by publicizing your intelligence objectives?

Your mechanism for gathering field intelligence is really a two-way communications program: if you want information back from the field, you have to send information to the field. Active involvement is required at both ends. For instance, if you want the salesperson to tell you what is going on at the point of sale, you have to ask him. But you do not have to tell him all the ways that the information he provides is going to be used, only those aspects that will be of direct benefit to the field person.

The opportunity exists to use the communications mechanism and the data base that are the heart of your intelligence program to achieve other objectives and get field intelligence as a by-product. Training and improving morale may be the only publicized objectives of the program initially. In the process of achieving other training and marketing objectives, a disguised intelligence-gathering mechanism is created at less cost than if it were undertaken independently.

## A FRAMEWORK FOR COLLECTING FIELD INTELLIGENCE

If the field intelligence network is recognized primarily as an interactive communications system that ties together the field sales force with headquarters through programs with mutual benefits for everyone, this simplifies the identification of the appropriate marketing and training programs that can serve as platforms for a field intelligence network.

## KEY FEATURES OF PROGRAMS APPROPRIATE FOR A FIELD NETWORK

### Well-defined Expectations

Expectations are clearly spelled out up front, at the beginning of the program. The participants know what they can expect in terms of their rewards and what is expected of them in terms of their input.

### Encompassing Theme

An appropriate program will have a theme, an overall concept supported by visual images that makes it easy for participants to identify with and to identify specific program communications.

### Thorough Integration with Job

All aspects of the program are well integrated with the participant's work activities. The program's activities relate directly to the doing of one's job, not just generically as a salesperson but specifically as a salesperson of a given product or products.

## High Visibility

The network is obviously a program of importance to the sponsoring firm. Top managers are identified in program communications. Often communications appear to come directly from top managers.

## Numerous Incentives

Individual and group incentives will work in a complementary fashion to keep an entire population involved throughout the program. Incentive types include the following:

A. Recognition incentives that show management's appreciation for taking part in the program. These incentives should have functional value to the recipient (examples include business card cases, desk sets, and portfolios) so that they can be used on the job and serve to stimulate continual awareness of the program's objectives.
B. Achievement to motivate an extra effort. Reaching specific goals results in participants earning cash, prizes, or trips as well as special recognition by top management.
C. Group participation and achievement incentives keep field managers involved in and supporting the program. Group incentives also serve to focus peer pressure on laggards unmotivated by individual incentives.

## Total Group Involvement

When possible and practical, the program should include everyone in the field. This is especially important when field staff work out of central locations rather than their homes. There is no faster way to turn people off than to exclude some from incentives that their workmates can receive.

## Clear Job-related Benefits

The knowledge by participants that involvement in the program will directly help them do their job better is essential.

## Adequate Response Time

Adequate response time reduces resentment of the program as adding an additional burden to an already-heavy work load.

## Administration Minimized

Administration requirements for participation are minimized. Personalized response forms, preaddressed, postage-paid business reply envelopes, and publicized fax and phone connections with program headquarters all help assure that program-participation time is quality time.

## MAINTAINING BALANCE: THE INTELLIGENCE "TELESCOPE"

Any field intelligence network carries with it the inherent risks of information overload. So much information enters the system that it is overwhelmed. The reaction is a net set up to sift out all but the "most valuable" information. The information flow is carefully structured to meet the requirements of the net. All information that does not meet the structure is excluded. The result is a loss of dynamism in the intelligence system. The means have become more important than the ends.

The failures of intelligence systems are not failures of the systems, but of managers who misunderstand or misuse them. The problem is often not that information is unavailable, but that it is not taken seriously by commanders who, once committed by bureaucratic consensus to a course of action, refuse to recognize the validity of contrary data and abandon the operation.[3]

Gerald Michaelson draws upon the intelligence-gathering techniques of Napoleon in suggesting an intelligence "telescope" as a balance to more formal intelligence-collection networks. Napoleon maintained a small personal staff of junior and senior officers to cut through the bureaucracy of information filters and find out true battlefield conditions. He relied on his personal assessment of the information provided to him so that he could interpret the information in relation to the orientation of the sender.

Michaelson suggests that the business executive balance his own formal information sources with an informal network of contacts. These may be special customers, key distributors with their own networks, or business "gurus" who have built their expertise in specific fields. Because of the personal nature of the communication, the network will necessarily be limited, a "telescope" allowing the executive to get a closer view of the action in the field and to judge what that action means to his business more clearly.

## TAILORING A PROGRAM FOR FIELD INTELLIGENCE

### Home Study Response Programs/Knowledge Competition: A Solid Foundation

Many basic requirements of a field intelligence system are in place when a home study response program is implemented.

The target-field population has an incentive to respond.

There is a common job-related basis for participation.

The program appeals to professionalism and intelligence.

Rewards are not given out by chance but earned.

The program has a dynamic existence over several months.

Additional lines of communication (telephone and fax numbers are captured and retained in the data base) are in place to follow up (headquarters to field) on specific items of intelligence.

"Hotline" to headquarters facilitates sharing of fresh information by the field.

Specific responses are evaluated and rewarded as part of the program.

A newsletter provides a feedback mechanism to the field.

The data base identifies respondents and serves as a foundation to assist in further analyzing and correlating responses.

## Integrated Customer/Prospect Response Programs Also Yield Intelligence

Up till now we have discussed an intelligence network that includes only the people selling products or services. That gives us intelligence from the seller's perspective. However, a sale includes at least two parties, seller and buyer. How about information from the buyer's perspective?

Building on the concept that a field response program can be a platform to gather field intelligence from the people selling your product, related customer/prospect programs can also contribute to the gathering of marketing intelligence from the customers' or the prospects' perspective.

The value of customer and prospect responses is to put the burden of proof on the participating salespeople themselves. As part of a program offering additional benefits for achievement, salespeople submit the names of noncustomer prospects to headquarters. Headquarters surveys the prospects for their buying preferences and feeds back the individual responses to the submitting salespeople. Incentives and personalized communication are used to enhance high returns.

During the course of the program, participants closely observe close the new business represented by the surveys. By the completion of the program, this new business can be measured and directly correlated to the impact of the competition. Applied product knowledge leads to sales.

The responses themselves become a source of marketing intelligence. Some clients have them tabulated to give geographic preference profiles. Comments on the individual responses often say much about the perception of the client's product and whether or not prospects will buy.

Tracking salesperson follow-up on these "enhanced" leads is another potential opportunity for grist for the intelligence mill. One can ask what salespersons did and how they did it. The new sales transaction has the additional perspective of up-front knowledge of buying motivations, thus providing possibilities for charting the application or lack of application of product knowledge.

### Relational Data Bases Offer Flexibility to Track and Analyze Field Responses

Minimizing administrative requirements helps assure a successful program. The data base must have the flexibility to emulate the organizational structure of the field sales force; it needs to be more accurate and more flexible than a personnel data base.

A relational data base format will meet the needs of the intelligence network. A separate record is created for each organizational layer that is to be tracked. If the field organization contains regions, districts, stores, and individuals, then a separate layer of records is created for each organizational layer. This offers two primary advantages over a flat-file data base with only one stand-alone record type. The first advantage is flexibility in adapting the program to the needs of many different clients or to the changing needs of an individual client. Consider a client that reorganizes its regions from four to five; in a flat-file data base, each individual record in the program would have to be edited to reflect the change. In the relational data base, an additional regional record would be created, and only those districts now becoming part of the new region would require editing.

The second advantage is the ability to add additional layers to the data base to look at individual response patterns in more detail. One has the capability to follow up on hunches by capturing and correlating additional facts without overwhelming an individual record. By adding an additional layer for encoding responses, that assumption can be tested with the facts without changing the overall structure of the data base itself.

The natural tendency of the information pack rat is to dump everything into one record. This is a direct transposition of the notebook approach to collecting intelligence. While it may release occasional pearls of wisdom, it does not give the big picture: the relationships between the individual items of information collected from the field and what they mean in light of the business. It does not translate into intelligence.

A relational data base categorizes information and then gives one the flexibility to look at the relationship of the different categories. A relational structure, such as that used for the Product Knowledge Competition, is a good start to setting up a more full-fledged field intelligence data base. The organizational breakdown makes correlation meaningful. Other important record groups—products, customers, and so on—can fit within this structure.

Sophisticated text-searching software used in conjunction with the relational data base offers the means to access all those items that do not fit the structure directly. Optical drives and other relatively inexpensive mass storage devices allow one to keep almost everything transmitted from the field. By keying on word groupings, rapid searching can unearth intelligence pearls in an information-dumping year and tie them together with more formal sources.

Time spent in conceptualizing the data base prior to initiating a program can be a valuable investment. The key criterion is flexibility. As a program continues, it inevitably will undergo evolution. The field environment and the perception of the field environment will require change; there will be new forms of information to collect, and new information relationships to explore. Flexibility will make evolution relatively painless. Inflexibility leads to irrelevance.

## Keep Communication With Users Clear and Brief

Hate the information glut? So does everyone else. Keep that in mind when your "pearls" of wisdom become planetary in volume. If your time is pinched to keep up with everything you think you should do, your audience both above and below has the same problem.

The criteria for the success of a field intelligence system are utilitarian; you and your users should get more out of it than you put into it. Since the nature of the field intelligence business is the big-net approach—capturing a lot of information with varying degrees of value—it depends on you to sort what you capture for value before communicating it further. Since value criteria for each group (participants, management, and executives) may be considerably different, different communication mechanisms must be created.

Rather than trying to anticipate all the needs of each group, it is better to sift for what seems to apply best, communicate that, and store the rest in a form easily accessible if the need should arise. This way you do not overwhelm people with information and thereby cause them to ignore or miss the value of what you have communicated.

Use the communication mediums most comfortable for each group. If executives respond best to memos rather than formal reports, then use memos. If salespeople like newsletters or phone messages or electronic mail, then those are what you use.

Ask people what they like best or feel is the most useful. It is easy to get in a routine and do the same thing time after time, and before you know it, you have lost your audience. Use surveys, visit the field, talk to people, and get opinions.

Intelligence gathering is not a static activity. It reflects what is going on in a dynamic environment. This includes everything, especially the means of communication. The fax machine is an interesting case in point. When Responsive Selling System (RSS) enrolls participants in its programs from dealership populations not recorded by the client, it has found that dealer principals and sales managers are more likely to transmit names via fax even though it is simpler and cheaper to use the postage-paid business reply envelopes that RSS includes with each mailing. Somehow the immediacy of the activity, the fact that the event is being completed at once rather than entrusted to the mails, appeals to busy businessmen. Test and try new communications mediums; you may be surprised at the results.

The bottom line in any case is to be brief and to the point. Consider your audience. Are you focusing on process rather than results in your communications? Review and cut. But keep everything, if possible, in case of value changes in the future. Today's information dump may be tomorrow's intelligence gold mine. Just be sure that your collection does not become identified as a garbage heap.

### Do Not Forget the Mission or the Incentives

Keeping your intelligence network productive requires the continued intelligent use of incentives, recognition, and innovative communication. Make recognition awards for participation. Give major awards for valuable responses, maybe cash payments. Vary the incentives to keep them interesting. Keep up with your population in terms of how they communicate. Restate your program objectives and management's commitment to these objectives. Never lose sight of the original program and its promises, no matter how long ago the promises were made. With that in mind, you will have a successful field intelligence network.

### NOTES

1. "Labor Letter" column, *Wall Street Journal*, January 1, 1989, 1.
2. Leonard M. Fuld, *Competitor Intelligence: How to Get It—How to Use It*, (New York: John Wiley and Sons, 1985), 21.
3. Gerald A. Michaelson, "Control Your Information Before It Controls You," *Marketing News*, November 6, 1987, 30.

# Part IV

## NEW AND OLD THREATS

# 10

# Computer Security

## Bruce Charnov

The final decades of the twentieth century have been characterized by a virtual explosion of information and can justly be considered the "age of information." The invention and proliferation of the computer in all its configurations, from the CRAY supercomputer to the now-common, relatively inexpensive desktop personal computer (PC), coupled with the creation of new communication technologies, have made it a reality for those engaged in decision-making to acquire, manipulate, and evaluate ever-increasing amounts of information. The increase in availability of computer technology is evident in the dramatic decline in the cost of this technology over the last forty years. By way of comparison, the first computer, ENIAC, weighed over 60,000 pounds, occupied two stories and 15,000 square feet of a building, and cost almost $487,000 in 1947. As impressive as this was in 1947, today's average digital watch, costing only a few dollars, has as much or more computing power; and this chapter was typed on an Apple Macintosh computer that costs less than $1,200 and can perform mathematical functions over twenty times faster than ENIAC.

Computers produce a tremendous volume of information, but the value of this application of technology extends far beyond the mere generation of information. The real potential benefit to management will be the improvement of the quality of information generated and thereby the improvement of the quality of managerial decision making dependent upon that information. The generation of better information and use of that information in managerial decision making can lead to advantages in the competitive arena. This emerging concept of "information for competitive advantage'' (IFCA), a term coined by the Management Information Consulting Division of Arthur Andersen and Company, is a dynamic view of information within the modern business enterprise. Some writers have even asserted that information is an increasingly important weapon in the business arena.

Whereas in the past managers had the luxury of time and a deficit of information, the contemporary executive is now confronted with the necessity of immediate decision making and a tremendous availability of information. Satellites placed in position approximately 22,500 miles above the earth in geosynchronous orbits remain stationary above a preselected locale and, when linked to other such communication satellites, are able to link any two points on earth. This means that a manager can now make decisions with real-time data from any location, no matter how distant. It is obvious that the company that acquires, analyzes, and employs current information in decision making will gain a competitive advantage that may prove crucial to business survival over competitors who do not have such access. The crucial task facing the corporation is to insure the security of its information. This chapter concerns itself with this vital task, from the mundane day-to-day safeguarding of hardware to the policies and practices that control access and entry to the corporate computer network.

## THE VIRUS

The "virus" is a dramatic example of the threat and the need to protect and safeguard computerized information. Several examples illustrate the problem. Froma Joselow, a financial reporter at the *Providence Journal-Bulletin*, lost several months' work that had been stored on a disk. The disk had been contaminated by a computer virus created in a Pakistani computer store in Lahore and passed along from disk to disk. Two brothers who owned the computer store in Lahore, Pakistan, had inserted the virus to "punish" tourists who bought the bootlegged software and then copied it for friends. Basit Farook Alvi, the programmer, claimed that it was originally inserted into a popular program and would only replicate itself if illegally copied. No one knows how it got from the Brain Computer Service in Lahore into the newspaper's computer system, but since a computer virus can travel via modem, it can spread rapidly and appear at locations remote from each other. The same virus that struck Joselow in Providence also struck 10,000 disks at George Washington University and an estimated 90,000 other computer disks across the nation, as well as computers in Israel and Europe.

Robert Morris, a 1988 Harvard graduate and graduate student at Cornell, invaded the Internet computer network with a virus that disrupted government and university research computers across America. This virus program caused computer hard disks to fill with extraneous data, and it is estimated that as many as 6,000 computers were affected. Fifty thousand computers could have been affected. The virus, in this case a complex series of instructions, replicated and sent itself as an electronic telegram to new computers. From Internet the virus penetrated unclassified military computing networks—MILNET and the Advanced Research Projects Agency Network. It took thousands of work hours to clean the virus out of the systems it thus infected.

A student at the State University of New York at Albany became the first college student to be fined and suspended for inserting a virus into the university's computer system. The fine was $2,000 to pay for the two and one-half days of labor to purge the virus from the system. The student claimed that he meant no harm and was merely responding to a perceived challenge. University officials were reportedly unconvinced.

The SCORES virus, designed to infiltrate the Apple Macintosh computer system, first appeared in Dallas but soon spread to other firms tied into common computer data networks. It has been found at Boeing and ARCO and in the computers of NASA, the IRS, and the U.S. House of Representatives.

The so-called "peace virus" created by Drew Davidson, a Texas programmer in his early twenties, illustrates how a virus spreads. This virus, which flashed a "peace greeting" on the Apple Macintosh computer screen and then erased itself and all its instructions, was given to Richard Brandow, a publisher of a Canadian computer magazine. Brandow and his colleague Pierre M. Zovilé transferred the virus to over 35,000 computers around the world, and on March 2, 1988, the screens of these Macintosh computers displayed a drawing of the planet earth and a message expressing the hope for universal peace. The epidemiology of this virus is only now coming to light.

Brandow had taken Davidson's program, added to it, and then inserted it into game disks that were given out at meetings of the local Montreal Macintosh Users Group. One of the individuals who thus unknowingly acquired a copy of the peace virus hidden in a game disk was Marc Canter, an employee of a local computer company that was doing subcontracted work for Aldus Corporation, a Seattle, Washington, software publisher renowned in the Macintosh world for its excellent graphic arts programs. Canter tried out the contaminated game disk on his office computer and then used the identical machine to work on the Aldus subcontract. Voilà—the virus spread to the Aldus disk, which was then sent to Seattle with the newly introduced virus hidden within its computer code. In Seattle the code was inadvertently duplicated in thousands of copies of the best-selling graphics program Aldus Freehand, the first known instance of a virus spreading to a commercial program.

In the IBM community a virus suddenly appeared around Christmas 1987 and instructed the user to enter a series of commands. Once that was done, the virus replicated itself and sent the identical programming to every name on the user's personal electronic mailing list. Within a matter of days, this E-mail (electronic mail) system was clogged with so many messages that its 350,000 terminals could not be used to provide normal message traffic. The virus spread to computers in 145 different countries around the world.

The virus is a piece of computer code that attaches itself to other programs and proceeds to alter or destroy data contained therein. Since, like a real virus, the computer variety has the power to replicate itself, even if the intent is benign, as with the IBM E-mail Christmas message, unbounded replication can result in a crowding out of other data or a mechanical lethargy that slows data processing and eventually chokes it off completely. Since Amjad Farook Alvi and Basit Farook Alvi introduced the first computer virus in their store in Lahore, Pakistan, several new varieties have emerged. A "retrovirus," contained on a supposed antivirus program, is designed to reappear in a system after memories have been wiped clean, while new viruses infect a disk and, although not altering the data contained within the computer system, cause disk drives to spin faster and thereby wear out more quickly.

This new plague has spawned a vocabulary of its own. As previously stated, a virus is a self-replicating code that can spread from computer to computer. A bomb is a program that, while not replicating itself, will cause a hard drive to crash and no longer function. A Trojan Horse program like its mythological counterpart, appears benign but actually contains a viral element that emerges and does destruction of some kind. However, it is not self-executing. It requires user help, and that aid is usually instructing the apparently safe program to execute itself. The hidden nastiness then goes to work. A variant of this is the worm program, such as the Brandow virus, that chews away at stored data until none is left.

## THE CORPORATE RESPONSE

Assuming that a company has taken steps to isolate its computer and data-storage facilities by means of portal protection, data encryption, internal port protection, and such, what can it do about the possibility that vital corporate data will be compromised or destroyed completely by a dedicated "hacker" who inserts a virus into that system? Realistically, any system can be penetrated, even by the employee who unwittingly plays a video game on the terminal at his or her own desk during lunch. But the following are some suggestions for, if not controlling, then at least containing the harm done by a virus:

1. Make regular use of the various commercial "vaccine" programs that examine disks and programs and search for the inserted virus.

2. Any program, but especially a noncommercial program that has been acquired from an electronic bulletin board, should always be tested for viruses before being introduced into a network where it may, if infected, carry a virus to other applications.

3. To accomplish the testing mandated in (2), keep all suspected (or untested) software on disk while testing, and do not introduce these programs onto the hard disk until testing is complete.

4. Do not assume that software acquired from others has been checked for virus infection—do it yourself. This testing should be over a period of time, not a one-shot test, as the virus may, like its human counterpart, lie dormant until activation at some later time.

5. Appoint a data security manager with the responsibility to follow the current developments in the area of data security. Remember that for every inventive mind solving problems, there are others equally dedicated to causing new ones.

6. If you lend disks, know where they have been.

7. Make frequent backups of your data disks.

Data security requires that a corporate climate be established that is dedicated to such security. The pragmatic steps stressed here are the proverbial tip of the iceberg. Individual situations will require individualized solutions, and data security requires that a company be open to dealing with its own unique problems. While the forms of portal protection may be the easiest to understand and implement, the most serious threat may come from the newly heralded virus. The forms of action discussed here represent only the most rudimentary of steps to be taken—this field is changing daily. Consider the following: West German expert computer "hacker" Bernd Fix claims to have created a virus program that could destroy all information in a large mainframe computer in minutes. The time required to create such a program was about twenty hours. The motivation was the intellectual challenge, "for the experience of doing it." He now claims that the program has been encrypted to prevent it from falling into the hands of someone intent upon loosing it upon an unsuspecting corporation. The task before the data security manager is to make it as difficult as possible for any individual to gain access to the corporate computer system.

The legislative/judicial establishment has also taken note of these emerging threats to data and is slowly responding. A bill was introduced into the House of Representatives on July 14, 1988, which would make it a federal crime to create a computer virus. This would augment the computer-crime laws currently on the books in forty-eight states. It is anticipated that the National Bureau of Standards, mandated by the Computer Security Act of 1987, will take the lead in establishing guidelines for computer security. Some commentators have suggested that the United States should enact a policy similar to that of Japan, which offers tax incentives to companies purchasing security equipment and software to safeguard corporate information. Alert data security directors will want to stay current on this developing legislative trend, for it will surely affect the way business is done and has the potential for dramatically changing the cost/benefit analysis of security decisions.

It should be emphasized that effective data security begins with an attitudinal posture: individuals must be sensitive and sometimes sensitized to the value of information. Information is the future of a business organization; it must be defined, acquired, managed, and secured. This final step with regard to effective data use is as important as the three that precede it. There is no magic bullet that will insure data security; this will be the result of many steps taken to insure that vital information remains available to those who require it and unavailable to those who would damage it. Effective security need not begin with the acquisition of the latest gadget to insure that purpose, but with frank conversation with employees and an invitation for their suggestions. Such courses of action as color coding of disks (detailed later) may emerge, easily accomplished and yet surprisingly effective in creating an atmosphere distinguished by security awareness.

If a company does not have anyone designated as manager of data security or anyone assigned to perform that function as part of a larger job description, it should consider making such a designation. If the business enterprise involves sensitive data, it is certain that others are considering data security and how to breach it. It goes without saying that these individuals do not have your corporate good as their goal. The remaining two sections of this chapter present practical suggestions for controlling and limiting hardware damage and preventing unwanted computer access and entry.

## HARDWARE SECURITY: THE AUDIT FUNCTION

Data is usually stored in a magnetic disk or tape format and is therefore highly vulnerable to physical damage. This potential damage extends from the exotic (magnetic interference, radiation, and so on) to the mundane run-of-the-mill catastrophic flood, fire, earthquake, or, as described by insurance companies, other ''acts of God.'' Although many of these cannot be prevented, damage can be minimized by anticipation to the extent possible. For example, it would be unwise to locate a computer facility or data-storage area in a lower floor of a building situated in a flood plain, as several companies in Chicago learned to their chagrin after an unusually high rainfall resulted in severe damage to the basement computer facility.

Extreme variance in temperature, fire, magnetic interference, and dirt are enemies of most forms of data-storage media. Storage facilities should be insulated from extreme temperature changes, thoroughly fireproofed (which may result in an insurance cost saving that will offset the additional construction and maintenance expenditures), and placed, insofar as possible, at a distance from water pipes that can leak or from sewer pipes that can back up. Such site-selection criteria are easiest to implement when they are made part of a company's design requirements in construction of an original facility. The advisability of adapting an existing facility and the amount of money to be spent should be decided using cost/benefit analysis.

The cost/benefit analysis should include a disaster-avoidance audit and an analysis and identification of potential sources of data damage. All parts of the system should be evaluated for potential design defects. This investigation will involve at least two foci: the current and evolving knowledge of the equipment itself and its performance under conditions of natural disaster. Manufacturers, both of the original equipment (OEMs) and of add-ons, along with insurance companies that routinely gather information regarding claims, will be valuable sources of information regarding the failure rates of your equipment. Many companies issue periodic bulletins announcing modifications and warnings concerning their equipment. Such bulletins should be consulted and incorporated into a company's knowledge base of a machine and its capacities. You may also wish to contact the OEM to determine how its equipment has fared in natural disaster, although if a company has discovered that its equipment has not done well in a hurricane or flood or fire, it may not want this information to become public knowledge. In such a case, a call to a similar company in an area that has suffered a natural disaster can often produce useful information. This information is particularly useful when setting up operation in a new or foreign environment.

While performing the disaster-avoidance audit, one should take care not to rely solely upon the records of equipment found in the company files. Such records, or even detailed guarantees or equipment specifications, may be outdated for several reasons: the equipment or building may have worn to a point where it no longer meets the original specifications, or it may have been modified several times so that it now exceeds those "specs." The current state of the equipment or building under consideration is what is important, not what is specified on paper.

Every audit should consider each piece of equipment, the system in which it interacts, and the physical plant or building in which it is based. It should identify single-point failure modes, such as a leaking ceiling sprinkler upon a main power supply or into a data-storage area, in which either the functioning of an entire data-processing system or a significant amount of data can be destroyed. These points should be deemed crucial in terms of prophylactic measures. Other systems and structural points are evaluated in terms of their ability to withstand disaster, and each facet of the system is double coded for potential vulnerabilities. Once these have been identified, organizations can direct disaster preparation to the most vital and most vulnerable operations.

## PORTAL PROTECTION AND SECURITY CONSCIOUSNESS

Organizations must address the issue of data security, of uninvited entry into a data-processing/storage system. Such security begins with limitations upon the ports of entry into the system. The number of individuals capable of effecting such entry and the possible pathways leading into the system have grown exponentially over the last decade due to the increase in computer literacy, availability of state-of-the-art references in almost every bookstore, and extensive networking characterizing all but the most routine of office layouts. This proliferation has created an imperative to limit such access in order to protect data and data-generation capacity. This limitation takes place on several sequential levels, from external access to the system to control of various levels within the system itself. This section will deal with portal protection, beginning with the external pathways by which an intruder could gain access to the computer system and compromise or destroy the stored data.

While the popular press represents the dedicated, highly talented "hacker" as the one most likely to "crack" the corporate computer system and romp unnoticed through the microchip fields, this is rarely the reality with a small company. There are usually few accessible modems, and such hackers pose little threat to the limited company. However, there may be a significant number of former employees who have experience with the computer system and who could profit from having company data. As more employees have modems, the various departments and divisions of a company are likely to be connected by data-transmission lines that also function to grant entry into the system, the very facets that lead to increased vulnerability. Companies such as financial institutions, insurance companies, and research companies that are data intensive are the most vulnerable. The worth of the data and the risk of compromise will determine the appropriate level of port protection.

A primary consideration in external port protection will be the dynamic tension between ease of entry for the authorized user but difficulty for the intruder. A port protection system that makes it overly difficult for the authorized user will be discouraging the very productivity that the system was designed to promote. The callback device is a common protection method used to verify user authorization. When a user calls into the computer, the device requests an identification code. The device then disconnects while it verifies the code in its memory and, when the verification has been completed, calls the authorized user back at a preprogrammed number and grants entry into the system. Such a system, of course, will contain a nonvolatile memory to store the phone numbers for the callbacks. A nonvolatile memory does not become erased when the power fails or is intentionally shut off. A password-verification sentry creates a lesser level of security in that it merely requests the identification code and then grants access to the system. Because they pass the user through to the computer after getting the correct identification/password, these devices are often called "pass-through verification systems." Either of these systems may be based on one of two technologies: an analog device that can accept an identification code entered on a touch-tone telephone, or a digital device that can accept an entry code from another computer terminal. Analog devices have an additional advantage of "port hiding." This means that they can be configured to conceal the fact that the caller has reached a modem pathway into a data system. (Modem is derived from the combination of *mo*dular *dem*odulator and indicates a connection to a telephone line that allows a computer to send and receive data.) This concealment will be accomplished by having a synthesized voice answer the caller or by having a silent connection that does not provide any sound. In the former the voice was highly distinctive, sounding tinny and brittle, but modern state-of-the-art technology has produced a voice that is increasingly able to mimic human speech. The latter concealment technique, the silent connection, provides no audio tone or answering voice and requires the user to be familiar with the procedure and to produce the required identification code without an obvious cue. Portal concealment will benefit the company in that potential intruders will not recognize the distinctive tone of a modem port into the data system. "Hackers" may use their own computers, modems, and programs that try thousands of phone numbers in an attempt to discover a modem line. When the modem line is discovered by this random phone search, the hacker will then use a variant of the same program to try thousands or hundreds of thousands of identification passwords in an attempt to gain entry. The programs that create this random search capacity are easily acquired and used on even the most rudimentary of computer systems.

In either of these portal sentry devices, when the appropriate password or identification is given, the user is then connected to the computer. (With a callback device, the individual is connected after the callback is completed. A second identification code/password may be required after the callback is completed, or a second identification code/password may be required during the callback to secure final analysis.) Access is granted in response to the correct identification code/password, so it is appropriate to address the issue of password security at this point. It should be remembered, however, that comments on password security also apply to the internal user as well. Passwords are also called "keys" in that they are necessary to secure data access. They may be used to create an entry barrier to the system itself or, within the system, to individual subsections (variously called files or partitions). There are advantages to using individual passwords to secure different partitions within the system. While every user can have a common password to enter the system, further entry to specific data can be restricted to those who need such access. If the common password becomes known or if an intruder gains the general entry, there are still barriers in place to prevent further entry. The use of passwords to create protective partitioning also allows a customization of data security—individual users can be granted access to specific data or combinations of data. If a particular employee is removed from a specific project so that access to a partition of data is no longer necessary, only the individual password need be changed, and instead of having to notify each user of the system of the changed password, only those individuals who use the specific partition of data need be notified.

A general problem with portal protection devices is that many, in order to be maximally "user friendly," will tell the potential intruder that a particular password attempt is in error and then allow further tries. If an unlimited number of tries is allowed, a computer programmed to serially attempt a dictionary of words could eventually gain entry. Any password protection device should allow only a reasonable number of attempts at entry before disconnecting. It is even possible to program a protection device, based on microprocessor technology, to keep track of the phone numbers of those attempting entry and, after a predetermined number of tries from a specific phone line, not to allow any further contact from that line. Although this is only a minor impediment to the determined intruder, who would then move to a different phone, it may be just enough of an inconvenience to discourage the would-be data vandal.

A final note of caution regarding portal protection devices is that the state-of-the-art technology is dynamic and constantly changing. Engineers and programmers are continually producing more sophisticated devices capable of more complex forms of protection. Consideration of such protection must necessarily entail a review of the latest offerings in devices. Out-of-date equipment may be a financial bargain concealing a potential protection disaster. Remember that what a creative mind can design, an equally devious mind can circumvent. For every form of portal protection in operation, there are those seeking to beat it. As each form is defeated by the dedicated intruder, new forms emerge. To the extent that such forms of protection can be trusted, the best bet will be the most current form available. However, a company will need to assess its needs. If the data to be protected is not very important, something less than the latest device may afford an acceptable level of data protection. Assuming that the portals are adequately protected, the security-conscious manager must turn to potential intrusion into data files by an individual who is inside the business organization. Safeguarding data on an internal basis presents a different set of problems to the corporate data security manager. Whereas the external focus entailed the frustration of dedicated efforts by a few intruders to penetrate the data-processing/storage system, the internal environment seeks to facilitate productivity by encouraging maximal use of that system by many users. As such, there exists a much greater opportunity for data tampering or destruction of data.

The first task confronting the data security manager is to convince workers that data security is a serious business, and the second is to create a climate that exhibits such a consciousness. The usual conceptualization of data as being reams of documents, even printouts, must give way to the recognition that the small three-and-one-half-inch disk lying on the desk or placed in someone's pocket is information vital to the business. It is now possible for someone to efficiently purloin hundreds of pages of vital data on a disk weighing a few ounces and easily concealed in a shirt pocket. If a data worker, and increasingly this category will include even the most modest of middle managers, is cavalier regarding data disks and regularly leaves them askew in a briefcase or on a desk, he or she is inviting the loss of that data. A clever and adept thief bent upon the compromise of company data can pocket, in a few seconds, enough to compromise a competitive advantage. Guard your disks! Protective efforts will, of course, take two forms: against accidents and against more malicious efforts.

For all the advantages of storing data on disks, the disks themselves are very fragile. Although there are now sophisticated "rescue programs" that can attempt to retrieve data from damaged disks, the use of such programs usually requires greater expertise than is possessed by the average user and will certainly require a costly investment of managerial/technical time. In addition to avoiding fingerprint smudges on the surface of data media, a worker should avoid placing a magnetic field or liquid anywhere near stored data.

A system to differentiate between high-security data disks and those reflecting a more routine content is usually valuable. Data-storage media, especially the three-and-one-half-inch semihard disks in rigid plastic cases with small sliding metal "windows" that allow access to the magnetic film inside, can be easily color coded. Other forms of data-storage media can also be color coded, and the effect will be to signal to even the most casual user that the data stored on this disk is to be treated with the utmost care. A common form of such coding would be to reserve red disks for the most valuable or sensitive data, yellow for an intermediate classification, and white for ordinary data disks.

If a central location is used to store data, it should be opened only to those who need access and secured to all others. If the number of individuals legitimately needing such access is significant, a company may wish to consider "internal" portal protection devices that grant access only upon presentation of identification or a password.

The latest internal entry protection technology is that of "biometric" security systems that are calibrated to recognize individual and unique physical traits and to grant entry only upon such recognition. The government makes use of "palm readers" at nuclear research laboratories that automatically scan finger and palm prints; entry is granted only after the scanned prints are matched to an existing data base and identification verified. Lest one think that such security is only for "atomic" institutions, a fingerprint reader is used to grant entry at the wine cellar of La Reserve Hotel in White Plains, New York, where the value of some of the bottles of vintage wine makes such security protection worthwhile. Other systems ask the potential entrant to peer into an eyepiece that scans the blood vessel pattern in the eye or employ other unique individual traits and characteristics to check for entry. Such traits as hand prints, blood vessel patterns on the retina of the eye, and jaw movements while speaking are so individualized as to be impossible to replicate, and so discrete as to be used to differentiate those approved for entry and those to be excluded. Each of these biometric characteristics has a distinct advantage over other forms of internal port protection since it cannot be lost, overheard, stolen, or duplicated.

Internal security must also protect against electronic eavesdropping. There has been a noticeable growth in number and activity of firms that specialize in discovering these unobtrusive electronic listening devices. (A recent advertisement for a security firm, quoting *Business Week*, estimated that over 100,000 bugs have been planted over the last several years.) Often calling themselves "security consultants," these firms offer a "high-tech" solution to eavesdropping and will "sweep" an office or an entire complex of offices for bugs for a fee. Companies may wish to consider this option as part of their data security system.

There are two important implications of eavesdropping for computer data security: (1) the unseen listener may learn computer passwords and protection processes via the "bug" and thus gain entry beyond the immediate eavesdropping; and (2) the bug may be attached to a dedicated telephone line with the computerized information being copied even as it is sent, to be deciphered later. Every individual in the business enterprise should be made aware of the potential for intrusion by electronic listening devices. Signs that may point to intrusion—such as furniture that has been moved or new paint or putty on a wall—may signal unwanted electronic visitors. Office personnel should be made aware of these signs and a procedure established for reporting them to responsible corporate officials for investigation. If you think that there is the remotest possibility that your office spaces have been compromised, do not discuss sensitive data in those spaces until they have been checked, and never order that security check over the phone. If there are bugs in place, the telephone conversation may only serve to notify those whom you are trying to catch in the first place.

A security consultant firm should be chosen based on a proven reputation—ask for and check references before letting these individuals onto your premises. An improperly done sweep will only foster the illusion of security while leading to more data leaks. Corporate managers must be vigilant and watchful for new ways by which data can be purloined. As embassy employees discovered several years ago in Moscow, a microwave antenna aimed at a glass window was capable of registering the extremely minute vibrations made by conversation from within the room on the pane. This technique allowed the listener to "sit in" on the conversation while being outside and several hundred feet distant. Computers also "leak" information in a similar manner. The disk drive, the keyboard, and the computer screen give off telltale electronic signals that can be decoded to learn the information being entered or retrieved. The National Security Agency refers to this as TEMPEST and requires that any computer used for security work be TEMPEST-hardened, that is, enclosed within a metallic case that makes it leakproof. Additionally, most computer programs allow for sections of entered data to be "erased," but this is a misnomer. This simply means that the disk space previously used for entered data is now made available to be written over, but until such rewriting takes place, the original data is still there. Computers used for sensitive purposes must have software routines that, when data are erased, actually write a series of random characters or ones and zeros over the erased section of disk. As you might imagine, the hardening of a computer and the software routines that provide for rewriting upon erasure can be extremely costly to implement, yet this cost may be indicated by cost/benefit analysis.

Assuming that a disgruntled former or current employee has gained entry into the data system, companies may make it harder for meaningful data to be extracted by means of computer programs that "scramble" or "encrypt" the entered data. Even if a disk of encrypted data is stolen, it will be meaningless without the key to decipher it. Once encrypted, files usually become random series of unreadable characters, a virtual mélange of letters, characters, and numbers. This process is often described as changing plaintext into ciphertext. These files can only be restored and thereby made meaningful by reversing the encryption process—employing the key to restore the data to its original format. This leads to a major source of data destruction—forgetting the key or password that allows the restoration of data to a meaningful form. While the use of the password to encrypt the data ("front door") protects it from prying eyes, the second use of the password (which can conceivably be a different word entirely) to restore the data protects the data from the user should that password be forgotten (back-door protection). If the password is assigned by another de-partment or the computer software company itself, it may even be possible for a dedicated intruder to contact the company or department, pretend to be a legitimate user, and obtain the supposedly forgotten password and thereby gain entry into the system.

Encryption programs alter data based on a complex set of instructions, called an algorithm, that changes data and keys that changed data to an assigned password. Even the simplest of these encryption programs, available for all but the most inexpensive personal computers, carry the warning that should a pass-word be forgotten, it will be virtually impossible to retrieve the scrambled data. The U.S. Bureau of Standards has created the Data Encryption Standard (DES) as a prototype to be used by commercial enterprises for transfer of sensitive data. As this methodology facilitates the creation of individual commercial ciph-ers, it is on the Department of State Munitions List, which means that you need a special export permit to take the computer program outside the United States—an important consideration for companies with overseas branch offices and the need to transfer data in a secure manner between that remote site and the home office. The DES methodology works by dividing data into eight-character blocks and scrambling them one after another, using a password as the basis for the encryption. The DES method is considered secure because is uses seventy-two possible keys and is deemed acceptable for commercial message traffic. In the world of political information gathering, however, even this level of security is unacceptable, and the U.S. government is now replacing DES with a self-contained "black-box" system that will code not only text, but also voice and video data.

Encryption and decipherment of encrypted data require a large amount of calculation time. Although such calculation time may be speeded by dedicated DES computer chips, it will still amount to a substantial cost factor. Also, data encryption algorithms are, by their very nature, sensitive to errors, and it is possible for a single error within a block of data to contaminate that chunk of data and make decipherment impossible. The source of error may be either mechanical (a wrong character entered) or physical (damage to a minute portion of the disk itself), but the end result would be the same—the data would be lost forever.

Additionally, encryption programs also attempt to balance security concerns and user friendliness. Thus a program may indicate when an incorrect password is entered to alert the potential user that he or she has made a mistake in typing the required key and to invite another try. This, however, is a weak spot because it invites another computer program to attempt thousands if not millions of potential keys to unlock the encrypted data, what one commentator called the "meat-cleaver" approach. Thus a good encryption program will limit the number of guesses before locking itself and requiring an additional password before entry can be gained.

Also, the fact that a password is employed to secure entry necessarily implies that the password itself is contained on the disk or in the document which it is protecting, so that it can be matched with the one keyed in. An intruder who is computer literate and fluent in the use of assembly language, making use of a disassembler that allows a program to be taken apart, may be able to discover the location and text of a password. However, even with all of the weaknesses described here, encryption makes it significantly more difficult to read data. An organization that sends data to remote locations should certainly make use of encryption programs so as to discourage the unintended listener or reader.

# 11

# Defense-related and Microcomputer Security

## Robert S. Redmond

We should begin by recognizing that spying is a fact of life.
Ronald W. Reagan, June 29, 1985[1]

President Reagan made his statement after a serious breach of security in the Department of Defense (DOD) had been discovered. Spying, or industrial espionage in the corporate world, is an everyday fact of corporate life. Keeping sensitive corporate information secure from hostile or competitive domestic or foreign organizations is an essential element of business success. The major corporations of the world expend significant resources protecting their proprietary technologies.

Smaller organizations that do not have the financial capacity to provide a separate organizational structure to protect their sensitive technologies must tailor their corporate management structure. Typically this will mean a choice between a very small security staff or the security function being assigned as an additional responsibility to the administrative section. In either case, all of the corporate managers must be familiar with the basic principles and procedures of industrial security. This chapter concerns itself with these basics and is intended to provide a point of departure for the manager with a need to protect company technology.

Security "is a condition which results from the establishment of measures which protect designated information, personnel, systems, components and equipment against hostile persons, acts or influence." This North Atlantic Treaty

Organization (NATO) definition of security fits well in the corporate environment. The DOD uses a similar but less detailed definition.

In the pages that follow, the approved U.S. military security definitions will be used. This approach is taken because the high volume of defense-related national security information, spread over much of corporate America (over 13,000 cleared defense industrial firms),[2] has made the DOD security procedures a standard for much of industry. DOD also manages industrial security for eighteen other executive branch agencies and departments.

Defense security specialists, in common with most other specialists, have a technical language, which is the point of entry for developing a working-level comprehension of the field. The linguistic starting points are definitions.

Physical security, operation security, and communications security are the three coequal sides of the triangle that supports effective corporate industrial security concepts, principles, and practices. Physical security concerns "physical measures designed to safeguard personnel, to prevent unauthorized access to equipment, facilities, material, and documents, and to safeguard them against espionage, sabotage, damage and theft."[3] Operations security (OPSEC) is the "protection of operations and activities resulting from the identification and subsequent elimination or control of indicators susceptible to hostile exploitation."[4] The last side of the security triangle is communications security (COMSEC), defined as "the protection resulting from all measures designed to deny unauthorized persons information of value that might be derived from the possession and study of telecommunications, or to mislead unauthorized persons in their interpretation of the results of such possession and study."[5] The arrival of the computer, and the personal computer (PC) in particular, has significantly increased the importance of this element of corporate security.

Managers traditionally view corporate security as a function that belongs to someone else, usually represented by a uniformed guard at the entrance to a company facility, or if the company is working on classified government contracts, by interruptions to the daily routine by inspectors checking compliance with a bewildering number of regulations and directives, usually referenced during discussions only by their numbers or initials, such as DOD 5200.28, ISM, ISR, 5220.22, XO 12356, and a number of other standard security publications that are part of the technical security language of the security community concerned with the government's classified information. These documents provide an important and proven base for a corporate security program.

There are two basic principles supporting all successful security programs. First, no individual can be completely trusted, and second, nothing is completely secure. Individual corporate security breaches may result from acts of omission or commission, but the results are the same. From a security standpoint the individual's motivation is material only from the perspective of additional security threats and risks. The important point to remember is that all employees who have access to sensitive corporate technology must be subject to the complete range of corporate security procedures. This should be made clear to the employee prior to authorizing access to the sensitive information. It is also necessary to remember that the basic divisions of corporate security (physical, operation, and communications) are interrelated and should not be addressed in isolation from each other.

Excluding information concerning national security matters and the clearance procedures for access to this information, there are significant differences in the security environment between U.S. corporate offices located within U.S. territory and those overseas. First let us look at the domestic environment and the key element in the security equation, the individual employee with access to sensitive company information. How does the manager know if an employee can be trusted with sensitive information? What happens if an employee with access to sensitive information resigns? Patents and proprietary information have a level of legal protection, but how can other less finite but important company information be protected from unauthorized dissemination? The free nature and high mobility of American society and our concept of individual privacy make effective corporate security policy and procedures difficult to develop and implement.

The trustworthiness of the individual is very difficult to determine. Background investigations can be conducted and psychological profiles developed and administered by in-house or private investigative organizations and industrial psychologists. But an in-depth investigation concerning one individual can cost many thousands of dollars, and there is no guarantee of the accuracy of the final product.

The simplest solution to the background investigation problem for a corporation with classified government contracts is to restrict the dissemination of sensitive corporate information to individuals who have current government security clearances. Because there are approximately 1.2 million cleared industrial employees who have access to national security information,[6] finding one who meets the required job description criteria should not be too difficult. However, a clearance to national security information does not guarantee loyalty to the nation or respect for company proprietary or sensitive technology. It is a good point of departure and a screening tool for the manager.

For those companies that do not have classified contracts and are subject to cost constraints that preclude commercial investigators, the evaluation of an individual devolves into a manager's subjective evaluation of the individual employee. This is not the best solution, but it is one that has been and is being used on a daily basis throughout the business community.

In the foreign environment the problem of access to sensitive corporate information is becoming much more important. Currently U.S. corporations are employing more foreign nationals than in the past, and this trend is forecast to continue. One international business expert, Lewis Griggs, reports that over 20 percent of all U.S. citizen international relocations end in premature returns to the United States. He also states that this rate in developing countries is as high as 70 percent.[7] Griggs estimates that this has cost companies over $2 billion per year in direct losses.[8] The move to hire foreign nationals can be expected to accelerate.

Fortunately, the United States and other Western-oriented countries have infrastructures of reputable employment agencies and executive search specialists or "head hunters" that can, for a fee, provide any level of employee skill. Usually these organizations can only provide references, not background checks, unless the prospective employer is willing to pay a substantial fee.

It would be unfair, inaccurate, and counterproductive to propose that all foreign employees should be excluded from access to sensitive information, regardless of the individual's requirement for the information—his need to know. If a foreign national is going to earn his keep, that individual must be given the tools to accomplish his job. The U.S. manager can establish both overt and covert control measures that will reduce the risk factor.

The control measures themselves can be a significant cost factor. Routine internal office controls (document logs, sign-in/out sheets, and so on) in a foreign environment are normally no more expensive than similar controls in the United States. However, if it is considered necessary to install sophisticated electronic equipment, security fences with sensors or television cameras and monitors, there could well be problems. Something as mundane as electrical power needs may require local or other-level governmental approval. These factors are essential corporate considerations for the releases of sensitive information to a company office on foreign soil.

Within U.S. boundaries the corporate security problems associated with the individual who has access to sensitive company information can be reduced. The prudent U.S. manager should institute internal control measures that will reduce the risk factor while not offending the employee.

In most cases the first place to start internal control is with the communications systems. The proliferation of computers in the United States, from mainframe to laptop, in the past few years has been remarkable. In 1984, 2,420 large-scale host computers (defined as machines serving more than 128 users in a normal commercial environment) were sold. In 1989 the estimated sales are projected to be 2,200.[9] In 1985 there were 26,682 mainframe computers in federal agencies.[10] The control of sensitive automated data is critical and the first element of a COMSEC program.

In general terms, the security of sensitive automated data centers on access to the information. Only properly authorized individuals or processes operating on their behalf will have access to read, write, create, or delete information.

There are six standard requirements that have been developed for a trusted computer system, that is, "a system that employs sufficient hardware and software integrity measures to allow its use for processing simultaneously a range of sensitive or classified information."[11] These requirements are extracted from the DOD "Trusted Computer System Evaluation Criteria."[12]

I. POLICY:

Requirement 1: Security Policy. There must be an explicit and well-defined security policy enforced by the computer system, and the system must include a mandatory security policy that can effectively implement access rules for sensitive information.

Requirement 2: Making access control labels must be associated with objects (each object must have a label that identifies the object's sensitivity level).

II. ACCOUNTABILITY:

Requirement 3: Identification. Individual subjects must be identified. Each access to information must be mediated based on who is accessing the information and what classes of information they are authorized to deal with.

Requirement 4: Accountability. Audit information must be selectively kept and protected. The system must be able to record the occurrences of security-related events in an audit log.

III. ASSURANCE:

Requirement 5: Assurance. The computer system must contain hardware and software that can be independently evaluated to provide sufficient assurance that the system enforces requirements 1 to 4. These mechanisms are typically embedded in the operating system and are designed to carry out the assigned tasks in a secure manner.

Requirement 6: Continuous Protection. The trusted mechanisms that enforce these requirements must be continuously protected against tampering.

In 1987 the U.S. Congress Office of Technology Assessment (OTA) published an analysis of the federal roles in information security.[13] Included in this document is a listing of common administrative, physical, and technical information security measures that provide for a reasonable implementation of these requirements. A tailored adaptation of the OTA measures that will meet the majority of needs for business computer security programs is provided here.

1. Administrative security measures

• Conduct background checks for all employees with access to sensitive, stored data.

• Require the authority of two employees for the retrieval of sensitive technology information.

• Assign passwords to each employee and change these passwords on an irregular basis.

• Remove the passwords of terminated employees quickly.

• Conduct mandatory security training.

• Establish backup files and contingency plans for disasters, the loss of telecommunications support, and the like.

• Designate a security policy, including criteria for establishing the sensitivity of data.

• Assign a senior individual to be responsible for designating specific data as sensitive.

• Provide visible senior management support for security.

2. Physical security measures

• Lock up diskettes and the room in which microcomputers are located.

• Install controlled key locks for microcomputers.

- Issue special badges for access to computer rooms.

- Protect the computer room from fire, water damage, and power outages.

3. Technical security measures

- Audit programs that log each individual on the computer.

- Access control systems that allow different layers of access for different sensitivities of data.

- Biometrics (fingerprint) user identification.

- Kernel-based operating systems, which have a central core of software that is tamper-proof and controls access within the system.

- TEMPEST shielding to eliminate readable emissions from the computers. Currently, this is an expensive addition to the hardware of the computer system and is appropriate only in extreme cases. In the near term, the cost for factory-installed tempested systems is expected to drop significantly.

- Encryption of the sensitive data.


The biometrics fingerprint user identification is a technology that has come of age and one that is very simple to operate. Access is granted to a restricted area only if the individual's fingerprint matches the digital characterization of an enrolled fingerprint previously stored in the host's memory.[14] It is fast, accurate, and fraudproof. Field tests indicate a false rejection rate of approximately 2 percent and a false acceptance rate probability of less than .0001 percent. This technology also provides the capability to capture forensic-quality, time-stamped fingerprint images during verification sequences. This capability can establish a positive audit trail.

"Encryption is the most important technique for improving communications security."[15] Encryption[16] must be used with other administrative, technical, and physical security measures, but it is the critical element. Encryption or cryptography is the process of transforming information (cleartext) into an unintelligible form (encrypted or ciphertext). A third party intercepting an encrypted text while it is being transmitted should not be able to understand the communication. This is the ideal.

In the real world few, if any, encrypted messages can remain secret if national resources are brought to bear on the decryption. F. W. Winterbotham's *The Ultra Secret* provides an excellent description of World War II cryptology and its effect on the outcome of the war. Cryptology has come a long way since 1946. It is probable that, given the necessary computer power and time, any encrypted message can be decrypted. However, it is not likely that any country's national resources will be allocated to breaking a business communication that has been encrypted.

Encryption is based on mathematical algorithms. The currently available ones differ in these areas:

- Mathematical sophistication
- Symmetric or asymmetric
- Length of the key
- Algorithm implanted in software or hardware
- Algorithm available for public scrutiny

Cryptology will not only provide protection for sensitive business communications but can also alert the manager to unauthorized modifications of the communication. It can detect modification or destruction, but it cannot prevent it.

To this point the personal computer (PC) has not been addressed as a separate COMSEC problem. It is not different in concept, but rather in application.

Most of the early PCs share a common security weakness in their built-in hardware. They are frequently single-state machines that will not support multiple processor states, privileged instructions that limit access to certain functions, and memory protection capabilities. PCs that are based on the Zilog Z80 series, the Intel 8086, 8088, or earlier central processing unit (CPU) chips, do not have the architectural capability to provide positive protection. MS-DOS does provide a limited capability for setting file status (read only, system, or hidden), but the switches that control these states are not protected and are relatively easy to change. Xenix and PC/IX are two Unix derivatives that provide the standard Unix access mechanism that allows restrictions to file manipulation. These can be defeated by an experienced PC operator by circumventing, modifying, or overwriting the operating system.

The vulnerability of the PC has been significantly reduced by the development of the 80286 and 80386 microprocessors. These have provided the newer PCs with the architectural capability to improve both hardware and software security capabilities. Unfortunately, though the architecture has improved, the willingness of the industry to develop, and of the customer to use, effective PC security safeguards is not widespread.

Ideally, a PC used for sensitive company information should be isolated in a controlled-access area and used only for sensitive information manipulation. This means that this PC will not be available for use in routine networking with other systems not cleared for the same-level data sensitivity. Unfortunately, the ideal case is not often found in the real world. The 286 and 386 systems are, in most companies, too useful to be dedicated to a very limited application. If this is the case, then the next-best solution is to remove the hard disk from the PC and use only removable disks. After use with sensitive information, the disks should be stored in a secure, limited-access container.

Threats to hardware and software may come from external or internal sources. The three most common forms of software attack are the following:

1. Trapdoor: "A hidden software or hardware mechanism that permits system mechanisms to be circumvented."[17]

2. Trojan Horse: "A computer program with an apparently useful function that contains additional (hidden) functions that surreptitiously exploit the legitimate authorizations of the invoking process to the detriment of security. For example making a 'blind' copy of a sensitive file for the creator of the 'Trojan Horse.' "[18]

3. Virus: "A virus is a software attack that infects computer systems in the same way as a biological virus infects humans. A computer virus is a small program that searches the computer for a program that is uninfected, or 'germ free'. When it finds one, it makes a copy for itself and inserts the 'germ' in the beginning of the healthy program."[19]

Unless constant care is taken, any PC or mainframe information-processing system can be vulnerable to attack by this type of software.[20] To avoid this problem, the manager should insist that no strange or bargain software be loaded on company systems and that company computers network only with approved systems. There is no guarantee that a hacker will not gain access via a modem, but the odds can be reduced.

To summarize, the purpose of computer system security is to accomplish or further three goals:

1. The confidentiality of the sensitive data
2. The integrity of the data
3. The availability of the data

All computers and their peripherals should be provided effective physical security. PCs should be locked to their work stations and each PC provided with an access key lock. Mainframes belong in an access-controlled area, and their tapes and disks should be secured in locked cabinets. All disks or tapes containing sensitive information should be controlled using a log and receipt system.

In a broader sense physical security concerns everything that is tangible in the corporate inventory, including the employees. A list for the typical small corporation might include the following assets to be protected:

- Employees
- Facilities
- Production equipment
- Inventory
- Supplies
- Data-processing equipment
- Documents and records
- Finished products

This list could continue for many pages, depending on the detail of the breakout. Each company is more or less unique and should develop a tailored list of critical physical assets, based on an in-depth risk analysis and the current situation.

The physical security systems that can be employed by any business include the following:

- Security guards
- Guard dogs
- Exclusion or limited-access areas
- Security fences
- Lighting systems
- High-security locking devices (including all biometrics systems, handwriting, card systems, and so on)
- Electronic sensors
- Electro-optical monitoring systems (TV, cameras)

The locks that actually secure the equipment or area are configured for every piece of equipment. The Locksmith Ledger lists fifty-seven categories of locks.[21] There is a lock for every purpose and environment. The National Bureau of Standards published a systematic review of locking devices in 1981.[22] This document provides a detailed presentation of what is available and what each type of lock does. A review of this document will probably convince the reader that an expert is required to make the right choice for a specific situation.

After the physical assets list has been developed and analyzed, the basic decisions are what level of physical security is necessary, what the funding levels are, and what the cost benefit is.

The last component of the security triangle is operation security. The definition of OPSEC used at the beginning of this chapter, the "protection of operations and activities resulting from the identification and subsequent elimination or control of indicators susceptible to hostile exploitation," is one that needs some expansion.

If a manager has been given a new product-development program, one of his or her first thoughts should be, "How do I keep a lid on this?" That is the beginning of an OPSEC program.

There are no longer-term secrets. All security systems eventually are compromised. The question is how long a specific technology can be kept secret. Until a patent, copyright, or other legal protection is in place? In other words, OPSEC is time sensitive.

OPSEC is maximized if management develops an OPSEC plan concurrently with the other planning associated with a sensitive project. It really does not work any other way. Plans and actions to establish a coordinated security program must be based on a detailed security review. The current or potential problems concerning security should be analyzed from the physical, operation, and communications security perspectives concurrently. The tool to accomplish this is the security review.

The security review can be conducted by in-house personnel or outside professionals who specialize in this area (there are many reputable ones). If the review is conducted in house, there are two basic potential problem areas that must be factored into the review output. These are a lack of experience in identifying the actual security threat and a lack of technical knowledge in the hardware and software of security systems.

The normal employee usually does not think in terms of security. The problem is further compounded because few of the actual cases of theft or misuse of company technology are publicized by the media. This lack of publicity is no accident. Most corporations are very reluctant to discuss these incidents in public, first because it is an embarrassment to the organization, and second because the company concerned does not want to give anyone else the idea that the theft of company technology can be profitable. A more professional approach to the conduct of a physical security review is to bring in a qualified consultant or a security firm.

Regardless of who conducts the physical security review, there is a methodology that should be followed. The basic methodology was developed for the Department of Justice's Bureau of Justice Statistics by SRI International.[23] This model has been modified to meet the needs of a security review. The methodology is as follows:

1. Organize the project: project design and scope, funding estimates, schedules, and company support requirements (work routine disruptions and employee time requirements).
2. Identify assets subject to loss; determine dollar value, the consequences of loss, and replacement cost.
3. Identify the security controls now in place.
4. Define the potential threat to each asset.
5. Identify the lack of controls that would facilitate the potential threats to the assets.
6. Combine the threat, assets subject to loss, and the lack of mitigating controls. Each triplicate constitutes a vulnerability.
7. Identify the security controls that would reduce the losses to an acceptable level.
8. Develop a plan to reduce the risk.
9. Evaluate the risk reduction plan in terms of cost to benefits.
10. Fund and manage the physical security project.

Senior management reaction to this structured approach to company security is often initially negative until the cost/benefit analysis demonstrates improvement in the company's position.

## NOTES

1. "Keeping the Nation's Secrets," *A Report to the Secretary of Defense by the Commission to Review DOD Security Policies and Practices*, Washington, D.C.: Government Printing Office, November 19, 1985.

2. Ibid., p. 19.

3. U.S. Department of Defense, *Dictionary of Military and Associated Terms*, Joint Chiefs of Staff, Publication No. 1, January 1972, p. 268.

4. U.S. Department of the Army, "Systems Acquisition Policy and Procedure," Washington, D.C.: Government Printing Office AR 70-1, November 12, 1986, p. 64.

5. *Dictionary of Military and Associated Terms*, p. 69.

6. "Keeping the Nation's Secrets," p. 19.

7. Nathaniel Gilbert, "The Ten Commandments of Global Management," *Management Digest*, July 1988, p. 2.

8. Ibid.

9. U.S. Congress, Office of Technology Assessment, "Defending Secrets, Sharing Data," OTA-CIT-310, Government Printing Office, October 1987, p. 40.

10. Ibid.

11. U.S. Department of Defense, "DOD Trusted Computer Systems," DOD 5200.28-STD, December 1985, p. 116.

12. Ibid., pp. 3–4.

13. "Defending Secrets, Sharing Data."

14. There is another major biometrics system that uses a scan of the individual's eye. This is also very effective. However, the fingerprint system is based on the worldwide recognized standard for identity verification. The recorded fingerprint can have other uses if criminality is suspected.

15. "Defending Secrets, Sharing Data," p. 54.

16. "Encrypt: to convert plain text into unintelligence form by means of a cryptosystem, (Note: The term encrypt covers the meanings of encipher and encode)." *Dictionary of Military and Associated Terms*, p. 112.

17. "DOD Trusted Computer Systems," p. 116.

18. Ibid.

19. "Personal Computer Security Considerations," National Computer Security Center, Government Printing Office, NCSC-WA-002-85, December 1985, p. 10.

20. A recent example of a virus infecting a mainframe information processing system was the November 1988 incident involving Internet. Internet, the main computer network used by the U.S. research community, encompasses over 500 autonomous unclassified national, regional, and local networks. The Internet virus differed from earlier viruses (that attacked personal computer programs) in that it was the first to use networks to spread to vulnerable computer systems. For a more detailed analysis of this virus, see "Computer Security, Virus Highlights Need for Improved Internet Management," U.S. General Accounting Office, GAO/IMTEC-89-57, June 1989.

21. "Locksmith Ledger and Security Register," Nickerson and Collins Co., Des Plains, Illinois, vol. 39, no. 2.

22. U.S. Department of Commerce, "High Security Locking Devices, A State-of-the-Art Report," National Bureau of Standards, National Engineering Laboratory, Center for Building Technology, Environmental Design Research Division, Washington, D.C., NBSIR 81-2233, June 1981 (issued January 1982).

23. U.S. Department of Justice, Bureau of Justice Statistics, "Computer Security Techniques," undated, p. 12.

# 12

# The Terrorist Threat to Corporations

## *Joseph E. Goldberg*

Despite the numerous incidents of terrorism since the 1960s, terrorism is not a modern phenomenon. In the medieval period, the Assassins, an Ismaili Shiite group believing that the line of Muslim leadership should descend from the line of Ismail, the seventh in line of succession from the Prophet's son-in-law, Ali, used murder and violence against Sunni rulers and officials. The fear of assassination, a word etymologically derived from the Assassins, often led rulers to modify their behavior. As one Islami proponent of assassination wrote, "By one single warrior on foot a king may be stricken with terror, though he own more than a hundred thousand horsemen."[1] The English word terrorism owes its origin to the Reign of Terror arising from the French Revolution.

Terrorism in its modern form is far more international in scope, and since the 1960s terrorism has been more commonly used to advance a variety of causes. Modern technological advancements have aided terrorists in carrying out their violent tasks. The existence of modern communications systems, especially television, has enabled terrorists to gain desired publicity for their objectives and increased the fear among the world at large that no individual or population is secure from the terrorist's arm. The uncertainty of terrorism enhances its effectiveness and influence.

But modern terrorism, unlike its ancient and medieval precursors, aims not

All views expressed are those of the author and do not necessarily represent those of the U.S. government.

simply at the assassination of selected leaders. Rulers and religious leaders have been murdered as well. Modern terrorists, especially those terrorist groups espousing Marxist objectives, but terrorists of the right as well, aim at society itself—its fundamental principles, its institutions, its very way of life. Though the Soviet bloc has not been immune from terrorism, the dominant targets of terrorism since the 1960s have been outside the Communist world. Western democracies have been a major target for the wrath of terror.

Western democracies share common fundamental principles that owe their origin to modern political philosophy, especially the writings of Thomas Hobbes and John Locke. Unlike the ancient democratic form, modern democracies hold governments responsible for the protection of inalienable rights that individuals possess at birth. Governments, consequently, are responsible for securing an arena whereby individuals can pursue their desired wants or objectives, that is, happiness. Liberal democracies, as such, secure a private realm for individual action and judgment.

Connected to an individual's pursuit of happiness is the assurance that life and limb will be protected. To pursue happiness, an individual must be alive. To pursue happiness, one must also have the liberty to pursue activities—to think and to act. Life and liberty, consequently, are vital preconditions for the pursuit of happiness itself. The responsibility of modern liberal democracies is to insure the existence of the vital necessary conditions for the pursuit of individual happiness.

Happiness is more than mere survival. For this reason, liberal democracies have been associated with the comforts of life as well. In the formulation of John Locke, governments must promote the comfortable self-preservation of their citizens. Comfortable self-preservation itself is associated with the fruits of individual and community labor—the very origins of property. Modern liberal democracy and modern commercial activity are closely intertwined in theory and practice.

Many have recognized the intricate relationship of the modern state and the modern economic system. The interrelationship of the two is a principal point of Marx's criticism of traditional political philosophy and modern life. Nor has the connection escaped the practitioner of modern terror. Fueled by numerous grievances, terrorist movements have identified the multinational corporation as the symbol of the state. As a representative of the modern commercial world, multinational corporations present themselves as a target for modern terrorism.

## THE NATURE OF TERRORISM

Terrorism not only poses a physical threat to our security, but the acts themselves threaten the most fundamental principles that the modern democratic state is dedicated to preserve. Terrorism threatens the foundation of economic and political life. Yet acts of terrorism have not resulted in the loss of large numbers of lives. According to the U.S. Department of State's annual report, *Patterns of Global Terrorism: 1988*, 658 deaths were attributed to acts of terrorism in that year—the most terrorist-related fatalities so recorded by the department. In contrast, more Americans, according to the National Safety Council, died in 1986 as a result of accidents: 47,900 as a result of motor vehicle deaths, 11,000 as a result of accidental falls, 5,600 as a result of drownings, and 3,600 as a result of the ingestion of food.

If terrorism has been responsible for so few deaths in comparison to accidental fatalities, why have so much attention and resources been devoted to understanding its causes as well as its prevention? What is there about terrorism that distinguishes this form of violence from crime, guerrilla activity, and conventional warfare?

The Department of State has defined terrorism as "premeditated, politically motivated violence perpetrated against noncombatant targets by subnational groups or clandestine state agents, usually intended to influence an audience." This is a useful definition that emphasizes the characteristics of the terrorist phenomenon so that terrorism can be distinguished from other forms of violence.

There is a mental willingness on the part of those nurtured on the ideals of Western civilization to explain brutal acts of violence as either spontaneous acts of vengeance from the oppressed or totally irrational acts of mad persons. Whether it is the murder of 25 Israeli schoolchildren in the village of Maalot by the Popular Democratic Front for the Liberation of Palestine in 1974, the death of 2 innocents in the lobby of the Hilton Hotel in London by a bomb planted by the Provisional Irish Republican Army in 1975, the massacre of 22 people aboard Bus No. PJG7284 in India's northern state of Punjab by Sikh separatists in 1986, or the murder of 259 passengers aboard Pan American World Airways Flight 103 over Lockerbie, Scotland, by a radio-cassette-recorder bomb placed in luggage probably by the Popular Front for the Liberation of Palestine, General Command, in 1988, the murder and maiming seem senseless.

Despite the brutality of acts of terrorism and the gross insensitivity that terrorists have shown toward humanity, most studies of terrorists "have not detected any striking psychological abnormality in the majority, although a range from normal through psychotic has been reported."[2] The brutality of the acts should not blind us to the fact that terrorist actions are advanced in the pursuit of an end, that is, such actions are premeditated. To be sure, the means employed to advance the desired objectives are misguided and should be stopped and condemned, but the actions themselves are logical.

Furthermore, terrorists are not contemplative. The objective of terrorists is to act, not to think or understand. Their message, in large part, is expressed through the act itself. Ulrike Meinhof, a leader of the infamous West German terrorist organization, the Baader-Meinhof gang, distinguished her actions from those of the intellectual left by her willingness to take the next step—that is, "to do that of which they talk."[3] Walter Laqueur traces the concept of "propaganda by deed" to the writings of the nineteenth-century anarchist Carlo Pisacane. The dramatic consequences of the "deed," according to the anarchists, could penetrate all segments of society—even demonstrating to the tired factory worker the importance of the issues of the day. Later anarchist writers, such as the Russian, Pyotr Kropotkin, came to believe that revolution would not follow in the path of a single heroic action.[4] Yet the message of contemporary terrorism is presented in such acts, and for that reason the victim can be innocent or guilty in the mind of the perpetrator: the victim is part of the deed.

As Nathan Leites has argued, such illegal acts as setting fire to a department store, robbery, and murder lead step by step to a complete rejection of accepted law and morality. There is a progressive "liberation" of the individual from the existing order. In its place, Leites observes, is generated a revolutionary consciousness that holds to the possibility of revolutionary change; that is, a belief is held that the existing order can and must be destroyed.[5]

Once an individual has crossed the separation between legal and illegal behavior, there is no turning back. An individual's entire life has been modified. The new terrorist becomes dependent upon the organization for direction, gratification, and protection.[6] The greater the risk to the terrorist group, the more the individual member is bonded to the organization.

## THE OBJECTIVES OF TERRORISTS

As premeditated violence, terrorism is the means to accomplish the goals or objectives of the organization. Those goals vary from terrorist group to terrorist group. *InTer*, the annual survey of international terrorism published by the Jaffee Center for Strategic Studies at Tel Aviv University, identified fifty-six organizations that were responsible for terrorist incidents in 1987.[7] Those terrorist organizations were motivated for distinct purposes. Some of the organizations articulated political objectives rooted in territorial claims. All segments of the Palestine Liberation Organization, for example, espoused the establishment of an independent Palestinian state in part or in all of Israel. The Euskadi Ta Askatasuna (Basque Fatherland and Liberty Movement, ETA) has insisted upon the establishment of an independent Basque nation in the northern regions of Spain or a greater share in making decisions that influence the Basque region. The U.S. Federal Bureau of Investigation identifies at least nine clandestine Puerto Rico–based terrorist groups that have engaged in terrorist activities since the early 1970s to gain Puerto Rican independence from the United States. The most active of the organizations, EPB-Macheteros, was founded in 1976. Their targets have been U.S. government facilities and personnel as well as businesses in the private sector. In the late 1980s Puerto Rican terrorists have been responsible for most of the domestic terrorist incidents within the United States.

Territorial claims are the political objectives of many terrorist groups throughout the world, and such desires are among the easiest to understand, though not necessarily the easiest to resolve. In some instances the political views are not articulated with great clarity. For example, in the 1970s one of the most active groups within the United States was the Weather Underground. The Weather

Underground and its associated group, the New World Liberation Front, claimed responsibility for bombing the U.S. Capitol in 1971 and the Department of State four years later. Arising from the national convention of the Students for a Democratic Society in June 1969, the organization espoused political views that constituted an amalgam of the teachings of Marx, Rousseau, Freud, and various anarchists. One of their chief theoreticians described the Weather Underground's purpose through the lyrics of a Bob Dylan song: " 'The pump don't work 'cause the vandals took the handles.' That's what we're about—being vandals in the mother country."[8]

Like the Weather Underground in the United States, the Japanese Red Army also arose from an extremist student organization, the Zengakuren. In the 1960s the membership of the Japanese Red Army, like the recruits to the Weather Underground, came dominantly from the student left. The Japanese Red Army, like the Weather Underground, believed that the basic pillars of modern society, the foundations of Western civilization and capitalism, had to be destroyed for the purification of contemporary life. Whereas the American Weather Underground also reflected the principles of romanticism—a purity in simplicity and individual expression, the Japanese Red Army coupled its Marxist teachings with the traditions of the Samurai. In both terrorist groups the appeal was ideological and often difficult to follow.

The stated objectives of two contemporary terrorist groups is to right historical wrongs. The Armenian Secret Army for the Liberation of Armenia (ASALA) has accepted responsibility for the killing of at least thirty-five Turkish diplomats or immediate family members since 1975. Their objectives are to gain Turkey's acknowledgment of and acceptance for the massacre of approximately a million and a half Armenians in 1915. A second terrorist organization, the Jewish Defense League, came into existence not to gain acknowledgment of the Holocaust perpetrated by the Nazis in World War II, but to insure that this would "never again" take place. Founded by Rabbi Meir Kahane in 1968, the JDL's activities moved from the protection of elderly New York Jews to bombings, arsons, and harassment of Soviet diplomats and Soviet delegations to publicize the plight of Soviet Jewry.

In the last quarter of the twentieth century, terror in the name of religion has been commonly experienced. Protestant and Catholic terrorist groups have been active in Northern Ireland for decades, and the Jewish terrorist organizations, Irgun Zyai Leumi and LEHI, had actively fought the British mandatory authorities in Palestine until Britain withdrew as the mandatory power. Religiously motivated terrorism of recent date has become associated with Shiite radicalism. One of the oldest of the Shiite groups, Hiab al-Da'wa al-Islamiyya, or the "Party of the Islamic Call," originated in Iraq. It took responsibility for the bombing of the American embassy in Kuwait in 1983. Al-Da'wa began operations within Iraq in the 1960s in reaction to the treatment of the Shiites by the Baathist regime.[9] With the rise of the Khomeini regime in Iran, other Shiite terrorist groups have been spiritually guided, supported, and aided by Iran. Amal and the Hizballah activities in the Bekaa Valley have been directed against the United States, Israel, and France as well as other Lebanese groups. In part, the rise of fundamental Islamic terrorism is a consequence of the impact of modernity upon traditional Islamic societies. Challenges to traditions bring severe dislocations, and with such disruptions there arises a desire to restore the purity of the traditional way of life.

Irrespective of the objective pursued by the terrorist group, the actions are politically motivated and violent. Furthermore, unlike conventional or guerrilla warfare, the terrorist is indiscriminate in the use of violence. As paradoxical as it may appear, the civilized nations of the world have adopted international conventions of warfare in an attempt to minimize the loss of innocent lives. The 1949 Geneva Conventions are the dominant body of international humanitarian law pertaining to armed conflict. One of the overriding principles of the conventions is the distinction between lawful combatants who are legitimate targets in warfare and civilians who are not legitimate targets. The 1949 Geneva Conventions recognized that those who engaged in the willful slaughter of innocents for politically motivated reasons would not be deterred by society's normal restraints. Those engaging in such actions, consequently, should not be extended the same privileges granted to soldiers, such as the protections given to prisoners of war. By recognizing the heinous nature of the offense, international conventions denied the right of a terrorist to justify the murder of innocents by the rightness of the cause. Causes may be just or unjust, but the justness of the cause does not legitimate the killing of innocents.

War is not neatly directed, and innocents do lose their lives in such conflicts. But when loss of life occurs as a consequence of misdirected fire, errors in intelligence, or accident, the deaths are an aberration from the norms of warfare. The often-repeated contention that ''one man's freedom fighter is another man's terrorist'' fails to appreciate that even the struggle for freedom is guided by limits. An unwillingness to make moral judgments of condemnation against those terrorists for whose cause you have sympathy opens a Pandora's box of moral relativism that ultimately undermines the ability to condemn all acts of terrorism—even those directed at causes that you support. For that reason, distinctions between terrorism on one hand and guerrilla warfare or freedom fighters on the other hand that use motives as the standard of definition are of little value. Such distinctions are more often than not used as rationalizations to support causes for which there is sympathy.

## TERRORISM AND THE CORPORATION

Terrorism, unlike criminal activity, is politically motivated. Unlike warfare, terrorism is indiscriminate in the selection of its victims. As a consequence, such indiscriminate violence nurtures a fear—partly based on a rational concern for safety and partly based on a fear of the unknown or unpredictability. The terror that is engendered in society by such acts exaggerates society's perception of the military capability of the terrorist as well as the actual number of casualties due to such incidents.

Of greater importance, the inability of a government to provide total security for its inhabitants calls into question its legitimacy. In nondemocratic countries, the claim to govern may rest simply on force. A demonstration that the existing governing body does not monopolize power and cannot offer security to the populace threatens to undermine the continued submission of that populace to its power.

Even the foundations of democratic rule are threatened by terrorist activity. Modern liberal democracies are founded on the doctrine of natural rights, the principles of which were first articulated in the writings of two English political philosophers, Thomas Hobbes (1588-1679) and John Locke (1632-1704). Perhaps the most familiar expression of the natural-rights doctrine is to be found in the American Declaration of Independence, where Thomas Jefferson wrote "that all Men are created equal, that they are endowed by their Creator with certain unalienable rights, that among these are Life, Liberty, and the Pursuit of Happiness." Jefferson goes even further by asserting that all humans possess these natural rights by virtue of their Creator—not as a result of governmental action. Governments, the declaration declares, "are instituted among Men" to secure such rights. Stated succinctly, the purpose of modern liberal democracy is to secure life, liberty, and the pursuit of happiness.

Central to the protection of these natural rights is property, which is an extension, in Chief Justice John Marshall's words, "from the right which every man retains to acquire property, to dispose of that property according to his own judgment, and to pledge himself for a future act. These rights are not given by society, but are brought into it."[10] Possessions are the consequence of human faculties, and the protection of those faculties is the responsibility of government. Understood in this way, the natural-rights doctrine encourages free enterprise, encourages individuals to seek labor and profit and in so doing to benefit the public as well as the individual. Security of property also provides benefit for individual and public security and encourages a general calm on society. Real production contributes to the general economic prosperity and power of the nation.

Because liberal economics and liberal democracy came forth from the same philosophical womb, we should not be surprised that the commercial activities of liberal democracies are inviting targets for terrorists' words and deeds. Gudrun Ensslin, of the West German Baader-Meinhof gang, wrote that "we set fires in department stores so that you will stop buying. The compulsion to buy terrorizes you." The Italian Red Brigades justified their acts of terrorism as punishing the servants of imperialism. In December 1973 the Italian terrorists kidnapped a personnel director of Fiat. Later the Red Brigades defined their adversaries as the "multinational imperialist state" (*stato imperialista multinazionale*).[11]

In the mind of left-wing terrorists, multinational corporations are part of the "imperialist state." The business community is perceived as an extension of the government and, consequently, a legitimate target for their violent actions. On January 15, 1985, two terrorist organizations, the West German Red Army Faction and the French Action Directe, issued a communiqué announcing a political-military front to battle against Western imperialism or predominantly U.S. imperialism.[12] The communiqué was followed by a number of terrorist incidents. Two Americans were killed and twenty others injured by a car bomb at the U.S. Rhein-Main Air Force Base in Frankfurt, Germany, in August 1985. In September of that year, bombs planted by the Red Army Faction destroyed three mobile radar units at a U.S. air base in West Germany. Other successful attacks against NATO installations followed, as well as assassinations. French Brigadier General Rene Audran had been murdered in January and West German industrialist Ernst Zimmerman on February 1, 1985. Altogether, the U.S. Department of State recorded 218 terrorist attacks in Europe during 1985.

The increased incidence of terrorism throughout Europe in this period was not limited strictly to military targets. The Belgium terrorist organization, the Fighting Communist Cells, took responsibility for attacking a Brussels gas and electric company headquarters. A Brussels steel company was bombed. In Hamburg, West Germany, six department stores were firebombed. The Revolutionary Cells, associated with the Red Army Faction, claimed responsibility for attacks on a botanical research institute and car dealership in Cologne. During the same period of time, multinational corporations distinctly identified with the United States came under attack as well. Honeywell, Motorola, and Litton were all attacked in Brussels.

European terrorists have not been the only ones to identify corporate targets as legitimate, that is, as critical institutions of a society that they hope to change if not destroy and as symbols of society itself. In the 1970s multinational corporations—especially American corporations—were the targets for attack and their executive leadership identified for kidnapping in Latin America. Stanley Sylvester, manager of a Swift meat-packing plant in Argentina, was abducted by the Argentinian terrorists, Rosario Group, in May 1971. The Rosarios insisted that the meat-packing firm rehire three hundred employees who had been released, reduce established work quotas, and distribute $50,000 worth of food to working-class neighborhoods. Swift and Company complied with the demands, and Sylvester was released one week later. The president of Fiat of Argentina, Oberdan Sallustro, was kidnapped in March 1972. He was killed when police stormed the hideout in an attempt to free him. In June 1972 the president of the Buenos Aires branch of the Italian Banco di Napoli was kidnapped; in September 1972 an Italian industrialist was kidnapped; and the kidnappings continued through 1974.

1986 was a year in which terrorist attacks were directed against oil companies in Venezuela and Colombia by the National Liberation Army, the ELN. The same terrorist organization kidnapped Richard Pauson, an official of the Occidental Petroleum Company, on March 9, 1987. American banks were bombed in Lima, Peru, on March 31, 1987, by the Movimiento Revolucionaria Tupac

Amaru (Tupac Amaru Revolutionary Movement, MRTA). Attacks against Western targets are not geographically limited.

Whereas left-wing terrorist groups throughout the world identify multinational corporations and industry as part of a political-economic exploitation of the deprived of the world, terrorist groups of the right also have viewed multinational corporations as part of an international exploitation of their nation's resources. This has been the cry of some West German neo-Nazi terrorist movements. The Volkssozialistische Bewegung Deutschlands-Partei der Arbeit (Popular Socialist Movement of German-Party of Labor, VSBD-PdA) sees multinational corporations as vultures who are out for their own profit.

For this reason, paradoxical though it may appear, terrorist movements of the left and right find common ground in their dispositions toward corporations. When, as in the 1980s, European political issues centered around the environment, the economy, and the positioning of nuclear arms in Europe, cooperation among European terrorist groups of both the left and the right against NATO and American troops, corporations, and interests became possible. In June 1985 Frankfurt officials were informed through a letter that a bomb that killed three people at the German city's airport had been placed to protest pollution. Karl-Heinz Beckurts, a fifty-six-year-old nuclear physicist and chief of research and development for Siemens Electrical Company, was murdered by a remote-controlled bomb in Munich in July 1986. In a seven-page letter signed by the Red Army Faction, the terrorists wrote, "Attack the current strategic projects of the political, economic and military formation of the imperialist systems in Western Europe!"[13] The letter also condemned the Siemens Company's role in planning a nuclear waste reprocessing plant in Wackersdorf. Later in the same month that Beckurts was murdered, a car bomb exploded outside the headquarters of a southern German aerospace firm, the Dornier Company in Immenstaad; and heavy damage was caused to the offices of the Fraunhofer Research Institute in Aachen, a firm engaged in research involving sensors in space. Following these attacks, Kurt Rebmann, a German federal prosecutor in charge of antiterrorist investigations, said that "evidence existed of a 'coordinated offensive' against companies and organizations that had military contracts, most notably those perceived as having a role in the United States anti-missile program as well as the European high-technology research program."[14]

## TERRORIST MEANS OF ATTACK

Over the years terrorists have used a variety of threats and attacks against corporations. Many of these means, of course, have been used against government and military targets as well.

Bombings, both threatened and actual, have been commonly used. The Jaffee Center's Project on Low Intensity Warfare estimates that of 377 terrorist incidents in 1987, 172 (46 percent) were bombings or arson.[15] The cheapest and easiest form is an incendiary bomb. A Molotov cocktail, a bottle filled with gasoline or other form of inflammable mixture and a rag to use as a fuse, can cause a major explosion. Explosive bombs constitute the second category of bombs. As in the case of an incendiary bomb, a cheap fragmentation device can be constructed from a lead pipe filled with black powder. Though pipe bombs are not difficult to construct, terrorist organizations have demonstrated a capacity to utilize more technical sophistication in the construction of explosive devices. Barometric bombs, plastic explosives, time-delay fuses, and combinations of these devices have been used—especially in bombs planted in airplanes.

Kidnappings constituted 54 (14 percent) of the 377 terrorist incidents in 1987. Businessmen and corporate executives have been a favorite target of terrorists. One of the reasons why corporate executives are such inviting targets is the willingness of multinational corporations to meet the demands and the desire of companies to do so rapidly and quietly. Abductions in Latin America were common in the 1960s and 1970s. The Tupamaros, an urban terrorist organization in Uruguay, carried out in the late 1960s a number of abductions of business executives to embarrass the Uruguayan government. Contrary to their expectations, the Tupamaros' activity ushered in a military government that proved successful in countering terrorism. It was in Argentina, however, that kidnappings were carried out from May 1971 through September 1974 in seemingly epidemic proportions. As discussed earlier, the demands made in the early 1970s were for corporations to support philanthropic causes—whether school supplies and shoes for poor children or food for the Argentine poor. Brian Jenkins, director of the Rand Corporation's program on terrorism, points out that terrorists then altered the nature of their demands from "philanthropy to cash payments paid directly to the terrorists."[16] Such payments were used to support future terrorist operations.

In those years governments also yielded to terrorist demands and paid ransoms or released prisoners. Brazil released prisoners on four different occasions between 1969 and 1971 to gain the release of kidnapped foreign diplomats. Greece capitulated to the demands of terrorists in July 1970 to free a hijacked Olympic Airways plane. Switzerland, Germany, and Great Britain released prisoners to obtain the release of their nations' citizens being held by Palestinians in Jordan. Similar instances can be recorded for West Germany, Guatemala, Haiti, and the Dominican Republic.[17] Argentina announced in March 1970 that its policy was not to pay ransom and became the first country to do so. Other nations followed Argentina's policy. The United States adopted a firm no-ransom policy in 1973, though changes in its policy can be traced back to 1971.[18]

A consequence of the many kidnappings in Argentina in the 1970s was the withdrawal and disinvestment from the country by a number of multinational corporations. ITT, IBM, Coca-Cola, John Deer, Otis Elevator, and Alcan all left Argentina at this time.

Hijackings of aircraft accounted for only 4 (1 percent) of the 377 terrorist incidents in 1987.[19] Although the number of hijackings is small, the hijackings of civil airplanes are highly publicized events involving a large number of hostages from different nations on airplanes that cost in the millions of dollars. In the air hijackings in the 1970s, many planes were commandeered in attempts to escape to other nations. Many of those hijackings originating in the United States had Cuba as their objective. These actions, like extortion attempts to gain money from airlines, were criminal activities and not terrorist activity in the strict sense of the definition. Those individuals, for example, who hijacked commercial airliners for travel to Cuba were not guilty of political crimes.

Like many corporations doing business outside their country's own borders, airlines are easily identified with a nation. National airlines, of course, are in themselves national symbols. Statistics from the Jaffee Center suggest that from 1983 to 1987 there were 206 terrorist attacks on civil aviation. France (36), United States (35), Japan (17), Iran (16), United Kingdom (15), Israel (14), West Germany (11), Jordan (10), and Saudi Arabia (10) led the list of nations whose planes were targeted by terrorists. Thirty-six percent of the total attacks took place in Western Europe.[20] Furthermore, most of the attacks on civilian aviation in Western Europe were carried out by terrorists outside of the region— primarily Palestinian and Shiite groups.[21] In fact, 68.4 percent of all attacks on civilian aviation in this period were carried out by these groups.

Hijackings of civil aviation planes and attacks on airports have resulted in a significant number of international forums being convened to act on this problem. Although the problem itself obviously has not been solved, the forums have adopted numerous international conventions. The adoption of such conventions and accords pertaining to terrorism and civil aviation is especially instructive as to why nations have or have not cooperated to control terrorism in general. When nations have been immune from the scourge of terrorism or have themselves been supportive of terrorist groups whose action is perceived as furthering their interests, cooperation to end terrorist activity cannot be obtained. When few nations, if any, are free from the dangers of attack, all nations perceive common advantage in cooperating against terrorism.

A case in point is the policy of the Soviet Union on the hijackings of civil airplanes. When an Israeli airliner was attacked in Zurich in 1970, the Soviet response was to describe the attack in mild tones as "regrettable." But when two Lithuanian citizens hijacked a Soviet domestic airliner and flew to Turkey, where they requested and received asylum in October 1974, the Soviets branded them "criminal murderers." The Soviet Union and Eastern European countries experienced 38 hijackings from 1977 to 1986—an indication that this form of activity is as common as it is in Western Europe.[22] The Soviets have been signators to many international conventions on civil aviation. Yet there have been other efforts by nations to obtain international cooperation against terrorism in which the Soviets and Warsaw Pact countries have not been cooperative.[23]

Product Contamination has also been used by terrorists to disrupt the economy of targeted nations or in attempts to extort sums of money from targeted corporations, though in most cases such crimes have been committed by extortionists without political aims. Poisoned products have been placed on supermarket shelves in extortion attempts. A Japanese group laced packages of candy and food with cyanide and demanded extortion money. The group, "The Man with 21 Faces," was never captured. The U.S. Food and Drug Administration reports that in 1985 there were 120 cases of food tampering reported, while the figure in 1986 increased to 1,720 cases.[24] The dramatic rise in reported cases may be a function of record keeping as well as a consequence of the "copycat" effect. In 1979 a Palestinian terrorist group identifying itself as the "Organization of Metropolitan Proletariat and Oppressed Peoples" injected poison into grapefruit exported from Israel to European markets. Poisoned grapefruits were in fact discovered in Rome and Naples. Chilean fruit marketed in the United States was suspected by U.S. authorities of being tainted by poison. Fruit from Chile was embargoed from leaving U.S. docks for shipment to markets. The consequence for the Chilean fruit industry in 1989 was a significant loss. Other threats to contaminate products on behalf of political causes have been made: in 1986 a threat was made to poison tea from Sri Lanka, and threats to various South African products have been made as well.

In the case of product contamination, the mere suspicion of danger to the consumer is sufficient to disrupt the normal buying pattern. Furthermore, once a consumer alters the traditional buying pattern, there is no certainty as to when the regular pattern of consumption will resume. When the product that has been altered is fruit, the natural biological results of spoilage aid the terrorist in accomplishing the objective.

Computer espionage and contamination are increasingly becoming a major concern of multinational corporations. As more and more of a corporation's daily activities are computer dependent, corporations find it difficult if not impossible to conduct business when their computers are down. This is especially true for banks, insurance companies, and any large corporation responsible for wide-ranging distribution of goods or services.

Protection of computer data itself is becoming of great concern and has resulted in a $3-billion-a-year industry devoted to this purpose. One of the concerns is the demonstrated capability of computer hackers to penetrate data banks to steal information. On March 3, 1989, West German authorities charged Marcus Hess with successfully infiltrating about 30 computer systems. Estimates from authorities indicate that he attempted to infiltrate at least 450 to obtain information that then was sold to the Soviet Union. According to accounts, Hess placed a telephone call in Hanover, Germany, that enabled him to connect through European lines and gain access across the Atlantic to networks within the United States. Inside the electronic system Hess apparently used key words to search for desired information. Computer systems at Lawrence Berkeley Laboratories, Thomson C.S.F., a French military and electronics manufacturer, and N. V. Philips, a Dutch electronics firm, were penetrated.[25]

Not only is there concern that vital information might be stolen, but concern exists as well that the introduction of computer "viruses" might destroy or even paralyze a computer system. At the present time, equipment and software to guard against such contamination are being designed and sold.

## CORPORATION SECURITY

Multinational corporations are not sovereign entities and are dependent upon states for security and legal protection. Though corporations most likely have their own security divisions and established procedures for the protection of personnel and property, corporation security activity is dependent upon the latitude of action permitted by a state. What is permitted varies from state to state.

States are ultimately responsible for securing their internal affairs. This important political fact—though obvious—must not be forgotten by corporation executives. The actions of governments are still the most obvious and critical factor affecting corporations. For this reason, the assessment of the dangers posed to the corporation by terrorism must begin with an assessment of the nature of the political regime itself.[26]

The economic activity that a corporation engages in within any country takes place within a context that is directly affected by the existing political conditions. Even if a corporation finds itself able to conduct business within a country after a revolution has taken place, the activities are now undertaken in a slightly different context with new political considerations. For this very reason, those responsible for the security of corporation personnel and physical plants or those responsible for assessing the political risks upon the business climate must concentrate upon the concrete—everyday political life.

From a political perspective, changes in the forms of government are not always to be feared. Changes—even violent ones—can take place for the better, but violent changes can also take place for the worse. Corporations do, of course, have a general understanding of what kinds of political climates are most conducive to successful economic operations and, like the thoughtful theorist, can be guided by some standard of better or worse. There is a consistency in values between those political regimes that promote political participation and individual initiative and place value on human rights and those forms of economic activity that are also dependent upon individual initiative and security for life, liberty, and the pursuit of happiness. In the same way, there has also been a congruence between regimes that limit individual action and initiative and an economic system that is planned with little allowance for private enterprise.

Change of any kind is consequently a sign that must concern those responsible for security. Again, the change must be assessed in light of the nature of the regime and the particular arrangement of offices that exist within that particular country. Changes can be consistent with existing conditions or can indicate a deviation from existing principle or practice.

An example will illustrate the importance of such an assessment. A particular Southeast Asian nation is interested in attracting multinational corporations to operate within its borders. The nation possesses an educated population and limited but useful natural resources, but it has not been as successful as surrounding nations in attracting foreign investment. In part, the difficulties are political. Once a colonial nation, it was successful in eliminating an indigenous terrorist movement that was aided by a larger middle power. Politically, our nation describes itself as a constitutional monarchy.

Among its most serious problems is communalism. Its people consist of three communal groups, and one of the communal elements constituted the former terrorist threat—though not all or even a majority of them supported the terrorists. Upon independence an agreement was made between the two largest communal groups to divide political and economic influence between them. The largest of the population groups would insure that it maintained dominant political control while the second-largest population group would maintain its hold upon the economic sectors of the country.

Over time the majority population group has expressed dissatisfaction with the existing relationship: a demand arises for increased economic influence and the rewards that accompany economic control. At the same time, a latent issue, always potentially troubling, comes of age: Islamic fundamentalism. An appeal is made by the Muslim population to guide life within the laws of the faith. The Muslim population and the majority communal group tend to be the same. Communal tensions, as a consequence, are fueled by growing religious tensions.

For those responsible for the security of any multinational corporation doing business in this nation, there are many changes that are significant, if not threatening for the moment. Because there is a past history of communal violence as well as terrorism, any change in the delicate balance between the elements constituting the nation must be taken seriously. These changes alter the economic and political arrangement of the nation. As such, they are changes that are more fundamental than cosmetic. What indicators and questions should be observed and asked by those responsible for corporate security?

The first question has been asked: do these changes usher in conditions that require more careful scrutiny? The answer is clearly yes. The second question must again relate back to the nature of the regime. To what extent does the existing regime protect the constitutional rights of all of the people? What mechanisms exist within the institutional structure to secure such rights? Have these mechanisms worked in the past and are they operative at the present? If the changes in the economic and political balance between the two largest communal groups suggest that the present administration is willing to ignore existing safeguards, then the analyst must carefully scrutinize newspapers, television and radio, public speeches, and communal newspapers for accusations that such safeguards are not being maintained. Another indicator that can be observed concerns the outward migration of populations. Who is leaving and where are they going?

At the same time, concern must be given to the reaction to these changes from other nations. In this case there is some concern for a neighboring nation that previously encouraged and aided terrorist activity. Are there indicators from sources external to our nation or internal to the nation that support is coming from abroad for the communal minority?

All of these assessments concern the possibility that communal violence might result in terrorist activity that ultimately would endanger present and future corporate activity. If communal terrorism does occur and the corporation is identified as a legitimate target, new questions concerning the character of the terrorist organization and the means of operation must be addressed.

First, the analyst must attempt to understand every piece of information that can be obtained about the terrorist organization. Again, many of the obvious considerations must be addressed. Who constitutes the membership of the terrorist organization? Is the membership strictly communal in character? Are the terrorists attracting recruits from all age groups, from both sexes, and from all areas of the country? Second, what are the objectives of the terrorist organization? Is it possible to discern from the organization's public statements or captured documents the stated objectives? Not all terrorist groups publicize their activities through publications. For example, the French Action Directe published very little, while the Italian Red Brigades wrote long explications about their actions.

In analyzing the documents of any terrorist organization, the analyst must show some care. The stated ideological beliefs are important to understand, but they may not reflect the attitudes of the entire terrorist organization. A document may reflect the particular views of one segment of the organization—perhaps the particular author of the document—and may not reflect differences in views that exist within the membership. Furthermore, a public document is public and not private. This means that the intention of the author(s) is to convey particular impressions to the audience that will gain or maintain public support for a cause. The nature of the document must be understood. Who is the document for? What is its purpose?

One of the major problems for any corporation attempting to acquire intelligence about a terrorist organization concerns the different levels or cells of the terrorist group itself. What is most visible to the outside world is not the operational structure of the terrorist organization but its support structure. The support system is much larger than the operational wing of a terrorist organization. It provides ideological support and economic aid and even acts as a conduit to provide legal and medical aid when necessary. Corporations must be alert not only to the general support structure within the nation, but to any specific signs that such support exists within the corporate organization itself. To what extent are the terrorists attempting to organize communal members within the corporation?

## PROGNOSIS

Unlike diseases, there is no vaccine for a corporation to immunize itself against terrorists. Nor can we expect to see acts of terrorism disappear in the future. As long as politically motivated elements perceive themselves as too weak politically or militarily to engage their adversary, the possibility of terrorism exists. Furthermore, as long as nations see the support of terrorist groups as furthering their objectives with little cost, state support of terrorism will continue, and international cooperation will be unable to solve the basic issues.

Corporations are not in a position to do battle with terrorists. The cost to personnel as well as corporation assets is too high. Most importantly, the purpose of corporations is not to be confused with that of governments. But corporations must be concerned with their own security and the extent to which terrorist activity disrupts their commercial ventures. For that reason alone, corporations must secure the kind of intelligence that will enable them to advise their personnel wisely as to the proper measures that they can implement for protection.

Personnel must be advised of the dangers of an overseas assignment and of travel in general. They must be advised of the dangers of kidnapping and of attack. Procedures must be established within the corporation that will enable it to work quickly and clandestinely with insurance agents and officials of foreign governments as well as officials of its own government.

Corporations, like governments, will never be able to control all of the factors that will enable them to dodge the terrorist arm. To promise such control would be to misrepresent the possible. Yet to act in ignorance is to invite disaster. There is no choice but to prepare for the unexpected.

## NOTES

1. Cited in Elie Kedourie, "Political Terrorism in the Muslim World," in *Terrorism: How the West Can Win*, ed. Benjamin Netanyahu (New York: Farrar, Straus, Giroux, 1986), 71.

2. Jerrold M. Post, "Hostilité, Conformité, Fraternité: The Group Dynamics of Terrorist Behavior," *International Journal of Group Psychotherapy* 36 (April 1986): 212.

3. Quoted in Nathan Leites, "Understanding the Next Act," *Terrorism: An International Journal* 3 (1979): 29.

4. Walter Laqueur, *The Age of Terrorism* (Boston and Toronto: Little, Brown and Company, 1987), 48ff.

5. Leites, "Understanding the Next Act," 8.

6. Jerrold M. Post, "It's Us against Them: The Group Dynamics of Political Terrorism," *Terrorism: An International Journal* 10 (1987): 23–35.

7. Ariel Merari, Anat Kurz, Maskit Burgin, Sofia Kotzer, Yoel Kozak, Tamar Prat, David Tal, Yael Treiber, and Orit Zilka, *INTER: International Terrorism in 1987* (Jerusalem: Jerusalem Post, 1988).

8. John Kifner, "That's What the Weathermen Are Supposed to Be . . . 'Vandals in the Mother Country,' " *New York Times Magazine*, January 4, 1970, 15.

9. See Martin Kramer, "The Structure of Shi'ite Terrorism," in *Contemporary Trends in World Terrorism*, ed. Anat Kurz (New York and Westport, Conn.: Praeger Publishers, 1987), 43–52; Yoram Schweitzer, "Terrorism: A Weapon in the Shi'ite Arsenal," ibid., 66–74; and Elie Kedourie, "Political Terror in the Muslim World," *Encounter* 68 (February 1987): 12–16.

10. *Ogden v. Saunders*, 12 Wheaton (U.S.) 346 (1827).

11. Quoted in Daniela Salvioni and Anders Stephanson, "Reflections on the Red Brigades," *Orbis* 29 (Fall 1985): 495.

12. *Facts on File*, January 18, 1985, p. 19, D1.

13. *Washington Post*, July 10, 1986, A1.

14. *New York Times*, July 26, 1986, 2A.

15. Merari et al., *INTER*, 124.

16. Brian Jenkins, "The Payment of Ransom," in *Terrorism and Personal Protection*, ed. Brian Jenkins (Boston and London: Butterworth Publishers, 1985), 225–26.

17. Ibid., 224–25.

18. Ibid.

19. Merari et al., *INTER*, 124.

20. Ibid., 75.

21. Ibid., 76.

22. Ibid., 83.

23. See Seymour M. Finger, "The United Nations Response to Terrorism," in *Political Terrorism and Business: The Threat and Response*, ed. Yonah Alexander and Robert A. Kilmarx (New York: Praeger Publishers, 1979), 257–80.

24. This discussion is based largely on Brian Michael Jenkins, "The Threat of Product Contamination," *TVI Report* 8, no. 3 (1989): 1–3.

25. "Computer Detective Followed Trail to Hacker Spy Suspect," *Washington Post*, March 4, 1989, A1; "Race to Secure Computers Threatens Free Exchange of Data," *Washington Post*, March 4, 1989, D11–D12; "West German Charged with Espionage in Computer Intrusion Investigation," *Washington Post*, March 4, 1989, A16; "Bonn Suspect Denies Espionage Was Goal of Computer Intrusions," *New York Times*, March 4, 1989, A1.

26. For a different perspective on the importance of assessing the country risk, see Patrick James and Jesse Goldstraub, "Terrorism and the Breakdown of International Order: The Corporate Dimension," *Conflict Quarterly* 8 (Summer 1988): 81–85.

# 13

# The Intelligence Approach to the Management of Corporate Intelligence: The Pragmatic Concerns of Terrorism

## Robert J. Kühne

Multinational companies doing business in the international arena are exposed to a variety of political risks, all affecting the profitability of the businesses. Examples of political risks companies face include expropriation or nationalization, currency devaluation or inconvertibility, involuntary divestiture, revolutions, coups d'état or civil disorder, export or import embargoes, and political terrorism. An evaluation of the experiences of companies with political risk over the last two decades indicates that the more successful the international expansion of the company, the higher the degree of political risk encountered. The success of the multinational, with the congruent high visibility and importance in a foreign country's economy, is often seen as a threat to the total economy or may easily be turned into the scapegoat for total social or economic problems.

The political risks companies are exposed to are not new or limited to certain parts of the world. As a result, management should plan for and anticipate these risks and adopt corporate policies and strategies to minimize the exposure. Multinationals with a high degree of local ownership but not contributing as much as before to the local economy or companies that negotiated unusually favorable arrangements are especially prone to changes in their business conditions. Under expropriation the host country forces the company to give up assets and operations for which the company receives compensation (often below the actual value) from the host country. Whereas expropriation may be limited to one company, nationalization refers to the taking of all corporate activities in a specific industry. It is often assumed that this type of political risk is limited to less developed countries, but this is not exactly true. Examples are the nationalization of the steel industry in the United Kingdom or the banks in France. According to the World Bank, by the early 1980s a total of 1,535 firms from 22 different countries had been expropriated in 511 separate actions by 76 nations.[1]

The risks of currency devaluation and inconvertibility are part of a company's foreign exchange exposure risk and may result in financial losses for the company. If the currency of the host country devalues in relation to the company's home-country currency, funds to be repatriated as profits and investment repayments will be worth less in terms of the home-country currency, and losses will be incurred. The most extreme risk is inconvertibility, whereby the local currency is not exchangeable for a foreign currency. Companies can manage this foreign exchange exposure risk through formulation of strategies aimed at anticipating changes in the political and economic environment of the host country and adapting the financial policies of the company and the subsidiary in the foreign country.[2]

Host-country governments may force foreign companies with subsidiaries in their countries into involuntary divestiture. This can range from requirements for the sharing of ownership in local subsidiaries with nationals to the sale of the commercial or technical side of the business to local investors.[3]

Revolutions, coups d'état, or civil disorder in the host country may affect the short- and/or long-term operations of the subsidiary, and not necessarily in a negative manner. The outcome depends on the new regime coming to power, which may have a more positive or negative attitude toward foreign-owned businesses than the regime it replaces, resulting in either an improved or worsened business climate. To avoid being taken by surprise by a change in the government or civil disorder, a company must monitor on a continuous basis the political trends in each country in which it operates. Monitoring of the political climate will allow the company to take the necessary steps in advance to reduce the risk to property and employees. For example, companies with a proper monitoring system were prepared for the overthrow of the political leaders in Iran, Nicaragua, and the Philippines, and could therefore reduce losses.

The continued success of the multinational corporation is influenced by the restrictions on trade and investment flows. Nations often try to reduce imports through protectionist legislation or import tariffs and may impose restraints on exports. Multinationals may benefit from protectionist legislation in the host country if this legislation was designed to protect the MNC's industry. However, the same legislation may make it impossible for the MNC to enter this local market by means of exporting. The difficulty will be to anticipate future protectionist legislation when determining the location of manufacturing facilities designed to supply multiple markets.

Recent carefully planned and executed terrorist attacks in Europe, the Middle East, and Latin America have renewed the corporate focus on terrorism as part of the company's exposure to political risk. It is suggested here that most writings on the topic of terrorism are too narrow in scope, sensationalize terrorism too much, and omit looking at normal corporate intelligence management as a means to deal with the terrorism risks. The latter should be part of the day-to-day business risk assessment.

The definition of terrorism as "the systematic use of terror especially as a means of coercion"[4] should be used in the broadest sense to include the forms of extortion actions against the organization by outsiders that may have a direct or indirect impact on the organization. The most publicized forms of terrorist activity are the kidnapping or harming of people and threats (and actual implementation thereof) against property and products. Examples of terrorist attacks against people include the blowing up of Pan American Flight 103 over Scotland in 1988 and the kidnappings and/or assassinations of well-known industrialists. Two of the more prominent U.S. executives kidnapped in South America were William F. Niehous, general manager of Owens-Illinois, who was kidnapped in Caracas, Venezuela, in 1976, and Victor Samuelson, the manager of the Esso Argentina oil refinery, kidnapped in Campana, Argentina, in 1973. In both cases ransom demands were extremely large and involved not only payments of money but also the distribution of food to the poor and the publishing of the terrorists' ideology in major international newspapers.

The demands of Samuelson's kidnappers were met and he was released unharmed. In the case of Niehous, the Venezuelan government forbade the publication of the terrorist doctrine in Venezuelan newspapers. Niehous was held by the terrorists for three years and finally discovered by the Venezuelan police. He was fortunately unharmed and in good spirits.

Highly publicized kidnappings of non–U.S. executives include those of Hans-Martin Schleyer, a German industrialist in 1977, and Baron Edouard Jean Empain, a French executive, in 1978. Again, exorbitant ransom demands were made and, in the case of Schleyer, the release of imprisoned members of Germany's notorious Baader-Meinhof gang was demanded. French compliance resulted in the safe release of Empain, but the German reluctance to free the imprisoned guerrillas led to the brutal execution of Schleyer. More recent examples are the kidnapping and murder in 1988 of Dutch supermarket executive Gerrit-Jan Heijn and the kidnappings for mostly political reasons of Americans and other Europeans in Lebanon.

Damage in the form of sabotage or explosions to corporate property is part of terrorist techniques. Even though attacks against corporate computer and communications centers have not been very prevalent, the risk exposure is enormous. It will be only a matter of time until terrorist groups will become more aware of the vulnerability of these centers and the important role they play in the management of multinational companies.

Extortion through product tampering is a dimension of terrorism that also exposes companies to major risks. Any actual or threatened product tampering, especially contamination of a consumer product, receives widespread press coverage, resulting in major financial losses for the company. As a result of the reports of deaths from cyanide-laced Tylenol capsules in 1982, Johnson and

Johnson incurred millions of dollars of lost sales and market share. The company regained market share later due to its excellent handling of this crisis. In another product tampering case in 1989, the finding of poison in only two grapes from Chile resulted in a U.S. government import ban against all tropical fruits from Chile. While the ban was only temporary due to the perishable nature of the product group, growers in Chile and middlemen incurred enormous financial losses.

Companies in the United States have been rather fortunate, as most of the terrorist activities against people, property, and products have been confined to the Middle East, Europe, and Latin America. But the scope of terrorism is changing, and more terrorist activities should be expected within the U.S. borders in the years to come. "While they [terrorist attacks in the United States] still are relatively rare (the FBI recorded only seven or eight incidents last year [1985], and other reliable estimates are only slightly higher), there is a consensus among American security experts that now is the time for U.S. corporations to reassess their domestic security programs and establish defenses not only against theft and vandalism, but also against the same type of terrorist acts that occur elsewhere."[5] The United States provides the perfect stage for terrorism violence. The ease with which people can enter the United States and move about, combined with the mobility and reactive resources of the press, make the United States an attractive target. As a result, terrorist attacks can come from a wide variety of sources within or outside the United States. "The Iranian network in the U.S. is the most dangerous and troublesome of all the terror groups in the U.S.," says L. Carter Cornick, head of the Washington-based Counter-Terrorism Consultants and a former FBI counterterrorism agent.[6] Increased terrorist activities will not be limited to Iranian groups and may include Libyan and Shiite groups and the Arab group, the Popular Front for the Liberation of Palestine. An example of how far these groups reach can be seen in the bombing in San Diego of the automobile driven by Sharon Rogers, wife of the captain of the USS *Vincennes*, which was responsible for the 1988 downing of an Iranian commercial airplane, killing over 300 people.

Multinational companies with multiple facilities and extensive distribution channels around the world are especially assailable and will find it very difficult to protect their interests. This, however, should be seen in terms of the scope of terrorist attacks against companies and the likelihood of an actual attack occurring. When reviewing the popular press, one may get the impression that terrorism against companies is widespread, but an evaluation of the real events clearly indicates the opposite. The total number of terrorist incidents is actually very low, but each incident receives extensive press coverage. Executives should take an intelligent approach to the management of corporate intelligence and be pragmatic about terrorism. Terrorism is indeed a risk that may result in losses for the organization, but it should be managed and planned for like any other possible event and risk the company is exposed to. Even though the current risk of actually becoming the victim of a terrorist attack is limited, extensive planning is needed, due to the size of the possible financial and humanitarian losses if an attack occurs. Kidnapping of an employee may result in a variety of problems for the company, depending on whether a safe release can be arranged. Problems include possible ransom payments, loss of intelligence or know-how and experience the employer may have possessed, legal ramifications in the form of lawsuits from the employee, the employee's family, or shareholders, morale problems among other employees exposed to similar risks, and public-relations aspects.

The management of the terrorism risk must be proactive, whereby the company assesses its current exposure to the risk factors and takes the necessary steps to reduce the risk. The company must appreciate the strength of the terrorist groups and the weaknesses of the company. Terrorists are very good at what they do. Only through careful planning can the company change the balance of power between the terrorist groups and the company's strengths and weaknesses.

Company executives must anticipate terrorist attacks and adapt corporate activities as part of the planning cycle. To properly prepare, a decision support system must be set up. Intelligence information must be collected on a continuous basis, and the organized information must be provided to the right person in a timely manner so appropriate decisions can be made. If properly executed, the decision support system will make it possible for the company to take the necessary preventive steps to avoid becoming a victim of a terrorist attack and to manage the situation and to make intelligent decisions when an attack takes place and thereafter.

The management of the terrorism risk can be divided into three phases: pre-event, event, and postevent. It should include intelligence gathering, training of the expatriate managers, guidelines as to the corporate response to a terrorist attack, and postevent considerations. If terrorism is properly planned for, the financial and humanitarian losses of terrorist activities can be controlled and minimized.

## THE PRE-EVENT PHASE

### Intelligence Gathering

To reduce the risk and effects of terrorist activities against the company, a data base must be developed that includes an assessment of the company's current situation and risk exposure in all areas in which the company has employees and facilities, an understanding of the goals and techniques of terrorist groups, an identification of the composition and profiles of terrorists, and an analysis of geographic-specific risks. The latter is needed because the goals, techniques, targets, and tactics vary widely from country to country or region to region.

After having assessed the company's risk exposure by carefully reviewing all facilities and employees, it is important to understand the goals and tactics of the terrorist groups. Terrorism has become a highly sophisticated means of conducting modern guerrilla warfare.[7] While in the distant past terrorists were motivated primarily by the desire to acquire material goods such as land, money, and other valuables, the motives for modern guerrilla warfare are primarily political and ideological. Terrorist acts are not, as they may appear to be, random and senseless, but rather are means toward the end of undermining the political system that the terrorists oppose. Kidnappings of foreign executives serve this larger goal in one or more of several ways.

Because the worst enemy of a subversive revolutionary doctrine is a strong, prosperous working class, terrorists may kidnap corporate executives with the intent of discouraging foreign direct investments, thereby undermining the financial stability of the government in power. This, the terrorists hope, will lead to a deterioration of the economic and social well-being of the people and will plant the seeds of revolution in the minds of the large and discontented working class.[8]

Another objective of terrorist activity is publicity. Due to sophisticated communications technology, news of every international terrorist incident spreads quickly and commands the public's attention. As a result, small groups of terrorists gain a worldwide forum for airing their grievances and setting forth their ideologies.

Short-range objectives may be the release of imprisoned comrades or the financing of future terrorist ventures by means of ransoming kidnapped executives. Sometimes terrorists hope that a kidnapping will elicit a retaliatory response from the authorities that will entail some reduction in personal liberties, such as curfews and security checks. This will tend to foster general discontent among the people, which may result in friction with the present government.[9]

The number of executive kidnappings is increasing rapidly because these kidnappings are usually successful in meeting the objectives of the terrorists. Furthermore, the international publicity offered by the media gives terrorists a global spotlight in which to operate and thereby encourages other dissident groups to become more active in their endeavors. The great number of successful attacks encourages future attacks.

Terrorist successes are due to several factors. With modern communications and powerful weaponry, it has become easier for small groups of terrorists to paralyze the normal activities of everyday life. By improving their communications systems and bringing their arsenals up to the technological standards of those of governments, the terrorists attain equal footing with their adversaries. Also, terrorist groups have certain advantages over their adversaries. Because their numbers are small and they are often the subject of constant police search, they use to the fullest these limited advantages:

### Surprise

Surprise is one of the terrorists' most effective weapons. They know the time, place, and procedures of the attack and the strengths and weaknesses of their victims. The victims, on the other hand, know nothing of the logistics of the operation in advance and often do not even know the size or strength of the organization that they are dealing with. Thus the terrorists start off with a tremendous advantage.[10]

### Fear

Terrorists try to make potential victims fearful so that they will be constantly on edge and more prone to awkward or irrational behavior. Fear also serves to distort the actual strength of the terrorist group.[11]

### Knowledge of the Terrain

Since the terrorists initiate the time and place of the incident, they have the opportunity to become familiar with the site far in advance of the time of operation. The victim and the forces involved in trying to save him may be relatively ignorant of the terrain and therefore overlook many of the details capitalized upon by the terrorists.

### Mobility and Speed

Given the time advantage usually conferred by surprise, mobility and speed become major factors in maximizing this advantage. If the terrorists can strike quickly and accomplish their objective before the victim can overcome the initial shock, their chances of success will be much greater.

### Information Network

The successful planning and implementation of operations depend on a sophisticated system of reconnaissance by which terrorists can obtain valuable information and monitor their victim's position, attitudes, strengths, and weaknesses. The more the terrorists learn about their adversaries, the greater their chance of circumventing retaliatory actions.[12]

Recent terrorist incidents have demonstrated that terrorist organizations have become highly adept at utilizing these advantages to the maximum extent. There is also evidence of collusion between sophisticated international terrorist organizations, which increases the likelihood that operations will be successful. The implementation of these five advantages to their fullest, coupled with the relative inability of the authorities or corporations to effectively combat these advantages, has contributed to a large extent to the recent success of terrorist activities.

Profiling terrorists will provide a better understanding of where and who the enemy is.[13] A distinction can be made between two types of terrorists: the "territorials" and the "nihilists." "Territorials" are like rural guerrillas and fight what is still essentially a territorial war with specific and limited goals in their respective nations. "Nihilists" are like urban guerrillas, who fight exclusively for psychological effect. The "nihilists" justify their actions on some vague concept of world revolution. Examples of the "territorials" are terrorist groups like the Irish Republican Army (IRA), the Puerto Rican independence group FALN, which frequently attacks power stations on the island, the Basque terrorist group ETA in Spain, which began a series of attacks on the Spanish Lemoniz nuclear power plant, and the Palestinian guerrillas who are fighting for a Palestinian homeland. The "nihilists" include groups as the Baader-Meinhof gang in West Germany, the Weathermen in the United States, the Japanese Red Army, the Red Brigades of Italy, and Germany's notorious Red Army Faction. The "nihilists" prime targets are leading industrialists.

These terrorist groups, however, do not work in isolation. The CIA reported that "the trend towards greater international contact and cooperation among terrorist groups that has already greatly enhanced operational capabilities of some of the organizations involved, seems likely to gain further momentum." The primary form of securing this type of international contact and cooperation among terrorists from different countries is at the elementary training stage, where they all get to know each other.

The Popular Front for the Liberation of Palestine (PFLP) training camp in South Yemen has trained Japanese, Dutch, North Americans, Latin Americans, West Germans, Irish, Spaniards, Scandinavians, Italians, Turks, and Iranians. Cooperation in the execution of terrorist acts can be illustrated by the attack on Israel's Lud Airport by four members of the Japanese Red Army. The four reportedly had received training in the PFLP camp, acquired weapons with the help of the Italian Red Brigades from Czechoslovakia, and travelled on false papers provided by the West German Baader-Meinhof gang.

The terrorist, as an individual, fits certain personal characteristics and personality parameters. Generally well educated, young (in the twenties or early thirties), from a well-to-do middle-class family, and unmarried best describes the profile of a terrorist. The terrorist is very dedicated, whatever the cause may be, idealistic, and prepared to sacrifice his life in the attainment of the objectives. The terrorist's dedication to the cause makes him a good "student"; there is no denying that terrorists are well trained, obedient, and loyal and thrive on an atmosphere of discipline and quasi-military social order.

Governments and businesses have not been prepared to combat terrorists on a sophisticated level and are only now developing the means of neutralizing the advantages terrorists have by gathering intelligence information on these terrorists and developing decision support systems to gather and process the intelligence information on a continuous basis. The next logical step in the pre-event stage is the taking of precautionary measures in an attempt to forestall terrorist attacks.

### Planning for Executive Protection

The pre-event stage must include, as already suggested, comprehensive intelligence gathering to anticipate and adapt to possible terrorist threats. This intelligence gathering is part of the corporate decision support system. The latter, however, must also include comprehensive planning to insure the safety of the corporate employees and their families, both at home and abroad. This planning for safety should be centered around the avoidance or minimization of risk where possible through precautionary security methods and the training of employees and their families as to proper response tactics in the event of an actual kidnapping.

The first step is the development of a "terrorist management team" consisting of personnel from different functional areas—legal, financial, security, personnel, and public relations. To work effectively, the team must be given the decision-making authority to prepare and institute precautionary security methods and handle (that is, make decisions about) any terrorist event. The size of this team must be limited to insure a rapid response in an orderly, calm, but speedy manner if an attack takes place. Extensive training and simulation must be part of the pre-event activities of the team.

The responsibility for the precautionary security methods lies both with the company and the employees. Companies must clearly indicate and give ample warning of the risks the employees and their families are exposed to, and through the "terrorist management team" they must provide a work environment as secure as possible and the training for employees and their families to protect themselves. Employees, on the other hand, must take the precautionary activities and tactics seriously without panicking. They must use their common sense and realize that their best defense weapon is being alert, aware, and attentive at all times.

Employees and the terrorist management team evaluating the risks should be cognizant of two factors that have a significant impact on the degree of risk: (1) the visibility of the company and (2) the visibility of the employee. Multinational companies often have a high visibility and are ideal targets for terrorists for several reasons:

1. Multinationals are often portrayed on the part of Communist and "nonaligned" governments, left-wing political parties, and "public-interest" groups as a symbol of the "ugly American" and as such are attractive targets for terrorists. Companies with very well known corporate names and a clear American connection are especially at risk.

2. Multinationals, as a result of their size and financial aspects, are perceived to be very rich, making them a perfect victim for extortion.

3. The type of business the company is in increases the degree of risk. For example, companies extracting raw materials, such as oil or mining companies, and companies in the defense industry are especially prone to terrorist attacks.

Employees need to be aware of how the terrorist group selects its targets. The overriding factor is visibility. The more prestige the person has within the local community, the higher the risk. This personal visibility, combined with a high visibility of the company, considerably increases the risk. Terrorists will also look for targets that are easily accessible and have a routine or pattern of life that is predictable, and those who are perceived to be rich themselves or work for rich companies. After studying what makes a perfect target, employees should be aware of the more common precautionary methods to avoid becoming a victim and what to do if one becomes the victim of a terrorist attack.

### Executive Protection: Precautionary Methods

Employees and their families can reduce the risk of becoming a target by taking a variety of precautionary steps. A few of the more important ones are discussed here, but it should be mentioned again that the number one and very best precautionary method is simply "common sense." By being aware of the risks and being alert and attentive, employees can significantly reduce the risk exposure. Next, they should implement the following steps:

- Maintain a low profile and avoid visibility. Executives and their families should try to keep their pictures out of the newspapers and off the television. Furthermore, the lifestyle should be modest and not give the impression of significant wealth.
- At the office and at home, executives should instruct their staffs never to divulge the whereabouts or general information on the executive or his family to strangers.
- The terrorist management team should prepare confidential files on the employees at risk and their offices and residences. This will make it possible to determine the authenticity of an alleged kidnapping and be useful in case of a hostage situation. These files should include the fingerprints, medical history, nicknames, hobbies, and other personal facts of the employees and their families. Information on the office and home, such as telephone numbers of neighbors, alarm systems, and location of telephone, gas, water, and electric lines should be included as well.[14]
- The accessibility of the executive can be significantly reduced by varying the routines. This includes modes of transportation, eating and recreational habits, routes travelled to and from work, and times of activities. The more variations and, therefore, reduced predictability, the better. Executives should be aware that most kidnappings and assassinations occur while the target is in transit.
- In very high risk areas the use of armed bodyguards, chauffeurs trained in defensive and offensive driving, and bulletproof cars is recommended. This type of protection is expensive and carries the risk that the executive puts the responsibility on others and drops some of his guard.
- Home security is an important aspect of self-defense. A patrolled neighborhood, or even better a patrolled apartment building, is a must. Furthermore, security devices, better lighting, motion-detection systems, and reinforcement of doors and windows will make it more difficult for terrorists to enter the home.
- When employees and their families are travelling by air, it is suggested to avoid airline companies that stand a higher risk of hijacking, that is, U.S., Israeli, and Arab airlines. Also, one should not flaunt one's affiliation with a major multinational or be dressed too American (jeans, sneakers).
- Personnel, especially those working in close proximity to the executive and the family, such as domestics, chauffeurs, bodyguards, and office personnel, should go through a very careful background investigation as part of the employee selection process and

should be trained in executive protection methods. They should be informed not to divulge information and to recognize and report any suspicious people or occurrences.

### Executive Protection: Insurance

Over time quite a number of kidnappings have taken place for the purpose of extorting a ransom from the victim's employer or family. Ransom demands have been at times very high, as in the case of Baron Edouard Jean Empain, who was held for $8 million ransom for sixty-three days. The amount will not be devastating for a multinational and is like any other risk the company is exposed to, and the purchase of special insurance should be considered.

A limited number of insurance companies offer kidnap and ransom insurance, and coverage can be obtained for directors, corporate officers, employees, and their families. While the ransom insurance insures corporations against the monetary demands made by kidnappers, the company is still exposed to loss of the executive's experience and knowledge in case of death when the kidnapping goes wrong. In many cases loss of information may be a larger financial loss than the actual ransom demand, and this factor should be taken into consideration when evaluating insurance policies.

The type of insurance coverage sold in response to terrorism has changed over time. Whereas in the past coverage focused only on kidnap and related ransom insurance, insurance companies have broadened the policies to include other extortion threats and incidents the company is exposed to, like product tampering and damage to property. The monetary losses from actual execution of these types of threats may be significantly more than ransom payments for kidnapping. Insurance coverage against the losses resulting from product tampering is expensive and covers product recall expenses, lost profits, and expenses associated with restoring the product's past market share. As can be expected, insurance coverage for kidnap, ransom, and extortion is also expensive. The need for this type of insurance is heavily dependent upon the visibility of the company and its products, including the areas of the world the company is operating in, and the financial strength of the company to sustain losses. The terrorist management team should carefully evaluate the financial implications of the terrorist risks the company is exposed to, analyze the insurance policies available and their premiums, and prepare a recommendation to the appropriate corporate executives with the decision-making responsibility.

## THE EVENT

An actual terrorist attack or threat can occur any day, any place, even though the risk of it happening may have been reduced through careful planning and precautionary methods. The terrorist management team should immediately come into action to avoid panic and to properly manage the corporate response. Since the team has been trained, it is best suited to handle the attack or threat thereof.

The team will set up its command center, analyze the situation, and set priorities. The team also can establish the necessary contacts with the national and local law enforcement authorities to insure local cooperation, logistical support, and decisions that meet the country's legal requirements pertaining to ransom or extortion payments and intracountry currency restrictions. The host government's policy may prohibit ransom payments or the importation or exportation of large sums of money.

The responsibility of a proper response to a kidnapping is equally shared between the terrorist management team and the victim. The team must do anything in its power to insure the safe release of the victim, but the victim, in turn, must draw on his earlier training as to personal behavior in a kidnap situation. It is suggested that the team structure a negotiating climate that is closer to the collective bargaining model, in which the mixed tactics of coercion and cooperation are used.[15] Since trust is a prime ingredient of the negotiating process, it should be thoughtfully cultivated by the team and the hostage. Minimal concessions to the terrorists should be made to extend the negotiations, to reduce the competitive aspects, and to build a more cooperative relationship. The more trust between the negotiators and the longer the time span of the negotiations, the higher the likelihood of a successful outcome.

## NOTES

1. Joseph V. Miscallef, "Political Risk Assessment," *Columbia Journal of World Business* 16 (January 1981): 47.

2. See Laurent L. Jacque, "Management of Foreign Exchange Risk: A Review Article," *Journal of International Business Studies*, Spring-Summer 1981, 81–101.

3. Examples of involuntary divestiture by U.S. companies are the Coca-Cola Company and IBM in India and United Fruit in Latin America. Under the Foreign Exchange Regulation Act of 1973 (FERA), the government of India required all foreign-owned subsidiaries operating in India to reduce the proportion of ownership held in foreign hands to 40 percent or below. Coca Cola and IBM decided not to accept shared ownership, and both companies withdrew from India in 1977. The United Fruit Company was forced to divest itself of its landholdings and banana-growing activities in Costa Rica. The company continued in the banana business by concentrating on its marketing and transportation operations.

4. *Webster's New Collegiate Dictionary*, 1976, s. v. "terrorism."

5. Rod Willis, "Corporations vs. Terrorism," *Management Review*, November 1986, 27.

6. See Brian Duffy, "Iran's Agents of Terror," *U.S. News and World Report*, March 6, 1989, 20–25.

7. This section is from Robert J. Kühne and Robert F. Schmitt, "The Terrorist Threat to Corporate Executives," *Business Horizons*, December 1979, 78-79.

8. Richard Clutterback, *Living with Terrorism* (London: Faber and Faber, 1975), 28–30.

9. For an in-depth analysis of the terrorist philosophy, see Anthony Burton, *Urban Terrorism* (New York: Free Press, 1975), chapter 12.

10. Carlos Marighela, "Handbook of Urban Guerrilla Warfare," in *For the Liberation of Brazil*, trans. John Butt and Rosemary Sheed (Baltimore: Pelican Books, 1971), 74.

11. Brian M. Jenkins, *Terrorism Works—Sometimes* (Santa Monica, Calif.: Rand Corporation, 1974), 3.

12. Marighela, "Handbook," 74–78.

13. This section heavily draws from Kenneth J. Miller, "Terrorism and the Multi-national" (Unpublished paper presented at the "Corporate Terrorism Seminar" at the University of South Carolina, September 20, 1978).

14. See F. X. O'Connor, "What to Do If You Are Kidnapped," *Saturday Evening Post*, May 1976, 6–9.

15. For an excellent analysis of the use of collective bargaining methods in hostage negotiations, see George S. Roukis, "Negotiating with Terrorists," in *Managing Terrorism: Strategies for the Corporate Executive*, ed. Patrick J. Montana and George S. Roukis (Westport, Conn.: Quorum Books, 1983).

# Part V

## STRATEGIC CHALLENGES

## 14

# Corporate Intelligence: The Key to the Strategic Success of Japanese Organizations in International Environments

## *Akira Tomioka*

Over the last two decades, a great deal has been written on the subject of successful management of the Japanese corporations. Thousands of executives, managers, and academicians have visited Japan in search of the secrets to its success. However, considerable disagreement exists as to the cause of the successful corporate behavior of Japanese organizations, particularly with respect to worldwide operations (Johnson 1988; Nonaka 1988).

The purpose of this chapter is to review the arguments and propose a new paradigm, a corporate intelligence model, based upon a social learning theory, to explain why some Japanese organizations are successful in worldwide operations. A review of the literature indicates that most arguments can be classified into two categories, sociocultural theory and government-industry conspiracy theory.

### SOCIOCULTURAL THEORY

This theory, popular in the late 1970s and early 1980s, simply indicates that Japan is a homogeneous and consensus-oriented country where Japanese work as a team, make decisions based upon group consensus, and work as hard as possible to maximize efficiency, thus achieving high productivity. This theory is basically derived from the strong conviction that Japan has a unique culture known as collectivism as opposed to individualism (Christopher 1983; Pascale and Athos 1981; Shimada 1985). Some researchers argue that ''Japanese are so homogeneous they share the same culture, ideologies, tasks, historical traditions, and even behavioral patterns'' (Shimade 1985, 42). This leads us to believe that Japanese value harmony among the members of an organization. According to Koprowski (1983), the Japanese believe that the cause of human suffering and miseries stems from human craving and selfish desire, and the way to alleviate them is to eliminate these cravings and desires. This is accomplished by practicing the middle way without judging things in terms of black and white, right and wrong, or good and evil, so that one's peace of mind is not being disturbed. The ultimate goal for Zen Buddhism is not to go to Heaven but to reach the state of Nirvana or to be free from sufferings by disassociating one's self from selfish ego or surrendering one's ego by becoming a part of an object that is valued most. Thus it is necessary for Japanese to differentiate *honne* or true intention and *tatemae* or official intention to maintain harmonious relations with other members of the society. This peculiar behavior has been criticized by Westerners as a double standard, but Japanese practice it with deep sincerity. This is mainly because Japanese society is vertically structured (Nakane 1972), while American society is horizontal with strong values of individualism and equality (Clark 1979; Graham 1981).

Graham (1981) believes that interpersonal relations in Japan are vertical in nature. Americans, however, size up one another and act accordingly. He argues that the ignorance and violation of such status distinction by American business-people trying to sell their products in Japanese markets through logical presentation, without establishing a vertical buyer (higher) and seller (lower) relationship, is a hidden cause of America's trade deficit with Japan. He emphasizes the importance of interpersonal relations as the essence of understanding successful Japanese organizational behavior, particularly in forming its corporate strategies in worldwide operations.

Gerlack (1987) states that ''the most significant but poorly understood feature of the Japanese economic landscape is the organization of firms into coherent groups which link them together in significant, complex, long-term ownership and trading relationships,'' which he refers to as ''business alliances.'' They operate ''through extended networks of relationships between companies, . . . on long-term reciprocity.'' Such relationships can be established through questionable means. One such incident, a ''Recruit'' scandal, came under government investigation in July 1988. According to a series of articles appearing in the *Wall Street Journal*, Recruit Cosmos, a real-estate unit of Recruit Company, a Japanese service firm, sold shares of stock at discount prices during 1984 and 1986 to a number of major business leaders, bureaucrats, and politicians or their aides, who were able to gain big profits when the company's stock was later offered to the public. Eight people, including the founder and chief executive officer (CEO) of Recruit Company, a government official, and other executives were arrested on suspicion of bribery or violation of securities laws in connection with the stock sales (*Wall Street Journal*, February 28, 1989). Even though such ''insider trading'' may not be illegal because the recipients were not expected to reciprocate with specific favors and thus did not meet the legal definition of bribery, in the long run, Recruit Company could have benefited from such arrangements and connections. In fact, H. Shinto, the former chairman (who resigned after the incident) of Nippon Telegraph and Telephone Corporation (NTT) was arrested on March 6, 1989. NTT, a Japanese public corporation, which ranked number one among the global 1,000 with its sales of $42.8 billion (*Business Week*, July 18, 1988), gave the real-estate company's parent, Recruit Company, special treatment, including selling two U.S.-made supercomputers NTT purchased from Cray Corporation. Shinto is a powerful figure in business circles and has close ties to politicians, including former Prime Minister Nakasone, who discussed the computer deals with former U.S. President Reagan (*Wall Street Journal*, March 7, 1989). The main idea was to establish a network and personal connections among the powerful leaders of big business firms, financial institutions, public corporations, government officials, and politicians so that Recruit Company could become a member of the big-business group in a very short period of time. This type of connection is critical to succeed in a vertically structured society. Government, the highest authority in Japan, gets higher status than the private sector, employers are perceived as higher than employees, husbands are treated as higher than wives, professors over students, and so on (Taylor 1983).

These unique Japanese cultural characteristics, in turn, are used to explain the specific nature of Japanese management. There are three factors most emphasized as to why Japanese firms are successful: lifetime employment, seniority-based wage systems, and collaborative labor unions. Ouchi (1982) and Vogel (1979) reinforced the belief that Japanese firms enjoy culturally unique systems. Ohmae (1987), however, argues that "despite our credo, . . . the Japanese are overconfident, even conceited about the management ability of Japanese firms. Foreign praise of Japanese management must not be taken at face value." Because this praise only focuses on the management methods of Japanese manufacturing, its validity is limited. Shimada (1985) agrees with the point that beneath the seemingly harmonious groupism there exist elements of "strenuous competition, confrontation, and conflicts." This is the key characteristic being argued by Benedict (1967). She states that "the Japanese are, to the highest degree, both aggressive and unaggressive, both militaristic and aesthetic, both insolent and polite, rigid and adaptable, submissive and resentful of being pushed around, loyal and treacherous, brave and timid," but she argues that these contradictions are "the warp and woof of books on Japan. They are true, and both the *sword* and *chrysanthemum* are a part of the picture" (Benedict 1967, 2; emphasis added).

It is important to behave according to one's hierarchical position to be accepted as a member of the society and to be supported by others. This naturally generates a unique cooperative society and a paternalistic corporate culture as a predominant pattern in Japan. In such a society employees tend to work hard to meet management as well as others' expectations, are more committed to their jobs, and are loyal toward their organization. As a result, they have higher productivity than American firms. This theory is quite convincing with regard to the reasons for economic success based upon unique Japanese culture. One puzzling question, however, is its transferability from one country to the other. More specifically stated, can Japanese-style management be transferred to U.S. firms? Some researchers believe that this is impossible (Sullivan 1983; Pascale and Athos 1981), but others are more optimistic (Lewis 1985; Ouchi 1982). Ouchi, in his *Theory Z*, argues that there is a striking similarity between Japanese firms and Theory Z–type American firms, such as Hewlett-Packard, Rockwell International, Intel, and Eli Lilly. Ouchi asserts that these American firms were successful because they had developed a corporate culture similar to that of Japanese firms except for responsibility, which resides in the individual in American firms but is held collectively in directive Japanese firms. Ouchi's theory does not respond directly to the question of transferability of the Japanese style of management but implies that it is possible to create a similar corporate culture, participative in nature, so that an existing organization, basically top-down and directive, can be changed to a Theory Z–type bottom-up and participative organization.

Sullivan (1983) challenged Theory Z that Japanese organizations developed a participative style of management due to their unique culture, but Theory Z–type American firms developed their management style based upon the top management's decision and corporate philosophy, which facilitated a no-layoff policy, collaborative work behavior, and worker involvement and generated a sense of trust among the members of such organizations. According to Sullivan, the basic assumptions of the Japanese and American styles of management are completely different. Both styles look similar, but it is impossible to transfer either style from one country to the other. Pascale and Athos (1981) warn that it is very hard or else a big mistake if American firms try to implant Japanese-style management in U.S. corporations. For example, the lifetime employment system, which has been considered as a core of Japanese participative management, is not feasible in the United States. Orr (1982) identified three factors, multiple skill training, flexible pay systems, and favorable labor unions, that make lifetime employment more difficult in the United States than in Japan.

In addition, some researchers argue that things are changing in Japan. Stanley S. Modic argues that "Japan's homogeneous culture is not all sunshine and roses. There is a dark side that indicated changes are coming" (*Industry Week*, October 5, 1987, p. 49). A recent *Wall Street Journal* article reports that "in Japan, employees are switching firms for better work and pay" (October 13, 1988). The article points out that "changing companies in mid-career is nothing less than revolutionary in Japan. And it is a revolution that more and more Japanese are joining. Last year about 2.2 million people or 4.4% of the labor force, jumped for greener pastures. That is up 80% from five years earlier." Because of slower economic growth, some Japanese firms started to force older employees to retire early, and employees quickly sensed that "the system of lifetime employment is not what it used to be and that self-interest may be the best policy." The article argues that "the relations between companies and individuals are becoming cool." A person who left Toyota after 16 years and joined BMW's Japanese subsidiary as an assistant senior manager stated that "if you count on corporate paternalism, you will be a loser." The article concludes its argument by stating that "the one-company-for-life era has come to an end."

The question of transferability of the Japanese style of management may be too broad, and a real question still remains unanswered, namely, why some Japanese firms operate their businesses successfully in the United States, employing thousands of Americans—more than 200,000 were estimated to be working at 574 Japanese manufacturing plants in 1987 (Japan External ' Trade Organization [JETRO] report, 1988)—where the culture is almost opposite to the one in Japan. This question will be discussed later, but the conclusion is that sociocultural theory is too simplistic to answer these puzzling questions. It does not properly address the cause of successful corporate behavior of Japanese organizations in international environments.

## GOVERNMENT-INDUSTRY CONSPIRACY

The government-industry conspiracy theory, popular in the mid-1980s, is basically an extension of sociocultural theory focusing on the argument that the success of Japanese corporations in the world market is the result of "Japanese conspiracy" (Wolf 1983) or "business alliance" (Gerlack 1987). According to this theory, government officials, politicians, business leaders, and executives of major banks agree on the primacy of economic objectives for the sake of the society as a whole, and on the means to achieve national goals and worldwide economic dominance. It argues that the Ministry of International Trade and Industry (MITI) assisted key or strategic industries by way of "administrative guidance" based on the government industrial policy and supported them through subsidies and protected them against foreign imports (Wolf 1983). MITI has been criticized as a ministry notorious for its protective policy, particularly its negative attitudes toward free trade and capital liberalization. Even today, as America's trade deficit with Japan soars ($79.7 billion in 1988), U. S. Trade Representative Carla Hills has kept berating the Japanese government.

It is true that after the Meiji Restoration in 1868 the Japanese government played the major role in facilitating the process of industrialization and modernization of Japan. After World War II it was again necessary for the government to set national industrial policy, to provide governmental funds, and to coordinate and implement specific plans for totally ruined Japanese industry to recover as quickly as possible. As a result, closely interwoven networks between government agencies and key industries were established to surpass the West. Such collective behavior has been known as "Japan Inc." (Abegglen 1970) or as "one superconglomerate" (Drucker 1981).

The expressions "Japan Inc." or "superconglomerate" are clearly an oversimplification and exaggeration. They are a misconception and misapprehension of Japanese corporate behavior based probably upon outdated assumptions. The industrial policy (particularly that of MITI) during the 1950s and 1960s encouraging and supporting private research and development (R & D) projects that required massive capital investments for many years was considered common practice and found in most countries. For example, the U.S. government's share of total national outlays on R & D expenditures was much larger than that of Japan (United States: 9 trillion yen or $70 billion; Japan: 1.7 trillion yen or $13 billion, *Nation's Business*, January 1985). As for the Japanese government's administrative guidance, it is up to the private sector to decide whether or not to follow such guidance. A typical example was the textile industry in Japan. During the 1960s it tried to control the importation of yarns and fabrics from developing countries and asked for government protection, which never happened, and the Japanese textile industry nearly vanished. At the same time, the car industry was pushing the government to promote free-trade and open-market policies, which were clearly against MITI's guidance that suggested merging many car-manufacturing firms into a few companies to enhance their competitiveness in the world car market (Clark 1979; Drucker 1981).

K. Mita, CEO of Hitachi, one of the largest electric and electronics manufacturers in the world, confirmed this point. He said in an interview that "most Japanese corporations before World War II were a part of the Zaibatsu, giant financial combine, groups. But we were totally unconnected with Zaibatsu and simply started as a modest repair factory in a small corner of the mine in 1910. This may have given us the characteristics of a *nobushi* or wandering chevallier, not part of a staid establishment" (*Wall Street Journal*, February 27, 1989). Drucker (1981) also argues that "the Japanese government is not always successful in making industries work together in the national interest. Despite 20 years of continued pressure, the supposedly all-powerful MITI has simply not been able to get the major computer manufacturers to pool their efforts—something that the governments of Germany, France, and Britain have all accomplished." He denounced the theory that the competitive success of Japanese industry is the result of some uniformity of thought and action. Instead, he points out that Japanese take competitiveness seriously, consider national interest first, make external relationships important, and do not seek final victory over opponents. He further states that these are ideals and concepts, "normative rather than descriptive of universal practice," and concludes, "Why Japanese management was able to respond to these ideals in such an effective manner no one yet really knows."

In order to clarify the cause of the successful international operations of Japanese corporations and their relationships with Japanese government agencies, the role of MITI and its trade promotional agency, the Japan External Trade Organization (JETRO) will be discussed next. After World War II Japanese manufacturing firms were operating without detailed information on what they should produce and export to foreign markets. They also did not have specific agents informing them of changes in tariffs and specifications for their products, as well as assisting in marketing their products (Johnson 1982). In order to cope with such problems, the Overseas Trade Promotion Association (Kaigai Boeki Shinkokai) was incorporated in 1951 by a group of people from the city of Osaka, the Osaka Chamber of Commerce, and major Kansai business enterprises (Johnson 1982). However, the activities of the association as an incorporated foundation (*zaidan hojin*) were not powerful enough to achieve the mission.

In 1954 MITI took over the association with more government funds and expanded its activities. Then it was transformed into a special corporation (*tokushu hojin*) under the Japan External Trade Organization law in 1958. Since then, JETRO has been playing an important role as an extended arm of MITI to accomplish the national policies, that is, to promote external trade. In 1980 MITI recognized that the period of catching up with advanced Western economies through industrial modernization had ended, and that the nation was about to go into the next phase of development. Japan needed to behave itself in the international community in a manner different from the past. When Japan was producing a small share of the world's GNP (3.6 percent in the 1950s, 4.4 percent in the 1960s, and 7.5 percent in the 1970s), Japan could afford to be passive to world economic developments and did not pay much attention to international implications. But in the 1980s Japan, producing more than 10 percent of the world's GNP, should act more positively and make a greater contribution to the international community. There was a growing demand for Japan to play a leading role not only in the economy but also in world politics (JETRO brochure, 1988).

Having made such national policy changes, JETRO has changed its mission from the promotion of exporting Japanese goods to importing foreign goods to Japanese markets. As of July 25, 1985, JETRO operated in fifty-seven countries, with twenty-five large Japan Trade Centers in key foreign cities as well as fifty-two additional offices throughout the world. Their functions are to investigate foreign markets, to publicize new Japanese products, to participate in international trade fairs, and to serve domestic and foreign businesspeople using the worldwide telex communication network. JETRO analyzes and evaluates collected data for its significance, and findings are reported to the public through various publications, such as *JETRO Sensor*, *JETRO Daily*, and monthly journals like *Focus Japan* aiming at Organization for Economic Cooperation and Development (OECD) countries and *Trade Scope* to help developing countries. JETRO also published white papers focusing on key issues for researchers and business people.

In its fiscal 1988 white paper focusing on world trade, JETRO states that world trade has been undergoing significant changes as the result of an agreement among finance ministries and presidents of central banks of major economic powers called G-7 in September 1985. According to the paper, overseas direct investments among Japanese firms in fiscal 1986 climbed 82.7 percent over the previous year, reaching the $20 billion level for the first time (accumulated total, $100 billion). A sharp rise of the yen against the dollar stimulated overseas direct investments in the United States, particularly in the parts and components

**Table 14.1**

**Distribution of Japanese Manufacturers' Factory Sites in the United States**

| States | Number of Plants | States | Number of Plants |
|---|---|---|---|
| California | 163 | Arkansas | 4 |
| New Jersey | 82 | Missouri | 4 |
| Georgia | 40 | Arizona | 4 |
| Illinois | 28 | Florida | 4 |
| Texas | 25 | Connecticut | 4 |
| Washington | 23 | Hawaii | 4 |
| Tennessee | 17 | Mississippi | 3 |
| Ohio | 16 | Oklahoma | 3 |
| Alaska | 16 | New Hampshire | 3 |
| Pennsylvania | 14 | Wisconsin | 3 |
| New York | 14 | Puerto Rico | 2 |
| North Carolina | 14 | Nevada | 2 |
| Indiana | 12 | Rhode Island | 2 |
| Kentucky | 10 | Iowa | 2 |
| Alabama | 9 | (Louisiana, Vermont, Maine, | |
| Massachusetts | 8 | West Virginia, Minnesota, | |
| Virginia | 7 | Colorado, | |
| Oregon | 7 | and Kansas have one plant | |
| South Carolina | 7 | each) | |
| Nebraska | 6 | | |
| Maryland | 5 | Total Plants | 564 |

*Source*: JETRO brochure, 1988, as of May 1987.

industries to meet the demand of Japanese firms operating plants in the United States. According to a JETRO brochure, Japanese firms have established 574 plants in the United States as of May 1987, as shown in table 14.1.

Intra-Japanese firms' trade, including overseas subsidiaries and affiliates, is expected to continue and contribute to improving Japan's trade imbalance with the United States. Japan's exports in 1987 grew 9.6 percent from the previous year to $229 billion, but imports surged 19 percent to $150 billion due to the yen's rise, which helped to reduce Japan's trade surplus almost $3 billion to $79.9 billion. As for U.S. firms, their direct investment in Japan accounted for 48.6 percent of the cumulative foreign investment at the end of fiscal 1986. Manufacturing industries, mainly chemical and machinery, took 71 percent of the total U.S. direct investment in Japan. JETRO's report urges that the United States encourage the export orientation of U.S. firms and that Japan open its market wider to foreign firms and promote Japanese direct overseas investment in an era of globalization (JETRO's special report, March 1988).

In order to alleviate foreign firms' complaints relative to government regulations, distribution systems, and nontariff barriers, JETRO created an Office of Trade ombudsman in 1982. JETRO has been active in providing consulting services to help overseas businesses to export their products to Japanese markets successfully by conducting market research through affiliated consulting firms and arranging meetings with prospective clients in Japan. Such services are

**Figure 14.1**
**Roles of MITI and JETRO**

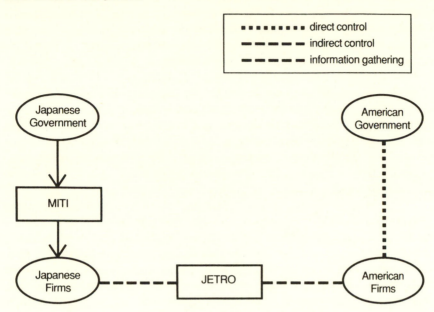

basically free of charge. JETRO has reversed its role from facilitating the process of information gathering and acting as a commercial intelligence agency for Japanese firms in the past to providing valuable information to American and other Western firms. Current relationships between the Japanese government and industries, including JETRO and American firms, are schematically shown in figure 14.1.

It is ironic that MITI used to be referred to as a notorious ministry, but more recently MITI and JETRO have been acting as trade-intelligence agencies for American and Western firms. Furthermore, the Japanese government has changed its role drastically. For example, the Japanese government has established a state agency, called the Japan Key Technology Center (JKTC), to provide venture capital to various research groups including foreign subsidiaries. The *Wall Street Journal* reports that "since its 1985 inception, the center has provided 32 billion yen or $256 million to research groups dealing with everything from biochemistry and steel production to futuristic aircraft engines" (February 6, 1989). In order to receive government venture funds, private research consortiums must come up with their own proposals by September each year. This is rather unusual and "almost radical" for the Japanese government, because, in the past, government agencies like MITI planners identified key industries and provided government funds, but now the government solicits research proposals from private research consortiums by placing a small advertisement in a government journal to foster "the kind of technology that Japan has been accused of not doing in the past"

(February 6, 1989). This scheme is not limited to Japanese firms. Japanese subsidiaries of Digital Equipment Corporation, IBM, F. Hoffman-La Roche and Company, and several other foreign firms have joined the JKTC-funded consortiums and are already a part of the Japanese government-industry research web. As long as foreign firms are set up to do research in Japan, "There is no discrimination between foreign and Japanese companies" (JKTC's deputy general manager, *Wall Street Journal*, February 6, 1989).

The government-industry conspiracy theory was probably appropriate in explaining the Japanese corporate behavior when Japanese companies were strongly supported and protected by the government in the 1950s and 1960s, but the theory is inadequate to explain today's successful Japanese corporate behavior in international environments. New paradigms are needed here.

## CORPORATE INTELLIGENCE THEORY

Recently Nonaka (1988) proposed an interesting model, a "self-renewal" theory. He argues that a Japanese firm "renews itself under constant metabolism with its environment." A self-renewing organization forms order out of uncertainty, confusions, and chaos while reacting selectively to information from the environment. According to this theory, the term "order" is used to imply not only physical patterns of organizational structures and systems, but also mental patterns such as visions, values, and conceptions. It is therefore critical to get meaningful information out of an unpredictable environment. For that reason, semantic information is more valuable than syntactic information. Syntactic information is quantitative by nature, such as interest rates, market shares, or sales revenues. Semantic information, in turn, is qualitative, such as a customer's perceptions of a product or societal value changes. Meaning can be generated out of semantic information that leads us to change our perceptions of products so that one can differentiate one firm's products from competitors' products.

Successful Japanese firms are constantly creating meanings throughout the organization based upon semantic information utilizing corporate intelligence, which is defined as the ability of an organization to create meaning out of semantic information. This seems to be the driving force of the self-renewing organizations.

It has been pointed out that the roles of middle managers are changing drastically, and some researchers say that they are an endangered species (*Business Week*, September 12, 1988). The article argues that "if today's middle managers feel threatened, they might as well feel nearly extinct as the corporation moves into the 21st century." Drucker (1981) envisions that in twenty years "the typical corporation will employ no more than a third of its current managers, with fewer than half the levels of management." Robert Tomasko argues that "we've got to be sure we don't create organizations with a CEO at the top, a computer in the middle, and lots of workers at the bottom" and suggests that "the job is not to wipe out middle management but to create a new role for managers; to be partners with top management in making the U.S. more competitive'' (*Business Week*, September 12, 1988, pp. 80–88). His suggestion is rather misleading regarding who is going to create such a new role. It should be rephrased so as to let middle managers think of their roles based upon their perceptions of their roles, levels of abilities, and career objectives. This is definitely something management is not going to do, but middle managers must find their new roles out of confusions and ambiguities.

Furthermore, Nonaka (1988) asserts that creation of such meaning is not limited to top management but is easily done at any level of organizational hierarchy. Toyota's invention of a ''just-in-time'' inventory-control system and successful implementation of Quality Control (QC) Circle activities among Japanese firms are examples of such a case. Imai (1986) argues that the essence of most unique Japanese management practices—be they productivity improvement, QC circles, or labor relations—can be reduced to one word, *kaizen*, or a process of constantly learning, changing, and improving their work. He believes that '' 'there should be unending improvement' is deeply ingrained in the Japanese mentality,'' and that this is the key to Japan's competitive success.

Nonaka (1988) points out that ''the systematic incorporation of the opportunity for creating information into daily work at the operator level has been precisely the major characteristic of Japanese organizations.'' The entire process is the self-renewal of an organization. There are, in fact, corporate intelligence officers serving as a trigger for this continuous process and transforming accumulated information into a form of knowledge. This becomes the basis of generating new visions, values, and conceptions of the organization's products and services. Such individuals are those who are able to get something valuable for the organization out of uncertain environments and who are making their organization a learning organization by constantly renewing their abilities. This seems to be the most effective way of operating business in turbulent international environments.

Based upon this argument, several factors can be identified as the cause of successful corporate behavior of Japanese corporations in international environments. First, the Japanese seem to place more value on feelings and emotions (semantic information) than on logic, written contracts, and return on investment (syntactic information) when they do business in domestic as well as foreign markets. Therefore, it is natural for the Japanese to pay attention to maintaining harmonious and cooperative relationships with government agencies like MITI and JETRO, customers, and banking institutions, and even among employees. Through such interactions and relationships they are able to exchange information and develop new meanings relative to future strategies for their organization, not because the Japanese government has direct control over industries through legal enforcements and penalties. However, it can be interpreted as a part of the Japanese government conspiracy if such constantly renewing corporate behavior of Japanese firms is ignored.

Second, successful Japanese firms seek information constantly. This is due to their attitudes toward the future, particularly as to international operations, which are perceived as uncertain and unpredictable instead of manageable and controllable variables. Therefore, Japanese are eager to get relevant semantic information constantly through various means of corporate intelligence activities. They are then able to create new meanings with regard to their future visions and change their corporate behavior to fit into the rapidly changing international environments. A typical example of such corporate behavior is Japanese firms doing business on imports and exports. T. Yahiro, president of Mitsui and Company, suggested at a U.S. and Japan video conference that "you have to make a very detailed, meticulous study of the sentiments and likes of the Japanese consumers, and you can not expect, simply because a product is popular in the U.S., that it is going to be as popular in Japan. When we export, the first thing we do is market research" (*Nation's Business*, April 1985). In fact, Japanese trading firms have been working hard to bring foreign goods to Japanese markets and are very successful. According to Yahiro, "Nine of the biggest trading companies operating in the U.S. are directly responsible for the sale of over $8 billion in American-made products to Japan" (*Nation's Business*, April 1985).

Third, the Japanese corporate philosophy tends to emphasize the importance of working for others, not for oneself. K. Mita, CEO of Hitachi, ranked 17th out of the global 1,000 with its sales of $39 billion (*Business Week*, July 18, 1988), talks about "global citizenship." He states that "contribution to the global community is the managerial keynote at Hitachi." Thus gaining customer trust is more important than making a profit (*Wall Street Journal*, February 27, 1989). Another example, Uni-Charm Corporation, a leading manufacturer of disposable diapers and sanitary products in Japan, has a unique corporate philosophy that clearly stipulates that the members of Uni-Charm should work for themselves to satisfy their own needs and wants through their work, not for the company. K. Takahara, CEO of Uni-Charm, is determined to make their jobs enjoyable and meaningful instead of simply assuming that they are paid to work for the company (Tomioka 1989). Kintetsu World Express (KWE), a subsidiary of Kinki Nippon Railway, ranked 77th among the global 1,000 with sales of $4 billion (*Business Week*, July 18, 1988), headquartered in Garden City, New York, is another example of such Japanese organizations. Since 1970 the firm has been very successful in an air cargo shipping business in the United States, employing 340 Americans and 38 Japanese (as of February 1989). There are three regional offices in the United States managed by American managers without direct control from the headquarters. According to T. Kunishi, vice president of administration, American managers are assigned to these offices with a broad mission, a general description of the situation, and no detailed instructions as to how to manage the office. However, through frequent face-to-face dialogues and discussions they are able to find out what to do by themselves instead of waiting for instructions from the headquarters. This management style is very consistent with KWE's corporate philosophy, which states that KWE seeks "to become a part of the community in which it is situated and to conduct its business in the manner most beneficial to that community'' (KWE USA brochure). Thus it is natural to assume that the headquarters is not in a position to give specific instructions to managers but simply expects them to find out what to do in a specific situation.

This type of management can be characterized as "outside-in" as opposed to "inside-out." KWE has been operating its business based on this "outside-in" philosophy not only in Japan but also in the world. Managers are given a broad corporate philosophy and exciting mission and try to realize KWE's long-term objectives through a daily trial-and-error method. Obviously some managers leave KWE due to a lack of clear job descriptions, hierarchical power structure, and broad corporate strategies. The management of KWE believes that those who remain in the organization are individuals who have learned how to create a proper way of managing business out of strategic ambiguities or chaos, and that they are continuously learning through their jobs. Such individuals are perpetual learners, keep increasing their abilities to do their jobs without specific instructions given by the management, and create new orders in the organization. Learning something new through one's job is the basic motivation for such individuals.

Fourth, the Japanese tend to manage their organizations and employees based upon self-motivation or bottom-up rather than management-oriented or top-down style of leadership. The Japanese believe that if the organization expects its employees to do their jobs exactly as they are told, then there will be no chaos, no motivation, and no learning. Organizational efficiency may be increased, but complacency is the result, and that type of organization cannot survive in the future. If managers are given specific orders and have clear ideas of what to do next, then they will do it efficiently as much as possible and will be rewarded, but nothing is learned. Such managers were needed in the past particularly in manufacturing industries, but in the future managers are needed who are constantly learning and able to create new orders in the organization. Bennis and Nanus (1985) argue that "the leader operates on the emotional and spiritual resources of the organization, on its values, commitment, and aspirations. The manager, by contrast, operates on the physical resources of the organization, on its capital, human skills, raw materials, and technology." A paradigm has been quickly shifting its major factors from hard variables like numbers, money, and technology to soft variables like feelings, perceptions, and emotions.

Jobs are mostly routine and are performed in a certain way, but successful Japanese firms demand of managers and operators a little more than routine job activities. Not provided with clear job descriptions, they are driven to find out what to do by themselves. Therefore, doing a job without clear instructions becomes an opportunity to learn what to do and how to do it by increasing one's job-related abilities. This is the major source of energy activating the corporate intelligence activities. It must be a frustrating experience for those who are used to taking orders from management, but without ambiguities and confusions, we tend to do our jobs the way they were done yesterday. K. Uesugi, vice president in charge of services at Canon USA, says that he would prefer to hire college graduates with a broad background, like those majoring in economics or philosophy, and let them learn through their jobs, than someone with experience, knowing what to do and how to do the job, because he has found that those with experience tend to do their jobs as given and do not change the way they are done even though they increase their abilities to do their jobs after they are placed to the job. This point clearly indicates that there are significant differences that exist between Japanese and American management not because of simple cultural differences and government conspiracy, but because of the fact that Japanese perform their jobs in unique ways, constantly learning to become a part of the environment. Therefore, a question of transferability of Japanese management to the United States should not be answered through simple and narrow-minded approaches but should be studied as part of a learning process. Bennis and Nanus (1985) argue, in a similar way, that the current management education that has been taught at elite business schools in the United States is outdated because it has been assumed that "the goals are clear, alternatives are known, technology and its consequences certain, and perfect information available," and these assumptions are completely wrong and "dangerously misleading" the students. The key is to experience confusions and ambiguities with regard to what to do today besides routines, and that is exactly the point of Uesugi's comment on hiring policy, Bennis and Nanus's criticism of management education, and the way jobs are handled at KWE and Canon USA.

To learn such work behavior, changing from other-directed to inner-directed, a model with detailed step-by-step procedures has been proposed (Tomioka 1975, 1989). The main idea of the model is to increase one's abilities of self-learning, internal attribution, and self-motivation using a to-do list that is normally considered as a tool to increase job efficiency and time management, but the model focuses on the way to satisfy one's need for self-actualization by going through a psychological identification between a job and one's ego (Tomioka 1984).

This leads to the last and most critical factor of successful Japanese organizations in international environments. Japanese are more reactive than proactive with respect to their attitudes toward environments. As discussed earlier, the process of learning cannot be completed without the experience of confusions and chaos that provide a chance to learn something new. When people have such a state of confusions and chaos, they simply have to give up their proactive approach because things happening are out of their control, and they are forced to change to a reactive approach. A reactive type of organizational behavior is like an amoeba changing its shape, constantly responding to the changing environments. I believe that this has been the basic corporate strategy of successful Japanese organizations. This argument can be summarized schematically in figure 14.2.

Taking the outside-in approach is forcing the Japanese management to accept the environment the way it is and make the organization a part of the environment. Japanese managements, therefore, must give up the proactive approach and surrender their selfish corporate egos because it is impossible for them to change

**Figure 14.2**
**A Corporate Intelligence Model**

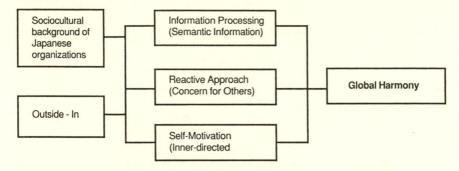

the environment to the way they feel comfortable and make it favorable to their business. Management must make the organization a learning organization by giving up management's ego to cope with changing and competitive environments.

By doing so, management is constantly learning from a confusing and unpredictable environment and is able to increase the level of abilities of corporate intelligence. Through a process of constant learning, management is able to accumulate knowledge and will be able to create a new order in the organization. Gerlack (1987) points out, regarding the strategic success of Japanese organizations, that "perhaps the strongest argument for the Japanese business system has been its remarkable ability and willingness to experiment, to try new things, and to look outside and learn." Management's ability to get relevant information out of turbulent environments utilizing corporate intelligence is the most critical factor affecting the future of the organization, regardless of whether it is American or Japanese. This is the key to understanding the strategic success of the Japanese organization in international environments.

## REFERENCES

Abegglen, J. C., and Stalk, G. 1985. *Kaisha: The Japanese Corporation*. New York: Basic Books.

Benedict, R. 1967. *The Chrysanthemum and the Sword*. Cleveland and New York: Meridian Books, World Publishing Co.

Bennis, W., and Nanus, B. 1985. *Leaders: The Strategies for Taking Charge*. New York: Harper and Row.

Christopher, R. C. 1983. *The Japanese Mind: The Goliath Explained*. New York: Linden Press/Simon and Schuster.

Clark, R. 1979. *The Japanese Company*. New Haven: Yale University Press.

Drucker, P. January–February 1981. "Behind Japan's Success." *Harvard Business Review*, 83–90.

Gerlack, M. Fall 1987. "Business Alliance and the Strategy of the Japanese Firm." *California Management Review*, 126–42.

Graham, J. L. Fall 1981. "A Hidden Cause of American Trade Deficit with Japan." *Columbia Journal of World Business*, 5–15.

Imai, M. 1986. *Kaizen: The Key to Japan's Competitive Success*. New York: Random House Business Division.

Johnson, C. 1982. *MITI and the Japanese Miracle*. Stanford, Calif.: Stanford University Press.

————. Summer 1988. "Japanese-style Management in America." *California Management Review*, 34–45.

Koprowski, E. J. Autumn 1983. "Cultural Myths: Clues to Effective Management." *Organizational Dynamics*, 39–51.

Lewis, J. 1980. *Excellent Organizations: How to Develop and Manage Them Using Theory Z*. New York: Wilkerson.

Nakane, C. 1972. *Japanese Society*. Berkeley: University of California Press. 1972.

Nonaka, I. Spring 1988. "Creating Organizational Order out of Chaos: Self-renewal in Japanese Firms." *California Management Review*, 57–73.

Ohmae, K. 1987. *Beyond National Borders: Reflections on Japan and the World*. Homewood, Ill.: Dow Jones-Irwin.

Orr, J. Autumn 1982. "Planning for Change: Employment Adjustments in the U.S. Japanese Companies." *National Productivity Review*, 408–15.

Ouchi, W. 1982. *Theory Z*. Reading, Mass.: Addison-Wesley.

Pascale, R., and Athos, A. 1981. *The Art of Japanese Management*. New York: Warner Books.

Shimada, H. 1985. "The Perceptions and the Reality of Japanese Industrial Relations." *The Management Challenge: Japanese Views*. Edited by L. C. Thurow. Cambridge, Mass.: MIT Press. 1985, 42–68.

Sullivan, J. 1983. "A Critique of Theory Z." *Academy of Management Review*, 8:132–42.

Taylor, J. 1983. *Shadows of the Rising Sun: A Critical View of the Japanese Miracle*. New York: William Morrow and Co.

Tomioka, A. 1975. *A Process of Developing Potential Abilities: Techniques of a T-Model* (in Japanese). Tokyo: Japan Productivity Center.

————. 1984. "A Comparative Study of Job Involvement as a Process of Ego-Surrender in an American and a Japanese Organization." Ph.D. diss., City University of New York.

————. March 30, 1989. "A Process of Becoming Involved in One's Work: A Japanese Way." Decision Science Institute, *Northeast Conference Proceeding*, Baltimore.

Vogel, E. F. 1979. *Japanese as Number One*. Cambridge, Mass.: Harvard University Press.

Wolf, M. J. 1983. *The Japanese Conspiracy: The Plot to Dominate Industry World Wide and How to Deal with It*. New York: Empire Books.

# 15

# Geography and Corporate Risk Assessment

## Ewan W. Anderson

Geography has been defined in numerous ways, but the all-embracing nature of the discipline defies the formulation of a generally accepted definition. However, in broad terms, geography can be considered the study of location and, in particular, the relationship between man and his environment. Since the total environment includes both the natural and the man-made, the subject matter of geography is drawn from both the physical and the social sciences. On the one hand, it is concerned with the atmosphere, the hydrosphere, and the lithosphere, which together comprise the physical world, and on the other, with the political, the economic, and the social, which between them provide a summary of man's activities. It is the interplay of these variables in the appropriate historical setting at a specific location that forms the core of geography. Thus a geographical factor can be any occurrence or event that happens at a known time in a specified place.

An example of the multifaceted nature of geographical concern can be illustrated with the case of minerals. Over the past decade, Western defense industrialists and planners have become particularly interested in the vulnerability of mineral supplies and in what constitutes a "strategic mineral."[1] For Western nations at the present time, the basic variables might be identified and weighted as in table 15.1.[2] It can be seen that half the relevant factors can be characterized as locational. Chromium, manganese, platinum-group metals, cobalt, and tungsten emerge with the highest risk factor and are in fact generally viewed as "strategic minerals."

**Table 15.1**
**Risk Factor for Minerals**

This is an initial attempt to quantify risk (or strategic importance), using the following analysis variables:

| | | | |
|---|---|---|---|
| S | substitution (1-4) | | most easily substituted = 1 |
| LE | life expectancy (1-3) | | most rapid depletion rates = 3 |
| SP | scale of production (1 or 3) | | thousands of tonnes + 1<br>millions of tonnes + 3 |
| MS | number of major sources (1-4) | | most sources = 1 |
| R | reliability of main sources (1-3) | | most reliable = 1 |
| WP | Warsaw Pact share of world production (0-2) | | no share = 0 |
| RF | risk factor: the total of scores with those for location factors (MS, R, WP) x 2 | | |

| | S | LE | SP | MS | R | WP | RF |
|---|---|---|---|---|---|---|---|
| ANTIMONY | 1 | 1 | 1 | 3 | 3 | 2 | 19 |
| CADMIUM | 1 | 1 | 1 | 2 | 1 | 1 | 11 |
| COBALT | 3 | 1 | 1 | 4 | 3 | 1 | 21 |
| COPPER | 2 | 2 | 3 | 2 | 1 | 1 | 15 |
| LEAD | 2 | 2 | 3 | 3 | 1 | 1 | 17 |
| MERCURY | 3 | 3 | 1 | 2 | 1 | 2 | 17 |
| PLATINUM | 3 | 1 | 1 | 3 | 3 | 2 | 23 |
| SILVER | 4 | 3 | 1 | 1 | 1 | 1 | 14 |
| TIN | 2 | 2 | 3 | 2 | 2 | 0 | 15 |
| TUNGSTEN | 3 | 1 | 1 | 3 | 3 | 2 | 21 |
| ZINC | 2 | 2 | 3 | 2 | 1 | 1 | 15 |
| CHROMIUM | 3 | 0 | 3 | 4 | 3 | 2 | 24 |
| MANGANESE | 2 | 0 | 3 | 4 | 3 | 2 | 24 |
| NICKEL | 2 | 1 | 3 | 3 | 1 | 1 | 16 |
| ALUMINUM | 1 | 0 | 3 | 2 | 1 | 1 | 12 |

Corporate risks may be of a spatial or of a nonspatial nature. Decisions about the establishment of a new plant or the penetration of a new market involve essentially locational concerns. A decision to increase production using existing facilities is, on the face of it, nonspatial. However, related problems such as the absorptive capacity of the market exhibit a definite geographical component. Indeed, since the field of geography is the surface of the earth, it is obvious that at some level in the process geography must be considered in most corporate decisions. Therefore, many of the risks assessed must be susceptible to geographical analysis.

The pervasive nature of geography poses a key practical problem. If, in assessments, the geographical factor is so frequently implicit, how can it be made sufficiently explicit that it is accorded due weighting? Resolution of the problem takes the form of a risk assessment.

## RISK ASSESSMENT

Risk assessment consists basically of two procedures: (a) dissection of the system under consideration into its key components and (b) assigning to each component the probability of a stated event occurring within a specific time period. The probability of such an occurrence expressed on a percentage scale or a numerical scale (usually zero to ten) is awarded either by the investigator or by adopting a variation on the Delphi method. The probabilities as percentages or numbers for several related occurrences are then combined to produce a "magic" number that is effectively dimensionless and believed to encapsulate all the nuances of risk. In fact, with such a multivariate problem, the magic number defies interpretation since it results from a large range of inputs, any of which may have dominated the calculation.

Producing one number has the advantage of simplicity and the apparently greater advantage of allowing comparability. However, if, for example, the risk to mineral supplies from Canada is given the magic number of one and that to supplies from Zaire eight, what exactly do these figures mean? For cobalt, the resource base of Zaire is greater than that of Canada for any individual mineral. It could be argued that Western industry suffered greater disruption from the Sudbury nickel miner's strike than from the insurrection in Shaba Province and the disruption of cobalt supply that ensued. Perhaps the government of Zaire is thought to be eight times as unstable as that of Canada. However, even if that were the case, there can be no direct correlation between governmental stability and interruptions to resource supplies. Furthermore, with its economy supported by International Monetary Fund (IMF) funding and its mining dominated by European expertise, the pro-Western character of Zaire may be less at risk than is commonly supposed. On the other hand, it is not beyond the bounds of possibility that a Canadian government could be elected on an antinuclear election platform or even one that aims at Canada's withdrawal from NATO.

Thus, given the conjectural nature of many of these probabilities, it is clear that a far more detailed "real-world" appreciation is required before a really useful risk assessment can be made. A strong geographical element reflecting the real world is a sine qua non of risk assessment. The geography needs to be explicit, and that is why the term "geopolitical" is preferable to "political." It is only by assessing the interplay of political, economic, and international factors at the specific location that the various risks identified can be monitored and even influenced by the foreign policy of the consumer country.

## THE MODEL[3]

Geopolitical factors arise from the interplay of geography and politics on various scales. For convenience, the scales can be designated as local, regional, and global; but it should be realized that the exact definitions, especially of the first two, vary from one particular problem to another. In the present context the term "local" is taken to mean "national," while the term "regional" refers either to areas encompassing contiguous states or to a region embracing different states according to a generally accepted understanding of it. The scope of the term "global" is intercontinental and worldwide. For certain problems one scale may be more important than another, whereas for others it may indeed be totally irrelevant. At the same time, the effect of a global political variable may well be felt on all three geographical scales; and by the same token, a local geographical factor may influence political variables at all three levels.

The key geographical elements are location or place and (as a consequence) distance, both of which have to be considered on all three scales. Location implies the total geography, physical and human, but specifically in this case it refers to scarce concentrations of strategic minerals. Distance varies according to the mode of transport and the route taken, but on all three scales there will be geographical influences. Depending on the scale of assessment, these may range from constraints at a particular port to problems of the regional infrastructure or a global choke point.

The relevant political input could be described as policy, a resultant of such factors as ideology, type of government, and leadership. Examples on the global scale are world trading, defense policies of major powers, and the attitudes of multinational corporations. Regionally, policies may result from a common stance such as that adopted by most of the "frontline states" against the Republic of South Africa. Locally, policies are either national or within national subdivisions and concern such aspects as labor, taxes, development, and environment. It is thus the interplay of decisions taken at different levels by the political actors—major and minor powers; transnational and multinational bodies; and even individuals—interacting with the factors of location on different scales that produces the geopolitical environment (see figure 15.1).

The full procedure for risk assessment of supply sources to the United States therefore begins with the establishment of the three criteria already discussed: (a) criticality, (b) import dependence, and (c) the concentration on limited sources. In applying the geopolitical part of the risk assessment model (figure 15.2), geopolitical factors, global, regional, and local, that affect the production of the strategic mineral at its location are examined. In turn, production of strategic minerals at a specific location exercises a geopolitical influence at the local, regional, and global levels. For example, superpower defense decisions, regional instability, and national mining policy are all factors that impinge on the production of a given mineral. Meanwhile, production may distort national economic development, affect the regional power distribution, and influence global diplomatic linkages. By separating the various activities onto different scales, the mechanisms involved can be clarified and more easily identified. However, this distinction is somewhat artificial because decisions made globally have a greater or lesser effect on regional and local geopolitics. For example, global strategic decisions affect world defense industries and generate demand for particular minerals. The interaction between these decisions and the geo-

**Figure 15.1**
**Risk Assessment Model for Strategic Minerals**

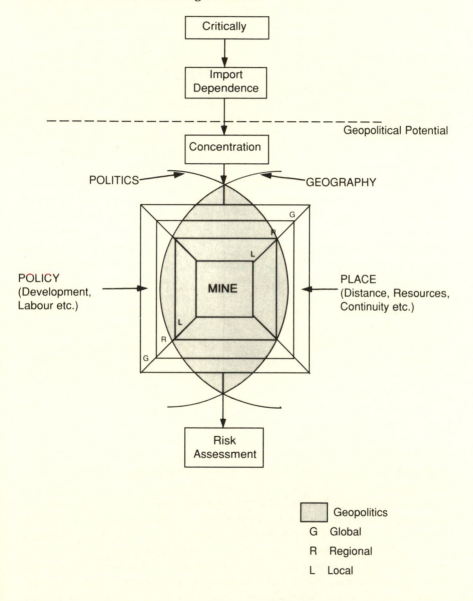

**Figure 15.2**
**Geopolitical Risk Assessment General Model**

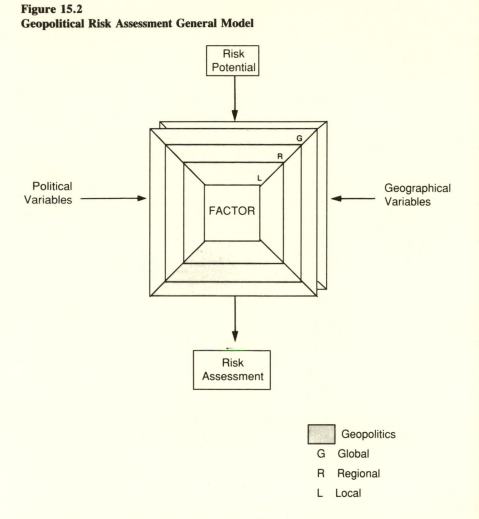

graphical pattern of resources can result in changes in the infrastructure on all three scales and can exert influence on developments down to the level of a single mine.

The extreme case of dependence on virtually a single mining complex occurs in the case of columbium. The United States obtains 75 percent of its imports from Brazil, and Brazilian production is limited solely to the mines of Araxa.

Similarly, local events are quite likely to exert an influence on the region and may even lead to global reaction. For example, industrial action or guerrilla activity may affect production at a given mine or in a mining region as a whole. The results will be felt regionally, and if the material is considered sufficiently crucial, a superpower may physically intervene. Thus the scales are not discrete, and the inputs from politics or geography on one scale may exercise a marked influence on a different scale.

Furthermore, when the time scale is taken into account, the general tendency to regard long-term events as global and short-term events as local should be viewed with a certain degree of caution. Considerations bearing on New International Economic Order (NIEO) or on changed supplier/consumer relationships may be global and long-term in character, but a price rise may be of global and short-term character. However, in general, price changes result from tendency disruptions, market manipulation, or political instability, all of which act in the short term and may well be local. These are the most likely ways in which supplies may be disrupted, and price is therefore a useful guide, since it encapsulates the range of influential factors: geological, technological, economic, and geopolitical. In the medium term, changing trade patterns, new sources of supply, and political alignment tend to operate on a larger scale, while in the long term, the reorganization of the world economic system or superpower military action have obvious global relevance.

The system is therefore very complex. It can be simplified objectively and rationally by the inputs of politics and geography on the various environmental scales. For each specific case under investigation, all inputs and all levels may not be relevant. By using the model, however, it should be possible to identify a series of key variables. From these a realistic assessment of risk can be made. It may be possible to assign probabilities to particular events, but in such a complicated situation, these must all be highly conjectural. It is obviously completely facile to assign numbers on a zero-to-ten scale for whole countries or whole industries. In order to produce a scenario of any value, the relevant factors require a detailed analysis; even such basic information as production statistics would need to be investigated.

## APPLYING THE RISK ASSESSMENT MODEL
## TO STRATEGIC MINERALS

United States companies operate a worldwide trading network, and the number of sources supplying strategic minerals is very large. Six major suppliers of key minerals, Canada, Australia, South Africa, Mexico, Jamaica, and Brazil will be analyzed to identify potential strategic or investment risk and vulnerability.[4]

### Canada

Canada is easily the most important source of U.S. minerals by volume of trade and the individual materials involved. Since it is a part of North America with the United States, the major forces involved at the regional level are those generated by its more powerful neighbor. Indeed, a major problem affecting all aspects of the national economy is Canada's lack of a separate identity. Bilateral trade between the United States and Canada is far greater than that between any

**Table 15.2**
**Strategic Minerals in Canada**

| Mineral | % of U.S. imports | % of world production | % of world reserve base |
|---|---|---|---|
| Ilmenite | 35 (2) · | c.18 (2) | 18 (2) |
| Nickel | 38 (1) | 19 (2) | 13 (4) |
| Tungsten | 19 (1) | 7 (3) | 19 (2) |

other two countries, each being the other's primary source of mineral imports. For different reasons, both countries have developed anxieties about mineral dependence, the United States on imports and Canada on exports.

Canada is the leading exporter of minerals in the world and, for the United States, a key supplier of three strategic minerals: nickel, titanium, (ilmenite), and tungsten. Furthermore, although Canada possesses in each case under 3 percent of the world reserves, significant amounts of cobalt, columbium, platinum-group metals, and tantalum are exported to the United States. For the United States, Canada is the leading source of nickel and tungsten and the second main supplier of ilmenite. Table 15.2 shows figures for (a) imports as a percentage of total U.S. imports of each mineral, (b) percentage of world production for which Canada is responsible, and (c) percentage of the world reserve base in the country. In each case the relative position of Canada is given in brackets. Thus for these three strategic minerals, Canada is not only a major supplier but has the great advantage of possessing long-term reserves.

For its size, Canada has a well-developed transportation network with a marked east-west orientation. There are direct road and rail links with the United States, but trans-Canadian movement tends to be the dominant route. The network comprises railways, roads, pipelines, and waterways, with minerals in many cases providing the minimum guarantee needed to establish these facilities. In particular, northern extensions tend to be built primarily for mineral transportation, while class-two railways are developed almost exclusively for mining. The Great Lakes–St. Lawrence Seaway (opened in 1959) is limited by the facts that it is only twenty-seven feet deep and that the size of the lock is restricted. With the increase in the size of ships carrying minerals, these limitations have become important. However, the overall infrastructure of transportation is good and is under expansion.

Canada is also well endowed with energy supplies ranging from petroleum (onshore and offshore) to tar sands, uranium, nuclear energy sources, and hydroelectric power. Mining development is not likely to be affected by the problems of water supply. The mining labor force, comprising some 1 percent of the total labor force, is highly unionized, and large losses have been sustained through industrial action. This was particularly evident in the nickel mines at Sudbury. In general terms, however, the geographical infrastructure is well developed and poses comparatively few problems.

Yet the impact of government policies upon this infrastructure has created a somewhat less favorable geopolitical environment. The level of direct U.S. investment is such that, particularly over the last ten years, Canadian anxiety over the maintenance of economic independence has steadily increased. This has been fueled by memories of American attempts to annex parts of Canada and by such postwar developments as defense agreements as well as American cultural and media infiltration. Canadians now feel that they have been deprived in many sectors of domestic industry. In particular, the mining industry has always been heavily dependent on foreign investment, about 80 percent of which comes from the United States. In fact, 65 percent of Canada's largest corporations are either wholly owned or principally controlled by foreign corporations. As a result, two pieces of government legislation, the Foreign Investment Review Act (1973) and the National Energy Program (1980), have been introduced.

The basic objectives of these pieces of legislation are to insure the continued development of the mining industry to Canada's benefit and to promote a policy of Canadianization (particularly of energy). This approach, along with the labor problems, has had a depressive effect on overseas investment. However, the diversification also promoted by this legislation has led to greater Japanese investment, particularly in the more favored joint ventures. Federal government interference is only one aspect of the mineral trade, since its operation depends also on the provincial governments, the mining corporations, the energy suppliers, and the consumers (both internal and external). Trade policy in general has been directed toward an increase in mineral processing, a diversification of secure markets, and improved competitiveness overall.

This political interest in mining is understandable when it is realized that minerals contribute some 9.5 percent of Canada's gross national product (GNP), over 30 percent of which is accounted for by nonfuel minerals. The provincial picture is, in many cases, far more compelling, with 85 percent of the GNP of the Yukon and Northwest Territories and 54 percent of the GNP of Alberta being directly attributable to minerals. Furthermore, minerals (fuel and nonfuel) account for between 28 and 30 percent of Canadian exports as a whole.

Thus, while Canada's geographical position is a strong positive factor, the political factor is complex, and the consequences of the interplay between the two are difficult to predict. This is largely a result of the involvement of three key actors—the federal government, the provincial government, and the mining corporations (which may well be foreign owned). Government policies directed toward improving economic growth, sovereignty, and the quality of life generally, together with tax legislation, have resulted in strong federal involvement in the market and have adversely affected investment. For the United States, this government intrusion appears to be the principal threat. Any attempt to reorient the economy along lines of nationalism and increased competitiveness and to improve the structure of mining would inevitably weaken the U.S. position. In particular, Quebec, the second most important mineral province, with its separatist tendencies poses special problems. However, it must be concluded that through the innate natural strength of the economy and especially in the light of some amelioration of government policies, Canada remains the most secure supplier of U.S. strategic minerals.

On the local scale, the siting of mines gives rise to a further series of issues. In Canada strategic vulnerability is usually a function of the geographical isolation of reserves, a good example of which is afforded by the location of tungsten deposits in the Northwest Territories. There are, however, exceptions. Titanium (ilmenite) and columbium are both mined in Quebec, where the political situation has recently been sensitive. A completely different kind of vulnerability attends the supply of nickel. Although the principal mining sites in Ontario (particularly the Sudbury region) and Manitoba are secure, the bulk of the refining takes place in Clydach (South Wales) and Kristiansand (Norway). This transportational vulnerability is, however, peculiar to nickel, with all other U.S. imports arriving directly from Canada by means of safe internal or coastal routes.

### Australia

Australia is in many ways similar to Canada as a major world mineral supplier, but it has its own brand of political problems. The key difference between the two countries lies in the extent of Australia's geographical separation from its major markets, particularly the United States.

Globally this isolation represents the main threat to the country, with many of its near neighbors potentially unstable and a number possessing centrally planned economies. Australia is an outpost of the West that is particularly handicapped by a low population (15 million) and an area the size of the continental United States to defend. Therefore, its underpopulated (indeed, largely unpopulated) northern and northwestern region is at strategic risk. With the very long sea lines involved, it would be difficult for the Western countries to coordinate aid to Australia.

On a regional level this sense of isolation is considerably enhanced by Australia's distinctive peculiarity in an otherwise largely homogeneous part of the globe. The Philippines and New Zealand are the only other English-speaking countries and also the only other predominantly Christian countries. Apart from New Zealand, most of the nearby states are comparatively small with a high population density. Several possess mineral wealth, though none on the scale of Australia. Only in the cases of Malaysia, Indonesia, and Thailand is the economy as dependent on minerals as the Australian economy. Furthermore, any shipment from Australia is bound to pass through a number of choke points, the vital sea lines to Japan being particularly vulnerable to regional pressures of various kinds.

Like Canada, Australia is a major exporter of a wide variety of minerals, but as far as the United States is concerned, three of these, bauxite, ilmenite, and rutile (both ores of titanium), are strategic (table 15.3). Other minerals of strategic significance are asbestos, manganese, nickel, and tin.

**Table 15.3**
**Strategic Minerals in Australia**

| Mineral | % of US imports | % of world production | % of world reserve base |
|---|---|---|---|
| Bauxite | | | |
| (as alumina) | 79 (1) | 32 (1) | 21 (2) |
| Ilemite | 58 (1) | c. 26 (1) | 6 (7) |
| Rutile | 68 (1) | c. 53 (1) | 9 (3) |

As in Canada, the mineral industry is a major user of the transportation network. The remoteness of many mines from the populated regions of the country has led to infrastructural investment problems. In many cases foreign capital, with or without state assistance, has been employed in the construction of the railway network. In fact, the east coast aside, there is effectively no rail network. Rather, there is a series of single lines to the coast from the various mining sites. While older ports tend to be relatively small, the new ones, principally constructed for iron-ore export, can accommodate the largest ore carriers. With its vast reserves of coal, Australia has abundant energy resources. Although it is a net importer of oil, domestic energy resources are sufficient to meet the requirements of the mining industry. In contrast, water is scarce throughout the continent except on its coastal fringes. However, due to the importance assigned to the developing mineral industry, a potentially serious water situation has been of less consequence than might otherwise have been the case. The Australian mining industry is more highly mechanized and therefore less labor intensive than its Canadian equivalent. Nevertheless, the Australian labor force is highly unionized, and the industry is subject to occasional disruption due to industrial action. However, as in the case of Canada, geographical factors in Australia have combined to produce a very strong mineral economy. Since mineral production accounts for 10 percent of the GNP and minerals make up 32 percent of total exports, government interest in the sector is considerable. As in the case of Canada, the structure is complex, involving not only the central government but also the various state governments, the mining corporations, and the consumers, domestic and foreign. Furthermore, with 52 percent of the industry foreign owned and as much as 60 percent under foreign control, there have been similar apprehensions regarding the extent of foreign capital investment. During the 1970s the government introduced legislation to insure Australian control of major investments in the future. However, although a large proportion of foreign investment originates in the United States, Japan rather than the United States is the principal market for the Australian mineral trade, unlike the situation in Canada.

The growth of Japanese industry, particularly its metallurgical sector, has generated the vast growth of Australian mining over the past twenty years. Rather than direct investment, the Japanese tend to favor long-term contracts, which are notoriously insensitive to price fluctuations. The Japanese prefer to import raw ores and concentrates, which are subject to refining and processing in Japan. However, it is worth noting that Japanese industry is changing (partly as a result of fuel costs) and is establishing plants offshore, particularly in North and South America. In the medium term such a change of orientation in Japan's metallurgical industry could exercise a decisive impact on the Australian mining industry. If present trends continue, the Australian mining industry will be compelled to develop other bases. Indeed, Australia is at present looking to Southeast Asian markets in an effort to offset the potential decline in Japanese demand. However, in this region it encounters considerable competition from Canada, the United States, and South Africa for the export of coal, and from Brazil and India for iron-ore export. Thus in many ways the Australian mineral industry resembles closely that of Canada, the major differences stemming more from length of sea lines and position on the globe than from internal geographical factors. Furthermore, the two governments approach the various problems facing the mining industry in a similar manner. In both cases legislation has been introduced to safeguard the national interest, to improve the competitiveness of the industry, and to diversify the trade pattern.

At the local level the processing of bauxite, the key strategic mineral, is divided between the Darling range in the south and the Gulf of Carpentaria in the far north. The latter location, which also includes a smelting facility, is all but indefensible. Ilmenite and rutile, together with zircon monazite, are mined from mineral sands around the core population regions of the east and west coasts.

### South Africa

Were it not for the internal complications posed by apartheid and its international ramifications, South Africa, the third-greatest supplier of minerals in the world, would appear in many ways similar to Canada and Australia. From the global viewpoint it contains a range of minerals vital to the West, but as in the case of Australia, sea lines are a source of problems. In fact, for various reasons, the Cape route is considered one of the most vulnerable sea lines of communication. Situated at the midpoint of this route, between the South Atlantic and the Indian oceans, South Africa is of great potential significance in view of the East-West confrontation.

On a regional scale South Africa differs geopolitically from Canada and Australia in that it has land frontiers with less developed countries. Moreover, the size of its armed forces and its probable possession of nuclear weaponry make it a relative superpower in the region. The "frontline states," while deploring the racial policies of South Africa, still maintain covert trading links and militarily are powerless to resist South African pressure. However, they represent a long-term threat to the South African regime, both by virtue of their very existence and by their ability to provide bases for guerrilla initiatives. Nevertheless, there

**Table 15.4**
**Strategic Minerals in South Africa**

| Mineral | % of U.S. imports | % of world production | % of world reserve base |
|---|---|---|---|
| Chromium | 55 (1) | 27 (2) | 84 (1) |
| Fluorspar | 28 (2) | 7 (5) | 17 (1) |
| Manganese | 31 (1) | 11 (2) | 71 (7) |
| (Ferro-manganese) | 39 (1) | | |
| Platinum | 49 (1) | 42 (2) | 81 (1) |
| Vanadium | 44 (1) | 30 (2) | 47 (1) |

is no doubt that central and southern African countries depend heavily on the South African infrastructure in general and the rail network and the ports in particular. Exports from Zaire, Zambia, and Zimbabwe are generally dispatched from East London, although since the Nkomatic accord (1984), Maputo (in Mozambique) is likely to remain open for such purposes. The other key influence on minerals is the need for labor, with repatriated wage earnings from the mines constituting a significant element in neighboring economies. Finally, the region is one of continuing turmoil, principally, though perhaps not totally, generated by South African policies.

South Africa is a major world source of seventeen minerals. It is no exaggeration to say that it is the main supplier of strategic minerals to the United States (table 15.4). The four most commonly recognized key strategics, chromium, cobalt, manganese, and platinum-group metals, are to be found in South Africa. Since by far the world's largest reserves of three of these key strategics are to be found in South Africa (cobalt being the exception), their very location warrants such a classification.

Furthermore, in each case, in the event of South African supplies failing, the next-largest (and in certain cases the only other significant) producer is the Soviet Union. Indeed, for chromium and platinum-group metals, the Soviet Union appears on the trading list of the United States. Thus, even were South Africa as potentially stable as Australia or Canada, these minerals would be considered more strategic than anything supplied by those two countries. South Africa is thus a supplier of more key strategics to the United States than any other country. Furthermore, for the four strategic minerals most dominated by South Africa, the Soviet Union is also a major producer, although it has comparatively limited reserves. Table 15.5 illustrates this point by listing the percentages of world production and of the world reserve base for both South Africa and the Soviet Union.

South Africa has a well-developed rail network linking mining centers with the major ports and also providing an outlet for countries to the north. At the same time, it has a series of magnificent deep-water ports, particularly the two newly developed bulk exporting ports of Saldanha and Richard's Bay. Richard's Bay, which is the major export point for chromite and ferrochrome, has some

Table 15.5

World Production and World Reserves: South Africa and the Soviet Union

| Percent of World Production | | | | Percent of World Reserve Base | | |
| --- | --- | --- | --- | --- | --- | --- |
| Mineral | SA | SU | Total | SA | SU | Total |
| Chromium | 27 | 29 | 56 | 84 | 2 | 86 |
| Manganese | 11 | 47 | 58 | 71 | 21 | 92 |
| Platinum | 42 | 54 | 96 | 81 | 17 | 98 |
| Vanadium | 30 | 33 | 63 | 47 | 25 | 72 |

of the most sophisticated handling devices in the world. Minerals from South Africa's landlocked northern neighbors and Zaire are shipped from East London, a river port, while the manganese ore from the northern Cape is exported through Port Elizabeth. All such transportation to the West of course uses the vulnerable Cape route. South Africa also has a well-developed road network that supplements the railways where necessary. With ample coal and uranium reserves, South Africa suffers no shortage of energy supplies for mining. However, the scarcity of water resources, particularly in the western part of South Africa, could well restrict future development. The labor problem arises from the fact that the vast majority of mine workers are black immigrants, either from neighboring states or from the various homeland regions within South Africa itself. Although wage differentials between whites and blacks have been improved (with the lesser-skilled grades increasingly open to blacks), equality of opportunity is still a long way off. Thus, despite a certain degree of unionization, a good deal of labor unrest persists. While wages account for approximately 50 percent of mining costs,[5] one of the major benefits offered by the South African minerals industry has been comparatively low prices. Thus, although geographically the industry to some extent resembles those in Canada and Australia, the problems facing South Africa are potentially more severe.

Since the minerals industry accounts for some 20 percent of GNP and provides approximately 50 percent of foreign exchange earnings, it is of great importance to the government. Although the state does operate directly in certain sectors (notably iron and zinc) and controls several others indirectly through the Industrial Development Corporation of South Africa, mining is generally left to private enterprise. Indeed, the mining laws and tax policies have been designed to encourage investment from abroad. Thus six multinational corporations account for most of the mining activity in South Africa, together constituting the Chamber of Mines of South Africa. Furthermore, through their provision of services, various state organizations, particularly the Geological Survey and the Council on Mineral Technology, have put the domestic mining industry at the forefront of technological advances.

However, in any risk assessment of South African mineral supplies, race-relations policies are probably of greater influence than those concerned specifically with mining. Since the sum of threats to South Africa, external and internal, is unique and exerts a crucial bearing upon the analysis, lengthier conclusions from field study are included here.

During the 1980s there have been no serious external threats to strategic mineral procurement from South Africa. International disunity and national self-interest have so far prevented any coordinated action against South Africa, and this situation is likely to continue for some time. However, extreme measures in South Africa itself might still provoke the international community to a more concerted effort against the present regime, though for the time being, internal threats seem to pose much the greater danger.

Despite its current depressed state, the mining industry has a great underlying strength, which results from the following factors:

1. The enormous scale of reserves

2. The highly developed infrastructure

3. The abundance of power for processing, beneficiation, and so on

4. The commercial stability

5. The technological expertise

Against this vast mining potential must be set the simmering resentment and frustration felt in particular by the black population. The key destabilizing factor appears to be the growth of an urban black population with a potential for conflict, ranging from civil disobedience to actual armed uprising. However, the South African security forces are so strong that it is doubtful whether internal unrest could, in the short term, become so serious as to affect the production of strategic minerals. It is more likely that the domestic populations of consumer countries will bring pressure to bear on their governments to discontinue the import of minerals from South Africa. If the situation in South Africa were to deteriorate to such an extent that a coordinated attack from the north occurred simultaneously with internal uprisings, the situation could well get rapidly out of control. In the background, the demographic composition of South Africa is rapidly changing due to the different birth rates of the black and white populations, changes in the physical environment, lack of water resources, and a steady encroachment of the desert.

Locally the position of the Bushveld Igneous Complex renders the platinum and chromium mines particularly vulnerable. Not only are they near the major urban concentrations of South Africa where major confrontations are on the increase, but they are also within easy striking distance of the "frontline state" borders. The northeastern border area is heavily forested, and the potential for infiltration by guerrilla forces is high. Unlike these mines, the open-cast manganese quarries of the northern Cape, albeit close to the frontier, are in a semiarid environment with next to no cover at all. Thus, while the major mines are all situated near the frontier area, there are considerable differences between the west and the east.

## Mexico

Superficially, Mexico and Canada appear to share certain locational characteristics. Mexico, however, is distinguished by the fact that it is the only developing country in North America and as such has more in common with Latin
and Central America. The United States takes a close interest in Mexico for a
number of obvious reasons. During recent years, however, there has been an
inclination by Mexico toward nonaligned nations, and with Cuba and Nicaragua
nearby, a question of supply vulnerability must remain. Nevertheless, it is difficult to believe that under existing political conditions Mexico could seriously
consider a future for itself completely free of the United States.

Mexico's economy is potentially the strongest in the Caribbean, although its
international debt has limited its scope for action. Furthermore, the Caribbean
region has been politically unstable for well over a decade.

Mexico supplies fluorspar, bismuth, graphite, silver, and strontium to the
United States, but of these, only fluorspar can be considered marginally strategic.
Mexico is the source for 54 percent of the total import of fluorspar by the United
States. It accounts for 14 percent of the total amount of fluorspar produced in
the world (second-largest producer) and has the fifth-largest reserve base (9
percent). The major fluorspar mining occurs near the border with the United
States. Although the mines are not connected to the main rail network, they are
situated in the most secure position within Mexico.

Mexico possesses a skeletal rail network with a line along the center of the
country and one or two branches to key mining areas. However, a high proportion
of the mining depends on road transport, although only 30 percent of the roads
are paved. Minerals are important in the transportation system, accounting for
just under 30 percent of the total traffic. In 1980 the World Bank approved a
loan to expand and develop Mexico's major rail network, while the government
is at present restoring the cargo land bridge across the country from the Atlantic
to the Pacific.

The transport network includes pipelines for petroleum and gas to the ports
as well as directly into the United States. Mexico is the third-largest oil producer
in the West. It also has large gas reserves. Indeed, the energy balance is dominated by gas and petroleum, which account for 88 percent of primary requirements. A mere 9 percent of the energy consumed originates in coal, the remainder
comes from hydroelectric power and the two nuclear power stations. However,
there is a fast-growing demand for energy, which is bound to create bottlenecks
in the future. Similarly, water resources, which are conspicuous by their extreme
scarcity in the north, could present problems for Mexico's continued development. Labor relations have been reasonably calm, especially in comparison with
a number of other Latin American countries. Mexico has experienced a major
difficulty in maintaining a supply of skilled workers. Thus, although the geographical infrastructure reveals a number of problems relating to communication,

energy, water, and labor, Mexico is comparatively well placed by the standards of other developing countries.

Minerals make up 74 percent of Mexican exports, of which nonfuel materials contribute 5 percent. Since the industry is highly critical for the economic development of the country, the government has been anxious to maintain foreign investment, mainly from the United States, Canada, and Japan. As a result of mining legislation (1975) and the policy of Mexicanization, the mineral sector consists of state-owned, partly state-owned, and private companies. Private mining companies contributed 49 percent of output and parastate companies 39 percent (1983). Almost 90 percent of all mining activity is conducted by the five largest mining companies, and these tend to account for well over 50 percent of output. The government furthermore provides various subsidies and incentives for mining, its policy being to reduce the ownership role of the state.

Governmental stability has been maintained since the Mexican Revolution (1910), with power kept in the hands of a party that has consistently represented the country's major economic and political interests. During the 1970s there was a trend toward nonalignment, but in recent years the government has tended to move closer to the United States. The advantage of friendly governmental policy has reinforced that provided by geographical contiguity.

## Jamaica

Though more distant than Mexico, Jamaica is close enough to the United States to be geographically or locationally comparable to it. It has had a relatively stable government, particularly in the recent past. Jamaica is important to the United States for the supply of bauxite and alumina. Its reserves of both minerals are more abundant than those held by either of its neighbors, Guyana and Surinam. Jamaica has been a leading source of U.S. bauxite imports, providing 37 percent (averaged over the three-year period 1981–84), and the second most important source of alumina with 11 percent. In 1984 it was the third-largest bauxite producer in the world, accounting for 9 percent of the total world production. It possesses 9 percent of the world reserve base in bauxite, making it the fifth-best-endowed country. However, since 1985 the Jamaican bauxite industry has been in some difficulty.

Bauxite and alumina are transported by rail, road, and conveyor belt to the various processing plants and export docks. Exports have to pass through the narrow Windward Passage to the sea line to the United States. For its size, Jamaica has an efficient transport network. However, for energy it is almost totally dependent on imported oil, although the energy requirements of the bauxite industry are kept separate from the national grid. In view of the difficulties involved in oil supply, there are plans to use coal in the industry. Two major companies, Alcoa and Alcan, recently completed conversion to coal. Jamaica's water-supply resources are sufficient to meet its needs but provide virtually no opportunity for generating energy. Jamaica suffers from high unemployment, but labor unrest among highly unionized workers has not reached serious proportions. The main problem posed by the geographical infrastructure relates to energy resources and to reduction of costs.

Since bauxite and alumina account for over 70 percent of export earnings, Jamaica is beset with problems commonly experienced by single-commodity economies. Five major North American corporations, of which the government has acquired an interest in four, control the production of these minerals. However, government policy necessarily places a premium on bauxite and alumina. Though Jamaica is conveniently located near to the United States, any depression in the alumina industry will set off considerable reverberations.

### Brazil

Brazil's geopolitical orientation differs considerably from that of both Jamaica and Mexico. While South America has long been linked with North America politically, economically, and strategically, recent changes in government in Argentina (1983), Brazil (1985), Peru (1985), and Uruguay (1986) from rule by the military to a popularly elected government have tended to generate a fresh political orientation. There has been an increasing desire on the part of these countries to regard themselves as part of a South Atlantic and South Pacific land mass. Brazil and Argentina in particular have cultivated links with southern African countries. In the case of Brazil, of course, the potential for development is so great that the country may well become a major world power in the next century. It is certainly the major regional power in South America at the present time.

Brazil's vast land area has only been surveyed in a limited fashion, and it would seem reasonable to suppose that major mineral deposits remain to be discovered. However, while the mineral sector has played an important role in the impressive economic growth of Brazil, it is not as significant as agriculture and manufacturing. Brazil possesses the world's largest reserves of at least three strategic minerals, of which columbium is the most important to the United States. It provides 75 percent of U.S. columbium imports and is the only relevant source of the mineral. Furthermore, in 1984 Brazil was the dominant producer of columbium (78 percent), and its reserves amount to 88 percent of the world base. Thus, despite Brazil's richness of mineral deposits, only one comparatively exotic metal possesses great strategic significance for the United States.

The transport network of Brazil is very thin and has been particularly developed to service the "iron quadrangle." A major line has also been constructed to Carajás, but the columbium mines are served only by a recently constructed branch line and road. The mineral is produced from three open-pit mines, and there is also a ferrocolumbium plant nearby at Araxa (Minas Gerais Province). Brazil uses a wide range of energy sources but is highly dependent on imported oil (which accounts for over 40 percent of the energy balance). However, the development of domestic coal and hydroelectric power should alleviate the situation. Thus, while energy may be a limiting factor locally, the long-term supply of it poses no big problems. Water conservation measures in operation should insure the supply required for mining purposes. Indeed, columbium mining uses mainly recycled water, with additions from a nearby lake. Labor relations in the mining industry are very good, but the work force is comparatively small because a high degree of mechanization has been achieved. Brazil, therefore, appears to be taking its place as one of the major mineral-source regions of the world, and with a more developed transport network, there would appear to be few impediments to its exportation of strategic minerals to the United States.

Government programs dominate the mining industry. A National Prospecting Program has been set up to oversee the development of the mineral industry. While state-owned companies account for about 70 percent of economic activity, government companies account for only 20 percent of total mineral output. The remainder is shared more or less equally between private Brazilian and foreign companies. Government policy can be described as supportive and is particularly active in metallurgical research and development of technology. However, mineral output accounts for only just over 2 percent of the GNP, and while future prospects are excellent, the economy is largely supported at present by other sectors. The mining industry in Brazil is in a strong position.

The fact that such a high percentage of columbium supplies to the United States have their origin in one small isolated area of Brazil must pose problems of vulnerability. In the total mineral portfolio of the United States, this is the most extreme case of concentration, since even in the medium term there appear to be no alternatives. Thus the effects of any constraint on supply, ranging from labor disruption to natural catastrophes, will be considerably magnified.

It can be concluded that geography furnishes a key element to be taken into consideration in any corporate risk assessment. However, owing to the all-embracing nature of the discipline, it is necessary to dissect it into its component parts and to consider each of these on a variety of scales. Unless geography is deliberately factored into the assessment in this fashion, its significant role may remain obscured. As a result, only a partial picture of the attendant risks will emerge.

## NOTES

1. C. De Vore, "Strategic Minerals: A Present Danger," *Signal*, January 1981, 63–68; P. Seabury, "Industrial Policy and National Defense," *Journal of Contemporary Studies*, vol. 6, no. 2 (1983): 5–15; E. W. Anderson, "Factors Affecting the Supply of Strategic Raw Materials with Particular Reference to the Aerospace Manufacturing Industry," in NATO, *Materials Substitution and Recycling* (Paris: NATO Advisory Group for Aerospace Research and Development, 1984), 2.1–2.20; D. James, ed., *Strategic Minerals: A Resource Crisis* (Washington, D.C.: Council on Economics and National Security, 1981).

2. E. W. Anderson, "The Need to Safeguard the Supply of Strategic Minerals to the

West,'' in *Global Collective Security in the 1980s*, G. Stewart-Smith (London: Foreign Affairs Publishing Company, 1982), 67–79.

3. This model was developed and tested during work on a number of projects for the British Ministry of Defence in 1984.

4. For the analysis at the regional level and particularly at the local level, where possible, personal experience was used. This was supplemented by data from a number of key sources, most importantly W.C.J. Van Rensburg, *Strategic Minerals* (Englewood Cliffs, N.J.: Prentice-Hall, 1986), vol. 1.

5. This figure was calculated following interviews at the Minerals Bureau and Chamber of Mines (Johannesburg) and the Rand Afrikaans University at the University of Stellenbosch.

6. Under the Trade and Development Program of the International Development Cooperation Agency.

# 16

# Financial Warfare

## Joshua N. Feinman, Peter M. Garber, and Michelle R. Garfinkel

To the extent that it has received academic attention, financial warfare has usually been relegated to a back chapter in primers on economic warfare.[1] Existing analyses aim chiefly at listing policies to prevent enemy countries from gaining resources abroad from exports of foreign financial securities.[2] The literature generally ignores the potential of financial warfare to disrupt internal taxation by an enemy government and, more generally, the credit allocation mechanism in an enemy country.[3] Apparently, the benefits from engaging in financial warfare are so obvious that economists have spent little effort to analyze how financial warfare contributes to a country's war aims. While application of financial weapons may hinder an enemy's acquisition of resources, it may also harm the country employing them, especially in the presence of retaliation by the enemy. To make the case that a country advances its war objectives by engaging in financial warfare requires a demonstration that financial warfare emerges as an equilibrium outcome in the gaming situation faced by the warring countries.

In this chapter we will develop a model to address whether countries behaving optimally in a war will employ financial warfare. We will pose financial warfare as an attack on an enemy's internal credit mechanism, resulting in inadequate funding of otherwise profitable investment projects and a decline in resources available for the war effort. We study financial warfare in the context of an unregulated, free-market financial and banking system.

To summarize our results, we find that financial warfare emerges as a Nash equilibrium prior to the major battles of the war. Since equilibrium levels of military activity fall after a financial attack, financial warfare serves as a substitute for construction of military goods. Also, attacks on assets of financial intermediaries through asset freezes are less disruptive to economic activity than are attacks on liabilities through counterfeiting. An economic system can avoid losses to financial attack by restricting activities of financial institutions. A government can impose either peacetime financial controls or a centrally directed allocation mechanism. Both methods might immunize the economy against financial attack. Since it restricts the dimensions of peacetime financial contracts, however, the immunization is not costless; and behavior in "normal," peacetime periods can be understood only in the context of potential warfare.

We divide the chapter into six sections. In the first section we present a brief history of financial warfare of the type postulated in this chapter. We concentrate our attention on the financial crisis that materialized at the start of World War I and on World War II plans to counterfeit an enemy's currency for the purpose of paralyzing its financial system. In the second section we derive a war-game model in which we determine the magnitude of wartime expenditure. The desire either to extract or to avoid extractions of tribute drives the choice of war expenditure, and the occurrence and magnitude of war emerge as endogenous variables.[4] In the third section we review a simple, off-the-shelf banking model due to Waldo (1985) in which a resource-destroying financial crisis is possible. In the fourth section we combine the war and banking models to derive the main results on the emergence of financial warfare. We consider attacks both on the liability and asset sides of the financial system. In the fifth section we consider how an economy might immunize itself against this form of attack. The final section contains conclusions.

## INCIDENTS OF FINANCIAL WARFARE

Financial warfare of the type considered here has appeared as a phenomenon of the large-scale wars of the twentieth century. Such activities have appeared in other episodes, notably the Napoleonic Wars, but the financial crisis triggered by the start of World War I serves as a prototype of modern financial warfare.[5] While the World War I crisis was an unintentional weapon for disrupting a country's mobilization plans, planned attempts to initiate a financial crisis emerged in World War II with the famous German effort to produce and circulate perfect counterfeit British five-pound notes.

### World War I Crisis

The sudden outbreak of World War I generated a five-month financial crisis in all the major participants and neutrals.[6] Centered in London, international short-term capital markets froze, forcing major liquidations of long-term securities and a consequent closure of all the major secondary securities markets. For example, the New York Stock Exchange remained closed for five months in 1914. The resulting collapse of markets for primary securities hindered the movement of capital from civilian to war production that one would expect in a rapidly mobilizing economy. Since the crisis delayed the transition to industrial mobilization in all the warring economies by five months, few resources were available for pursuing the war in the first half of 1915 after the warring countries had exhausted previously accumulated munitions in the initial 1914 battles.

The crisis emerged because of potential balance-sheet problems for short-term lenders. Since London was the center of international finance, most short-term international credit assumed the form of sterling loans, accepted by British acceptance houses and held by British discount banks. In particular, many assets held by British financial institutions were liabilities of institutions and individuals in the Central Powers, who would obviously not pay once their governments initiated financial warfare in the form of a prohibition of capital movements to enemy countries. Since acceptance houses were necessarily insolvent and since no one knew the condition of individual discount houses or even of the clearing banks, the short-term credit markets locked up, with everyone scrambling for sterling. In an effort to convert to sterling, foreigners dumped their holdings of U.S. securities on the New York Stock Exchange, forcing its closure. Similar problems emerged in France and Germany.

Though central banks served as traditional lenders of last resort to end the crisis after several months, financing of new investment projects was retarded. The crisis was an unintentional effect of the unexpected explosion of war among participants in an unregulated international capital market. The warring countries, however, learned the effectiveness of fomenting a financial crisis for disrupting the mobilization of an enemy country.

## World War II Financial Attacks: Hyperinflationary Warfare

Though much larger battles impended with the outbreak of World War II, an initial financial crisis of the World War I sort did not occur. By the beginning of the war, the warring countries had insulated their capital markets from potential financial attacks through capital and exchange controls. Some disturbances occurred on London secondary markets, but they did not disrupt the mobilization since allocation of capital to the war industries had shifted to a central planning apparatus.

Defensive counters to financial warfare in the form of capital controls developed in the 1930s. Simultaneously, some countries attempted to develop offensive methods to trigger financial crises. Notably, the Germans planned to disrupt the British economy by dropping perfect counterfeit five-pound notes on Great Britain.[7] Gathering the best European counterfeiters and providing them with engraving and paper technologies available to a technologically advanced government, the Germans succeeded in producing perfect counterfeits within a year of the outbreak of the war.[8]

Placed under the control of the SS, the original plan was quickly subverted.

The SS decided to circulate the counterfeits in occupied territory to serve as an auxiliary source of revenue for SS operations. This change implied a limitation on the quantity of counterfeits placed in circulation, as would any "for-profit" counterfeit operation. Thus, although the Germans developed the potential for an attack on British currency, they did not unleash the weapon in the most potentially destructive manner.

What disruption could the Germans have caused if they had followed through on their original plan? They could have delivered the currency at low cost, since their bombers would not need to approach defended targets. Once the population realized that the currency supply was subject to sudden increases in arbitrary amounts, the demand for currency would have collapsed. The population would have switched to an accounting-based method of transactions. For smaller transactions, the government would have had to provide a commodity-based currency like gold and silver coins. As an ultimate result, this form of financial attack would have removed part of the government's inflation tax base. It would also have caused losses for currency holders and transfers between debtors and creditors (to the extent that the government did not redefine the unit of account in contracts). In the transition this hyperinflationary attack might have disrupted transactions mechanisms and credit markets, hindering the channeling of resources into the war machine.


## A WAR MODEL

In this section we will present a two-period, two-country model in which a war will occur with certainty after the first period. No war will occur in the second period. The two countries, labeled $E$ and $G$, are identical in tastes, technology, and endowments. In each country at the start of period 1, representative consumers receive an endowment of $Z$ units of goods, of which they consume $C_1$ and save the remainder to produce consumption goods $C_2$ in period 2. The intertemporal utility function $U(C_1) + U(C_2)$ depends on consumption in both periods.

An economy can generate consumption goods for period 2 in two ways. A peaceful investment technology $f(i)$, with $f' > 0$ and $f'' < 0$, allows the transfer of goods from period 1 to period 2, where $i$ represents the number of endowment units invested.

War provides an alternative means of transferring goods from the present to the future. In this model success in war translates into an increase in future goods consumption through the imposition of tribute on a defeated enemy.[9] A unit of endowment can be converted into a unit of war goods. War goods do not enter directly into the utility function. The outcome of the war at the end of period 1 depends on the relative amounts of war goods, $W^E$ and $W^G$, constructed by the two countries in period 1. The outcome is reflected in the amount of tribute one

**Figure 16.1**
**Tribute Collected versus Military Expenditure**

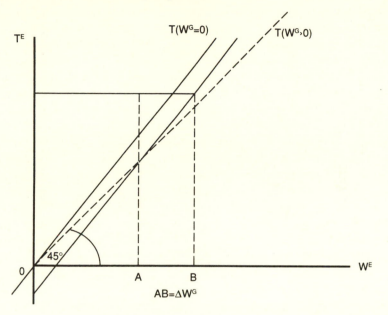

country can collect from the other in period 2. Specifically, tribute $T$ is determined by

$$T^E = \begin{cases} a(W^E - W^G) \text{ if } -f(i^E) < a(W^E - W^G) < f(i^G), \\ -f(i^E) \text{ if } a(W^E - W^G) \le -f(i^E), \\ f(i^G \text{ if } f(i^G) \le a(W^E - W^G), \end{cases}$$

$$T^G = -T^E,$$

where the constant coefficient $a$ exceeds unity.

The amount of tribute exacted depends linearly on the difference in war effort, but it cannot exceed the amount of second-period goods available in the defeated country. Ignoring magnitudes of warfare that trigger these kinks in the tribute function, we represent the tribute for country $E$ as a function of $E$'s war expenditure in figure 16.1.

The position of the tribute function depends on the magnitude of $G$'s war expenditure. The slope of the tribute function is $a$. When $W^G = 0$, the function passes through the origin. An increase in $W^G$ shifts the tribute function to the right by the change in $W^G$. Since our assumption of symmetric countries will imply a stalemated war in any equilibrium, attempts to gain future goods by investing in a war machine will always be fruitless.

We will assume that governments gain resources to fight the war through lump-sum taxation in period 1 and make lump-sum transfers of tribute to their

**Figure 16.2**
**Optimal Peaceful and Military Investment**

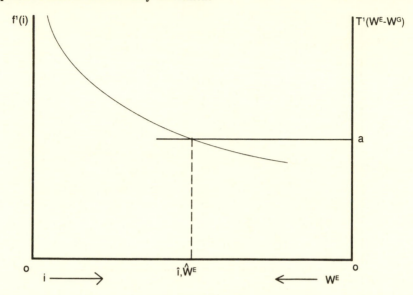

citizens in period 2. Each government selects the magnitude of the war effort to maximize the utility level of its representative consumer.

Country $E$'s problem is to maximize

$$U(C_1) + U(C_2)$$

By its choice of $W^E$ and $i$, country $E$ maximizes its welfare such that

$$C_1 = Z - W^E - i,$$
$$C_2 = f(i) + a(W^E - W^G).$$

Country $G$ solves a similar problem. Each government solves its problem taking the other country's war effort as given.

The first-order conditions for this problem are $U'(C_1)/U'(C_2) = a = f'(i)$. We graph the second equation, which determines the optimal mix between peaceful investment and war goods in both countries, in figure 16.2. The intersection of the marginal payoff curves of peaceful and military investment determines the optimal mix of peaceful investment $\hat{i}$ and war goods production $\hat{W}^E$ for a given $Z - C_1$. Because of the constancy of the marginal payoff on war investment, increases in $Z - C_1$ generate only increased war expenditure, provided that $f'(Z - C_1) \leq a$.

Combining the two methods of transferring goods from the present to the future, we can plot country $E$'s production-possibility frontier for first-period and second-period goods, assuming momentarily that $W^G = 0$ (figure 16.3). The curved segment of the production frontier starting at $Z$ represents the allocation of first-period goods to peaceful investment. At point B, where $f'(i) = a$, the linear, tribute-extraction segment begins. Until $f'(i) = a$, investors allocate

**Figure 16.3**
**Two-Period Consumption Choice**

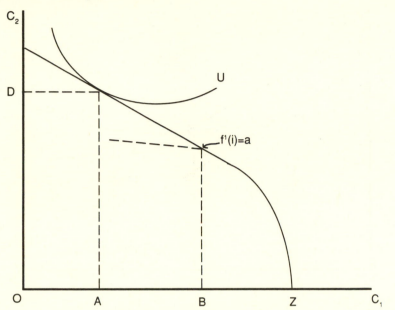

all goods not consumed in period 1 to peaceful investment. If consumers prefer to save more than *BZ* goods in period 1, a government acting to maximize the representative consumer's welfare will allocate all savings above *BZ* to constructing armaments. As usual, the tangency between the representative consumer's indifference curve and the opportunity set determines the optimal allocation: $C_1 = OA$, $C_2 = OD$, $WE = AB$, and $i = BZ$. If marginal returns on peaceful investment decline fast enough with investment increases, each country will construct positive amounts of war goods.

If $W^G$ increases, *E*'s production-possibility frontier shifts downward by the change in $W^G$ multiplied by *a*, with one exception. Because the change in $W^G$ has no impact on *Z*, the shifted opportunity set still begins at *Z* on the $C_2 = 0$ axis, following the axis until the payoff from peaceful investment suffices to pay tribute to *G*.

In figure 16.4 we depict the effect of a shift in $W^G$ on *E*'s optimal allocation. If consumption goods in both periods are normal goods, the increase in $W^G$ causes $W^E$ to rise, (represented by the shift from A to A'), but by less than the increase in $W^G$. This last result is crucial for deriving *E*'s reaction function, which indicates *E*'s military expenditure for each level of *G*'s war expenditure. In turn, the reaction function will determine the Nash solution to this problem. We plot the reaction functions of both countries in figure 16.5. The slope of *E*'s reaction function is less than one. Symmetry requires that the slope of *G*'s reaction function exceed one and that the intersection of the reaction functions occur on the 45° line. The intersection depicts a Nash equilibrium of identical war ex-

**Figure 16.4**
**Consumption Possibilities with Positive Foreign Military Expenditure**

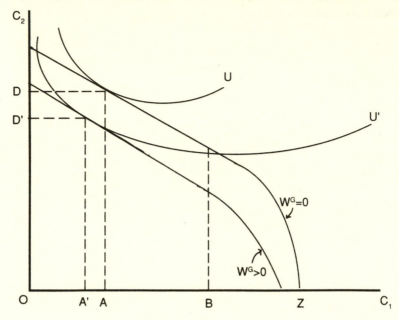

**Figure 16.5**
**Countries G and E Reaction Functions**

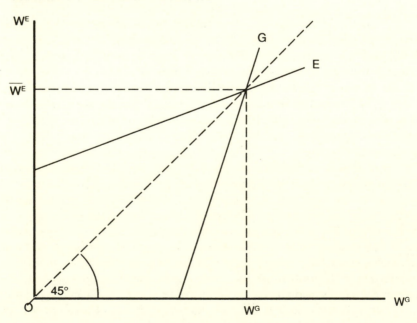

**Figure 16.6**
**Equilibrium with No Military Expenditure**

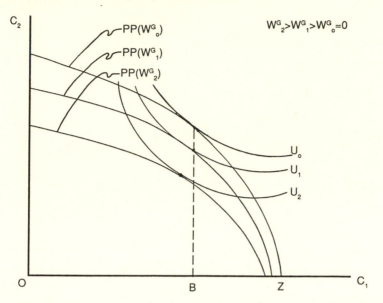

penditures, $W^E$ and $W^G$ implying a stalemated war. Consequently, consumption in period 2 for both countries is simply the gross return on the peaceful investment.

## Peaceful versus Warlike Outcomes

For the previous graphical example, we assumed an interior solution for military expenditure, so the Nash equilibrium necessarily involved a war. Tastes, technology, and the endowment magnitude determine whether or not the governments of $E$ and $G$ will select positive military expenditure. For a given technology, if consumers have strong-enough preferences for present consumption or if they have small-enough endowments, their governments will have no incentives to invest in war goods.

In figure 16.6 we have diagrammed production possibility frontiers for three different levels of foreign-war expenditures. At the outer frontier, where $W^G = 0$, no war goods are produced by country $E$. As country $G$'s level of war-goods production rises, country $E$'s production frontier shifts downward. Beyond a threshold level $W^G$, country $E$ engages in war-goods production.

In figure 16.7 we depict the reaction functions for the two countries for this case. Neither country $E$ nor country $G$ produces war goods until its enemy's war production exceeds the threshold level. Since the reaction functions intersect at the origin, the Nash solution precludes war-goods production. Although war is possible, neither country chooses to fight.

**Figure 16.7**
**Non-Intersecting Reaction Functions**

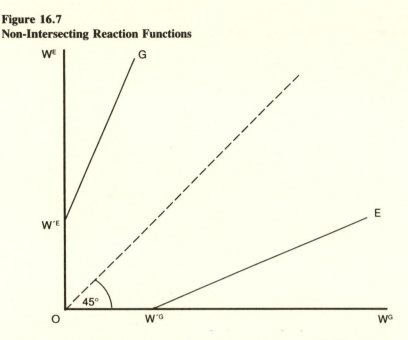

As a country's endowment $Z$ rises, its production-possibility frontier shifts rightward for a given amount of foreign-war production. For large-enough endowment increases, a country will choose to construct positive quantities of war goods as the marginal payoff of peaceful investment declines. In figure 16.7 endowment increases would shift country $E$'s reaction function to the left and country $G$'s reaction function to the right. There exists a threshold endowment level $Z'$ for both countries below which no war occurs in the Nash equilibrium. Above $Z'$ both countries construct positive quantities of war goods.

## A Depression-Induced War

Introducing a stochastic peaceful investment technology, we can account for the observation of intermittent belligerent and peacetime periods. For example, let peaceful technology for both countries be given by $f(i, e) = \Theta g(i)$, where $g' > 0$, $g'' < 0$, and $\Theta$ has mean 1 ($g$ is a specific function for $f$ where the disturbance enters as a multiplier). In figure 16.8, with a good draw $\Theta_1$, both countries would choose not to produce war goods. In contrast, a poor draw $\Theta_2$ rotates the production frontier downward sufficiently to make the production of war goods part of the optimal strategy. To explain the observable succession of war and peace, we imagine that the game described in this section is repeatedly played every two periods. The games differ only in the realization of the random payoff parameter for peaceful production $\Theta$.

From the realization of a high $\Theta$ would emerge a period of peace. A low $\Theta$ would trigger a war. For example, the economic contraction of the 1930s might

**Figure 16.8**
**Effect of Productivity Shift**

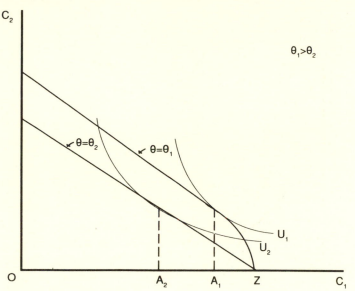

be interpreted as a low realization of the payoff parameter to investment that made military construction optimal. Hence the outbreak of World War II might be explained in this framework.

## A War Induced by Advances in War Technology

In figure 16.9 we depict a shift in military technology that increases the ability of a country to extract tribute for a given level of war effort. This shift, represented by an increase in $a$, the marginal payoff parameter in the tribute function, changes $E$'s consumption from $A'B'C$ for a zero level of $G$'s war effort. With the old technology, $E$ would have selected zero military construction. The advent of the new technology, however, precipitates an arms race.

## A REVIEW OF WALDO'S BANK-RUN MODEL

To produce an environment in which we can examine the effects of financial warfare, we will attach our simple war model to Waldo's (1985) model of a bank run.[10] In Waldo's model, bank runs emerge from the potential for multiple equilibria; a panic occurs because of a belief that a panic will occur rather than because of market-fundamental insolvencies in the banking system. Since financial warfare works by attacking one of the sides of the financial system's balance sheet to force insolvency, we will consider only market-fundamental collapses of the financial system.

**Figure 16.9**
**Effect of a Shift in Tribute Gathering Technology**

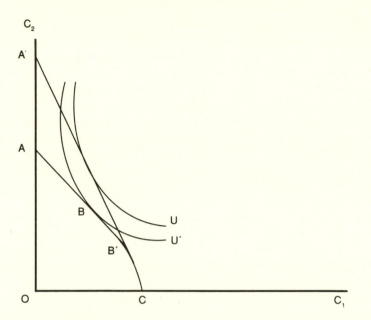

Waldo sets his model in a three-period world populated by small depositors, entrepreneur investors with access to short-term projects, investors with access to long-term projects, and bankers who can lend funds to investors and receive deposits from savers. Small savers cannot lend directly to investors.

Savers are identical and have initial endowments $X$ in period 1 ($X$ is used to designate endowments in Waldo's period 1, a period which precedes those for which $Z$ endowments have been identified). They consume only in the third period with tastes given by utility function $U$. They could store their endowments in amounts $S_1$ or deposit them in banks in amounts $d_1$ with payoff after the first period of $r_{d1}$ per unit deposited. Funds deposited in period 2 earn a payoff $r_{d2}$ in period 3. Deposits can be withdrawn after period 2 or left in the bank.[11] Typically, deposit returns will dominate storage so savers will initially deposit $X$ in banks.

Waldo assumes that for every $N$ savers there is one short-term investor, one long-term investor, and one banker. Short-term investors have projects which pay out $f(i_1)$ in period 2 and $f(i_2)$ in period 3, where $i_1$ and $i_2$ are the amounts invested in the project in the given period. Similarly, the long-term investor has a project that pays out $F(B)$ in period 3, where $B$ represents both the amount invested in period 1 and the number of long-term bonds sold to finance the project. The payoff functions have the following properties: $F(0) = f(0) = 0$, $f' > 1$, $F' > 1$, $F'' < 0$, and $f'' < 0$. Investors finance their projects by selling to banks $b_1$ short-term bonds at interest rates $r_1 - 1$ and long-term bonds $B$ at interest rates $R - 1$ in period 1. Short-term investors also sell $b_2$ bonds to banks in period 2 at interest rate $r_2$. Profit maximization generates sufficient investment that $F'(B) = R$, $f'(b_1) = r_1$, and $f'(i_2) = r_2$, where $i_2 = f(b_1) - r_1 b_1 + b_2$. $b_2$ may be negative if short-term lenders buy securities from banks in period 2.

Competition among banks and interest-rate arbitrage will guarantee that $r_{d1} = r_1$, $r_{d2} = r_2$, and $R = r_1(r_2)$. Banks have no capital and earn zero profits.[12]

In a bank run, banks can pay off second-period withdrawals from receipts from short-term loans in period 1. If these receipts are insufficient, banks can sell long-term securities on the secondary market to short-term investors who purchase the securities with profits from their first-period investments. If the short-term investor spends ($-b_2^* < 0$) in acquiring long-term securities, the short-term interest rate will be $r_2^* = f'(f(b_1) - r_1 b_1 + b_2^*)$. (An asterisk indicates the value of a variable in the presence of a bank run.) Since long-term securities are now one-period loans, their yields must equal the yields on short term projects, that is, $-RB/b_2^* = r_2^*$.

The level of second-period real investment will decline in a bank run because depositors hoard the liquid resources of the bank plus any proceeds from selling the bank's bond portfolio. Short-term investors, who would otherwise have borrowed from the bank, purchase bonds from it in period 2. Since short-term investors use some of their liquid resources to purchase bonds, the level of investment falls in a bank run, thereby reducing the amount of resources available to the economy in period 3. Moreover, the decline in real investment causes a rise in the marginal payoff of investment and in the short-term real interest rate.

## A HYBRID FINANCIAL WARFARE MODEL

We now combine our simple war model with Waldo's (1985) bank-run model. Each country in our war model can incite a bank run in its opponent's financial system by driving asset values below liability values, thereby forcing a fundamental insolvency of the banking sector. A bank run reduces resources available for prosecuting a war by reducing the scale of short-term investment projects.[13]

We consider a four-period model where events in the first three periods are similar to those in Waldo's model. We assume, however, that two identical countries will fight a war between the third and fourth periods. Neither country anticipates the outbreak of the war until the second period, and long-term investment projects are available only in period 1. When they realize that a war will occur, both countries contemplate a financial attack designed to reduce the resources available to their opponent in the war.

In the first two periods decisions are made by individual savers, bankers, and short-term and long-term investors. By period 3 each agent has accumulated a stock of goods generated by his or her investment activities in the first two periods. In our extension of Waldo's model, however, each government acquires resources from its citizens at the beginning of period 3 through lump-sum taxation.[14] To maximize total utility, governments choose an optimal resource allocation among third-period consumption, short-term investment projects maturing in the fourth period, simple storage, and war goods, as in the section "A War Model." This optimal allocation will in turn determine consumption in the fourth period.

We consider two types of financial warfare, both of which can incite a second-period bank run by triggering a fundamental insolvency in the enemy's banking sector. The first type is a counterfeiting operation; this serves as a metaphor for an attack that expands enemy financial liabilities beyond enemy assets. We assume that bank liabilities consist of circulating notes and that each country has the technological capability of expanding the amount of paper liability claims against an enemy's banking system at no cost.[15] This type of financial warfare is similar to the operation contemplated by the Germans in World War II.

As an alternative form of financial warfare, we examine an attack on the asset side of the enemy's banking system that also forces insolvency and a resource-destroying bank run. We assume that in period 1, when neither side anticipates the outbreak of war, banks lend to short-term investors both at home and abroad.[16] Half of each bank's asset portfolio consists of claims on foreigners. In period two, when the inevitability of the war becomes apparent, each country chooses whether or not to enforce the loan contracts between its investors and the foreign banks, imposing, for example, either capital controls or default. We design this analysis to capture the key features of the financial panic triggered by the start of World War I, as described in the section "Incidents of Financial Warfare."

Under either form of attack, a bank run reduces the resources available for war-goods production in the attacked country by reducing second-period investment. We assume, however, that third-period investment opportunities remain intact.[17]

To determine whether either form of financial warfare will emerge in a unique Nash equilibrium, we must examine outcomes in all possible moves of the game: when neither country employs financial warfare, when they both use financial warfare, and when only one country engages in a financial attack. By comparing these outcomes, we can find the noncooperative equilibrium strategies.

For this analysis, we employ the graphical techniques developed in "A War Model." Figure 16.10 depicts the effects of financial warfare on a nation's resources. If Country $E$ is subjected to a financial attack in period 2, its production frontier, drawn here for a given level of foreign-war-goods production $W^G$, will shift to the left. The financial attack destroys the banking system and reduces available resources in period 3 from $OZ$ to $OZ'$.[18]

If third- and fourth-period consumptions are normal goods, the financial attack will reduce consumption in these periods. This implies that the pool of resources devoted to peaceful investment and war production must decline. In our simple war model, this decline will be effected solely through a reduction in the amount of war expenditure. Consequently, the levels of peaceful investment with an attack, $B'Z'$, and without an attack, $BZ$, will be identical.

**Figure 16.10**
**Financial Attack Reduces Initial Endowment**

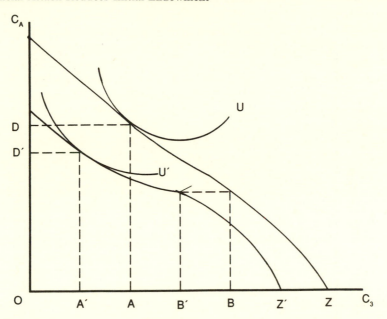

If country *G* employs financial warfare, country *E* will produce fewer war goods for any given level of war expenditure by country *G*. In terms of figure 16.10, $A'B' < AB$. Thus a financial attack precipitates a downward shift in the attacked country's reaction function, as indicated in figure 16.11. A financial attack shifts *E*'s reaction function from $E_1$ to $E_2$. Country *E* will respond to any $W^G$ with a smaller war effort after a financial attack. Analogously, *G*'s reaction function shifts from $G_1$ to $G_2$ if *E* unleashes a financial attack.

Each country chooses whether or not to launch a financial attack. The points *A, B, C,* and *D* represent outcomes for each possible pair of choices. A comparison of these outcomes will determine which pair of choices will emerge as noncooperative equilibrium strategies.

When neither side engages in financial warfare, the outcome is indicated by point *A*. While the magnitude of each country's war effort is relatively large, the war is stalemated, and the two countries attain equal levels of consumption in periods 3 and 4. Point *B* indicates a situation in which *E* does not employ financial warfare while *G* does. By engaging in a financial attack, *G* improves its welfare over that of point *A*. It experiences an increase both in fourth-period consumption through positive receipts from tribute and in third-period consumption through a reduction in war expenditure. By an identical argument, point *D* dominates point *A* for country *E*. Consequently, point *A* cannot be a Nash equilibrium.

At point *C*, both countries engage in financial warfare. Country *E* prefers the

**Figure 16.11**
**Shift in Reaction Functions from Financial Attack**

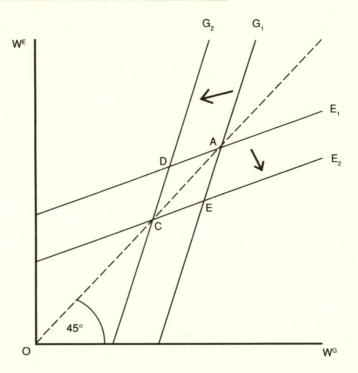

outcome at *C* to that at *B*, since it will spend fewer goods in period 3 on war and pay less tribute in period 4. Similarly, country *G* prefers the outcome at *C* to that at *D*. Therefore, point *C* emerges as the unique Nash equilibrium in this game.

In the equilibrium represented by *C*, a stalemated war will once again occur. The scale of the war measured in terms of war-goods production is smaller at point *C* than at point *A*. Thus financial warfare serves as a substitute for the production of war goods. The smaller magnitude of the war, however, is illusory, since it does not account for the prewar real output losses in the measurement of war costs.

We have considered two different forms of financial warfare: attacks on assets, represented by defaults on foreign loans or asset freezes, and attacks on liabilities, represented by counterfeiting. We will now demonstrate that a default is less damaging than counterfeiting.

The percentage of savers who beat the bank run is smaller under a default-induced run than under a counterfeiting-induced run. In a second-period default domestic short-term investors, freed from a requirement to export liquid resources to foreign banks, experience an increase in available liquid resources. Conversely, half of the contracted inflow of liquidity to domestic banks is cut off and half of domestic bank holdings of long-term bonds is unsaleable in a default. Consequently, savers can withdraw and hoard fewer resources from a banking system subjected to a default, leaving more liquid resources available for short-term real investment projects. The increase in short-term projects in period 2 will increase total resources available just before the war in period 3. The default generates a transfer of goods from savers to investors that does not occur under counterfeiting. For this reason, fewer liquid resources are immobilized by hoarding.

In terms of figures 16.10 and 16.11, greater immobilization of liquid resources implies that a country's production frontier and reaction function shift by a greater amount under counterfeiting than under default. Therefore, both the measured magnitude of the war and the levels of third-period and fourth-period consumption will decline by more in a counterfeiting attack.

## DEFENSIVE FINANCIAL WARFARE

We have examined the problem of financial warfare between undefended economies. Against attacks on either side of its financial system's balance sheet, a country can readily mobilize defensive measures. Such measures, however, would always involve prewar restrictions on the country's financial activities and would burden the country with inefficient institutional arrangements, viewed from a permanent peace perspective.

Examples of defensive financial operations include lender-of-last-resort responsibilities of a central bank, the use of blocked accounts and special payment accounts for debt to foreigners, peacetime capital controls, restriction or suspension of bank payments to depositors, nationalization of capital markets and centralized allocation of capital in an emergency, deposit insurance financed by taxation, and the use of accounting systems of exchange and full-bodied commodity currencies.

While combinations of such measures would secure an economy against damage in a financial attack, each might impose additional costs on the peacetime operation of an economy. In turn, these defensive institutions would reduce the amount of war goods constructed to prosecute a war.

For example, suppose that at time 1 everyone knew that there was some chance of an outbreak of war, with a financial attack in period 2 and a battle between periods 3 and 4. Under a bank policy to suspend payments in a financial attack, savers might originally hoard part of their endowments through the storage technology, thereby precluding some productive investment projects. In turn, this would reduce resources available for consumption goods if war did not break out and for war goods if war occurred.

Also, we might assume that each economy is subject to an idiosyncratic macrodisturbance affecting investment projects but not storage technology. Then each bank would want to hold an international portfolio to diversify risk, even if there were a positive probability of a war. The imposition of capital controls would push resources into storage to recover some diversification, thereby reducing goods available when the war breaks out.

## CONCLUSION

Analyses of the management of wartime economies consist of a set of prescriptions for centralized market control with little consideration of how policies fit into the objectives, technology, and strategy of a country engaged in war. Our objective has been to construct a general equilibrium war-game model in which particular war policies emerge in a Nash equilibrium. Specifically, we have integrated a war model with an existing model of financial crisis to examine the emergence of the use of financial weapons. We have found that financial warfare in the form of an asset freeze or a counterfeiting attack will emerge as an equilibrium outcome of a war game. In the narrow case represented by our model, financial warfare, by precluding potential industrial projects, will reduce the measured magnitude of the war, defined as the total amount of resources converted to war goods. We have also found that a counterfeiting attack is more damaging to war potential than an asset freeze.

## NOTES

1. Such books generally appear opportunistically in the second year of major wars. A partial list includes Chandler and Wallace (1951), Stein and Backman (1942), Steiner (1942), Backman (1952), and Brown University Economists (1942). Though these books serve as advice manuals for how to operate an economy in a major war, they present no systematic analysis of why recommended policies are optimal in a general-equilibrium war environment.

2. Asset freezes, blocked accounts, war-zone-stamped money, occupation currency, counterfeiting, and secret accounts comprise a collection of financial weapons employed in major wars.

3. Shubik and Verkerke (1986) have recently suggested that financial weapons might be employed to spark a financial crisis in an enemy country.

4. This is in contrast to many authors in macroeconomics who treat war expenditure as exogenous. For example, the riveting examples in Lucas and Stokey (1983) concern the exogenous outburst and magnitude of war. In many cases, assuming the exogeneity of war is simply a theoretical convenience. Hall (1989), however, argues that military expenditures are among the few exogenous macroeconomic variables that can be used to identify macroeconomic structural models.

5. A financial crisis also emerged during the first year of the U.S. Civil War. See Hammond (1970).

6. See Sprague (1915), Morgan (1952), or Laughlin (1918) for descriptions of the crisis and its control in the United States, Great Britain, and Germany.

7. The use of counterfeiting in warfare was not a new phenomenon. The British themselves employed this method in counterfeiting continentals during the Revolutionary War. The British openly advertised that they would distribute quality counterfeits to anyone at the cost of the paper. See Newman (1957) (Ron Michener pointed out this

source). In addition, the British maintained a printing operation with four hundred employees in London to counterfeit French assignats during the wars of the French Revolution. Eventually, two of every three assignats in circulation were counterfeits. On the assignat, see Harris (1930). While counterfeiting was employed in succeeding wars, it was used mainly as a method of raising revenue. However, before World War II the possibility of massive counterfeiting was raised by the U.S. Secret Service leadership in making contingency plans about defensive responses. See SS Circular 181 (July 22, 1938).

8. For details, see Pirie (1962).

9. Whether or not the ability to extract tribute provides sufficient motivation to endure the costs of major modern wars is a matter of controversy. Milward (1977, 140) calculates that from 1940 to 1944 Germany extracted from France an average of 25 percent of French 1938 national income per year. Since the actual invasion of France cost relatively little, this was an enormous return on investment for Germany. The German war machine of 1940, the product of the cumulating expenditures from 1934, had already accomplished the conquests of Austria, Czechoslovakia, Poland, Belgium, Luxembourg, the Netherlands, Denmark, and Norway. Milward (p. 145) estimates the cost of the German war machine through 1940 at 13.3 billion reichsmarks per conquered territory, a sum smaller than the 1943 payments from France alone. As a percentage of German wartime GNP from 1940 through the first six months of 1944, French payments were 3 percent, 5.3 percent, 5.5, 9.1, and 6.7 percent, respectively.

10. Diamond and Dybvig (1983) and others have provided a different model of a run on a financial system. However, their model contains features that make its use inconvenient here. Most importantly, the banking contracts and banks that emerge in their model could not be supported in economies that also have functioning securities markets. Since the banks also directly hold real investment projects as the sole assets in their portfolios, in a run they must terminate the long-term projects because of their inability to sell claims against the projects in the nonexistent securities market. Thus we cannot explore such phenomena as the collapse of the long-term secondary bond market or the jump in short-term interest rates in the Diamond and Dybvig context. Waldo's model provides a rationale for banks by granting them access to entrepreneur borrowers that small lenders lack. This allows the coexistence of banking contracts and securities markets that we exploit in our problem.

11. To create a rationale for contracts allowing withdrawal after only one period, Waldo assumes a random, unobservable, idiosyncratic liquidity requirement that materializes for each saver in period 2. This creates a demand for insurance that demand deposits satisfy. Diamond and Dybvig (1983) use the same insurance argument to justify the existence of demand-deposit contracts. To keep notation and analysis simple, we will not carry along this random term. We simply assume the existence of demand-deposit contracts as optimal outcomes. Our qualitative results would not change if we carried along this disturbance term so that demand-deposit contracts could emerge as an optimal outcome.

12. Waldo assumes that banks have capital $K$, which serves a role in the case of a panic. For simplicity we set $K = 0$.

13. By generating a bank run in Waldo's framework, a financial attack will raise short-term interest rates. Hence we would expect that at the outset of a war in which financial attacks occur, short-term rates would rise. This contrasts with the work of others (Benjamin

and Kochin 1984; Barro 1986) who argue that short-term rates would decline at the outbreak of war because of declines in future consumption.

14. To simplify our analysis, we assume a taxation scheme that preserves the incentives of short-term investors to undertake second-period investment projects.

15. In a system in which liabilities consist of accounting entries, this would amount to a capability of electronic invasion of the bookkeeping system. Moreover, adding a cost of counterfeiting would require withdrawals from the banking system in the second period to supply the government with resources to undertake counterfeiting. We ignore this complexity here.

16. If either country were to anticipate the outbreak of the war in period 1, defensive measures would be taken to insulate the economy against financial attacks. In this section we abstract from these defensive measures and study the effects of financial warfare on an unprotected economy. In the next-to-last section of this chapter, we consider defensive financial warfare designed to immunize a nation from the effects of a financial attack.

17. We might assume that banks immune to further attack reemerge in period 3 or that governments nationalize the capital markets, using centralized decision making to protect the war mobilization from further financial attack.

18. A financial attack can be severe enough to preclude the future production of war goods. To see this, recall from our discussion of peacetime versus wartime periods that there exists a threshold endowment level below which no war occurs in the Nash equilibrium. If the financial attack drives an enemy's resources below this threshold level, zero war expenditure emerges as the equilibrium outcome.

## REFERENCES

Backman, J., ed. 1952. *War and Defense Economics*. New York: Rinehart and Co.

Barro, Robert J. August 1986. "Government Spending, Interest Rates, Prices, and Budget Deficits in the United Kingdom, 1701–1918." Cambridge: National Bureau of Economic Research. Working Paper 2005.

Benjamin, Daniel, and Levis Kochin. 1984. "War, Prices, and Interest Rates: A Martial Solution to Gibson's Paradox." In *A Retrospective on the Classical Gold Standard, 1821–1931*, ed. Michael D. Bordo and Anna J. Schwartz. Chicago: University of Chicago Press.

Brown University Economists. 1942. *Introduction to War Economics*. Chicago: Richard D. Irwin.

Chandler, Lester V., and David H. Wallace. 1951. *Economic Mobilization and Stabilization*. New York: Henry Holt and Co.

Diamond, Douglas, and Phillips Dybvig. 1983. "Bank Runs, Deposit Insurance, and Liquidity." *Journal of Political Economy* 91, no. 3: 401–19.

Hall, Robert E. 1989. "Consumption." In *Modern Business Cycle Theory*, ed. Robert J. Barro. Cambridge: Harvard University Press.

Hammond, Bray. 1970. *Sovereignty and an Empty Purse*. Princeton, N.J.: Princeton University Press.

Harris, Seymour. 1930. *The Assignats*. Cambridge: Harvard University Press.

Laughlin, W. Laurence. 1918. *Credit of the Nations*. New York: C. Scribner's Sons.

Lucas, Robert, and Nancy Stokey. July 1983. "Optimal Fiscal and Monetary Policy in an Economy without Capital." *Journal of Monetary Economics*.

Milward, Alan. 1977. *War, Economy, and Society, 1939–1945*. Berkeley: University of California Press.

Morgan, Edward V. 1952. *Studies in British Financial Policy*. London: Macmillan.

Newman, Eric. January and February 1957. "Counterfeit Continental Currency Goes to War." *Numismatist*.

Pirie, Anthony. 1962. *Operation Bernhard*. New York: Morrow.

Shubik, M., and J. H. Verkerke. April 1986. "Defense Economics and Economic Warfare Revisited." Cowles Foundation Discussion Paper No. 789. New Haven: Yale University Press.

Sprague, O. M. W. September 1915. "The Crisis of 1914 in the United States." *American Economic Review*, 499–533.

Stein, E., and J. Backman, eds. 1942. *War Economics*. New York: Farrar and Rinehart.

Steiner, George, ed. 1942. *Economic Problems of War*. New York: John Wiley and Sons.

U.S. Secret Service Archives. July 22, 1938. SS Circular 181, Box 17, File 125, U.S. National Archives, Suitland, Maryland.

Waldo, Douglas G. May 1985. "Bank Runs, the Deposit-Currency Ratio, and the Interest Rate." *Journal of Monetary Economics*.

*17*

# The Soviet Foreign Intelligence Service: An Overview

*Marshall Lee Miller*

## THE NECESSITY FOR INTELLIGENCE

When there is as much difference and misunderstanding between two societies as there is between the USSR and the West, a lack of accurate intelligence could be a menace to world peace. For corporations involved in the global economy, particularly high-technology firms, understanding the nature, structure, and objectives of Soviet intelligence could be of inestimable value to their operations. Depending upon where business is conducted, initiatives can be taken to identify areas of vulnerability, and security measures can be implemented to preclude theft of trade secrets. The acquisition of high-technology research and products via thoughtful espionage activities remains a top priority of Soviet intelligence. The purpose of this chapter is to provide corporate leaders and their strategic planning and intelligence staffs with the needed insights to avoid embarrassing and costly surprises.

During the Cuban missile crisis in 1962, President Kennedy learned from a high-ranking agent, Colonel Oleg Penkovsky, that the USSR's strategic arsenal was much weaker than the United States had believed. In particular, a manual he provided on Russian medium-range ballistic missiles showed that they were far less capable than the CIA had believed. Consequently, instead of feeling compelled to launch a preemptive military strike against Soviet missiles in Cuba, Kennedy was able to call Khrushchev's bluff, knowing that the Soviet leader would have to back down.[1]

During the same crisis, an intelligence defect on each side that could have led to war involved the downing of an American U–2 reconnaissance plane over Cuba on October 27, 1962. President Kennedy assumed that Khrushchev had ordered the firing of the Soviet surface-to-air (SAM) missile and considered an all-out air attack to take out the SAM sites. Khrushchev, however, curiously assumed that the Cubans had fired the missile. In fact, according to a recent article by the former Soviet ambassador to Cuba, Alexander Alexeev, in the magazine *Planetary Echo*, the local Soviet missile commander had ordered the attack on his own, but the Soviet military had concealed this from Khrushchev. Neither his KGB nor the GRU told him otherwise.[2]

Another instance supposedly occurred in 1984, according to the former KGB station chief (*resident*) in London, Oleg Gorzdievski. Somehow the Russians misread the significance of routine NATO maneuvers in Central Europe and became alarmed that the West was planning a surprise attack on them. This led the USSR to put its agents on alert around the world. The naivete of this notion, assuming that Gorzdievski's account is accurate, raises serious doubts about the quality of the KGB's analysis and its understanding of the outside world. Fortunately, Gorzdievski, who had been a double agent for several years, tipped off the West about the misconception, and the crisis was apparently defused.[3]

The Soviets apparently also panicked in October 1984 following President Reagan's remarks about bombing the Soviet Union, although any reasonable person should have realized that these were clearly facetious. Japanese intelligence deciphered a message of the Soviet Far East Army in Vladivostok that war between the United States and the USSR appeared imminent and that the army should be on special alert because of American plans for a surprise attack.[4]

The United States has also had its panics. In 1980, at the height of the Iranian turmoil, American analysts looking for warning signals that the USSR might move troops into Iran were stunned to see ultrasecret code messages indicating that nuclear weapons in the Caucasus were being readied for action. The president and National Security Council decided not to respond, and the incident was kept from the press, but the significance of the Soviet move is still debated. Such faulty intelligence analysis could bring the world to the brink of war. How could it occur?

## THE KGB: SWORD AND SHIELD OF THE PARTY

On the desk in my office is a red and black coffee mug, an exact copy of one on Yuri Andropov's desk when he was director of the KGB.[5] On the side is the organization's motto, "Sword and Shield of the Party." This is a surprisingly honest admission that the KGB's real purpose is not to safeguard the country but to protect its ruling party. Although we usually think first of its foreign intelligence functions, the KGB's primary function is internal security.

The KGB combines the functions of not only the American CIA and the FBI but also the National Security Agency (NSA) (codebreaking), Secret Service (bodyguards), the border patrol, and several other American agencies thrown in for good measure. On occasion in the past, it has been combined with the Soviet Ministry of Interior (MVD), which, unlike its American namesake, is responsible not for national parks but for various aspects of police, fire, and other public security.

Directly or indirectly the KGB employs over a million personnel. (The CIA has less than 20,000.) The KGB also has its own army, comprised of several divisions of elite troops with tanks and artillery. During World War II, KGB military units amounted to over 60 divisions, each larger and better equipped than the standard army division, comprising in total between one and two million men. The force, now of course much smaller, still performs an important role as the praetorian guard protecting the Kremlin and other sensitive sites. With such resources, it could not help but be a powerful organization.

In the Soviet system, power rests on the forces of coercion, the army and the security services, but control resides with the Party. Since the former have the weapons, the latter must resort to ideology, vigilance, guile, and playing one group against another in order to preserve the Party's monopoly of power.

The greatest fear historically has been of "Bonapartism" from the army. Although the army has never once posed a serious threat to the regime, this fear may explain why Stalin ruthlessly destroyed the Soviet officer corps on the eve of World War II. Following the war, the Soviet commander, Marshal Georgi Zhukov, was humiliatingly dismissed not once but twice, the first time by Stalin immediately after the war, so the generalissimo would not have to share the glory of victory with the "conqueror of Berlin," and the second time by Khrushchev in 1958 shortly after Zhukov showed his power by playing a crucial role in saving Khrushchev from attempted ouster by a group of Party rivals.

Control over the military is exercised through the Main Political Administration (Glavnoye Politicheskoe Upravlenie, GPU), which is the successor to the political commissar system set up after the Bolshevik Revolution, and by the Third Directorate of the KGB. Most army officers, and virtually all senior officers, are Party members, and there are always a number of military officers among the Communist Party's Central Committee. In the Politburo itself, however, the military is only indirectly represented. The late Marshal Dimitri Ustinov, the minister of defense, was on the Politburo until his death, but he was a civilian who was given military rank. On the present Politburo there are no military officers.

The KGB was dealt with in a similar fashion. At the same time that he was purging the Red Army and killing millions of innocent civilians as spies and saboteurs in the 1930s, Stalin also was periodically decimating the leadership of the KGB. Genrikh Yagoda and most of his assistants were executed as traitors, as was Nikolai Yezhov, whose name was given to the most brutal period of the purges, the Yezhovshchina. The replacement in 1938 was a brutal and perverted fellow Georgian of Stalin, Lavrenti Beria, who was a member of Stalin's ruling circle until the dictator's death in 1953. Beria thereupon sought to seize power for himself.

The KGB's foreign intelligence function is the responsibility of the First Chief Directorate.[6] Although it comprises only about 5 to 10 percent of the organization, this Chief Directorate is perhaps the most prestigious.[7] It consists of almost a dozen alphabetically named directorates, whose composition and titles have varied over time but typically include the following: Directorate S, for illegal agents, is the centralized control for the Soviet Union's vast network of spies around the world. Directorate T, for scientific and technical espionage, has become increasingly important as the Soviet Union has sought to pursue Western military and industrial technology. This section was elevated to a separate directorate in 1963 and is now the second-largest of the First Chief Directorate's alphabetical directorates. It alone is reportedly as large as the entire CIA. Its industrial and economic espionage operations abroad are conducted through an organization called "Line X."[8]

Directorate K, for counterintelligence, has, despite its name, more of an offensive than a defensive mission.[9] It is designed to neutralize opposing intelligence services. It also serves as the watchdog over all Soviet officials traveling or serving abroad. (This organization's defensive counterpart is another chief directorate, the Second, the largest of the chief directorates and the one that is responsible for internal security of the USSR itself.)

The First Chief Directorate's activities abroad are organized into eleven geographical and linguistic sections. The most important are the First Department for the United States and Canada; the Third Department, covering Great Britain and Scandinavia, as well as Australia and New Zealand; and the Fourth Department, responsible for the Germanic countries. The Sixth and Seventh departments cover the Far East.[10]

The First Chief Directorate also has three special branches called services (*shluzhby*). Service A, a unit that has received particular attention in recent years, has the mission of disinformation (*dezinformatsiya*).[11] Although a part of its activity is to confuse Western observers by sending out false signals and misleading information, what the Russians call *maskirovka*, the basic role of this section is to produce spurious rumors and forged documents that will fan anti-Western feelings in gullible Third World nations. The service works closely with the International Department of the Soviet Communist Party's powerful Central Committee and with the news agency Novosti.[12]

The most notorious unit is popularly known as "Smersh." It was founded in 1942, though with considerable antecedents, to deal with the wholesale desertion of Russian troops,[13] and its name comes from *smert shpionam* (death to spies). It has alternately been a separate counterintelligence organization, sometimes called the Osobye Otdel, and a part of the KGB.[14] There is a third service, Service R, which supervises the activities of the covert espionage case officers, but it is more administrative than tactical.[15]

The KGB has several other chief directorates. They include the Second Chief Directorate, mentioned earlier, which has charge of internal security; the Fifth Chief Directorate, a relatively new organization that deals with dissidents inside the Soviet Union; and the Eighth Chief Directorate, which is concerned with communications security, both offensive and defensive.[16]

One rank below the chief directorates, but not subordinate to them, are the directorates. The Third Directorate is probably the most important. It keeps watch over the loyalty of the armed forces, whether threatened from within or without, and is a logical continuation of an organization that was designed originally to deal with the wholesale collapse and desertion of Soviet troops at the onset of the German invasion.[17] The border guards (the Ninth Directorate) and the praetorian guards for the Soviet leaders[18] are other directorates, as are the groups responsible for surveillance of foreigners and others.[19]

## FUNCTIONS OF THE FOREIGN INTELLIGENCE SERVICE

### Threats from Abroad

The Soviet intelligence system's secondary function, after internal security, is to deal with threats to the regime from abroad. In the first several decades of Communist rule, its activity was largely an extension of its domestic role against opponents, or purported opponents, of Stalin. This meant the penetration and neutralization, generally by assassination, of opposition groups.

One was the remnants of the White armies and other proczarist groups that the Bolsheviks had defeated militarily but that continued their ineffectual plotting as refugees in Paris and elsewhere. The Paris-based veterans group, the Russian General Military Union (Russkiy Obshche-Voyenskiy Soyuz, ROVS), was a special target. In January 1930 its commander, Gen. P. A. Kutyepov, was abducted by the KGB's predecessor, the OGPU.[20] His successor, Gen. Yevgeniy Miller, met a similar fate in September 1937. Key to both operations was ROVS's chief of counterintelligence and security, Gen. Nikolay Skoblin, who was secretly working for the KGB as well as also being a double (or triple) agent supposedly cooperating with the Nazi intelligence organization, the Sicherheitsdienst (SD).[21] The most noted murder was the assassination of Stalin's archenemy, Leon Trotsky, in Mexico in 1940.

### Collection and Analysis

The emphasis in the Soviet system is on the collection of data; there is much less attention devoted to its subsequent analysis. Thus raw, unprocessed intelligence data is reportedly often served directly to Soviet leaders, and as someone once said about FBI investigation files, "Raw data can be very raw indeed."

The result is that the Soviets are very good indeed at collection, though they seem to work harder at it than necessary, given that the West can be a very soft target for espionage. The imbalance between easy collection and inadequate analysis has created a problem for the Soviets. In the words of former CIA Deputy Director Bobby Inman, "We drown them in detail which they're unwilling to trust or believe."

## Assassinations

The Soviets have never had scruples about terminating real or purported enemies. Whether that is due to their "oriental" tradition, their ideology, or the personality quirks of their leaders, the Communist regime that has murdered twenty or even thirty million of its own citizens cannot be expected to quibble about a few more.[22]

Much of the early effort of the KGB abroad was directed against opponents of the regime, or at least of Stalin. That expanded to include defectors from the KGB and GRU itself, many of whom had fled to avoid being caught up in the purges back home. Other than that, however, there was no clear pattern of using assassinations as a weapon of foreign policy. No foreign leaders were targeted, not even Hitler, despite a widespread use of political assassinations during the prewar period by others (particularly Balkan terrorists) with fewer scruples.[23] There is no clear explanation for these scruples, although one suggestion is that Stalin may have hesitated to strike back at Hitler too.[24]

Despite periodic reports that Smersh has been abolished, it turns up hidden in some other section. The Russian euphemism for assassination squads is *mokrye dela* (wet affairs), traditionally called Department V, then Department Eight of Directorate S, which handles illegals.[25] According to one KGB defector from this section, Ilya Dzhirkvelov, the current code word for wet affairs is *voyennaya podgotovka*, literally "military preparation or drill."[26]

It was assumed a few years ago that Soviet wet affairs activities had been sharply curtailed since their heyday in the 1930s, but this proved optimistic. One mark of a successful assassination is for no one to know that it has occurred. Such were the deaths of two anti-Soviet émigré leaders in West Germany who apparently died of natural heart attacks in 1957 and 1959. Subsequently, their assassin, Bogdan Stasinsky of the KGB's wet affairs bureau, defected in 1961 and revealed that he had killed them with a vapor gun firing prussic acid. Another KGB officer, Nikolai Khokhlov, had defected in 1954 rather than kill his assigned victim; Khokhlov later survived an attempt to kill him using radiation.[27]

Radiation is also a favorite weapon of the Rumanian secret service, according to its former deputy director, Ion Pacepa. More direct methods, however, are preferred, especially faked automobile accidents arranged with French gangsters.[28] Sometimes, however, as with the Russians, the Rumanian agents defected rather than carry out their missions, as did Matei Haiducu when ordered to silence Rumanian émigré writers Paul Goma and Virgil Tanase in France.[29]

A less subtle approach was used in 1979 when a paramilitary unit assaulted the presidential palace in Afghanistan, killed President Hafizullah Amin, and ushered in the Russian invasion. More clandestine activities were carried out by the Bulgarian intelligence service, Durzhavna Sigurnost, with crucial Soviet technical assistance. Knowledgeable Bulgarians who had fled abroad and were writing or broadcasting about the flaws of the regime were hunted down. After the deaths of several dissidents attributed to natural causes and an unsuccessful attempt on Bulgarian defector Vladimir Kostov in Paris, the mystery was revealed when a broadcaster for the BBC's Bulgarian news service, Georgi Markov, fell fatally ill in 1978 after being jabbed with an umbrella. This time the doctors finally found a tiny pellet with a cavity containing the potent poison ricin.[30]

The most controversial wet affair was the attempted murder of Pope John Paul II on May 13, 1981.[31] The would-be assassin, a Turk named Mehmet Ali Agca, was captured and implicated the Bulgarian intelligence service, acting at Soviet behest to remove the popular Polish pope, who, it was feared, could galvanize his homeland's resistance to the Soviets. The matter became murkier at the trial, however, when the defendant purposefully (and probably prudently) sought to discredit his own testimony. The puzzle therefore cannot be said to be conclusively solved, and many Westerners, including the CIA, shrank from the full implications.[32] If true, however, it would mean that the highest Soviet leadership, including Andropov, deliberately approved the attempt on the pope's life.

## Active Measures (Disinformation)

The Soviets may appreciate the power of deception better than almost any other nation. To an unprecedented degree, therefore, they have emphasized *maskirovka* (deception) in their military maneuvers to mislead foreign intelligence. The KGB has a whole section concerned with the more political aspects of deception, called "disinformation." This is not a novel notion; the ancient Chinese writer Sun Tzu in the fifth century B.C. wrote of undermining an enemy by "leaking information which is actually false."[33] The Soviets, however, have raised this art to new heights. This effort, which they call "active measures" (*aktivnye myeropriyatiya*), is directed by Service A of the KGB's First Chief Directorate. The service's standard procedure is to prepare forgeries purporting to be official Western documents and then to leak them to the press. Foreign journalists are also wooed and fed misleading stories, usually designed to portray the West, especially the United States, in a negative light.

For example, a letter supposedly on White House stationery was sent from President Ronald Reagan to the king of Spain to induce that country to destroy its left-wing opposition. That document was quickly exposed as bogus, as were others written in ungrammatical English, but the Soviets have had more success in planting false documents in Third World countries. These included supposed CIA lists of journalists on the agency payroll and a phony U.S. National Security Council document professing secret support for South African repression.[34] These clumsy efforts could fool only the gullible before they were exposed, but other Soviet disinformation has become accepted history. For example, even most

Americans believe that the CIA engineered the coup that brought the downfall and death of Salvador Allende's Communist regime in Chile in 1973, although in fact the CIA had nothing to do with that coup.[35]

Our knowledge of these KGB activities is considerably better than in most other areas because of the relatively large number of defectors familiar with these operations. These include such KGB officers as Ilya Dzhirkvelov and Stanislav Levchenko, as well as the deputy of the Czech disinformation department, Ladislav Bittman, and a number of other satellite intelligence officers.[36]

The Soviets succeeded in recruiting what might be more important than espionage agents—"agents of influence." These are people who, because of their prominence or position, can affect their government and nation. According to the former head of the Communist International (Comintern), Georgi Dimitrov, "A university professor who, without being a party member, supports the interest of the Soviet Union, is of more value than a thousand people with a membership card."[37] For example, in France the KGB recruited Pierre-Charles Pathé, a prominent journalist and member of the famous Pathé newsreel family. In Denmark they used an influential journalist, Arne Herlov Petersen, to coordinate with KGB-financed antinuclear groups in Scandinavia.[38]

### Countering Foreign Counterintelligence

Nowhere has Soviet intelligence achieved a more remarkable success than in penetrating those Western organizations devoted to counterespionage against the Soviet threat itself. The KGB's most famous case agent was Kim Philby, who became head of the Russian section of the British MI6 and thus was in a position to betray or undermine countless Western operations. For example, when a high-ranking Soviet official in Turkey sought to defect to the West, Philby tipped off the KGB and then dawdled long enough for them to bundle the would-be defector back to Russia.

Similarly, when the British and Americans made a joint clandestine military effort to oust the Communist regime of Enver Hoxha from Albania in the late 1940s and early 1950s, it was Philby again as head of the British force that insured that the parachuting agents and naval landing parties encountered Communist welcoming parties, so that few Western guerrillas survived.[39] Philby was recommended to become head of MI6 by its retiring director, Stewart Menzies. This would have been equivalent from a security viewpoint to a Russian spy becoming head of the CIA. Fortunately, Philby's public drunkenness and other erratic behavior kept this from happening.[40]

The West German intelligence services have also been riddled, perhaps with greater ease, by the Soviets working through their East German puppets. In the immediate postwar years intelligence against the Soviet Union was conducted by the so-called Gehlen Organization, headed by General Reinhard Gehlen, who had directed the Foreign Armies East department of the wartime German OKW, the German high command.[41] The effectiveness of this organization in penetrating the USSR was vastly overrated by its American patrons, but in those early years there was no ready alternative. In 1963 it turned out that three of the top men in the organization were long-time Soviet agents, including the head of Gehlen's counterespionage department, Heinz Felfe.[42]

In 1954 the head of West German counterintelligence, Otto John, disappeared to the East under mysterious circumstances.[43] He claimed at a subsequent press conference that he had defected, but the mystery deepened eighteen months later when he suddenly reappeared in the West with the claim that he had been kidnapped by East German agents. The West Germans nevertheless sentenced him to a four-year prison term in solitary confinement.[44] His account of abduction is now given greater credence,[45] but the scandal greatly tarnished the reputation and credibility of the West German services.

West Germany suffered another severe blow with the defection to the East in August 1985 of Hans Joachim Tiedge, the head of the Soviet division of the country's counterespionage organization. He had fallen heavily into debt and drank but, despite several years' evidence of instability, had been left in office by his superiors.[46]

American intelligence has not been plagued by such high-level wholesale penetration as its allies (or such penetration has yet to be uncovered), but it has not been completely immune either. At one time the CIA claimed that not one of its thousandscore employees had proved disloyal, but in recent years several serious cases have been uncovered. A junior watch officer, William Kampiles, entrusted as a duty officer in the agency's command center, walked off with the technical manual for the billion-dollar, supersecret KH–11 spy satellite and, after being dismissed, peddled it to the Russians for the paltry sum of $3,000.[47] Another dismissed junior CIA officer, Edward Lee Howard, fled to the USSR with information about American agents in Russia that led to their apprehension and execution.[48]

The FBI suffered the humiliation in 1984 of having one of its counterintelligence officers, Richard W. Miller, fall into a sex trap with an obvious Soviet agent in San Francisco.[49] The resulting accounts of disorganization and mismanagement in the FBI's West Coast operations make one wonder whether that case was really a solitary. There were also rumors for years of high-level leaks in the FBI offices in New York, but nothing was ever proved.

## THE LITTLE-KNOWN GRU

The GRU (Glavnoe Rasvedyvatelnoe Upravlenie), the intelligence arm of the Soviet General Staff, is the KGB's big little brother. Almost unknown in comparison with the KGB, the GRU is almost exclusively directed toward espionage abroad, with little internal role.[50] The GRU, which is primarily concerned with military and technical matters, is roughly the counterpart of the American Defense Intelligence Agency (DIA), combined with the Office of Naval Intelligence (ONI) and the army and the air force intelligence organizations.[51]

## Comparison of the GRU with the KGB

Although the GRU is nowhere near as large as the KGB, it has no internal security or other quasi-political functions, so it rather than the much better known KGB is responsible for most of the traditional Soviet espionage. There is considerable bad feeling between the KGB and the GRU. This is more than the rivalry (and sometimes mild contempt) that exists between the CIA and the DIA. It is a bitter feud, stemming from the bloody purges of the GRU by the KGB (then called the NKVD) in the 1930s and sustained by a thousand slights and insults since then. This hostility, according to some commentators, may be deliberately encouraged by the Party since it prevents the two organizations from ganging up on the Party leadership.

The GRU, however, because of its more external role and its lack of a strong paramilitary capability, is not really a counterweight to the KGB. (The GRU's "Spetsnaz" units will be discussed later.) It is probably more accurate to say that the KGB is seen as a balance to the armed forces as a whole, of which the GRU is but one facet. To keep the GRU in rein, for decades the commanders of the GRU have come from the KGB.

A KGB defector, Major Peter Deriabin, has observed:

The GRU was and is an organization which hulks as large as the State Security's [KGB] Foreign Intelligence Directorate in the business of information-gathering, subversion, and terror outside the Soviet Union. In fact, the GRU is far larger in size than the Second [*sic*] Directorate. It has often proved more formidable to the West from the sheer comprehensiveness of its activities.[52]

The difference between the KGB and the GRU was described by a former GRU officer as follows:

The basic function of the KGB may be expressed in one guiding phrase, not to allow the collapse of the Soviet Union from inside. . . . The function of the GRU may also be stated in one parallel, but quite different phrase: To prevent the collapse of the Soviet Union from an external blow.[53]

## GRU Exploits

Reportedly, the GRU also has a much larger espionage budget than the KGB. Many of the espionage successes credited to the KGB were, in fact, achieved by the GRU.[54] The famous Sorge spy ring, for example, that learned that the Japanese would not invade Russia from the rear and that thereby enabled Stalin to switch crucial reserves against the Nazis, was part of the GRU.[55] So too were the penetrations of the German High Command, notably the famous "Red Orchestra" led by Leopold Trepper that enabled the Russians to surprise the Germans at Kursk in the biggest tank battle in world history.[56] In the United States, so were the atom bomb spies: Julius and Ethel Rosenberg, Harry Gold, David Greenglass, and Klaus Fuchs, as well as the famous Whittaker Chambers and Alger Hiss.[57]

There is, by history and by design, considerable antagonism between the KGB and the GRU that goes far beyond the bounds of normal interagency rivalry. The antagonism is kept alive in a dozen different ways, not the least being the overbearing attitude for which the KGB is often notorious. On each exam for GRU trainees the question is reportedly asked, "How many marshals of the Soviet Union were annihilated by Hitler—and how many were eliminated by our KGB friends? The correct answer is none and three, respectively.[58] In this fashion the memory of the bloody purges of the 1930s is kept alive.

The GRU uses "illegal" espionage agents by the thousands. This is in sharp contrast to the American DIA, which principally employs electronic techniques or uniformed military attachés. A second major difference is that the GRU does not limit itself to order of battle, weapons systems, and other specifically military information but also seeks almost any other kind of technological or economic information. This includes commercial and trade secrets and devices sought by other ministries wishing to keep up with the West on the cheap.

### The Structure of the GRU

The organization of the GRU is simpler than that of the KGB because the GRU does not have the security responsibilities inside the Soviet Union, but it is complex enough.[59] Reporting to the GRU head is the first deputy, who controls a number of geographical directorates, such as the first (Europe) and Third (the Americas), along with the Fifth, which handles operational intelligence (discussed later), and the Sixth, which is responsible for electronic surveillance. Also reporting to the GRU head is the chief of information, who is responsible for six directorates; the Directorate of Personnel; the Technical Directorate; the Directorate of Space Satellite Reconnaissance; and a number of administrative departments.[60]

Three other organizational features should be mentioned. First, each of the sixteen Soviet military districts, four naval fleets, and groups of forces has its own GRU units, which are subordinate to the Fifth Directorate for operations intelligence. Second, the individual GRU directorates run their own "illegal" agents, rather than having them directed through a specialized single organization, as does the KGB. Third, the GRU controls a large and highly capable military commando force, the Spetsnaz (Spetsialnoe Naznachenie, "Special Designation"), for covert missions.

### Spetsnaz

The Spetsnaz is a large but elite unit of around 30,000 troops, designed for sabotage, peacetime reconnaissance, assassinations, and wartime missions against nuclear facilities and other key installations.[61] These troops are active even in peacetime. For example, Spetsnaz officers are reportedly driving large commercial trucks on deliveries and extended detours around strategic routes in Western Europe. They have infiltrated "peace" demonstrations around air bases in England and explored Scandinavian harbors in midget submarines.[62] Spetsnaz works with units such as the KGB's Department V of the First Chief Directorate, which has agents, such as former KGB officer Oleg Lyalin in Britain, designated for sleeper sabotage networks in case of war.

## THE ROLE OF INTELLIGENCE IN RUSSIAN SOCIETY

The intelligence services under the czars, first the Oprichina and later the Third Department and the Okhrana, were merely a secret police, not very effective, and hampered by an inability to distinguish revolutionaries from their own agents provocateurs, one of whom was probably Stalin himself.[63] The nineteenth-century Russian czars sentenced a few individuals to death, notably after the army "Decembrists" rebellion in 1825 and the assassination of Czar Alexander II in 1881, but only a few were executed, and many others served prison terms and were released. More common was to send dissidents off to Siberia, not to harsh penal colonies where death was expected and almost welcomed, but (like Lenin) to towns or villages where they lived in private houses and could read and write at leisure. In the half a century before the 1917 revolution, the czarist governments executed a total of approximately 14,000 people.[64] Stalin murdered well over a thousand times this number in much less time.

Foreign intelligence under the czars was given but slight attention. Russian intelligence during the Crimean, Balkan, and Russo-Japanese wars was virtually nonexistent. During the intervening peace times it was, if possible, even worse. On the eve of World War I, czarist Russia did score one notable success in recruiting as an agent Colonel Alfred Redl of the Austro-Hungarian army, who supplied the Russians with invaluable military plans.[65] Considering the heterogeneous ethnic nature of Austro-Hungary, however, including the many Slavs who regarded Russia most sympathetically, this meager success only highlights the general failure of the lackadaisical Russian effort.

An intelligence service is not an end in itself, even though in the Soviet system it and the Communist Party have each acquired somewhat of a self-perpetuating life of their own. Intelligence must serve the foreign policy interests of its country. For the Soviet Union, that has meant, above all, protecting the regime from hostile outside forces, whether political dissidents abroad or countries that posed a possible military threat.

Those would seem obvious goals for any intelligence service. But what would happen if the two were in conflict? Under Stalin, the former goal took priority. He used the KGB (then called the OGPU, or NKVD, or often the Cheka) to methodically wipe out his opponents abroad. With the rise of Hitler, he was given a choice between supporting Communist opposition to Nazism inside Germany or cooperating with Hitler. He chose to cooperate, even when that meant turning over local Communist Party members to the Nazis. There are many facets to this controversial collaboration between the two dictators, including a link between the German and Russian armies that predated Hitler's ascension to power and (Russian accounts emphasize) Stalin's need to bide for time.

Two aspects of this relationship are worth noting. First, the Soviet Union established a clear pattern of sacrificing local ideological interests for the sake of broader national goals. That was the rule followed in postwar Europe, when the powerful French and Italian Communist parties were restrained from a push for power. It continues to be the typical Soviet approach wherever local Communists are jailed or executed by governments, such as Syria, with which the Soviet Union wants to maintain close relations.

Second, ideological concepts and personal preconceptions often took precedence over mere facts. Thus in 1940 and 1941 Stalin disregarded numerous intelligence indicators that the Germans were planning to attack him. The warnings did not fit his notion that Hitler could be trusted, so he chose to overlook evidence that inescapably led to the contrary conclusion. Yet he had readily accepted phone information, planted by the Germans, that his senior army officers were German agents, because this is what he wanted to believe.[66]

The present KGB is less rigidly ideological and, under Andropov's tenure beginning in 1967, became a thoroughly professional organization recruiting the cream of the Soviet elite. The neckless clods in the baggy blue suits were gradually replaced by younger and more urbane officers with more subtle approaches. The means have thus changed, but not the goals.

## TECHNIQUES OF SOVIET INTELLIGENCE

The Soviet Union has traditionally placed a higher premium on HUMINT (human intelligence, that is, spies) than has the United States or even the British. This is due to historical experiences, the Russian lack of equivalent technology until recently, the (earlier) advantage of a ready group of potential fifth columnists in the Communist parties of most countries, and the fact that this method has worked best for them.

### The Keys to Betrayal

There is an enormous difference between conducting espionage, on the one hand, in an open, democratic society where even suspect Soviet agents can wander freely and newspapers carry the latest state secrets, and on the other, in a totalitarian society where the most innocent information is kept a state secret and where millions of citizens have been liquidated for fabricated claims of espionage. It is thus natural that the Soviets have had an easier and more successful time in enlisting and utilizing agents in the West than the West has had in the Soviet Union.

There are different kinds of "spies." The Soviet Union, like most other countries, sends military attachés, diplomats, and others to ferret out information from their host country. Sometimes, as with attachés, there is no pretense otherwise; sometimes these are intelligence officers with another cover. These are called "legals." There are also quasi-legals, such as employees of the Soviet state airline Aeroflot or the press agencies TASS and Novosti serving abroad. Technically these are "illegals," but as government employees, albeit without diplomatic immunity, in positions in which a third to a half of the employees are KGB or GRU, their link to intelligence surprises no one.

The true illegals, particularly those in "deep cover" who often pose as loyal citizens of the host country, are in another category. These are men like Rudolph Abel, a KGB colonel who posed as an ordinary New York photographer, or the English bookshop owners, "Peter and Helen Kroger" (Morris and Lona Cohen). In most cases these are not actually spies, however, but "case officers" who recruit those who actually do the spying. These true spies, who almost always are genuine citizens or legal residents of the target country, have somehow been persuaded to become traitors to their own nation.

The classic motivations for spying have been given the mnemonic MICE. This represents money, ideology, compromise, and ego. A former British intelligence officer, Chapman Pincher, has suggested that more complex motivations should be added, including "flouting of authority and disrespect for the law, which have arisen out of the 'permissiveness' encouraged in the 1960s by those who felt it to be 'progressive.' "[67] These seem, however, to be but variations on the traditional themes.

In the decade before and that after World War II, ideology was the primary motivation for the Soviet Union's top agents in the West. Their fanatical devotion to the Communist Party and Stalin, despite an awareness of the evil they had wrought, seems inconceivable today, but it gave the Soviet Union a disciplined group of disciples who subordinated everything—country, family, friends—to the demands of the Party.

Ideology was a factor that impelled the privileged Cambridge University students in the 1930s to join the Communist spy ring that, two decades later, led Donald McLean, Guy Burgess, George Blake, and others of their group to penetrate the deepest recesses of the British government and led Soviet agent Kim Philby to the brink of becoming head of all British counterintelligence. Betrayal was not merely a British phenomenon. The American atom bomb spies, such as Julius and Ethel Rosenberg, were inspired by a belief. Not all were naive immigrants; among them were senior State Department official Alger Hiss and Justice Department clerk Elizabeth Bentley, who was told by her Moscow controller, "That's the function of the American Communist Party; it's the reservoir from which we draw most of our agents."[68]

Compromise is not the factor it once was. In our permissive society blackmail is more difficult than previously, when sexual entrapment snared both the British and French ambassadors to Moscow.[69] The Rumanians trapped the wife of an American ambassador who later became head of personnel at the State Department.[70] A British diplomat in Prague handed over his country's diplomatic codes in exchange for an exit visa for his mistress,[71] and a Czech contract employee with the CIA in Washington, Karl F. Koecher, and his attractive wife involved a number of CIA and other governmental officials in "swinging sex" parties until they were arrested in November 1984. Czech defector Josef Frolik told a U.S. Senate committee, "Sex exploitation is an important weapon used by the Czech intelligence service in its daily life, as it is with all the Soviet satellite services."[72]

Homosexuals have long been considered security risks because of their vulnerability to blackmail, and indeed they have constituted a disproportionately large share of the KGB's Western agents. But in almost none of those cases was blackmail involved, so there must be some other explanation. In any case, in the future the nonsexual types of compromise, such as faked auto accidents and phony arrests, will become more important in compromising target candidates.

With the decline of both ideology and compromise, money has overwhelmingly become the main motivation for Western traitors. Virtually every case in recent years has involved greed, gross greed. Ironically, the Soviets are notoriously chintzy paymasters.[73]

Ego, the last element in the MICE formula, is harder to assess. Several cases, such as the CIA's Kampiles and Sweden's Colonel Stig Wennerstrom, claimed to have begun feeding secrets without authorization to Soviet intelligence to entice it into a double-agent game at which they could become heroes. Wennerstrom, who had been passed over for promotion by the Swedish air force, was craftily handled by the GRU; he was told that he had been made a major general in the Soviet service and given the designation of "top agent," although this was completely spurious.[74]

### The Dilemma of Defectors

Defectors are a window into the soul of an opponent's intelligence agency. By comparison, all the satellite photographs, radio intercepts, and other devices are but viewing the institution from the outside. In this respect there is a crucial difference between the Soviet and American approaches.[75] The KGB, with patience, favors penetration agents who, like Kim Philby, may take many years or even decades to reach positions of influence and importance.[76] Besides, the Soviets have to make a virtue of necessity, for virtually no defectors to the Communist side, whether for greed or ideology, have really wanted to flee to the Soviet Union for the rest of their lives. The CIA, sharing the American proclivity toward more immediate results, favors defectors, officials who switch to the Western side after they have already achieved prominence, although an effort will be made to keep the defector in place for as long as possible.

Nevertheless, the handling of defectors (*perebezhchiki*) can be a real problem even under the best of circumstances. They have abandoned home, friends, careers, and often their hostage families in pursuit of a dream of freedom that they cannot initially be certain is real. Economically, their standard of living takes a plunge, and their feeling of self-respect may drop even more. They go from being a member of the intelligence, military, or governing elite into a system that gives less deference to such positions or their recent, often heroic escapes.

For example, Rumania's Ion Pacepa, described as the highest-ranking Soviet-bloc intelligence officer ever to defect to the CIA, was offered a job driving a school bus. Soviet diplomat and KGB officer Vladimir Sakharov, the son of a Kremlin physician, was urged to train as a motel clerk in a Los Angeles red-light district. Naval commander Alexander Ushakov, a professor and the author of four books, escaped by a three-week climb through the treacherous Caucasus Mountains into Turkey. After extensive CIA debriefing, he lived for a time in a Harlem slum and, at this writing lives in Washington, D.C. Other well-educated senior defectors have wound up as dishwashers and typewriter repairmen.

In contrast to the KGB, the CIA has really never been comfortable with turncoats. This may be due, in part, to the agency's long-standing ambivalence about the value of HUMINT (human intelligence) itself. The advent of high-resolution overhead photography and sophisticated communication intercepts has meant that secret installations deep in the enemy's heartland can be penetrated on short notice, without the danger, unreliability, and complication of cultivating an inside agent for years. This also reflects the American preference for gee-whiz technology over eccentric and devious foreigners. Ironically, the far greater expense of these technological methods, requiring mammoth organizations and huge investments (NSA's codebreaking budget is many times higher than the CIA's budget) creates a vested interest in their favor.[77]

### Espionage Technology

The Soviets are also fond of electronic eavesdropping. All intelligence services use such devices, of course, but the Soviets have had certain advantages. First, they have fewer scruples about the right of privacy than do most Western countries, and certainly no judicial warrants are required. Second, whereas bugging itself is relatively simple, arranging teams of continuous eavesdroppers and the voluminous transcribing are very labor intensive. The high priority for such activities in a totalitarian state and the usual labor surplus historically there have given the Soviets a significant advantage.

Nowhere is this clearer than in Rumania, where not only every leading hotel's rooms are bugged—not just selected ones or on an ad hoc basis, as in most other Communist states—but the special ceramic ashtrays at every table in most leading restaurants are special transmitters.[78] Such wholesale bugging requires enormous resources and manpower and reflects more the fears for internal security than the likely incidence of foreign intelligence activity.

In the past several decades "overhead" intelligence, that is, aerial and satellite reconnaissance, has assumed overwhelming importance. The U-1 and U-2 spy flights during the 1950s gave the United States virtually its only window into the tightly closed societies of the USSR and China. This loss was keenly felt after Gary Powers's aircraft was shot down over Svedlovsk in May 1960, because efforts to get espionage agents into the Soviet Union were repeatedly frustrated by KGB ruses and the nature of that police state itself. Thus the development of photographic satellites helped answer a desperate need.

As the resolution of the cameras has become so sharp that a baseball could be filmed from three-hundred kilometers in the sky, and real-time coverage has become possible with high-resolution television cameras, the U.S. reliance on this form of intelligence threatens to dominate all other forms of intelligence. Many observers think our reliance has grown too great, for there is much that a "recky bird" cannot see; it can help identify capabilities but cannot determine intentions.

The KGB has been less tempted to rely so heavily on overhead, partly because it has had HUMINT and other alternatives and partly because its satellites have been technically less sophisticated than their Western counterparts. Now that Soviet overhead resolution is itself becoming so fine, it will be interesting to see if the Soviets are tempted to follow the American pattern.

The Soviets, like the Americans and British, place great emphasis on another, more advanced type of eavesdropping, namely the breaking of the diplomatic and military codes of other nations. This is the responsibility of the KGB's Eighth Chief Directorate, which is the counterpart of the U.S. National Security Agency (NSA) and the equally vaguely named British Government Communications Headquarters (GCHQ). The United States has an edge because of its possession of superior Cray and other supercomputers. The United States has also had some success in the past in "black-bag" jobs to purloin foreign codebooks.

But codes can also be lost by betrayal, and here the Russians have apparently been more successful. They got the codebooks and equipment that the North Koreans captured from the USS *Pueblo*, and they obtained agents such as Geoffrey Prime in the British GCHQ, the defectors Bernon Mitchell and William Martin from NSA in 1960, Army cryptographer Joseph George Helmich, and the far more serious NSA Staff Sergeant Jack E. Dunlap, whose treachery was discovered only after he had committed suicide in 1963.[79]

Few spies could have been more seemingly insignificant than two twenty-one-year-old, drug-dealing, dropout flower children, Christopher Boyce and Andrew Daulton Lee. Through family connections they got access to a dull and low-lying facility at TRW in Redondo Beach, California, that just happened to be the focal point for America's spy satellites. The secrets they gave away to the

Russian embassy in Mexico City were priceless.[80] John Walker was a retired navy petty officer, but his network of greedy agents, which included his son and brother, gained access to vast quantities of American cryptological documents that were supposed to be burned. The Russians got them instead.[81] The Soviets' most recent success was apparently the bugging of the typewriters and transmission equipment in the American embassy in Moscow, so that all messages, coded or uncoded, could be read.[82]

## CURRENT TRENDS IN SOVIET INTELLIGENCE

### The Shift from War Plans to Technical Secrets

The emphasis in Soviet intelligence is shifting from the traditional "secret plans" type of espionage to political disinformation ("active measures") and a new type of espionage—acquisition of high technology that is useful not only for the military but also for the economy in general. Under Gorbachev, whose fate rests so much on revitalizing the Soviet economy, the acquisition of Western technology has achieved a markedly higher priority. Products that can be bought or purloined and then copied can save the USSR billions in research and development costs.[83]

For example, the Soviets have tended to lag far behind the West and Japan in almost every phase of computers. They have thus placed a premium on their intelligence agents acquiring advanced Western hardware and, more recently, the sophisticated equipment needed for manufacturing integrated computer chips.[84]

The United States and its NATO allies (minus Iceland but plus Japan) have organized a coordinating committee (COCOM) specifically to deny advanced technology to the Soviet Union and other Communist countries. Circumvention of these controls is the responsibility of the KGB and the GRU, which operates through fronts in such favored countries as Austria and Sweden or through NATO countries such as Germany and France who do not always share America's concerns about trade with the Soviets.

The economic conditions that gave rise to *perestroika* also have led to a tempering of Soviet adventurism abroad. The USSR is annually contributing $7 billion to Cuba and billions more to Ethiopia, Angola, and other famine-ridden countries. The unsuccessful war in Afghanistan cost many billions more, in addition to the costs in blood. All this is apart from the subsidies provided to the Eastern European satellites to restrain them from further straying and the long-term loans and credits to countries such as Egypt or Libya that may never be repaid. These expenditures are a serious drain upon the meager hard currency resources of the Soviet Union. They have made the USSR a player on the world stage, but it is unclear what benefit other than psychological this has provided to either the country or its hard-pressed citizenry. Moreover, communism has wrecked the economies of these already-poor nations, bringing famine to Ethiopia and making the other nations not a shining model for socialism but international charity cases.

Under Gorbachev a major "peace offensive" has been launched for both strategic and conventional arms reduction. Fanning support for these campaigns through the Soviet-controlled peace groups, as well as through the more independent organizations, is now a prime KGB goal. Earlier efforts against deployment of the U.S. Pershing missiles and other systems in Europe were heavy-handed, but with Gorbachev's popularity rating higher than that of the U.S. president in European esteem, prospects are better for this new campaign.

Likewise, the USSR's role in the Third World will need to change from a direct role of collecting poverty-stricken vassal states, like Angola and Ethiopia, with all the concomitant costs and obligations, to a more indirect and less entangling influence. This means suborning political leaders in these states and developing "agents of influence." Development of such agents for influence, not espionage, is a higher form of intelligence activity, for after all, what information is really desired from such benighted countries? On the other hand, they can be useful for providing military bases, centers of subversion against neighboring countries, and political support in denouncing "imperialism" at the United Nations and elsewhere. Thus the KGB may have an even more important, though different, role in the future. The country targets themselves, however, will probably not change. They will continue to be nations along the world's maritime checkpoints, ones with vital raw materials, and increasingly those countries, such as Japan, with coveted modern technology.

The priorities of Soviet intelligence collection are known to us. According to CIA Director William Webster,

The highest Soviet priority is information on U.S. strategic nuclear forces. Other high-priority subjects are key foreign-policy matters, congressional intentions, defense information, advanced dual-use technology . . . and, not surprisingly, U.S. intelligence sources and methods.[85]

There are no surprises here, for political intelligence will continue to be the goal of the KGB, as military intelligence is the chief task of the GRU. In recent years, however, the priority of economic and industrial espionage has soared. If Gorbachev's survival depends upon economic revitalization and modernization, then acquiring Western technology and equipment, either to use or to copy, is a necessity.[86] The USSR cannot afford the costs, nor would it have sufficient hard currency even if it could. Thus clandestine acquisition, carried out by the GRU and other Soviet organs, must play a crucial role in fostering the continued economic development of the USSR.

### Soviet Intelligence after Gorbachev

The long-term prognosis for Gorbachev the reformer is not good.[87] The support of the intelligentsia and, for now, the average Soviet citizen will avail him little if the economy fails to improve, ethnic groups clamor increasingly for independence, and Party officials see their privileges continue to erode.[88] Gorbachev's days may well be numbered.

What would be the result of Gorbachev's departure from power as it affects Soviet intelligence functions? Probably very little, although the loss of Gorbachev's astute, warm public-relations image would make recruitment a bit more difficult. The recent emphasis on economic and technological espionage would continue or even increase as the need becomes ever greater. For this, Japan and the Pacific Rim will loom ever larger, with a consequent slightly lesser attention paid to the main enemy, the United States, and its Western European allies. Africa (except for South Africa) and the Middle East will also receive less attention, though their essential ores and minerals will continue to merit a watch for targets of opportunity when they arise. Involvement in South and Central America will have little importance other than as an occasional prod to keep the United States off balance in its own backyard. But will there be less of a role for the KGB? For the foreseeable future, one can rest assured that this powerful organization will continue to play a pivotal role in the Soviet system.

## NOTES

1. Oleg Penkovsky, *The Penkovsky Papers* (Garden City, N.Y.: Doubleday, 1965); John Dziak, *Chekisty: A History of the KGB* (New York: Random House, Ballantine, 1988), p. 163. Considerable controversy still swirls about this highly regarded American spy known as "Ironbark," including whether he was fully genuine (the usual assumption) or a Soviet plant. The latest, but not the most plausible, theory is that he was indeed a plant by a faction of the KGB opposed to Khrushchev that wanted an alternative channel to the United States. Phillip Knightly, *The Second Oldest Profession: Spies and Spying in the Twentieth Century* (New York: Penguin, 1987), pp. 324–25.

2. Michael Dobbs, "Soviets and Cubans to Give Their Versions of '62 Missile Crisis," *Washington Post*, January 9, 1989.

3. Gorzdievski was spirited out of Moscow, where he had been recalled for "consultation," after Soviet double defector Vitaly Yurchenko tipped off the CIA that he had come under suspicion.

4. Howard Kurtz, "Reagan Joke Said to Cause Soviet Alert," *Washington Post*, October 12, 1984; Jeffrey T. Richelson, *Foreign Intelligence Organizations* (Cambridge, Mass.: Ballinger, 1988), p. 258.

5. At different times in its history the KGB has been called the Cheka (extraordinary committee), the OGPU, NKVD, MVD, and other names. For convenience, the term KGB is used here even when it may be anachronistic.

6. The leading work on the KGB structure and functions is Amy W. Knight, *The KGB: Police and Politics in the Soviet Union* (Boston: Unwin Hyman, 1988).

7. William Kennedy, *Intelligence Warfare: Penetrating the Secret World of Today's Advanced Technology Conflict* (New York: Crescent, 1987), pp. 8, 204.

8. Jay Tuck, *The T Directorate: How the KGB Smuggles NATO's Strategic Secrets to Moscow* (New York: St. Martin's Press, 1986); William R. Corson and Robert T. Crowley, *The New KGB: Engine of Soviet Power* (New York: William Morrow, 1986),

p. 342; John Barron, *KGB Today: The Hidden Hand* (New York: Reader's Digest Press, Berkley, 1983), p. 54.

9. John Barron, *KGB: The Secret Work of Soviet Secret Agents* (New York: Random House, Bantam, 1974), p. 109. The former name for this unit, before it was elevated to a directorate, was Special Service II.

10. Jeffrey T. Richelson, *Sword and Shield: Soviet Intelligence and Security Apparatus* (Cambridge, Mass.: Ballinger, 1986), p. 25.

11. This unit, created in 1958, was elevated from the status of a department, Department A, in the 1970s. Ibid., p. 24.

12. Ibid.

13. A. I. Romanov, *Nights Are Longest There: A Memoir of the Soviet Security Services* (Boston: Little, Brown, 1972). The pseudonymous author was a member of Smersh's wartime operation before defecting to the Americans in 1947; he may have been murdered in London in 1984.

14. In 1946 Smersh became part of the KGB, technically then the MVD (Ministry of Internal Affairs), under the name Otdel Kontra-Razvedka (OKR), or Counter-Intelligence Section. Richelson, *Sword and Shield*, pp. 14–15.

15. Ibid., p. 24.

16. Ibid., p. 22.

17. Aleksei Myagkov, *Inside the KGB* (New York: Ballantine, 1981). The Third Directorate is separate from the political commissar system, which dates from the days of the Revolution, and is overseen by the Main Political Administration (GPU), which itself is not to be confused with military intelligence, the GRU, or an earlier name for the KGB, the OGPU.

18. Peter Deriabin, *Watchdogs of Terror: Russian Bodyguards from the Tsars to the Commissars* (New Rochelle, N.Y.: Arlington House, 1972; Frederick, Md.: University Publications of America, 1984).

19. See chart 2–1 in Richelson, *Sword and Shield*, p. 22; and chapter 8 in Knight, *KGB*.

20. The Soviet Union denied any knowledge of the disappearance, but on September 22, 1965, an article by Col. Gen. N. Shimanov in the Soviet military's newspaper, *Krasnaya zvezda* (Red Star), praised the OGPU agent responsible for the abduction. See Dziak, *Chekisty*, pp. 110, 218n. 75.

21. Dziak, *Chekisty*, pp. 109–14.

22. Robert Conquest, *The Great Terror: Stalin's Purge of the Thirties*, rev. ed. (New York: Macmillan, 1973); M. Lewin, *Russian Peasants and Soviet Power: A Study in Collectivization* (New York: W. W. Norton, 1968); Robert Conquest, *The Harvest of Sorrow: Soviet Collectivization and the Terror-Famine* (New York: Oxford University Press, 1986).

23. The more notable murders included the assassination in Marseilles of King Alexander of Yugoslavia and French Foreign Minister Barthou in October 1934.

24. This rather unconvincing theory has also been raised in connection with Stalin's (probable) murder of his close associate, Sergei Kirov, in 1934, which served as the pretext for the first major Soviet purges.

25. Our information comes from, among others, Oleg Lyalin, who defected from the London embassy in 1971, and Vladimir Kuzichkin, who came over a decade later. Dziak, *Chekisty*, p. 180.

26. Dziak, *Chekisty*, p. 223 n. 42; Ilya Dzhirkvelov, *Secret Servant: My Life with the KGB and the Soviet Elite* (London: Collins, 1987).

27. Dziak, *Chekisty*, p. 158; Nikolai Khokhlov, *In the Name of Conscience: The Testament of a Soviet Secret Agent* (New York: David McKay, 1959); Brian Freemantle, *KGB: Inside the World's Largest Intelligence Network* (New York: Holt, Rinehart and Winston, 1982), p. 42.

28. Ion Pacepa, *Red Horizons: Chronicles of a Communist Spy Chief* (Washington, D.C.: Regnery Gateway, 1987).

29. Matei Pavel Haiducu, *J'ai refusé de tuer: Un agent secret roumain révèle les dessous de l'affaire* (Paris: Plon, 1984).

30. The sophistication of the device revealed a capability beyond that of the Bulgarian service, although assassinations by bomb and gunfire were a real Bulgarian specialty in the pre-Communist period. Vladimir Kostov, *The Bulgarian Umbrella* (New York: St. Martin's Press, 1988); BBC videotape and other documentation in the author's personal research files. A popular account is given in Freemantle, *KGB*.

31. Claire Sterling, *The Time of the Assassins: Anatomy of an Investigation* (New York: Holt, Rinehart and Winston, 1984); Paul Henze, *The Plot to Kill the Pope* (New York: Charles Scribner's Sons, 1984).

32. A contrary view, that the entire "pope plot" was the result of irresponsible journalism and Western deception, is given in Edward S. Herman and Frank Brodhead, *The Rise and Fall of the Bulgarian Connection* (New York: Sheridan Square Publishers, 1986).

33. Sun Tzu, *The Art of War*, Ed. by James Clavell (London: Oxford University Press, 1963), pp. 144–49; Richard H. Shultz and Roy Godson, *Dezinformatsia: The Strategy of Soviet Disinformation* (New York: Berkley, 1986).

34. House of Representatives, *Hearings before the Permanent Select Committee on Intelligence*, 97th Cong. 2nd Sess., 13–14 July 1982, pp. 96–97, 170ff., 230, et al.

35. See David Atlee Phillips, *The Night Watch* (New York: Ballantine, 1977), pp. 367–68. Phillips was the head of CIA's Western Hemisphere division at the time.

36. Ladislav Bittman, *The Deception Game: Czechoslovak Intelligence in Soviet Political Warfare* (Syracuse: Syracuse University Research Corporation, 1972); Chapman Pincher, *The Secret Offensive* (London: Sidgwick and Jackson, 1985), pp. 34ff.

37. Chapman Pincher, *Traitors* (New York: St. Martin's Press, 1987), p. 34. Dimitrov, although he had acquired Soviet citizenship, became Party boss of Bulgaria after World War II.

38. Soviet Active Measures, *Hearings*, p. 69.

39. Nicholas Bethell, *The Great Betrayal: The Untold Story of Kim Philby's Biggest Coup* (London: Hodder and Stoughton, 1984). The episode was actually much more complicated, in that the operation leaked like a sieve from many different sources, so that the failure of the Albanian affair cannot be attributed solely to Philby.

40. Purists might object that MI5 is not the equivalent of FBI, since the latter has a number of functions akin to Scotland Yard, of which counterespionage is only one. But in terms of status, the equivalency is a fair one.

41. Among the many books on or about General Gehlen are E. H. Cookridge, *Gehlen: The Spy of the Century* (London: Hodder and Stoughton, Corgi, 1972); Heinz Hoehne and Hermann Zolling, *The General Was a Spy: The Truth about General Gehlen and His Spy Ring* (New York: Coward, McCann and Geoghegan, 1972); and Reinhard Gehlen,

*The Service: The Memoirs of General Reinhard Gehlen* (New York: World Publishers, 1972).

42. Knightly, *Second Oldest Profession*, pp. 274–75.

43. There are two German intelligence organizations, corresponding to the FBI-CIA or MI5-MI6 dichotomy. For foreign intelligence there is the Bundesnachrichtendienst (BND, or Federal Information Service). For counterespionage there is the Bundesamt für Verfassungsschutz (Federal Agency for Protection of the Constitution).

44. Otto John, *Twice through the Lines: The Autobiography of Otto John* (New York: Harper and Row, 1972).

45. Ibid., introduction by H. R. Trever-Roper, who theorizes that the Soviets arranged John's "defection" to cover their real penetration of the Gehlen organization.

46. Pincher, *Traitors*, pp. 174, 177, 210.

47. Ibid., pp. 52, 81, 272, 286.

48. David Wise, *The Spy Who Got Away: The Inside Story of Edward Lee Howard, the CIA Agent Who Betrayed His Country's Secrets and Escaped to Moscow* (New York: Random House, 1988). The betrayal of American agents in the USSR that was blamed on him, however, may have actually been due to Soviet penetration of the supersecret code room on the ninth floor of the U.S. embassy in Moscow.

49. Anatole Verbitsky and Dick Adler, *Sleeping with Moscow: The Authorized Account of the KGB's Bungled Infiltration of the FBI by Two of the Soviet Union's Most Unlikely Operatives* (New York: Shapolsky Publishers, 1987). I do not agree with this conclusionary title. See also Corson and Crowley, *New KGB*, p. 391.

50. A computer search by this author of the recent reports of the Soviet news agency TASS found forty-seven articles mentioning the KGB secret police; not one mention was found of the GRU.

51. Among the books about GRU defectors or describing the GRU organization, albeit often dated, are William Hood, *Mole* (New York: W. W. Norton, 1982); Viktor Suvorov, *Inside Soviet Military Intelligence* (New York: Macmillan, 1984); Elizabeth Poretsky, *Our Own People: A Memoir of Ignace Reiss and His Friends* (Ann Arbor: University of Michigan Press, 1970); Walter G. Krivitsky, *In Stalin's Secret Service: An Exposé of Russia's Secret Policies by the Former Chief of Soviet Intelligence in Western Europe* (Westport, Conn.: Hyperion Press, 1979); Igor Gouzenko, *The Iron Curtain* (New York: E. P. Dutton, 1948); Alexander Foote, *Handbook for Spies* (Garden City, N.Y.: Doubleday, 1949); and Ismail Akhmedov, *In and out of Stalin's GRU: A Tatar's Escape from Red Army Intelligence* (Frederick, Md.: University Publications of America, 1984). To my knowledge, the only Western book about the GRU that is not merely anecdotal or a defector's account is Pierre Villemarest, *GRU: Le plus secret des services soviétiques, 1918–1988* (Paris: Stock, 1988).

52. Peter Deriabin and Frank Gibney, *The Secret World* (New York: Random House, Ballantine, 1959), p. 286.

53. Suvorov, *Inside Soviet Military Intelligence*, pp. 51–52.

54. For example, former FBI counterespionage author Robert J. Lamphere's book about his battles with the GRU-led atom spy ring is entitled *The FBI-KGB War: A Special Agent's Story* (New York: Random House, Berkley, 1986).

55. Frederick W. D. Deakin and Richard G. Storry, *The Case of Richard Sorge* (New York: Harper and Row, 1966).

56. Leopold Trepper, *The Great Game: Memoirs of the Spy Hitler Couldn't Silence* (New York: McGraw-Hill, 1977); Anthony Read and David Fisher, *Operation Lucy* (New

York: Coward, McCann and Geoghegan, 1981); Giles Perrault, *The Red Orchestra* (New York: Simon and Schuster, 1969).

57. Kennedy, *Intelligence Warfare*, p. 12; Oliver Ramsay Pilat, *The Atom Spies* (New York: Putnam, 1952); Norman Moss, *Klaus Fuchs: The Man Who Stole the Atom Bomb* (New York: St. Martin's Press, 1987); Robert C. Williams, *Klaus Fuchs: Atom Spy* (Cambridge, Mass.: Harvard University Press, 1987); Whittaker Chambers, *Witness* (New York: Random House, 1952); Allen Weinstein, *Perjury: The Hiss-Chambers Case* (New York: Alfred A. Knopf, 1978); Lamphere, *FBI-KGB War*. The GRU link is obscured, however, because even the books about its episodes refer to the KGB.

58. Foreword by Viktor Suvorov, "The GRU: An Insider's View," in William Kennedy, *Intelligence Warfare*, p. 10. The GRU returned the favor in 1953, after the deaths of Stalin and KGB chief Beria, when the GRU assisted the new Soviet leaders in torturing and executing Beria's closest followers.

59. Kennedy, *Intelligence Warfare*, pp. 8–13.

60. Ibid.

61. John J. Dziak, "The Soviet Approaches to Special Operations," in Frank R. Barnett et al., *Special Operations in US Strategy* (Washington: National Defense University Press, 1984), Richelson, *Sword and Shield*, p. 162. This force originated as a behind-the-lines partisan force during World War II.

62. Viktor Suvorov, *Spetsnaz* (New York: W. W. Norton, 1987); John M. Collins, *Green Berets, Seals, and Spetsnaz: U.S. and Soviet Special Military Operations* (New York: Pergamon, 1987); see also Viktor Suvorov, "Spetsnaz: The Soviet Union's Special Forces," *International Defense Review* (Geneva), September 1983; John Adams, *Secret Armies: Inside the American, Soviet, and European Special Forces* (New York: Atlantic Monthly Press, 1987).

63. Isaac Don Levine, *Stalin's Great Secret* (New York: Coward-McCann, 1956). The historical background is set forth in, among others, Sidney Monas, *The Third Section: Police and Society in Russia under Nicholas I* (Cambridge, Mass.: Harvard University Press, 1961); A. T. Vassiliev, *The Okhrana: The Russian Secret Police* (London: G. G. Harrap, 1930); George Backer, *The Deadly Parallel: Stalin and Ivan the Terrible* (New York: Random House, 1950); and Alexander Yanov, *The Origins of Autocracy: Ivan the Terrible in Russian History* (Berkeley: University of California Press, 1981).

64. Dziak, *Chekisty*, app. A, pp. 191–92.

65. Knightly, *Second Oldest Profession*, pp. 49–52.

66. Stalin may have planted the evidence himself, to be fed back to the KGB by the Germans, in order to justify his own pathological desire to purge the Red Army.

67. Pincher, *Traitors*, pp. xiv–xv.

68. Elizabeth Bentley, *Out of Bondage: KGB Target: Washington, D.C.* (New York: Ballantine, 1988), p. 177.

69. Pincher, *Traitors*, pp. 92–93.

70. Pacepa, *Red Horizons*, pp. 9–12.

71. Pincher, *Traitors*, p. 93.

72. Corson and Crowley, *New KGB*, p. 394.

73. Thomas B. Allen and Norman Polmar, *Merchants of Treason: America's Secrets for Sale from the Pueblo to the Present* (New York: Doubleday, 1988).

74. Thomas Whiteside, *An Agent in Place* (New York: Random House, Ballantine, 1966).

75. See Vladislav Krasnov, *Soviet Defectors: The KGB Wanted List* (Stanford, Calif.: Hoover Institution Press, 1986).

76. See, for example, Knightley, *Second Oldest Profession*, pp. 296–339.

77. The defectors' murmurings of discontent reached the Senate Intelligence Committee, and in 1981 a staff working group was established to look into two issues, whether the discontent was substantial and whether there was a problem because the CIA was "offering unsustainable assurances of assistance prior to debriefing and failing to deliver fully afterwards."

Former CIA deputy director Robert Gates, in his confirmation hearings on April 10, 1986, admitted to Sen. Frank Murkowski (R-Alaska) that the defection program had been unsatisfactory and stated that organizational reforms were under way. One reform was to place all defector matters, both interrogation and resettlement, under a single boss. The other was a new policy of having a single case officer remain with a defector throughout, to provide personal continuity and to prevent the first team promising what the second team could not deliver.

A private organization, the Jamestown Foundation in Washington, D.C., has been established by attorney William Geimer to help nonintelligence defectors adjust to American life. The organization has often been privately critical of the agency's resettlement program; but, according to former CIA director William Colby, concerned organizations like this can provide more personal assistance than government bureaucrats, however well intentioned. (A similar organization, SPARC, headed by a descendant of Lev Tolstoy, to help Soviet soldiers captured in Afghanistan, exists in London.)

78. Pacepa, *Red Horizons*.

79. Wayne G. Barker and Rodney Coffman, *The Anatomy of Two Traitors: The Defection of Bernon F. Mitchell and William H. Martin* (Laguna Hills, Calif.: Aegean Park Press, 1981); James Bamford, *The Puzzle Palace* (Boston: Houghton Mifflin, 1982), pp. 177ff. Pincher, *Traitors*, pp. 18, 76.

80. Robert Lindsay, *The Falcon and the Snowman: A True Story of Friendship and Espionage* (New York: Simon and Schuster, 1979).

81. John Barron, *Breaking the Ring: The Rise and Fall of the Walker Family Spy Network* (Boston: Houghton Mifflin, 1987); Jack Kneece, *Family Treason: The Walker Spy Case* (Briarcliff Manor: Stein and Day, 1986); Howard Blum, *I Pledge Allegiance: The True Story of the Walkers: An American Spy Family* (New York: Simon and Schuster, 1987).

82. Ronald Kessler, *Moscow Station: How the KGB Penetrated the American Embassy* (New York: Charles Scribner's Sons, 1989).

83. Lauran Paine, *Silicon Spies: The Implications of Soviet Acquisition of Western Technology* (New York: St. Martin's Press, 1986); August Bequai, *Techno-Crimes: The Computerization of Crime and Terrorism* (Lexington, Mass.: Lexington Books, 1987).

84. See, for example, Tuck, *The T Directorate*, pp. 151–79.

85. Speech by William H. Webster to the American Bar Association, Toronto, Canada, August 9, 1988.

86. See also Joseph Finder, *Red Carpet: The Connection between the Kremlin and America's Most Powerful Businessmen* (New York: Holt, Rinehart and Winston, 1988).

87. At a recent meeting of middle-level officials from the United States and the USSR, the different outcomes of Gorbachev's reforms were explored in detail. The Soviet delegates felt strongly that the reforms had to succeed because all of the other courses, whether a return to bureaucratic and economic stagnation or a centrifugal disintegration

of the union, were unacceptable. The American delegates were unanimous in believing that *perestroika* would fail, that its success (in thereby strengthening the Soviet Union) would not necessarily be in the interests of the United States or world peace, and that the most likely outcome in the short run was indeed a relapse to unimaginative economic and political leadership dominated by the conservative factions of the Communist Party.

88. There are other views of Gorbachev, of course, including the hypothesis that he is "neither a liberal nor a bold reformist" but rather possesses "the proper combination of orthodoxy, efficiency, toughness and political and diplomatic skill" to survive, even if his current policies do not. Zhores A. Medvedev, *Gorbachev* (New York: W. W. Norton, 1986), pp. 245–46.

# Select Bibliography

## BOOKS

Abegglen, J. C., and G. Stalk. *Kaisha: The Japanese Corporation*. New York: Basic Books, 1985.

Adams, Frederick Upham. *Conquest of the Tropics*. Garden City, N.Y.: Doubleday, Page and Co., 1914.

Adams, James. *Secret Armies: Inside the American, Soviet, and European Special Forces*. New York: Atlantic Monthly Press, 1987.

Ady, Peter H., ed. *Private Foreign Investment and the Developing World*. New York: Praeger Publishers, 1972.

Aguilar, Francis J. *Scanning the Business Environment*. New York: Macmillan, 1967.

Aharoni, Yair. *The Foreign Investment Decision Process*. Boston: Harvard University, Graduate School of Business, 1966.

Aharoni, Yair, with Clifford Baden. *Business in the International Environment*. Boulder, Colo.: Westview Press, 1977.

Aho, A. V., J. E. Hopcroft, and J. D. Ullman. *Data Structures and Algorithms*. Reading, Mass.: Addison-Wesley, 1983.

Akhmedov, Ismail. *In and out of Stalin's GRU: A Tatar's Escape from Red Army Intelligence*. Frederick, Md.: University Publications of America, 1984.

Aldrich, H. E. *Organizations and Environments*. Englewood Cliffs, N.J.: Prentice-Hall, 1979.

Alexander, Garth. *The Invisible China: The Overseas Chinese and the Politics of Southeast Asia*. New York: Macmillan, 1973.

Alexander, Yonah, David Carlton, and Paul Wilkinson, eds. *Terrorism: Theory and Practice*. Boulder, Colo.: Westview Press, 1979.

Allen, A. M. *Guide for Investment in Developing Countries*. London: Brown, Knight and Truscott, 1973.

Allen, Thomas B., and Norman Polmar. *Merchants of Treason: America's Secrets for Sale*. New York: Delacorte Press, 1988.

Ambrose, Stephen E., with Richard H. Immerman. *Ike's Spies: Eisenhower and the Intelligence Community*. Garden City, N.Y.: Doubleday, 1981.

Anderson, E. W. *Strategic Minerals: The Geopolitical Problem for the United States*. New York: Praeger Publishers, 1988.

———. *Strategic Raw Materials and Geopolitical Risk Assessment: A Model*. London: Ministry of Defense, 1984.

———. *The Structure and Dynamics of United States Government Policy-Making: The Case of Strategic Minerals*. New York: Praeger Publishers, 1988.

Apter, David E., and Louis Wolf Goodman, eds. *The Multinational Corporation and Social Change*. New York: Praeger Publishers, 1976.

Arendt, Hannah. *The Origins of Totalitarianism*, 3rd ed. London: George Allen and Unwin, 1966.

Ariel, Dan. *Explosion*! Tel-Aviv: Olive Book of Israel, 1972.

Ascher, William. *Forecasting: An Appraisal for Policy-Makers and Planners*. Baltimore: Johns Hopkins University Press, 1978.

Aybar de Soto, Jose M. *Dependency and Intervention: The Case of Guatemala in 1954*. Boulder, Colo.: Westview Press, 1978.

Ball, G. W. *Global Companies: The Political Economy of World Business*. Englewood Cliffs, N.J.: Prentice-Hall, 1975.

Bamford, James. *The Puzzle Palace*. Boston: Houghton Mifflin, 1982.

Banks, Arthur S. *Cross-Polity Time-Series Data*. Cambridge, Mass.: MIT Press, 1971.

Banks, Arthur S., and Robert B. Textor. *A Cross-Polity Survey*. Cambridge, Mass.: MIT Press, 1963.

Barr, A., and E. A. Feigenbaum. *The Handbook of Artificial Intelligence*. Vols. 1–3. Los Altos, Calif.: William Kaufman, 1981.

Barron, John. *Breaking the Ring: The Rise and Fall of the Walker Family Spy Network*. Boston: Houghton Mifflin, 1987.

———. *KGB: The Secret Work of Soviet Secret Agents*. New York: Random House, 1974.

———. *KGB Today: The Hidden Hand*. New York: Reader's Digest Press, Berkley, 1983.

Bar-Zohar, Michael. *Spies in the Promised Land: Iser Harel and the Israeli Secret Service*. Translated from the French by Monroe Stearns. Boston: Houghton Mifflin, 1972.

Becker, George. *The Deadly Parallel: Stalin and Ivan the Terrible*. New York: Random House, 1950.

Becket, Henry S. A. *The Dictionary of Espionage: Spookspeak into English*. New York: Dell Publishing Co., 1986.

Bennis, W. and B. Nanus. *Leaders: The Strategies for Taking Charge*. New York: Harper and Row, 1985.

Bentley, Elizabeth. *Out of Bondage: KGB Target: Washington, D.C.* New York: Ballantine, 1988.

Berg, T. L. *Mismarketing: Case Histories of Marketing Misfires*. New York: Anchor, 1970.

Bergier, Jacques. *Secret Armies: The Growth of Corporate and Industrial Espionage.* New York: Bobbs-Merrill, 1975.

Bethell, Nicholas W. *Gomulka: His Poland and His Communism.* Rev. ed. Harmondsworth: Penguin, 1972.

————. *The Great Betrayal: The Untold Story of Kim Philby's Biggest Coup.* London: Hodder and Stoughton, 1984.

*Bibliography of Intelligence Literature: A Critical and Annotated Bibliography of Open-Source Literature.* Washington, D.C.: Defense Intelligence School, 1981.

Bittman, Ladislav. *The Deception Game: Czechoslovak Intelligence in Soviet Political Warfare.* Syracuse, N.Y.: Syracuse University Research Corp., 1972.

Blackstock, Paul W. *The Secret Road to World War Two: Soviet versus Western Intelligence, 1921–1939.* Chicago: Quadrangle Books, 1969.

————. *The Strategy of Subversion: Manipulating the Politics of Other Nations.* Chicago: Quadrangle Books, 1964.

Blackstock, Paul W., and Frank L. Schaf, Jr. *Intelligence, Espionage, Counterespionage, and Covert Operations: A Guide to Information Sources.* Detroit: Gale Research Company, 1978.

Blank, Stephen, with John Basek, Stephen J. Kobrin, and Joseph La Palombara. *Assessing the Political Environment: An Emerging Function in International Companies.* New York: Conference Board, 1981.

Blasier, Cole. *The Hovering Giant: U.S. Responses to Revolutionary Change in Latin America.* Pittsburgh, Pa.: University of Pittsburgh Press, 1976.

Blum, Howard, *I Pledge Allegiance: The True Story of the Walkers: An American Spy Family.* New York: Simon and Schuster, 1987.

Blum, Richard H., ed. *Surveillance and Espionage in a Free Society.* New York: Praeger Publishing, 1972.

Blumberg, Stanley A., and Gwinn Owens. *The Survival Factor: Israeli Intelligence from World War I to Present.* New York: Putnam, 1981.

Bouza, Anthony V. *Police Intelligence: The Operations of an Investigative Unit.* New York: Am's Press, 1976.

Brewer, Thomas L., ed. *Political Risks in International Business.* New York: Praeger Publishers, 1985.

Brus, Wlodzimierz. *Socialist Ownership and Political Systems.* London: Routledge and Kegan Paul, 1975.

Bulloch, John. *M.I.5.: The Origin and History of the British Counter-Espionage Service.* London: A. Barker, 1963.

Bunge, Fredrica A. *Philippines: A Country Study.* Foreign Area Studies. 1982.

Bunyan, Tony. *The Political Police in Britain.* New York: St. Martin's Press, 1976.

Burnham, David. *The Rise of the Computer State.* New York: Random House, 1983.

Burstein, Daniel. *Yen: Japan's New Financial Empire and Its Threat to America.* New York: Simon and Schuster, 1988.

Calvert, Peter. *Guatemala, A Nation in Turmoil.* Boulder, Colo.: Westview Press, 1985.

Carroll, John M. *Secrets of Electronic Espionage.* New York: E. P. Dutton, 1966.

Castro Hidalgo, Orlando. *Spy for Fidel.* Miami, Fla.: E. A. Seemann Publishers, 1971.

Chambers, Whittaker, *Witness.* New York: Random House, 1952.

Christopher, R. C. *The Japanese Mind: The Goliath Explained.* New York: Linden Press/Simon and Schuster, 1983.

Clark, R. *The Japanese Company.* New Haven: Yale University Press, 1979.

Clinard, Marshall B., and Peter C. Yeager. *Corporate Crime*. New York: Free Press, 1980.

Cline, Marjorie W., ed. *Teaching Intelligence in the Mid–1980s: A Survey of College and University Courses on the Subject of Intelligence*. Washington, D.C.: National Intelligence Study Center, 1985.

Collins, John M. *Green Berets, Seals, and Spetsnaz: U.S. and Soviet Special Military Operations*. New York: Pergamon, 1987.

Conquest, Robert. *The Great Terror: Stalin's Purge of the Thirties*. Rev. ed. New York: Macmillan, 1973.

————. *The Harvest of Sorrow: Soviet Collectivization and the Terror-Famine*. New York: Oxford University Press, 1986.

Constantinides, George C. *Intelligence and Espionage: An Analytical Bibliography*. Boulder, Colo.: Westview Press, 1983.

Cook, Blanche. *The Declassified Eisenhower: A Divided Legacy of Peace and Political Warfare*. Garden City, N.Y.: Doubleday, 1981.

Cookridge, E. H. *Gehlen: The Spy of the Century*. London: Hodder and Stoughton, Corgi, 1972.

Copeland, Miles. *Without Cloak or Dagger: The Truth about the New Espionage*. New York: Simon and Schuster, 1974.

Corson, William R., and Robert T. Crowley. *The New KGB: Engine of Soviet Power*. New York: William Morrow, 1986.

Cowan, Paul. Nick Egleson, and Nat Hentoff with Barbara Herbert and Robert Wall. *State Secrets: Police Surveillance in America*. New York: Holt, Rinehart and Winston, 1974.

Crane, Dwight B., ed. *Financial Management*. New York: John Wiley and Sons, 1983.

Cyert, R. M. and J. G. March. *A Behavioral Theory of the Firm*. Englewood Cliffs, N.J.: Prentice-Hall, 1963.

Deacon, Richard. *The Israeli Secret Service*. New York: Taplinger Publishing Company, 1977.

Deakin, Frederick W. D., and Richard G. Storry. *The Case of Richard Sorge*. New York: Harper and Row, 1966.

Deriabin, Peter. *Watchdogs of Terror: Russian Bodyguards from the Tsars to the Commissars*. New Rochelle, N.Y.: Arlington House, 1972; Frederick, Md.: University Publications of America, 1984.

Deriabin, Peter, and Frank Gibney. *The Secret World*. New York: Random House, 1959.

Derogy, Jacques, and Hesi Camel. *The Untold History of Israel*. New York: Grove Press; distributed by Random House, 1979.

DeVore, Ronald M. *Spies and All That . . . Intelligence Agencies and Operations: A Bibliography*. Los Angeles: Center for the Study of Armament and Disarmament, 1977.

Donner, Frank J. *The Age of Surveillance: The Aims and Methods of America's Political Intelligence System*. New York: Alfred A. Knopf, 1980.

Dulles, Allen. *The Craft of Intelligence*. New York: Harper and Row, 1963.

Dunlop, Richard. *Donovan: America's Master Spy*. New York: Rand McNally, 1982.

Dunning, J. H. *The Multinational Enterprise*. London: Allen and Unwin, 1971.

Dvornik, Francis. *Origins of Intelligence Services*. New Brunswick, N.J.: Rutgers University Press, 1974.

Dzhirkvelov, Ilya. *Secret Servant: My Life with the KGB and the Soviet Elite*. London: Collins, 1987.

Dzienwanowski, M. K. *The Communist Party of Poland*. 2nd ed. Cambridge, Mass.: Harvard University Press, 1976.

Dziak, John J. *Chekisty: A History of the KGB*. New York: Random House, Ballantine, 1988.

Eckstein, Harry. *Internal War*. New York: Free Press, 1964.

Eells, Richard, and Peter Nehemkis. *Corporate Intelligence and Espionage*: *A Blueprint for Executive Decision-Making*. New York: Macmillan, 1984.

Elliff, John T. *The Reform of FBI Intelligence Operations*. Princeton, N.J.: Princeton University Press, 1979.

Epstein, Edward Jay. *Legend: The Secret World of Lee Harvey Oswald*. New York: Reader's Digest Press, 1978.

Feierabend, Ivo K., and Rosalind L. Feierabend. *Cross-National Data Bank of Political Instability Events*. San Diego, Calif.: Public Affairs Research Institute, 1965.

Feigenbaum, E., and P. McCorduck. *The Fifth Generation: Artificial Intelligence and Japan's Computer Challenge to the World*. Reading, Mass.: Addison-Wesley, 1983.

Feigenbaum, E., H. Penny Nii, and P. McCorduck. *The Rise of the Expert Company*. New York: Times Books, 1988.

Finder, Joseph. *Red Carpet: The Connection between the Kremlin and America's Most Powerful Businessmen*. New York: Holt, Rinehart and Winston, 1988.

Flam, Henry, and Stan Persky. *The Solidarity Source Book*. Vancouver: New Star Books, 1982.

Foote, Alexander. *Handbook for Spies*. Garden City, N.Y.: Doubleday, 1949.

Fraser, Peter. *The Intelligence of the Secretaries of State and Their Monopoly of Licensed News, 1660–1688*. London: Cambridge University Press, 1956.

Freedman, Lawrence. *U.S. Intelligence and the Soviet Strategic Threat*. Boulder, Colo.: Westview Press, 1977.

Freemantle, Brian. *KGB: Inside the World's Largest Intelligence Network*. New York: Holt, Rinehart and Winston, 1982.

Fuld, Leonard M. *Competitor Intelligence: How to Get It—How to Use It*. New York: John Wiley and Sons, 1985.

Gabor, Dennis. *Inventing the Future*. New York: Alfred A. Knopf, 1969.

Galbraith, J. *Designing Complex Organizations*. Reading, Mass.: Addison-Wesley, 1973.

Galland, Joseph S. *An Historical and Analytical Bibliography of the Literature of Cryptology*. Studies in Humanities Series. Evanston, Ill.: Northwestern University Press, 1945.

Gallenkamp, Charles. *Maya: The Riddle and Rediscovery of a Lost Civilization*. 3rd rev. ed. New York: Viking Penguin, 1985.

Gehlen, Reinhard. *The Service: The Memoirs of General Reinhard Gehlen*. New York: World Publishers, 1972.

Geyikdagi, Mehmet Yasar. *Risk Trends of U.S. Multinational and Domestic Firms*. New York: Praeger Publishers, 1982.

Gibney, F. *Miracle by Design: The Real Reasons behind Japan's Economic Success*. New York: Times Books, 1982.

Gilad, Benjamin, and Tamar Gilad. *The Business Intelligence System: A New Tool for Competitive Advantage*. New York: American Management Association, 1988.

Godson, Roy. *The Kremlin and Labor: A Study in National Security*. New York: Crane, Russak and Company, 1977.

———, ed. *Comparing Foreign Intelligence: The US, USSR, UK, and the Third World*. Washington, D.C.: Pergamon-Brassey's, 1988.

———. *Intelligence Requirements for the 1980s: Analysis and Estimates*. Washington, D.C.: National Strategy Information Center, 1980.

———. *Intelligence Requirements for the 1980s: Clandestine Collection*. Washington, D.C.: National Strategy Information Center, 1982.

———. *Intelligence Requirements for the 1980s: Counterintelligence*. Washington, D.C.: National Strategy Information Center, 1980.

———. *Intelligence Requirements for the 1980s: Covert Action*. Washington, D.C.: National Strategy Information Center, 1981.

———. *Intelligence Requirements for the 1980s: Elements of Intelligence*. Washington, D.C.: National Strategy Information Center, 1979.

———. *Intelligence Requirements for the 1990s: Collection, Analysis, Counterintelligence, and Covert Action*. Lexington, Mass.: D. C. Heath and Company, 1989.

Gouzenko, Igor. *The Iron Curtain*. New York: E. P. Dutton, 1948.

Gunzhauser, Max. *Geschichte des geheimen Nachrichtendienstes (Spionage, Sabotage, und Abwehr)* (History of secret services—espionage, sabotage, and counterintelligence). Frankfurt: Bernard und Graefe Verlag für Wehrwesen, 1968.

Haendel, Dan. *Foreign Investments and the Management of Political Risk*. Boulder, Colo.: Westview Press, 1979.

Haendel, Dan, with Gerald T. White and Robert G. Meadow. *Overseas Investment and Political Risk*. Philadelphia: Foreign Policy Research Institute, 1975.

Haiducu, Matel Pavel. *J'ai refusé de tuer: Un agent secret roumain révèle les dessous de l'affaire*. Paris: Plon, 1984.

Hamburg, M. *Statistical Analysis for Decision Making*. 2nd ed. New York: Harcourt Brace Jovanovich, 1977.

Haner, Frederick T. *Global Business Strategy for the 1980s*. New York: Praeger Publishers, 1980.

Hargreaves, D., and S. Fromson. *World Index of Strategic Minerals*. Aldershot: Gower, 1984.

Harmon, P., R. Maus, and W. Morrissey. *Expert Systems: Tools and Applications*. New York: John Wiley and Sons, 1988.

Harris, William R. *Intelligence and National Security: A Bibliography with Selected Annotations*. Cambridge, Mass.: Harvard University Center for International Affairs, 1968.

Hasegawa, K. *Japanese-style Management: An Insider's Analysis*. Kodansha International, 1986.

Hayes-Roth, F., D. A. Waterman, and D. B. Lenat. *Building Expert Systems*. Reading, Mass.: Addison-Wesley, 1983.

Heims, Peter. *Countering Industrial Espionage*. London: 20th Century Security Education, 1982.

Henze, Paul. *The Plot to Kill the Pope*. New York: Charles Scribner's Sons, 1984.

Herring, Richard, ed. *Managing International Risk: Essays Commissioned in Honor of the Centenary of the Wharton School*. New York: Cambridge University Press, 1983.

Hersh, Seymour M. *The Target Is Destroyed: What Really Happened to Flight 007 and What America Knew About It*. New York: Random House, 1986.

Heuer, Richards J., Jr. *Quantitative Approaches to Political Intelligence: The CIA Experience*. Boulder, Colo.: Westview Press, 1978.

Hilsman, Roger. *Strategic Intelligence and National Decisions*. New York: Free Press, 1956.

Hingley, Ronald. *The Russian Secret Police: Muskovite, Imperial Russian, and Soviet Political Security Operations*. New York: Simon and Schuster, 1971.

Hoehne, Heinz, and Hermann Zolling. *The General Was a Spy: The Truth about General Gehlen and His Spy Ring*. New York: Coward, McCann and Geoghegan, 1972.

Hood, William. *Mole*. New York: W. W. Norton, 1982.

Hougan, Jim. *Spooks: The Haunting of America: The Private Use of Secret Agents*. New York: Morrow, 1978.

Jackson, P. *Introduction to Expert Systems*. Reading, Mass.: Addison-Wesley, 1986.

Jacobs, Neil H., Peter Nehemkis, and Richard Eells. *Bribery and Extortion in World Business: A Study of Corporate Political Payments*. New York: Macmillan, 1977.

James, D., ed. *Strategic Minerals: A Resource Crisis*. Washington, D.C.: Council on Economics and National Security, 1981.

James, Peter N. *The Air Force Mafia*. New Rochelle, N.Y.: Arlington House, 1975.

Jodice, David A. *Political Risk Assessment: An Annotated Bibliography*. Westport, Conn.: Greenwood Press, 1985.

John, Otto. *Twice through the Lines: The Autobiography of Otto John*. New York: Harper and Row, 1972.

Johnson, Chalmers. *Japanese Public Policy Companies*. AEI-Hoover Policy Studies, 24. Washington, D.C.: American Enterprise Institute for Public Policy Research, 1978.

————. *MITI and the Japanese Miracle*. Stanford, Calif.: Stanford University Press, 1982.

Johnson, Lock K. *A Season of Inquiry: The Senate Intelligence Investigation*. Lexington: University Press of Kentucky, 1985.

Kane, William Everett. *Civil Strife in Latin America: A Legal History of U.S. Involvement*. Baltimore: Johns Hopkins University Press, 1972.

Kapp, D., and J. F. Leben. *IMS Programming Techniques*. New York: Van Nostrand Reinhold Company, 1978.

Karnes, Thomas L. *Tropical Enterprise: The Standard Fruit and Steamship Company in Latin America*. Baton Rouge: Louisiana State University Press, 1978.

Keen, P. G. W., and M. S. Scott-Morton. *Decision Support Systems: An Organizational Perspective*. Reading, Mass.: Addison-Wesley, 1978.

Kelly, Marie Wicks. *Foreign Investment Evaluation Practices of U.S. Multinational Corporations*. Ann Arbor: UMI Research Press, 1981.

Kennedy, William. *Intelligence Warfare: Penetrating the Secret World of Today's Advanced Technology Conflict*. New York: Crescent, 1987.

Kent, Shermon. *Strategic Intelligence*. Princeton, N.J.: Princeton University Press, 1949.

Kepner, Charles David, Jr. *Social Aspects of the Banana Industry*. New York: AMS Press, 1967.

Kessler, Ronald. *Moscow Station: How the KGB Penetrated the American Embassy*. New York: Charles Scribner's Sons, 1989.

Khokhlov, Nikolai. *In the Name of Conscience: The Testament of a Soviet Secret Agent.* New York: David McKay, 1959.

Kimche, Jon. *Spying for Peace: General Guisan and Swiss Neutrality.* 3rd ed. New York: Roy Publishers, 1962.

Kirkpatrick, Lyman B. *The U.S. Intelligence Community.* New York: Hill and Wang, 1973.

Kneece, Jack. *Family Treason: The Walker Spy Case.* Briarcliff Manor: Stein and Day, 1986.

Knight, Amy W. *The KGB: Police and Politics in the Soviet Union.* Boston: Unwin Hyman, 1988.

Knightly, Phillip. *The Second Oldest Profession: Spies and Spying in the Twentieth Century.* New York: Penguin, 1987.

Kobrin, Stephen J. *Foreign Direct Investment, Industrialization, and Social Change.* Greenwich, Conn.: JAI Press, 1977.

Kolde, Endel J. *Environment of International Business.* Boston: Kent Publishing, 1982.

Kostov, Vladimir. *The Bulgarian Umbrella.* New York: St. Martin's Press, 1988.

Krasnov, Vladislav. *Soviet Defectors: The KGB Wanted List.* Stanford, Calif.: Hoover Institution Press, 1986.

Krivitsky, Walter G. *In Stalin's Secret Service: An Exposé of Russia's Secret Policies by the Former Chief of Soviet Intelligence in Western Europe* (Wesport, Conn.: Hyperion Press, 1979.

Kroeber, D., and H. Watson. *Computer-based Information Systems.* 2nd ed. New York: Macmillan, 1987.

Kroenke, D. M. *Database Processing.* 2nd ed. Chicago: Science Research Associates, 1983.

Kwak, N. K. *Mathematical Programming with Business Applications.* New York: McGraw-Hill, 1973.

LaFeber, Walter. *Inevitable Revolutions: The United States in Central America.* New York: W. W. Norton, 1983.

Lamphere, Robert J. *The FBI-KGB War: A Special Agent's Story.* New York: Random House, 1986.

Lapham, L. H. *Money and Class in America.* New York: Weidenfeld and Nicolson, 1988.

Laqueur, Walter. *A World of Secrets: The Uses and Limits of Intelligence*, New York: Basic Books, 1985.

Law, A. M., and W. D. Kelton. *Simulation Modeling and Analysis.* New York: McGraw-Hill, 1982.

Lawrence, P., and J. Lorsch. *Organization and Environment.* Boston: Harvard Business School, Division of Research, 1967.

Levine, Isaac Don. *Stalin's Great Secret.* New York: Coward-McCann, 1956.

Levite, Ariel. *Intelligence and Strategic Surprises.* New York: Columbia University Press, 1987.

Lewin, M. *Russian Peasants and Soviet Power: A Study in Collectivization.* New York: W. W. Norton, 1968.

Lewis, J. *Excellent Organizations: How to Develop and Manage Them Using Theory Z.* New York: Wilkerson, 1980.

Lindsey, Robert. *The Falcon and the Snowman: A True Story of Friendship and Espionage.* New York: Simon and Schuster, 1979.

Lipset, Seymour Martin. *Political Man*. Garden City, N.Y.: Doubleday, 1960.

Loomba, N. P., and E. Turban. *Applied Programming for Management*. New York: Holt, Rinehart and Winston, 1974.

McCann, Thomas P. *An American Company: The Tragedy of United Fruit*. New York: Crown Publishers, 1976.

McLeod, R., Jr. *Management Information Systems*. 3rd ed. Chicago: Science Research Associates, 1986.

McMillan, C., Jr. *Mathematical Programming*. 2nd ed. New York: John Wiley and Sons, 1975.

Madden, Carl H. *Clash of Culture: Management in an Age of Changing Values*. Washington, D.C.: National Planning Association, 1972.

Martin, David C. *Wilderness of Mirrors*. New York: Harper and Row, 1980.

Matejko, Alexander. *Social Change and Stratification in Eastern Europe*. New York: Praeger Publishers, 1974.

Medvedev, Zhores A. *Gorbachev*, New York: W. W. Norton, 1986.

Melvern, Linda, David Hebditch, and Nick Anning. *Techno-Bandits: How the Soviets Are Stealing America's High-Tech Future*. Boston: Houghton Mifflin Company, 1984.

Meyer, Herbert E. *Real World Intelligence: Organized Information for Executives*. New York: Weidenfeld and Nicolson, 1987.

Miliband, Ralph. *Marxism and Politics*. Oxford: Oxford University Press, 1977.

Miller, D., and P. H. Friesen. *Organizations: A Quantum View*. Englewood Cliffs, N.J.: Prentice-Hall, 1984.

Minsky, M., ed. *Semantic Information Processing*. Cambridge, Mass.: MIT Press, 1968.

Monas, Sidney. *The Third Section: Police and Society in Russia under Nicholas I*. Cambridge, Mass.: Harvard University Press, 1961.

Montana, Patrick J., and George S. Roukis, eds. *Managing Terrorism: Strategies for the Corporate Executive*. Westport, Conn.: Quorum Books, 1983.

Morgan, Richard E. *Domestic Intelligence: Monitoring Dissent in America*. Austin: University of Texas Press, 1980.

Moss, Norman. *Klaus Fuchs: The Man Who Stole the Atom Bomb*. New York: St. Martin's Press, 1987.

Myagkov, Aleksei. *Inside the KGB: An Exposé by an Officer of the Third Directorate*. New Rochelle, N.Y.: Arlington House, 1976.

Nakane, C. *Japanese Society*. Berkeley: University of California Press, 1972.

Needler, Martin C. *Political Systems of Latin America*. Princeton, N.J.: Van Nostrand, 1964.

Nehrt, C. L. *International Finance for Multinational Business*. Scranton, Pa.: Intext Educational Publishers, 1972.

Nilsson, N. J. *Principles of Artificial Intelligence*. Los Altos, Calif.: Morgan Kaufmann, 1980.

O'Leary, Michael K., and William D. Coplin. *Quantitative Techniques and Foreign Policy Analysis and Forecasting*. New York: Praeger Publishers, 1975.

Ouchi, W. *Theory Z*. Reading, Mass.: Addison-Wesley, 1982.

Pacepa, Ion. *Red Horizons: Chronicles of a Communist Spy Chief*. Washington, D.C.: Regnery Gateway, 1987.

Paine, Lauran. *Silicon Spies: The Implications of Soviet Acquisition of Western Technology*. New York: St. Martin's Press, 1986.

Penkovsky, Oleg. *The Penkovsky Papers*. Garden City, N.Y.: Doubleday, 1965.

Perrault, Giles. *The Red Orchestra*. New York: Simon and Schuster, 1969.

Persky, Stan. *At the Lenin Shipyard: Poland and the Rise of the Solidarity Trade Union*. Vancouver: New Star, 1981.

Phillips, David Atlee. *The Night Watch*. New York: Ballantine, 1977.

Pilat, Oliver Ramsay. *The Atom Spies*. New York: Putnam, 1952.

Pincher, Chapman. *Inside Story: A Documentary of the Pursuit of Power*. New York: Stein and Day, 1979.

———. *The Secret Offensive*. London: Sidgwick and Jackson, 1985.

———. *Traitors*. New York: St. Martin's Press, Viking, 1987.

Platt, Washington. *National Character in Action: Intelligence Factors in Foreign Relations*. New Brunswick, N.J.: Rutgers University Press, 1961.

Pooley, James. *Trade Secrets: How to Protect Your Ideas and Assets*. Berkeley, Calif.: Osborne/McGraw-Hill, 1982.

Porter, Mutual E. *Competitive Strategy: Techniques for Analyzing Industries and Competitors*. New York: Macmillan, 1980.

Prados, John. *Presidents' Secret Wars: CIA and Pentagon Covert Operations since World War II*. New York: William Morrow, 1986.

———. *The Soviet Estimate: U.S. Intelligence Analysis and Russian Military Strength*. New York: Dial Press, 1982.

Ra'anan, Uri. *Hydra of Carnage: The International Linkages of Terrorism and Other Low-Intensity Operations*. Lexington, Mass.: Lexington Books, 1986.

Ranson, Harry Howe. *The Intelligence Establishment*. (Rev. and enl. ed.) Cambridge, Mass.: Harvard University Press, 1970.

Rauch-Hinden, W. B. *Artificial Intelligence in Business, Science, and Industry*. Vol. 1. Englewood Cliffs, N.J.: Prentice-Hall, 1986.

Read, Anthony, and David Fisher. *Operation Lucy*. New York: Coward, McCann and Geoghegan, 1981.

Reitman, W., ed. *Artificial Intelligence Applications for Business*. Norwood, N.J.: Ablex, 1984.

Richelson, Jeffrey. *American Espionage and the Soviet Target*. New York: William Morrow, 1987.

———. *Foreign Intelligence Organizations*. Cambridge, Mass.: Ballinger, 1988.

———. *Sword and Shield: Soviet Intelligence and Security Apparatus*. Cambridge, Mass.: Harper and Row, Ballinger, 1986.

———. *The U.S. Intelligence Community*. 2nd ed. Cambridge, Mass.: Ballinger, 1989.

Robinson, P. R. *Using Turbo Prolog*. Berkeley, Calif.: Osborne/McGraw-Hill, 1987.

Rocca, Raymond, and John Dziak. *Bibliography on Soviet Intelligence and Security Services*. Boulder, Colo.: Westview Press, 1985.

Romanov, A. I. *Nights Are Longest There: A Memoir of the Soviet Security Services*. Boston: Little, Brown, 1972.

Rositzke, Harry. *The CIA's Secret Operations: Espionage, Counterespionage, and Covert Action*. New York: Reader's Digest Press, 1977.

*The Rote Kapelle: The CIA's History of Soviet Intelligence and Espionage Networks in Western Europe, 1936–1945*. Washington, D.C.: University Publications of America, 1979.

Schmid, Alex P. *Political Terrorism: A Research Guide to Concepts, Theories, Data*

*Bases, and Literature*. Amsterdam, Holland: Transaction Books, North-Holland Publishing Company, 1983.

*Scholar's Guide to Intelligence Literature: Bibliography of the Russell J. Bower Collection*. Frederick, Md.: University Publications of America, 1983.

Scott, Peter Dale. *The War Conspiracy: The Secret Road to the Second Indochina War*. Indianapolis: Bobbs-Merrill, 1972.

Senn, J. A. *Information Systems in Management*. 2nd ed. Belmont, Calif.: Wadsworth Publishing Company, 1982.

Shackley, Theodore. *The Third Option*. New York: Reader's Digest Press, 1981.

Shaw, E. M. *Hydrology in Practice*. London: Van Nostrand Reinhold International, 1988.

Sherman, K. *Data Communications: A Users Guide*. Reston, Va.: Reston Publishing Company, 1983.

Shulman, David. *An Annotated Bibliography of Cryptography*. New York and London: Garland Publishing, 1976.

Shultz, Richard H., Jr., and Roy Dodson. *Dezinformatsia: Active Measures in Soviet Strategy*. New York: Pergamon Press, 1984.

———. *Dezinformatsia: The Strategy of Soviet Disinformation*. New York: Berkley, 1986.

Simon, H. A. *The New Science of Management Decision*. Englewood Cliffs, N.J.: Prentice-Hall, 1977.

———. *The Science of the Artificial*. Cambridge, Mass.: MIT Press, 1982.

Sprague, R. H., and H. J. Carlson. *Building Effective Decision Support Systems*. Englewood Cliffs, N.J.: Prentice-Hall, 1982.

Sterling, Claire. *The Time of the Assassins: Anatomy of an Investigation*. New York: Holt, Rinehart and Winston, 1984.

Steven, Stewart. *The Spymasters of Israel*. New York: Ballantine, 1980.

Stevenson, William. *A Man Called Intrepid*. New York: Ballantine, 1977.

Strong, Kenneth, Sir. *Intelligence at the Top: The Recollections of an Intelligence Officer*. Garden City, N.Y.: Doubleday, 1969.

Sun Tzu. *The Art of War*. Edited by James Clavell. New York: Delacorte Press, 1983.

Suvorov, Viktor. *Inside Soviet Military Intelligence*. New York: Macmillan, 1984.

Sweeny, Allen, and Robert Rachlin, eds. *Handbook of International Financial Management*. New York: McGraw-Hill, 1984.

Taylor, J. *Shadows of the Rising Sun: A Critical View of the Japanese Miracle*. New York: William Morrow, 1983.

Tennant, H. *Natural Language Processing*. New York: Petrocelli, 1981.

Thurow, Lester C., ed. *The Management Challenge: Japanese Views*. Cambridge, Mass.: MIT Press, 1985.

Tomioka, A. "A Comparative Study of Job Involvement as a Process of Ego-Surrender in an American and a Japanese Organization." Ph.D. diss., City University of New York, 1984.

———. *A Process of Developing Potential Abilities: Techniques of a T-Model* (in Japanese). Tokyo: Japan Productivity Center, 1975.

Trepper, Leopold. *The Great Game: Memoirs of the Spy Hitler Couldn't Silence*. New York: McGraw-Hill, 1977.

Tuck, Jay. *The T Directorate: How the KGB Smuggles NATO's Strategic Secrets to Moscow*. New York: St. Martin's Press, 1986.

Turban, E. *Decision Support and Expert Systems: A Managerial Perspective*. New York: Macmillan, 1988.

Turner, Stansfield. *Secrecy and Democracy: The CIA in Transition*. Boston: Houghton Mifflin, 1985.

U.S. Congress. House. Committee on International Security. *Domestic Intelligence Operations for Internal Security*. vol. 5 House of Representatives. 93rd Cong., 2nd sess. Washington, D.C.: U.S. Government Printing Office 1974.

———. Senate. Judiciary Committee. Subcommittee to Investigate the Administration of the Internal Security Act and Other Internal Security Laws. *Combined Cumulative Index, 1951–1971, to Published Hearings, Studies, and Reports. 2 vols. Washington, D.C.: U.S. Government Printing Office, 1972.*

———. *Combined Cumulative Index Supplemental to Published Hearings, Studies, and Reports, 1972–1975*. Washington, D.C.: U.S. Government Printing Office, 1975.

U.S. Library of Congress. Congressional Research Service. *Soviet Intelligence and Secret Services: A Selective Bibliography of Soviet Publications with Some Additional Titles from Other Sources, 1964–1970*. Prepared for the Subcommittee to Investigate the Administration of the Internal Security Act and other Internal Security Laws, Senate Judiciary Committee, 2 vols. Washington, D.C.: U.S. Government Printing Office, 1971–1972.

Vernon, Raymond, ed. *The Oil Crisis*. New York: W. W. Norton, 1976.

Vogel, E. F. *Japanese as Number One*. Cambridge, Mass.: Harvard University Press, 1979.

Volkman, Ernest. *Warriors of the Night: Spies, Soldiers, and American Intelligence*. New York: Morrow, 1985.

Wallender, Harvey W., III. *Technology Transfer and Management in the Developing Countries: Company Cases and Policy Analyses in Brazil, Kenya, Korea, Peru, and Tanzania*. Cambridge, Mass.: Ballinger, 1979.

Waterman, D. A. *Building Expert Systems*. Reading, Mass.: Addison-Wesley, 1982.

———. *A Guide to Expert Systems*. Reading, Mass.: Addison-Wesley, 1986.

Weinstein, Allen. *Perjury: The Hiss-Chambers Case*. New York: Alfred A. Knopf, 1978.

Westin, Alan F. *Data Banks in a Free Society*. New York: Quadrangle Books, 1972.

Whiteside, Thomas. *Computer Capers: Tales of Electronic Thievery, Embezzlement and Fraud*. New York: Thomas Y. Crowell and Company, 1978.

Whyte, W. H., Jr. *Is Anybody Listening?* New York: Simon and Schuster, 1952.

———. *The Organization Man*. New York: Simon and Schuster, 1954.

Wilcox, Laird M. *Bibliography on Espionage and Intelligence Operations*. Kansas City, Mo.: Editorial Research Service, 1980.

———. *Terrorism, Assassination, Espionage, and Propaganda: A Master Bibliography*. Olathe, Kan.: Laird Wilcox Editorial Research Service, 1988.

Wilensky, Harold L. *Organizational Intelligence: Knowledge and Policy in Government and Industry*. New York: Basic Books, 1967.

Williams, Robert C. *Klaus Fuchs: Atom Spy*. Cambridge, Mass.: Harvard University Press, 1987.

Winks, Robin. *Cloak and Gown: Scholars in the Secret War, 1939–1961*. New York: William Morrow, 1987.

Wise, David. *The American Police State: The Government against the People*. New York: Random House, 1976.

———. *The Spy Who Got Away: The Inside Story of Edward Lee Howard, the CIA*

*Agent Who Betrayed His Country's Secrets and Escaped to Moscow*. New York: Random House, 1988.

Wohlstetter, Roberta. *Pearl Harbor: Warning and Decision*. Stanford, Calif.: Stanford University Press, 1962.

Wolf, Charles. *The Costs of the Soviet Empire*. Santa Monica, Calif.: Rand Corporation, 1983.

Wolf, M. J. *The Japanese Conspiracy: The Plot to Dominate Industry Worldwide and How to Deal with It*. New York: Empire Books, 1983.

Woodward, Bob. *Veil: The Secret Wars of the CIA, 1981–1987*. New York: Simon and Schuster, 1987.

World Bank. *Guatemala: Economic and Social Positions and Prospects*. Washington, D.C.: World Bank, 1978.

Wright, Peter. *Spy Catcher*. New York: Bantam Doubleday Dell Publishing Group, 1987.

Yakovlev, Nikolai. *CIA Target—The USSR*. Moscow: Progress Publishers, 1984.

Yardley, Herbert O. *The American Black Chamber*. New York: Ballantine, 1981.

Yavitz, Boris, and William H. Newman. *Strategy in Action: The Execution, Politics, and Payoff in Business Planning*. New York: Macmillan, 1982.

Zaltman, G., R. Duncan, and J. Holbek. *Innovations and Organizations*. New York: John Wiley and Sons, 1973.

Zink, D. W. *The Political Risks for Multinational Enterprise in Developing Countries*. New York: Praeger Publishers, 1973.

## ARTICLES

Aliber, R. A. "Exchange Risk, Political Risk, and Investor Demands for External Currency Deposits." *Journal of Money, Credit, and Banking* 7, no. 2 (May 1975): 161–79.

Armstrong, Larry, and Laxmi Nakarmi. "Korea's Elections: High Stakes For the Economy." *Business Week*, December 14, 1987, 52.

Artandi, Susan. "Computers and the Postindustrial Society: Symbiosis or Information Tyranny?" *Journal of the American Society for Information Science* 33, no. 5 (September 1982): 302–7.

Baglini, N. A. "Political Risk." *National Underwriter: Property and Casualty Insurance* 86, no. 51 (December 17, 1982): 16–20.

Bajackson, Rick. "Reaping the Rewards of Improving Security Programs to Comply with DOD Requirements." *Security Management* 30, no. 7 (July 1986): 85–89.

Bass, Bernard M., Donald W. McGregor, and James L. Walters. "Selecting Foreign Plant Sites: Economic, Social, and Political Considerations." *Academy of Management Journal* 20, no. 4 (December 1977): 535–51.

Beach, Linda M. "Data and Information Controls." *Information Management* 19, no. 1 (January 1985): 17–18.

Beck, Sanford E. "Risk Managers Can Help Win the War against White Collar Crime." *Risk Management* 28, no. 8 (August 1981): 24–27.

Bequai, August. "The Industrial Spy—Red Flags and Recourse." *Security Management* 29, no. 8 (August 1985): 93–94.

———. "Management Can Prevent Industrial Espionage." *Advanced Management Journal* 50, no. 1 (Winter 1985): 17–19.

Berkowitz, Harry. "The Spy Who Came into the Office." Part 3. *Newsday*, March 17, 1986, 1, 8–9.

Bethell, Nicholas. "Lunch with Lech." *New Republic*, November 2, 1987, 13–14.

Betts, Mitch. "Safeguarding Privacy: MIS Confronts a Sensitive Challenge." *Computerworld* 20, no. 27 (July 7, 1986): 53–54, 56–57, 59, 62.

Betts, Richard K. "Analysis, War, and Decision: Why Intelligence Failures are Inevitable." *World Politics* 31, no. 1 (October 1978): 61–89.

Bologna, Jack. "Security Managers Take Heart—Help Is Coming." *Computerworld* 18, no. 44 (October 29, 1984): Special Report 6.

Boulton, N. R., W. M. Lindsay, S. G. Franklin, and L. W. Rue. "Strategic Planning: Determining the Impact of Environmental Characteristics and Uncertainty." *Academy of Management Journal* 25, no. 3 (1982): 500–509.

Bozel, Patricia B. "The Secret of Solidarity." *National Review* 39, no. 3 (February 19, 1988): 39–41.

Bratkowski, Stefan. "A Revolt for the Possible." *Dissent*, Winter 1981, 31–38.

Brewer, Thomas L. "Political Risk Assessment for Foreign Direct Investment Decision: Better Methods for Better Results." *Columbia Journal of World Business* 16, no. 1 (Spring 1981): 5–12.

Brown, Stanley H. "United Fruit's Shotgun Marriage." *Fortune* 79, no. 4 (April 1969): 132–34.

Brumberg, Abraham. "A New Deal in Poland?" *New York Review of Books*, January 15, 1987, 32–36.

Brzezinski, Zbigniew. "Poland: Reflections on Solidarity." *Yale Review*, Spring 1985, 345–52.

Bunn, D. W., and M. M. Mustafaoglu. "Forecasting Political Risk." *Management Science*, November 1978, 1557–67.

Bussolati, U., and G. Martella. "Security Design in Distributed Database Systems." *Journal of Systems and Software* 3, no. 3 (September 1983): 219–29.

———. "Treating Data Privacy in Distributed Systems." *Information and Management* (Netherlands) 4, no. 6 (December 1981): 305–15.

Carson-Parker, John. "The Thief Executive—How Serious Is Fraud in the Executive Suite?" *Chief Executive*, No. 26 (Winter 1984): 26–33.

Chenoweth, Eric, and Jerzy B. Warman. "Why Reagan Didn't Help: Solidarity Abandoned." *New Republic*, 195, no. 2 (July 14, 1986): 18–20.

Chesnoff, Richard Z., and Douglass Stanglin. "From a U.S. Mole: Inside Story of What Might Have Been." *U.S. News and World Report*, 102, no. 4 (April 20, 1987): 32–33.

Chira, Susan. "South Korea: The Next Wave." *New York Times Magazine*, December 14, 1986, p. 30, col. 1.

Chua-Eoan, Howard G. "Sputtering Back to Life." *Time*, August 21, 1987, 30.

Clark-Gerald. "South Korea: A Nation in High Gear." *Canadian Reader's Digest*, July 1987, 68–72.

Cohen, Suleiman. "Industrial Performance in South Korea: A Descriptive Analysis of a Remarkable Success." *Developing Economies* (Tokyo), December 1978, 408–33.

"Competitive Intelligence Gathering: Keeping Ahead of Competition." *Small Business Report* 10, no. 8 (August 1985): 52–56.

"Computer Security: What Can Be Done." *Business Week* (Industrial Edition), no. 2809 (September 26, 1983): 126–30.

Cooper, Nancy. "South Korea: Labor Pains." *Newsweek*, August 31, 1987, 26.

Crapnell, Stephen G. "Award-Winner Reveals Security Strategy." *Occupational Hazards* 42, no. 5 (May 1980): 43, 46, 48.

Culnan, M. J. "Environmental Scanning: The Effects of Task Complexity and Source Accessibility on Information Gathering Behavior." *Decision Sciences* 14 (1983): 194–206.

"Data Communications: When Privacy Laws Hurt Trade." *Business Week* (Industrial Edition), no. 2632 (April 14, 1980): 104D–104H.

Dean, Clifford W. "Establishing an Information Center." *Best's Review* (*Property and Casualty*) 82, no. 5 (September 1981): 80–86.

de Gruchy, William. "Security and Integrity: They're in the Hands of the CIO." *Computerworld* 19, no. 38a (September 25, 1985): 46–47.

Derr, Kenneth T. "Security Management in Transition." *Security Management* 26, no. 10 (October 1983): 27–31.

Desta, Asayehgn, "Assessing Political Risk in Less Developed Countries." *Journal of Business Strategies* 5, no. 4 (Spring 1985): 40–53.

DeVore, C. "Strategic Minerals: A Present Danger." *Signal*, January 1981, 63–68.

Dickey, Sam. "Is Getting In Getting out of Control?" *Today's Office* 20, no. 4 (September 1985): 28–36.

Dobbs, Michael. "Soviets and Cubans to Give Their Versions of '62 Missile Crisis." *Washington Post*, January 9, 1989.

Downs, J. E. "Fifth Generation Computing Promises Optimistic Outlook for 1990's." *Data Management* 22, no. 7 (July 1984): 178–200.

Drake, Rodman L., and Allan J. Prager. "Floundering with Foreign Investment Planning." *Columbia Journal of World Business* 12, no. 2 (Summer 1977): 66–77.

Drucker, P. "Behind Japan's Success." *Harvard Business Review*, January–February 1981, 83–90.

Dubofsky, Melvyn. "The Extension of Solidarity Conflicts with the Spirit of Individualism." *Monthly Labor Review*, August 1987, 36–37.

Duckworth, Donald R. "Is Security Indispensible?" *Security Management* 27, no. 2 (February 1983): 65–66.

Duff, Ernest A., and John F. McCamant. "Measuring Social and Political Requirements for System Stability in Latin America." *American Political Science Review* 62, no. 4 (December 1968): 1125–43.

Dutton, J. E., and R. B. Duncan. "The Creation of Momentum for Change through the Process of Strategic Issue Diagnosis." *Strategic Management Journal* 8, no. 3 (1987): 279–95.

———. "The Influence of the Strategic Planning Process on Strategic Change." *Strategic Management Journal* 8, no. 1 (1987): 103–16.

Ebel, Karl H. "The Impact of Industrial Robots on the World of Work." *International Labour Review* 125, no. 1 (January–February 1986): 39.

Echikson, William. "Gorbachev May Be Setting the Stage for More Unrest in Poland." *Business Week*, January 19, 1987, 53.

Ellis, P. "Expert Systems—A Key Innovation in Professional and Managerial Problem Solving." *Information Age*, January 1983, 2–6.

Fahey, Liam, and William R. King. "Environmental Scanning for Corporate Planning." *Business Horizons* 20 (1977): 61–71.

Feierabend, Ivo K., and Rosalind L. Feierabend. "Aggressive Behavior in Politics, 1948–1962: A Crossnational Study." *Journal of Conflict Resolution* 10, no. 3 (September 1966): 249–71.

Fersko-Weiss, H. "Expert Systems: Decision-Making Power." *Personal Computing*, November 1985, 97–105.

Fey, Tom. "Establish Your Own Security Library." *Security Management* 29, no. 10 (October 1985): 71–77.

Finney, Martha I. "The Battle over a Plant-Closing Bill." *Nation's Business*, October 1987, 84.

Fitzpatrick, Mark. "The Definition and Assessment of Political Risk in International Business: A Review of the Literature." *Academy of Management Review* 8, no. 2 (1983): 249–54.

Flournay, Don M. "Satellite in the National Interest." *Satellite Communications* 10, no. 2 (February 1986): 33–34.

"Foreign Investment: The Post-Shah Surge in Political Risk Studies." *Business Week*, December 1, 1980, 69.

Franz, C. R., and D. Robey. "Organizational Context, User Involvement, and the Usefulness of Information Systems." *Decision Sciences* 17, no. 3 (1986): 329–56.

Fredrickson, J. W., and J. Mitchell. "Strategic Decision Processes: Comprehensiveness and Performance in an Industry with an Unstable Environment." *Academy of Management Journal* 27, no. 2 (1984): 399–423.

Fuld, Leonard. "Don't Confuse Corporate Intelligence with 'I Spy.' " *Marketing News* 20, no. 19 (September 12, 1986): 38, 45.

Gadacz, O. "Third World: Lower Costs Higher Risks: Korean, Mexican Strikes Shut Firms." *Automotive News*, August 24, 1987, 1.

Galbraith, J. K. "From Stupidity to Cupidity." *New York Review of Books*, November 24, 1988, 12.

Garton, Timothy. "Poland: The Use of Adversity." *New York Review of Books*, June 27, 1985, 5–7.

Garvin, David A. "Japanese Quality Management." *Columbia Journal of World Business*, 19, no. 3 (Fall 1984): 3–12.

Ghosal, Sumantra, and Seok Ki Kim. "Building Effective Intelligence Systems for Competitive Advantage." *Sloan Management Review* 28, no. 1 (Fall 1986): 49–58.

Gilad, Benjamin, and Tamar Gilad. "Business Intelligence—The Quiet Revolution." *Sloan Management Review* 27, no. 4 (Summer 1986): 53–61.

———. "Strategic Planning: Improving the Input." *Managerial Planning* 33, no. 6 (May/June 1985): 10–13.

———. "A Systems Approach to Business Intelligence." *Business Horizons* 28, no. 5 (September/October 1985): 65–70.

Girsh, Jodi Lynne. "How Security Gets Around/Ask the Right Questions." *Security Management* 27, no. 6 (June 1983): 63–66.

Gladwin, Thomas M., and Ingo Walter. "How Multinationals Can Manage Social and Political Forces." *Journal of Business Strategy* 1, no. 1 (Summer 1980): 54–68.

Graham, J. L. "A Hidden Cause of American Trade Deficit with Japan." *Columbia Journal of World Business* 16, no. 3 (Fall 1981): 5–15.

Gunawardare, G. "Implementing a Management Information System in an Extremely

Dynamic (and Somewhat Hostile) Environment—A Case Study." *Interfaces* 15 (1985): 95–99.

Haeckel, David A. and Bruce B. Johnson. "Complete the Cycle of Information Security Planning." *Security Management* 28, no. 5 (May 1984): 54–58.

Hamilton, Dennis C. "New Technology Adds New Worries." *Computing Canada* (Canada) 10, no. 7 (April 5, 1984): 17, 25.

Helm, Leslie. "The Unrest That Could Stall Seoul's Growth Empire." *Business Week*, August 5, 1985, 4–41.

Henkel, Tom. "New Technology Seen Threatening Security." *Computerworld* 14, no. 52 (December 22, 1980): 21.

Hoving, Per L. "To Install an Access Control System, Activities and Checklists." *Computers and Security* (Netherlands) 2, no. 2 (June 1983): 163–70.

Howard, N. "Doing Business in Unstable Countries." *Dun's Review* 115, no. 3 (March 1980): 48–55.

"How Japan Will Finance Its Technology Strategy/The Business Intelligence Beehive." *Business Week*, December 14, 1981, 50–52.

Howe, Charles L. "Coping with Computer Criminals." *Datamation* 28, no. 1 (January 1982): 118–28.

Hu, Hic. "Compensation in Expropriation: A Preliminary Economic Analysis." *Virginia Journal of International Law* 20, no. 1 (Fall 1979): 61–69.

Hulnick, Arthur S. "The Intelligence Producer–Policy Consumer Linkage: A Theoretical Approach." *Intelligence and National Security*, May 1986, 215.

"Imperialism with A Human Face." *Progressive* 50, no. 4 (April 1986): 10–11.

"Industrial Espionage—A Company's Viability, Even Survival, Is at Stake." *Small Business Report* 11, no. 9 (September 1986): 44–47.

Janson, John J., Jr. "The Search for Private Eyes." *Security Management* 29, no. 1 (January 1985): 64–69.

Johnson, C. "Japanese-style Management in America." *California Management Review*, Summer 1988, 34–45.

Jones, Randall J., Jr. "Empirical Models of Political Risks in U.S. Oil Production Operations in Venezuela." *Journal of International Business Studies* 15, no. 1 (Spring/Summer 1984): 81–95.

Kalbacker, Warren. "Attacking New Markets." *Computer Decisions* 15, no. 10 (September 15, 1983): 42–53.

Kelly, Laurence. "Undercover Agents at Work." *Worklife* (Canada) 3, no. 4 (1983): 14–15.

Kennedy, C. R. "The External Environment–Strategic Planning Interface: U.S. Multinational Corporate Practices in the 1980s." *Journal of International Business Studies* 15, no. 2 (1984): 99–108.

Kirtland, Monika. "Designing Corporate Information Systems." *Information and Records Management* 16, no. 3 (March 1982): 28–32.

Kitchener, Alan. "The Impact of Technology on the Information Systems and Operations Research Professions." *Interfaces* 16, no. 3 (May–June 1986): 20–30.

Kobrin, Stephen J. "Political Risk: A Review and Reconsideration." *Journal of International Business Studies* 10, no. 1 (1979): 67–80.

Kobrin, S. J., J. Basek, S. Blank, and J. LaPalombara. "The Assessment and Evaluation of Non-Economic Environments by American Firms: A Preliminary Report." *Journal of International Business Studies* 11 (Spring/Summer 1980): 32–47.

Komisar, Lucy. "Life on the Plantation." *Progressive*, June 1986, 15.

Korzeniowski, Paul. "A Threat from Without." *Network World* 3, no. 13 (June 2, 1986): 13, 16.

Kossov, V. V., and R. V. Tatesosou. "Geographical Mobility of Manpower in the USSR." *International Labour Review* 123, no. 1 (January–February 1984): 87–97.

Kraar, L. "The Multinationals Get Smarter about Political Risks." *Fortune* 101, no. 6 (March 24, 1980): 86–100.

Krause, James R. "Auditing the Integrated Data Base." *Computerworld* 14, no. 7 (February 18, 1980): 1–7.

Kravitz, Marjorie, "NCJRS: Security Information at Your Fingertips." *Security Management* 26, no. 10 (October 1983): 10–14.

Kull, David. "Protecting Information Resources." *Computer Decisions* 16, no. 11 (September 1984): 50–63.

Latta, Geoffrey W., and Bellace R. Janice. "Making the Corporation Transparent: Prelude to Multinational Bargaining." *Columbia Journal of World Business*, Summer 1983, 73–80.

Leibholz, Stephen W. "Legislative Action Makes Data Protection Hard to Ignore." *Computerworld* 18, no. 44 (October 29, 1984): Special Report 2, p. 4.

LeMoyne, James. "In Long-suffering Central America, the Workers Suffer Most." *New York Times*, September 8, 1987, p. A14, col. 2.

Leonard-Barton, D., and J. J. Sviokla. "Putting Expert Systems to Work." *Harvard Business Review*, March–April 1988, 91–98.

Levis, Mario, "Does Political Instability in Developing Countries Affect Foreign Investment Flow?" *Management International Review* 19, no. 3 (1979): 59–68.

Lewin, Robert E. "Securing and Managing Dial-in Networks." *Telecommunications* 18, no. 10 (October 1984): 52–59.

Lewis, Oscar. "The Culture of Poverty." *Scientific American* 215, no. 4 (October 1966): 19–26.

Liew, Chong Kiew. "The Impact of Higher Energy Prices on Growth and Inflation in an Industrializing Economy: The Korean Experience." *Journal of Policy Modeling* 2, no. 3 (September 1980): 389–408.

Liggett, Rosy. "Info Resource Management Aids Data Security." *Computerworld* 18, no. 18 (April 30, 1984): Special Report, pp. 49–50.

Linder, Jane. "Harnessing Corporate Culture." *Computerworld* 19, no. 38 (September 23, 1985): 1–10.

Linowes, David F. "Communications Satellites: Their Impact on the CPA." *Journal of Accountancy* 152, no. 3 (September 1981): 58–64, 66.

Lydecker, Toni H. "Computer Crime." *Association Management* 36, no. 11 (November 1984): 62–66.

MacDonnell, Arthur. "Getting the Word on the Competition: Plain . . . or Fancy." *New England Business* 5, no. 15 (September 19, 1983: 37.

"Maintain Control of Company Information." *Small Business Report* 9, no. 3 (March 1984): 72.

Miscallef, Joseph. "Political Risk Assessment." *Columbia Journal of World Business* 16, no. 2 (Summer 1981): 47–52.

Mikill, Frederick J., II. "MIS Security: Trade-offs and Risk Assessment." *Journal of Information Management* 7, no. 3 (Summer 1986): 9–13.

Minch, R. P., and G. L. Sanders. "Computerized Information Systems Supporting Multicriteria Decision Making." *Decision Sciences* 17, no. 3 (1986): 395–413.

Montgomery, David B., and Charles B. Weinberg. "Toward a Strategic Intelligence System." *Journal of Marketing* 43 (1979): 41–52.

Murray, John P. "Protecting Corporate Data with Off-site Vault Storage." *Computerworld* 15, no. 11 (March 16, 1981): 15–24.

Murray, Kevin D. "The Corporate Counterspy." *Security Management* 25, no. 4 (April 1981): 48–53.

Nakarmi, Laxmi. "Korea's New Corporate Bosses: Made in America." *Business Week*, February 23, 1987, 58–59.

———. "What Kind of Korea Will the New Labor Movement Build?" *Business Week*, October 12, 1987, 56–57.

Nehemkis, Peter. "Expropriation Has a Silver Lining." *California Management Review* Fall 1974, 15–22.

Nonaka, I. "Creating Organizational Order Out of Chaos: Self-renewal in Japanese Firms." *California Management Review*, Spring 1988, 57–73.

Norton, John H. "A Systematic Approach to Microcomputer Security." *Personnel* 63, no. 6 (June 1986): 8–12.

"Notes and Comment." *New Yorker*, October 20, 1986, 35(2).

Obermeier, K. K. "Natural-Language Processing." *Byte*, December 1987, 225–32.

O'Brien, Thomas J. "Classification Management: The Keystone of Industrial Security." *Security Management* 26, no. 3 (March 1982): 29–30.

O'Connor, Walter F. "Information—The Next Trade Problem?" *Data Communications* 15, no. 3 (March 1986): 186–91.

Oestreicher, Richard Jules. "Solidarity and Fragmentation: Working People." *Monthly Review* 8, no. 39 (January 1988): 53–59.

Perlmutter, H. V. "The Tortuous Evolution of the Multinational Corporation." *Columbia Journal of World Business* 4, no. 1 (1969): 9–18.

Perschke, Gerhard A., and Stephen J. Karabin. "Four Steps to Information Security." *Journal of Accountancy* 161, no. 4 (April 1986): 104–11.

Phelan, M., and J. Uieira. "Korean Turmoil Means Headaches in Detroit and Tokyo." *Ward's Auto World*, September 1987, 117.

"Philippine Assembly Passes a Bill Aimed at Preventing Violence Caused by Strikes." *Asian Wall Street Journal* (Hong Kong), June 2, 1982, 3.

Polis, Richard I. "Information Security: Reality and Fiction." *Computers and Security* (Netherlands) 3, no. 3 (August 1984): 225–28.

Porter, Grover L. and James E. Gauntt, Jr. "Safeguarding MIS Assets—A Management Responsibility." *Management Accounting* 65, no. 5 (November 1983): 10, 83.

Radcliffe, J. "The Way to Cope with Political Risk." *Euromoney*, May 1980, 147–48.

Rapoport, Roger. "South Korea Crosses Economic DMZ." *California Magazine*, November 1986, 42.

Riley, Tom. "Canada's Access to Information Act." *Canadian Manager* (Canada) 10, no. 3 (Fall 1985): 26–27.

Robock, Stefan H. "Political Risk: Identification and Assessment." *Columbia Journal of World Business*, July–August 1971, 6–20.

Root, Franklin R. "U.S. Business Abroad and Political Risks." *MSU Business Topics*, Winter 1968, 73–80.

Rowan, Richard L., and Duncan C. Campbell. "The Attempt to Regulate Industrial

Relations through International Codes of Conduct.'' *Columbia Journal of World Business*, Summer 1983, 64–72.

Rucks, A. C., and P. M. Ginter. ''Strategic MIS: Promises Unfulfilled.'' *Journal of Systems Management*, March 1982, 16–19.

Rummel, Rudolf J., and David A. Heenan. ''How Multinationals Analyze Political Risk.'' *Harvard Business Review* 56, no. 1 (January–February 1978): 67–76.

Samuel, A. L. ''Some Studies in Machine Learning Using the Game of Checkers.'' *IBM Journal of Research and Development*, July 1959, 211–30.

———. ''Some Studies in Machine Learning Using the Game of Checkers. II—Recent Progress.'' *IBM Journal of Research and Development*, November 1967, 601–17.

Sanger, David E. ''A High-Tech Lead in Danger: Japan Threatens to Overtake the U.S. in Supercomputers, a Critical Technology.'' *New York Times*, December 18, 1988, sec. 3, pp. 1, 6.

Schell, Jonathan. ''A Better Day.'' *New Yorker*, February 3, 1986, 47–67.

Schweitzer, James A. ''A Management View: Computer Security as a Discretionary Decision.'' *Computers and Security* (Netherlands) 4 (May 1985): 13–22.

Scoma, Louis, Jr. ''Developing a Healthy Security Posture.'' *Information Strategy: The Executive's Journal* 2, no. 3 (Spring, 1986): 45–46.

''Security: Striking a Balance.'' *Infosystems* 33, no. 1 (January 1986): 22–23.

Shapiro, Alan C. ''Managing Political Risk: A Policy Approach.'' *Columbia Journal of World Business* 16, no. 3 (Fall 1981): 63–69.

Sheridan, Peter J. ''Security Planning Cushions Future Shock.'' *Occupational Hazards* 47, no. 6 (June 1985): 43–46.

Simon, Jeffrey D. ''Political Risk Assessment: Past Trends and Future Prospects.'' *Columbia Journal of World Business* 17 (Fall 1982): 63–71.

Sizer, Richard. ''Key Issues in Managing Information.'' *Long Range Planning* (United Kingdom) 16, no. 5 (October 1983): 10–18.

Spooner, David L., and Ehud Gudes. ''A Unifying Approach to the Design of a Secure Database Operating System.'' *IEEE Transactions on Software Engineering Use* 10, no. 3 (May 1984): 310–19.

Srinivasan, Cadambi A., and Paul E. Dascher. ''Access Control Assures Network Security.'' *Internal Auditor* 43, no. 4 (August 1986): 40–45.

Stobaugh, Robert B. ''How to Analyze Foreign Investment Climates.'' *Harvard Business Review*, September–October 1969, 100–108.

Swick, Thomas. ''Private Lives.'' *American Scholar* 55, no. 3 (Summer 1986): 381–90.

Tormey, John C. ''Managing Government Security Programs in the 80s.'' *Security Management* 27, no. 5 (May 1983): 12, 14, 26–27.

Waldrop, M. ''The Necessity of Knowledge.'' *Science*, March 23, 1984, 6–9.

Westermeir, J. T. ''Trade Secret Protection.'' *Information Strategy: The Executive's Journal* 2, no. 2 (Spring, 1984): 40–43.

''Why Business Must Wait.'' *Industry Week*, March 17, 1986, 28.

Wilkinson, Bryan. ''Auditing Clients Who Use Service Bureaus.'' *Journal of Accounting and EDP* 2, no. 1 (Spring 1986): 8–18.

Wilson, John O. ''Measuring Country Risk in a Global Context.'' *Business Economics* 14, no. 1 (January 1979): 23–27.

Wood, Charles Cresson. ''Enhancing Information Security with the Information Resource-

Management Approach." *Computers and Security* (Netherlands) 2, no. 3 (November 1983): 223–29.

Wood, C., E. B. Fernandez, and R. C. Summers. "Data Base Security: Requirements, Policies, and Models." *IBM Systems Journal* 19, no. 2 (1980): 229–52.

Yanchinski, Stephanie. "The Multinationals That Are Sticking with the Philippines." *International Management*, May 1987, 81–82.

Yaprak, Attila, and Keith T. Sheldon. "Political Risk Management in Multinational Firms: An Integrative Approach." *Management Decisions* 22, no. 6 (1984): 53–67.

Zais, Arnold M. "Financial Executive's Guide to Blocking Electronic Espionage." *Financial Executive* 49, no. 9 (September 1981): 44, 46, 48.

# Index

# About the Contributors

EWAN W. ANDERSON is Senior Lecturer in the Department of Geography and the Centre for Middle Eastern and Islamic Studies at the University of Durham, England, and is Visiting Lecturer in the Department of Politics at York University. He is a consultant to the British Ministry of Defense and the World Court at The Hague. He is also a consultant on aspects of water reserves to several Middle Eastern and African Countries. His recent publications include *Strategic Minerals: The Geopolitical Problems for the United States* (Praeger, 1988) and *The Structure and Dynamics of United States Government Policymaking: The Case of Strategic Minerals* (Praeger, 1988).

HENRY S. BERSZINN has been engaged in developing more refined methodologies for identifying and capturing accurate information about specific events. As Director of the Management Review and Corruption Prevention Bureau of New York City's Department of Investigation, he helped shape his unit's strategy in addressing the sources of corruption. As a consultant with executive database developer Strategic Intelligence Systems and Big 8 accounting firm Touche Ross and Company, he refined his overall concept that a successful competitive intelligence approach to marketing requires more than just well-organized secondary information. Presently Vice President of Development at Responsive Selling System (RSS, Inc.), he specializes in tailoring RSS programs to the needs of a variety of industries.

MAHESH CHANDRA is an Associate Professor in Business Computer Information Systems and Quantitative Methods at Hofstra University. Prior to coming to Hofstra, he taught at the University of Iowa in the Department of Industrial and Management Engineering and at the University of Delhi in the Department of Operations Research. His research interests include reliability and maintainability, failure data analysis, quality control, operations research, and expert systems. Dr. Chandra has published papers in *Mathematics of Operations Research*, the *Journal of the American Statistical Association*, and other journals. He has a D.Sc. degree in operations research from the University of Delhi and a B.S. from Agra University. Dr. Chandra is an American Society for Quality Control certified reliability engineer and certified qualified engineer.

BRUCE CHARNOV is currently a tenured Assistant Professor of Management and General Business at Hofstra University. He is a widely published author in the areas of management, organizational ethics, and labor law and maintains an ongoing interest in computer/data security. Dr. Charnov possesses a B.A. from the University of Michigan, an M.B.A. from Fairleigh Dickinson University, a Ph.D. in clinical and organizational psychology from the United States International University, and a J.D. from the Hofstra University School of Law.

HUGH CONWAY is the Director of Regulatory Analysis, Occupational Safety and Health Administration, U.S. Department of Labor, in Washington, D.C. He writes on a broad range of economic issues. He recently edited a text, *Economic Issues of Defense Spending*, for the National Defense University, Institute for Higher Defense Studies (1990). He received his B.S. from Cornell University, his M.Sc. (economics) from the London School of Economics, and his Ph.D. from the University of London.

MAMDOUH FARID received his Ph.D. degree in organizational behavior and business policy from Baruch College, City University of New York. Currently he is an Assistant Professor of Management in the School of Business at Hofstra University. His professional career involved serving for years in the Egyptian presidency (with the late President Sadat). He also had worked in the maritime industry and is a licensed ship captain in the merchant marine.

JOSHUA N. FEINMAN is an economist at the Board of Governors of the Federal Reserve. He received his Ph.D. in economics from Brown University.

DAVID M. FLYNN is an Associate Professor of Management at Hofstra University. He has published in the areas of entrepreneurship in China and the United States, innovation in Japan and the United States, organizational commitment, personal values of Japanese managers, and information processing in international markets. He has been a grant recipient for the development of a strategic plan for the New York State Capital District. Professor Flynn has also received funding for his research on regional economic development and innovation in organizations.

PETER M. GARBER is a Professor of Economics at Brown University. He has been on the faculties of the University of Virginia and the University of Rochester and received a Ph.D. in economics from the University of Chicago.

MICHELLE R. GARFINKEL is an economist at the Federal Reserve Bank of St. Louis. She received her Ph.D. in economics from Brown University.

JOSEPH E. GOLDBERG is Professor of Research at the Institute for National Strategic Studies at the National Defense University, Washington, D.C., and Adjunct Professor of Political Science at the George Washington University. He formerly taught at the University of Virginia and Hampden-Sydney College (Virginia). He has written extensively on national security issues as well as on political philosophy.

ROBERT F. GORDON is Research Staff Member for IBM at the Thomas J. Watson Research Center and Executive-In-Residence in the Business Computer Information Systems and Quantitative Methods Department of the Graduate School of Business at Hofstra University. He received his B.S. degree in mathematics and physics from the City College of New York in 1964, his M.S. in mathematics from Carnegie Institute of Technology in 1965, and his Ph.D. in mathematics from Carnegie Mellon University in 1969. Prior to joining IBM in 1983, he was Manager of Mathematics and Programming for Hoffmann–La Roche, Inc., and then Director of Information Management Services at Avis, Inc. His work in the application of mathematics and computers to solve business problems has been used as a basis for corporate decisions in manufacturing, marketing, and finance for the past twenty years. He has been awarded several corporate honors, and his results have appeared in numerous publications and conference proceedings. Dr. Gordon is a member of Phi Beta Kappa, Sigma Xi, and the Operations Research Society of America.

ROBERT J. KÜHNE, a native of the Netherlands, received his Ph.D. and M.B.A. degrees from the University of Georgia. He also holds diplomas from Nijenrode University in the Netherlands and Institute Valcreuse in Switzerland. He is Professor and Dean at the School of Business Administration, Philadelphia College of Textiles and Science. Professor Kühne is an editorial review board member of both *Essays in International Business and Journal of Business Research*. His publications include a book, *Co-Determination in Business*, and over thirty articles in such prestigious publications as the *Journal of International Business Studies, Columbia Journal of World Business, Compensation Review*, and *Business Horizons*. Before joining Hofstra University, Dr. Kühne was Director and Chief Administrative Officer of the Master in International Business

Studies Program at the University of South Carolina (USC). He built this program into a leading graduate program with operations in sixteen countries. In 1984 Dr. Kühne was named the outstanding professor of USC's International Business Department. At Hofstra he received two research grants. He is a member of the Academy of International Business, the Academy of Management, and the Eastern Academy of Management.

MARSHALL LEE MILLER, a former senior governmental official, is now a Washington, D.C., lawyer specializing in international and environmental issues. Educated at Harvard, Oxford, Heidelberg, and Yale, he has authored or edited a number of books, including *Bulgaria in the Second World War* and the *Environmental Law Handbook*, and has been editor for Soviet military developments at *Armed Forces Journal International*.

SHIVAJI RAO received his M.B.A., M.Phil., and Ph.D. in management science from the City University of New York. He received his B.A. with honors in economics and mathematics from the University of Delhi in 1983. He was granted an M.Sc. in management science by the University of Durham in England in 1985. He is currently a Senior Research Associate responsible for equity/portfolio valuation systems at Bridge Research. He has published articles in the *Journal of the Operational Research Society* and the *Proceedings of the National Decision Science Institute*. His current interests include portfolio valuation problems, option pricing models, expert systems, and stochastic programming.

ROBERT S. REDMOND, Colonel, USA, (Ret.), has a wide range of experience in special operations at both the operational and senior-staff levels. He is a recognized expert in the life-cycle management of counterterrorist equipment and in terrorist vulnerability analysis. He currently consults in special operations logistics and operational security.

GEORGE S. ROUKIS received his Ph.D. in history and Russian area studies from New York University. He is a Professor of Management at the Hofstra University School of Business and a professional labor arbitrator. He formerly served as United States Deputy Assistant Secretary of Labor (1973–1975) and presently serves as a neutral referee on the National Railroad Adjustment Board and numerous public law boards in the railroad industry. He is a contract arbitrator in several industries, including the United States Postal Service. In 1986 he was appointed by the president of the United States as chairman of an emergency board to resolve a nationwide labor dispute between 93 percent of the nation's class I railroads and 38 percent of the total rail work force. In recent years he has coedited two books, *Managing Terrorism: Strategies for the Corporate Executive* (Quorum Books, 1983) and *Workforce Management in the Arabian Peninsula: Forces Affecting Development* (Greenwood Press, 1986). He has also published articles in *Labor Law Journal, Journal of Collective Negotiations in the Public Sector*, and the *Arbitration Journal*. He is a member of the National Academy of Arbitrators and has settled over two thousand labor disputes.

AKIRA TOMIOKA received his Ph.D. degree in organization behavior from City University of New York. He is Professor of Organization Behavior at the Tokyo University of Information Sciences. He is also a management consultant and Managing Director of the Japan Organization Behavior Institute. He is a member of the Academy of Management.

JOHN E. ULLMANN is Professor of Management and Quantitative Methods in the School of Business at Hofstra. An industrial engineer, he is the author of more than sixty books, monographs, and articles on industrial change, community development, product innovation, and product management. His recent books include *The Anatomy of Industrial Decline, The Prospects of American Industrial Recovery*, and *Social Costs in Modern Society*, all published by Quorum Books.

PAUL G. ZURKOWSKI is Founding President of the Information Industry Association, located in Washington, D.C. Since 1968 he has worked to define industry interests and represent those interests before the U.S. Congress and international organizations. He has written numerous articles and has lectured extensively on the information industry. He received his B.A. and L.L.B. from the University of Wisconsin.